Convening Black Intimacy

NEW AFRICAN HISTORIES

SERIES EDITORS: JEAN ALLMAN, ALLEN ISAACMAN, DEREK R. PETERSON, AND CARINA RAY,

David William Cohen and E. S. Atieno Odhiambo, *The Risks of Knowledge*
Belinda Bozzoli, *Theatres of Struggle and the End of Apartheid*
Gary Kynoch, *We Are Fighting the World*
Stephanie Newell, *The Forger's Tale*
Jacob A. Tropp, *Natures of Colonial Change*
Jan Bender Shetler, *Imagining Serengeti*
Cheikh Anta Babou, *Fighting the Greater Jihad*
Marc Epprecht, *Heterosexual Africa?*
Marissa J. Moorman, *Intonations*
Karen E. Flint, *Healing Traditions*
Derek R. Peterson and Giacomo Macola, editors, *Recasting the Past*
Moses E. Ochonu, *Colonial Meltdown*
Emily S. Burrill, Richard L. Roberts, and Elizabeth Thornberry, editors, *Domestic Violence and the Law in Colonial and Postcolonial Africa*
Daniel R. Magaziner, *The Law and the Prophets*
Emily Lynn Osborn, *Our New Husbands Are Here*
Robert Trent Vinson, *The Americans Are Coming!*
James R. Brennan, *Taifa*
Benjamin N. Lawrance and Richard L. Roberts, editors, *Trafficking in Slavery's Wake*
David M. Gordon, *Invisible Agents*
Allen F. Isaacman and Barbara S. Isaacman, *Dams, Displacement, and the Delusion of Development*
Stephanie Newell, *The Power to Name*
Gibril R. Cole, *The Krio of West Africa*
Matthew M. Heaton, *Black Skin, White Coats*
Meredith Terretta, *Nation of Outlaws, State of Violence*
Paolo Israel, *In Step with the Times*
Michelle R. Moyd, *Violent Intermediaries*
Abosede A. George, *Making Modern Girls*
Alicia C. Decker, *In Idi Amin's Shadow*
Rachel Jean-Baptiste, *Conjugal Rights*
Shobana Shankar, *Who Shall Enter Paradise?*
Emily S. Burrill, *States of Marriage*
Todd Cleveland, *Diamonds in the Rough*
Carina E. Ray, *Crossing the Color Line*
Sarah Van Beurden, *Authentically African*
Giacomo Macola, *The Gun in Central Africa*
Lynn Schler, *Nation on Board*
Julie MacArthur, *Cartography and the Political Imagination*
Abou B. Bamba, *African Miracle, African Mirage*
Daniel Magaziner, *The Art of Life in South Africa*
Paul Ocobock, *An Uncertain Age*
Keren Weitzberg, *We Do Not Have Borders*
Nuno Domingos, *Football and Colonialism*
Jeffrey S. Ahlman, *Living with Nkrumahism*
Bianca Murillo, *Market Encounters*
Laura Fair, *Reel Pleasures*
Thomas F. McDow, *Buying Time*
Jon Soske, *Internal Frontiers*
Elizabeth W. Giorgis, *Modernist Art in Ethiopia*
Matthew V. Bender, *Water Brings No Harm*
David Morton, *Age of Concrete*
Marissa J. Moorman, *Powerful Frequencies*
Ndubueze L. Mbah, *Emergent Masculinities*
Judith A. Byfield, *The Great Upheaval*
Patricia Hayes and Gary Minkley, editors, *Ambivalent*
Mari K. Webel, *The Politics of Disease Control*
Kara Moskowitz, *Seeing Like a Citizen*
Jacob Dlamini, *Safari Nation*
Alice Wiemers, *Village Work*
Cheikh Anta Babou, *The Muridiyya on the Move*
Laura Ann Twagira, *Embodied Engineering*
Marissa Mika, *Africanizing Oncology*
Holly Elisabeth Hanson, *To Speak and Be Heard*
Paul S. Landau, *Spear*
Saheed Aderinto, *Animality and Colonial Subjecthood in Africa*
Katherine Bruce-Lockhart, *Carceral Afterlives*
Natasha Erlank, *Convening Black Intimacy*

Convening Black Intimacy

*Christianity, Gender, and Tradition
in Early Twentieth-Century South Africa*

Natasha Erlank

OHIO UNIVERSITY PRESS

ATHENS, OHIO

Ohio University Press, Athens, Ohio 45701
ohioswallow.com
© 2022 by Ohio University Press
All rights reserved

To obtain permission to quote, reprint, or otherwise reproduce or distribute material from Ohio University Press publications, please contact our rights and permissions department at (740) 593-1154 or (740) 593-4536 (fax).

Earlier versions of chapters 2 and 5 appeared as Natasha Erlank, "'Brought into Manhood': Christianity and Male Initiation in South Africa in the Early 20th Century," *Journal of Southern African Studies* 43, no. 2 (2017): 251–65, https://doi.org/10.1080/03057070.2017.1295644; and Natasha Erlank, "The White Wedding: Affect and Economy in South Africa in the Early Twentieth Century," *African Studies Review* 57, no. 2 (September 2014): 29–50, https://doi.org/10.1017/asr.2014.46.

Printed in the United States of America
Ohio University Press books are printed on acid-free paper ∞ ™

Library of Congress Cataloging-in-Publication Data

Names: Erlank, Natasha, author.
Title: Convening Black intimacy : Christianity, gender, and tradition in early twentieth-century South Africa / Natasha Erlank.
Other titles: New African histories series.
Description: Athens : Ohio University Press, 2022. | Series: New African histories | Includes bibliographical references and index.
Identifiers: LCCN 2022028022 (print) | LCCN 2022028023 (ebook) | ISBN 9780821424995 (paperback) | ISBN 9780821424988 (hardcover) | ISBN 9780821447840 (pdf)
Subjects: LCSH: Black people—Marriage customs and rites—South Africa—Religious aspects. | Marriage—South Africa—Religious aspects—Christianity. | Families, Black—South Africa—Religious aspects. | South Africa—Social life and customs—20th century.
Classification: LCC HQ693.4 .E76 2022 (print) | LCC HQ693.4 (ebook) | DDC 306.85089/96068—dc23/eng/20220613
LC record available at https://lccn.loc.gov/2022028022
LC ebook record available at https://lccn.loc.gov/2022028023

Contents

	List of Illustrations	vii
	Some Notes on Terminology	ix
	Acknowledgments	xi
	Abbreviations	xv
	Introduction	1
Chapter 1	Convening Christian Publics *Churches, Newspapers, and Customary Courts*	22
Chapter 2	Modern Masculinity	50
Chapter 3	Love, Sex, and Consequence	74
Chapter 4	Marriage and Lobola and the Imagining of Black Intimate Life	111
Chapter 5	Weddings and Status, Consumption and Reciprocity	141
Chapter 6	Polygamy, Multiple Conjugality, and Masihlalisane	161
	Conclusion *Black Intimacy into the Present*	187
	Notes	197
	Bibliography	241
	Index	267

Illustrations

FIGURES

1.1	Front page of a case lodged in the appeal court in the Cape in 1929	42
1.2	"Town and Country News," *Umteteli wa Bantu*, 30 October 1937	45
2.1 and 2.2	Initiates dancing during the circumcision ceremony, ca. late nineteenth century	55
3.1	Letter "K," Dorothy Kabane to Selbourne Bokwe, 3 January 1933	78–79
3.2	Letter "L," Selbourne Bokwe to Dorothy Kabane, 9 February 1933	80
3.3 and 3.4	Pieces of paper tendered as evidence from a case about restoration of lobola, Wellington Gwavu v. Henry Lubambo Case 18/1929	86
5.1	Photographs of church weddings, ca. 1925	143
5.2 and 5.3	A church wedding in the Eastern Cape in the 1920s	145

TABLE

3.1	Kabane letter register	88

Some Notes on Terminology

When I wrote this book, I did not capitalize "Black" but rather used the lowercase, which is accepted practice in South Africa and other parts of the world. While I do not agree with some of the reasonings for the capitalization of the word, linked particularly to linguistic politics in the Global North and put forward by scholars in the US, I followed the Ohio University Press editorial convention. I would further add that, following Black consciousness thinking from the 1970s in South Africa, the adjective "Black" commonly refers to all those subject to the oppression of apartheid. Rather than adopting universal definitions of meaning for particular words, even fraught ones, academic scholarship should be alert to the kinds of nuance conferred by context.

South Africa as a nation-state came into existence only in 1910. Prior to this, the region consisted of four separate colonial entities—two British colonies and two Afrikaner territories—and a range of independent African kingdoms that lost territorial independence over the course of the nineteenth century. For the purposes of this book, which is about Black South Africans of African descent, the most relevant independent kingdoms were those in the South African provinces of the Eastern Cape and KwaZulu-Natal. Zululand, the northern part of what is today the province of KwaZulu-Natal, lost its independence to the British in 1879. All the Xhosa-speaking (where this is a reference to language and not ethnicity) chiefdoms are today part of the Eastern Cape, a province created after South African democracy in 1994. During the period of time covered by this book, some of these regions were also known as the Ciskei and the Transkei (*cis-Kei*, the region on "this side of the Kei River," and *trans-Kei*, the region on "the other side of the Kei River," or east of the Kei). The border between the Transkei, or the old Transkeian Territories (the Mpondo formally lost their independence to the British in 1894), and the colony of Natal lay at the Umzimkulu River. The border between the Transkei and Zululand has always been an artificial one, remarkable for both the extent to which it is still contested and the extent to which the historiographies of the two regions seem to imagine a vast chasm between themselves. I use the term "Eastern Cape" to refer to a historical region, which is not a common usage in academic work.

I omit prefixes for references to groups of people, so—the Xhosa, the Mfengu, the Thembu, the Mpondo, the Tswana, the Tshangaan, the Pondo, and the Sotho. I use the appropriate linguistic prefixes when referring to languages rather than ethnic groups, unless the meaning is immediately evident in the text. IsiXhosa was and is spoken by large numbers of people in what is today the Eastern Cape, though in the past it existed as several different dialects of the same language. Not all isiXhosa speakers are ethnically Xhosa. Likewise, not all isiZulu speakers were ethnically Zulu.

In the early part of the twentieth century, both isiZulu and isiXhosa underwent orthographic revision. An important literature exists on this subject. Roughly speaking, the Xhosa revisions substituted an unaspirated "Xosa" with an aspirated "Xhosa." With the sources that predate this shift, I use the spelling "Xosa." Over the course of the twentieth and twenty-first centuries, further shifts have occurred. For nonspecialist readers, keeping up with these shifts can require too much explanation; moreover, I do not reflect all the shifts. Instead, I try to follow the usage as it was in the early twentieth century (so "Umzimkulu" rather than "uMZimkhulu," and "Umtata" rather than "Mthatha").

More generally, I use words in a way that reflects their popular, historical use. For instance, I use "circumcision" for Xhosa surgical circumcision of the foreskin and "polygamy" instead of the more correct "polygyny." I do not italicize indigenous language words unless they appear infrequently in the text. For example, "lobola" has become part of South African English, and so it should not be italicized at all. The "Bible" is a reference to the proper noun, rather than anything else. All biblical references are to the King James Version, which was the version used in early twentieth-century South Africa.

This book is about a particular intersection between Black South Africans who practiced lobola-marriage and their adaptation to Christianity. It should be apparent that much of what I write about intimate life applies also to South Africans of Indian and Coloured descent or those who identify as Indian or Coloured. The discussion of intimacy in South African history is complicated and fraught for several reasons, but I mention only two here. Firstly, the nature of South African racial politics, both during the colonial and apartheid periods, meant that people's intimate lives coincided at many different levels. Separating them out can be an artificial exercise. Secondly, contemporary South African identity politics makes using terms like "African," "Black," "White," "Coloured," and "Indian" intensely contested (see the first paragraph in this section). The level of complication is further enhanced by differences in global identity politics, where practices in the Global North often outweigh those in the Global South.

Acknowledgments

I am very grateful to all those who assisted me, firstly, in discussing and debating the ideas and practices constituting this book and, secondly, in helping put this book together. They were remarkably patient! I would like to thank my colleagues at the University of Johannesburg Department of History, who supported me through the vicissitudes of research. Elsje Bonthuys, colleague, friend, and family law expert, thank you for the conversations about so-called customary law, including my questions about the minutiae of which children belonged to which house and how marital regimes have changed over time. For variously energetic conversations, historiographical debates, and essential fact-checking, thank you, Nafisa Essop Sheik and Stephen Sparks. Liz Gunner engaged me in many excellent conversations about power, orality, and sources created by women. Shireen Hassim pulled me out of more historical rabbit holes and into a broader perspective than would have been possible on my own. Isabel Hofmeyr was an on-tap resource for questions about romantic genre fiction in Africa. Akwasi-Kwarteng Amoako-Gyampah has been an excellent correspondent and interlocutor on African history more generally.

For the last fifteen or so years, I have belonged to a supremely supportive group of female colleagues in Johannesburg, laterally distributed internationally. To Elsje Bonthuys, Sarah Charlton, Shireen Hassim, Isabel Hofmeyr, Liz Gunner, Catherine Burns, Alison Todes, Barbara Buntman, Cathi Albertyn, Srila Roi, Caroline Jeannerat, and Nafisa Essop Sheik, thank you very much for advising me on marriage, lobola, historicity, and the serendipity of a well-found phrase, and for always telling me I had two papers, if not three. And for never reserving felicitous critique. Sadly, in 2019, Tessa Hochfeld, a very good friend and colleague, and also a member of the group, died unexpectedly. Tessa could always see to the heart of a piece.

In a research project from about 2016 to 2018, Joel Cabrita and I argued about the relationship of belief to Christianity, the nature of Christianity, and the rupture in thinking about the nature of divisions in Protestant evangelicalism. Sarah Emily Duff debated affect and other issues at length with me, and members of the South African history community in the US, especially Liz Thornberry, submitted to my in-depth questioning about consent and sexual violence. Susanne Klausen and I debated histories of sexuality long into the night on more than one occasion. Robert Ross, also a longtime interlocutor, stepped in on several occasions with just the right primary source and reference. Deborah Gaitskell was an informal mentor and source of all things Christian and African. I also benefited from discussions with Jochen Arndt, Ben Carton, Bob Edgar, and Robert Trent Vinson around issues like language and Zulu masculinity, the gaps in South African historiography, and transatlantic connections. Thank you, too, to Derek Peterson for encouraging me in much of my thinking in this project and encouraging me in the production of the book. I am also immensely grateful to Wendy Urban-Mead and my second Ohio University Press reader for their generous and constructive feedback on my original manuscript. Thank you, Paul Landau, for being so quick and helpful with answers to questions about manuscript layout.

African studies and African history are rich and vibrant fields of engagement. There are many people to whom I owe an intellectual debt, although they may not be directly referenced in this book. Thank you to all the colleagues I have shared conference panels, workshops, journal editions, and other space with over the last ten years. Unbeknownst to these colleagues, I have been having regular conversations with them in my head about their work for many years; I thank them for inspiring me in my academic journey.

I also benefited from the support, advice, and creative thinking from the two sabbaticals that covered the span of this book. I found my thinking stretched by Florence Bernault and others at the University of Wisconsin-Madison Department of History. And at the University of Sheffield Department of History, I benefited from colleagues working on Southeast Asia, South Asia, and medieval Europe. Paula and Glynn supplied the menu and dog walks. Thank you also to them.

My archival and research visits were made much more comfortable by the archival staff at several institutions: Erika van Zyl at the Cape Archives Depot; Michele Pickover, Zofia Sulej, and Gabi Mohale at Wits Historical Papers; and Riette Zaaiman and Atline Malukeke at UJ Historical Papers. Others aided my obsessive love for paper in different ways. Many of them have since retired or moved on, but I am still very grateful for the help they have provided, including allowing me into the stacks and behind the scenes to satisfy my archival curiosity. I was also greatly assisted in translation work by Hlumela Sondlo and Sibonisiwe Moyo. I am also very grateful to all the staff at Ohio University Press who have guided me through this process: the editors of the New African Histories series (Jean Allman, Allen Isaacman, Derek Peterson, and Carina Ray), as well as Rick Huard, Laura André, Sally Welch, and Beth Pratt. Dana Johnson and Tyler Balli were most patient and gracious with my text editing and South Africanisms. Elaine Williams skillfully prepared my index. Thank you. Any errors in the book belong to me or to Eskom, the South African electricity provider, since much of my copyediting occurred in the dark.

I would also like to remember the students whose paths intersected with mine over the last ten years or so, some of whom have become colleagues. I have truly been inspired by them. So thank you to Akwasi-Kwarteng Amoako-Gyampah, Charmaine Hlongwane, Mark Hackney, Koena Mashala, Busi Nxongo, Phindi Gumede, Kyle Harmse, and Shokahle Dlamini.

Funding for this research has come from several sources, including the Oppenheimer Foundation, the National Research Foundation, and the British Academy.

My mother, who died, sadly, during the writing of this manuscript, was an unpaid research assistant, a role she played for many years. My sisters, Dominique Erlank and Vanessa Leborgne, offered emotional support and a Cape Town base of operations for the duration of my work. Nella Opperman gave me a bed and much more in London. Neil, my partner, and our children, Daniel and Ella, kept sanity close at hand and offered both the necessary support and skepticism (as well as exercises in prioritization) along the way. Thank you.

Abbreviations

CAD	Cape Archives Depot (Western Cape Archives and Record Service), Cape Town
CBMS	Conference of British Missionary Societies, School of Oriental and African Studies, London
Cory	Cory Library for Historical Research, Grahamstown (or Makhanda, as the more recent name is not yet in wide usage)
FMCNA	Foreign Missions Conference of North America, Burke Theological Library, New York
IMC	International Missionary Council (Microfiche Collection from the IMC Archives, World Council of Churches, Geneva)
IMC/CBMS	International Missionary Council/Conference of British Missionary Society Joint Records, School of Oriental and African Studies, London
Imvo	*Imvo Zabantsundu*
Intlalo	*Intlalo xa Xosa,* the MS in the Cory Library (see the discussion in chapter 2)
Isigidimi	*Isigidimi sama Xosa*
NLS	National Library of Scotland, Edinburgh
Qayiso	The Qayiso interviews reference the collection in the Cory Library for Historical Research MS16891. The collection contains many interview transcripts. These are supplied with details of the person being interviewed and also generally a page number. However, page numbers are often duplicated. In the text, these interviews are referred to as "Qayiso, Interview with [name of interviewee]," along with the page number (though

	the page number may appear elsewhere in the collection).
SOAS	School of Oriental and African Studies, London
Umteteli	*Umteteli wa Bantu*
Wits	Department of Historical Papers, University of the Witwatersrand, Johannesburg

Introduction

IN 1917, Tiyo Burnside Soga, a second-generation Xhosa Christian, minister in the Presbyterian Church, and brother's son of the better-known Tiyo, wrote a historical ethnography of the Xhosa entitled *Intlalo xa Xosa*. It is a fascinating and eloquent piece of writing, touching past and present via an incipient Xhosa nationalism and a qualified critique of white society. In it, he comments upon the relationship between Xhosa tradition and Christianity. "Xosa's laws were many & very good although there were some dreadful ones. The strange thing about them was that they resembled the Ten Commandments of the Almighty."[1] While Reverend Soga may have been venturing toward grandiloquence, his suggestion that a congruence existed between Xhosa custom and Christianity was a commonly held view among Bible-familiar Africans in South Africa in the early twentieth century.

By the time T. B. Soga compared Xhosa custom to the Ten Commandments, Christianity—understood as a range of beliefs and dispositions—had fed solidly into Black society. In addition to its other effects, Christianity brought about considerable change in patterns of love, courtship, and marriage, a field I refer to as "Black intimacy." I use the term to capture an interlinked and interlocking set of thinking, behavior, and feelings tied to sexuality, fertility, the moral dispositions associated with both of these, conjugal and family life, and the gendered roles that shape them. A consideration of Black intimacy would include ideas about sexual morality, changes in patterns of marriage, commodification of private life, people falling in or out of love, emotions felt and then responded to (including love, shame, and loss), and also the public generation and sharing of ideas about these.[2]

Crucially, Black intimacy is impossible to understand without considering it in relation to Christianity. Nthana Mokale, a resident of Phokeng interviewed in the early 1980s, remembered organizing sexual trysts at school during the interwar period. "He wrote a letter to you if he wanted to know you intimately. Didn't we go to school so that we could learn how to write? If a man saw you at the church or anywhere and was interested in you, he would write and propose to you through the post."[3] Her recollection charts the complicated, conflictual, and often messy shifts that occurred when intimate lives, sexuality, Christianity, and literacy coincided, both in private and in public.[4]

PRECOLONIAL INTIMACY AND LINEAGE POLITICS

From their first concerted encounter with Christian missionaries in the nineteenth century, Black South African Christians, often referred to as "Kholwa" or "school" people, struggled to bring indigenous gendered social practice into the practice of Christianity. Christianity taught different ways of thinking about sexuality and marriage. The way in which precolonial southern African society was structured carries a number of implications for a study of Black intimacy in the twentieth century, indeed, for the very definition of Black intimacy.

Southern African precolonial cultural and political economy placed a premium on lineage politics, patriarchal privilege, and wealth in women. When women married, their fertility and labor power were transferred to their husband's family at the same time as their marriage created alliances between the families. Women carried the privilege and burden of lineage reproduction. Behavior that sustained the reproduction of a lineage, including its links to a family's ancestors, constituted appropriate sexuality; other behavior, as long it did not compromise reproduction, was allowable, usually as long as it was discreet. Polygamous and multiple-marriage relationships were acceptable according to this thinking, because these practices could grow and cement the status of their families. Practices like lobola—bridewealth—both created and performed the bonds that were built between families. Because of the centrality of bridewealth exchanges to marriage, it is almost impossible to consider histories of marriage in South Africa without some consideration of the role of lobola. This book is concerned with those who marry, or aspire to marry, via lobola.

Further, the priority placed on fertility meant these societies were heterosexual in outlook. Lauren Berlant and Michael Warner refer to social formations like these as heterosexual cultures, though they caution that these only ever have a provisional unity, or only ever give the appearance of an overarching heterosexuality.[5] This is evident in South Africa, where sexual cultures have always been historically and racially contingent. Same-sex sexual activity has consistently had a regional historical presence, including in precolonial African society, but its inability to promote social and biological reproduction has meant it generally needed to occur alongside biologically reproductive sexualities to be sanctioned.

However, Black intimacy is inadequate as a concept if it concerns itself only with sex and marriage considered as aspects of domestic or private life. In precolonial South Africa, the concepts of private and public were understood differently than they would have been in nineteenth-century Europe. A division existed between matters internal to the generational politics of a lineage—including marriage transactions, succession, and inheritance—and external matters of concern to the broader clan or chiefdom. Further, private and public, understood rather as internal and external, were not distinct realms that mapped onto feminine and masculine attributes. Instead, ideas about the respect owed to elders or in-laws in marriage were more determinative of status. Young wives followed complex rules of avoidance around the cattle kraals in their new married homes that gradually diminished over time, finally disappearing largely at menopause. When women did wield overt political power, it was generally when they were past the age of having children.

In Xhosaland, a chief's first wife might have been of his own choosing and exchanged for cattle under his personal control. All the men who offered patronage to him would contribute advice on an appropriate choice of wife and cattle for her when he married his principal, or great, wife. Little in the choice of a great wife was private, but it was intimate.

My definition of Black intimacy must, therefore, include the understanding that it is simultaneously what happens between sexual and/or married partners and what is created in public spaces that debate and dissect the nature of intimate life. It was a continual mediation between acts and feelings that occurred out of the sight of others and the same acts as subjects of public scrutiny.[6] More recently, Berlant and others have written about an intimate public sphere, where ideas about intimacy gain public currency partly because they present themselves as forces rooted in affect rather than other political motivations.

A history of intimacy also allows for a different presentation of South African history, one that offers new explanations for social change beyond those offered by race and class alone. Some of the earliest histories of intimacy range freely between private and public life, with historians not forced into a choice between investigating one or the other. For instance, they investigate intimate practices and behavior in the public spaces of ancient Greece while in other parts of the world, archaeologists speculate about intimate behavior in prewritten times on the basis of artifactual remains.[7]

AFRICAN ENCOUNTERS WITH CHRISTIANITY

It is impossible to separate the shaping of Black intimacy from its connections to Christianity. As Africans encountered Protestant ecumenical Christianity, they encountered different and Christian thinking about proper masculine and feminine behavior, sexual morality, and beliefs about how marriages ought to look and function. While Christianity affected African society in diverse ways, its moral and gendered teachings produced some of its most lasting effects.

Nineteenth-century Britain almost seamlessly merged ideas in Protestant Christianity with the values of industrial capitalism. As the British middle class expanded in response to the growing importance of industrial capital, ideas about a separation of spheres—of women ideally placed to be mothers and wives and men suited to public life—folded smoothly into ideas about Christian religious life. By the middle of the century, it would have been almost impossible to separate what people understood as Christian piety and its requirements of behavior and belief from what they viewed as social convention and propriety. But religion did not merely offer ideas about proper gender roles; it fixed expectations about the role of faith in daily life that made faith essential to everyday life. "Church and chapel were central to the articulation and diffusion of new beliefs and practices related to manliness and femininity."[8]

Much attention has been paid to the intersection of these ideas with African ideas in the context of colonial conquest, which I discuss in later chapters. However, the imposition of new ideas about gendered practice and moral codes did not go unchallenged, not only among Africans who continued to practice traditional forms of marriage but also among Christian converts. While it is generally the former who are historically viewed as most resistant to moving away from traditional practices, I argue that few converts were uncritical in their acceptance of Christianity. During the late nineteenth and early twentieth centuries, African converts adopted, molded, and selectively appropriated many Christian ideals, both in daily life and in ritual, refashioning them as part of new intimate practices.

This first occurred among those educated Africans who aspired to middle-class status and belonged to the historic mission, or mainline, churches or those closely associated with them—Anglicans, Presbyterians, Methodists, and Lutherans—as well as some of the larger of the independent

African churches, including the African Methodist Episcopal Church. These were first-, second-, and third-generation Christians who had early on aligned themselves with mission church procedures and practices, as well as with English literacy and education. As a group, they are described in the literature as a Black "petty bourgeoisie," an older term used less today; a Black "elite," by virtue of the group's relationship with other Black South Africans; or an emergent Black "middle class." The Black elite, or middle class (my preferred terms), was inseparable, historically, from its adherence to Christianity, and its members collectively shared an identity of being both Christian and educated. As Hlonipha Mokoena notes, for adherents—referred to as "amaKholwa" in isiZulu and "amaGqoboka" in isiXhosa—this was a political and social identity as much as it was a religious identity.[9]

While the literate and converted Africans who made up the Black elite were the first to experience and adopt intimate practices and a sexual morality rooted in Christianity, these ideas and practices soon spread to include most Black Christians, irrespective of denominational allegiance or membership in a mainline or independent church. By 1951, just under 5.1 million Black South Africans out of an enumerated Black population of just over 8.5 million identified themselves as Christian.[10]

But Christianity's sphere of influence in South Africa went beyond its institutional membership. It had what I refer to as "an institutional thickness," constituted through the relational connections it created among its adherents and their social worlds, which extended Christianity's footprint to include also traditional communities and structures. Especially after industrialization and urbanization had firmly linked countryside to city by the 1920s, sometimes supportive but often fractious debates around the relative merits of Christianity and custom were a characteristic of all sectors of Black society. The debates were always mutually constitutive. Although sexual morality and gendered roles were not the only sources of conflict between Black South Africans, these concerns populated and vitalized the contested zone that existed between Christianity and modernity, and tradition and custom. As a result of this contestation, by the 1950s, Black sexual modernity had gained extensive traction and legitimacy within Black society.

Chapter 4 shows, for instance, the tenacity with which Black Christians defended lobola. Christian support for lobola gradually became so widespread through the twentieth century that in postcolonial South Africa support for lobola emanated as much from its continued practice by successive generations of Black Christians as it did from so-called traditional practice. What Black South Africans regard today as tradition has been altered unequivocally by Christianity.

Moreover, Christianity and its imprint on Black intimacy is partly responsible for the ideal of family life that remains central to Black social aspirations, even in the twenty-first century. While the impact of migrant labor was a powerful vector in shifts in family life, the changes wrought by a Christian sexual modernity were at least as consequential. Migrant labor and the differences between city and country life dominate discussions of Black social change in South African history, a point I return to in a later subsection. The destabilizing effects of migrant labor wrenched families apart. By the 1960s and 1970s, Black marriage rates had declined and migrant labor patterns had resulted in the growth of female-headed households spatially stretched over country and city.

However, migrant labor was not the only source of social change in African life. While this book concerns itself with family and intimate life constituted through Christianity, I also need to make a more general argument for the impact of Christianity in South African history. The diverse impacts of Christianity are regularly overlooked in South African history, including in the literature on migrant labor. The large-scale oscillation of women between city and countryside might have been caused by the needs of migrant labor or, later on, by forced removals, but concerns around labor and how to generate income were not the total of people's daily lives. Christianity also has played a powerful role in how people understand their place in this world and the actions they take as a result.

ANALYTICAL FIELDS IN PUBLIC INTIMACY, CHRISTIANITY, AND SOUTH AFRICAN SOCIAL HISTORY

In the next few sections I consider some of the analytical fields, theoretical directions, and historiographical writing that inform my larger argument about the constitution of Black intimacy in South Africa between 1919 and 1948. The first section details how ideas about Black intimacy gained a constituency and purchase through public discussion. This is followed by a reflection on current writing in relation to Christianity, including debates about its material and spiritual purchase on African imagination and practice. While African Christianity is not the primary focus of this book, some consideration of its larger appeal and constituency in South Africa is necessary to understand the book's argument. The final portions of this chapter consider the reasons for locating my argument in the period between 1910 and 1948 as well as describe my sources and chapter content.

A Convention of Publics

New ideas about intimate life were possible because of the spread of mission-driven written literacy in South Africa, which provided both the forms necessary to share these ideas and the spaces where these ideas could be shared—the "convening" of the title of this book.

The church constituted the first and most powerful of those spaces. Whatever else it did, church life provided people with the tools and a shared repertoire of experience to behave in ways legible to public life in the early twentieth century. This occurred at the level of people's daily lives but also in relation to how church institutions operated in conjunction with the state. The institutional life of the Christian church—its round of rituals and meetings and its ordering of time—facilitated the entry of Black men (not women) into the governmentality of colonial life. Institutional church life had a grammar that allowed Black and white Christians to share meeting spaces and, to a limited extent, the decision-making not open to Black South Africans in a racially divided society.

Further, men who worked as chiefs and headmen within the edifice of indirect rule had often served an organizational apprenticeship in a men's council in the church or worked as lay clergy. Indeed, many of the remunerated positions available to Africans within rural districts hinged upon either their possession of mission literacy or their status as a Christian.

The associational and bureaucratic experience that Africans gained through church structures was not limited to South African borders. Several notable figures among the Black elite attended international ecumenical conferences about the future of Christianity. The same status and experience in church governmentality benefited the early twentieth-century leaders of the African National Congress through rounds of conferences in London in the 1910s.

Magisterial courts were another space for the performance of Black modernity. All precolonial southern African societies had chiefly forums where senior men (and occasionally senior women) debated matters of relevance to the chiefdom, including succession and, by the nineteenth century, relations with the British colonial state. (These were the matters I previously described as external to the family.) When the British established district law courts in the nineteenth century, these chiefly courts largely lost their power, and the adjudication of both internal kin and external chiefly matters passed to the colonial courts.[11] Interpersonal relations and customary obligations thereafter came under the purview of these, including cases of seduction, lobola, and inheritance and succession disputes, establishing a precedent for the kinds of cases that shaped Black intimate life in the twentieth century.

While customary law applied across the whole southern African region, when Union occurred in 1910, the two provinces with the most extensive customary court networks were the Cape and Natal. In the Eastern Cape, where the customary courts began operating much earlier than elsewhere in the later South Africa (and which correspondingly have a denser archival record), complex adjudications occurred around whether or not a person's status as a Christian affected their personal and intimate matters. The processes involved in bringing a case to court were similar to those that structured the operation of precolonial chiefly courts. The elders of a lineage were familiar with arguing cases of succession and disputes around the occupation of land, even if the setting had shifted from the kraal of a chief to the square brick structure that served to house a magisterial court. Like church proceedings, court cases were doubly formed—both oral and textual—first, because of their instance as a performance and, second, because every court case generated a written record. Indeed, many of the legal texts that subsequently acquired life through the action of a typewriter began as oral performance.

This double formation present in church and court proceedings is important. While some African history tends to privilege oral forms as more authentic than written, the impact of an oral performance is necessarily limited by its particular audience. Mission literacy took oral performances and re-created them for multiple audiences, not just those physically present. It allowed Africans to transform their considerable oral skill into words written on pages, increasing the accessibility of that content. It also made it possible for those whose voices were not usually heard in public—junior men and women—to be heard more extensively. Alec Ryrie would refer to this as one of the democratic outcomes of Protestant Christianity.[12]

Further, content captured on paper, as in the case of the Black press, became the joint property of a public, in a way that the words of a performed text, like an *isibongo* (a praise poem), could not.[13] This held particularly for newsprint agreement and discord over the content and shape of Black intimate life and sexual modernity. In articles and letters about the loss of parental authority, the importance of lobola, or the morality (or immorality) of polygamy, family life was rendered public in new ways, making its concerns national concerns.

African Christianity as a Field of Social Inquiry

The mission literacy that embedded ideas about intimacy in the Black Christian imagination has a history that can be written as the spread and influence of Protestant Christianity in South Africa. However, since the early 1990s, with the publication of John and Jean Comaroff's two-volume history of Protestant nonconformism among the Sotho-Tswana, studies of African Christianity have moved from an exclusive focus on mission effort to a greater understanding of the purchase and status of multiple forms of Christianity across sub-Saharan Africa.

The first of some of the more relevant and current debates in African Christianity concerns the relative importance of Christianity in contemporary South Africa. According to the 2001 census, 79.8 percent of South Africa's roughly forty-two million inhabitants were self-professing Christians.[14] In 2015, this figure was 86 percent, with 52.5 percent claiming some form of frequent religious observance and a further 22.5 percent claiming once- or twice-monthly church attendance.[15]

The self-profession of Christianity can mean many things. Africa is not reducible to one variant of Christian spirituality; all Africans who are Christian are not Christian in the same way. Indeed, more Africans have found practical strategies and ways of living in the diverse set of practices and beliefs tied to Christianity than in the century's only comparable nonpartisan and non-nationalist philosophy, socialism. But where socialism provided little practical assistance for the maintenance of structures like the family, which it regarded as a bourgeois myth, Christianity had a wealth to offer fathers, mothers, sons, daughters, and other sorts of kin. Much of the literature that accounts for the conversion of Africans to Christianity in the nineteenth century locates reasons for conversion in the material benefits associated with Christianity. Still, to leave the explanation for conversion at material reasons is a reductive assessment of Christianity's historical impact.

Most historians today, however, discount the historical impact that Christianity has had on South African lives. They find it difficult to consider experiences of faith, including the religious reasons people provide for their actions, as valid categories of historical evidence. As a result, rather than viewing belief or faith as historically causative, South African historians have underplayed the impact of Christianity on regional historical developments.

I shall return to this point later, but it is interesting to note that this idea is counter to the historical treatment of Christianity in other parts of the continent. David Gordon explains Zambian political developments in the twentieth century as crucially mediated by the visible effects of invisible spirits exerting "power in this world."[16] And Stephen Ellis and Gerrie ter Haar explain the way that the spirit world constitutes a motivating force behind African political life.[17] While some see an identification of spiritual agency in everyday life as an essentialization of African Christianity, this is not a sufficient criticism for discounting how belief, however we understand it, acts as a historical force.[18] As Ruth Marshall notes, it is important to "restore intelligibility to religion in its irreducibility, to make sense of the inherent rationality of its disciplines and practices, over and above its social, cultural, or political functions."[19]

Most South African Christians (about 8.5 million of them) now belong to Zionist or Pentecostal churches, but many remain members of the mainline churches, where three denominations (Methodist, Anglican, and Presbyterian) account for approximately 5.5 million South Africans. Until the 1950s, most African Christians, about 59 percent of the total African population, were members of the mainline churches.[20] From the 1960s onward, more African Christians belonged to Pentecostal or Zionist churches than belonged to the mainline churches. This was both because of the expansion of South Africa's African population and because people were switching denominational allegiance.

Denominational allegiance is, though, something of a red herring in histories of South African Christianity. In 1948, Bengt Sundkler published his seminal work, *Bantu Prophets in South Africa*. In it, he distinguished between mainline, or historic mission, churches and a variety of churches he identified as Ethiopianist or Zionist. The former includes African-founded and African-led churches similar in structure to the mainline churches, and the latter includes the churches theologically derivative of the late nineteenth- and early twentieth-century holy spirit revivals in the US. It is now commonplace to distinguish between mainline, African independent, and Pentecostal Christianity.

But there are issues with this typology that overstate the importance of denominational difference and that link authenticity and political virtue to the independent churches only. Africa's religiocultural heritage, according to the theologian Mercy Oduyoye, needs to be viewed as contributing to the shaping of world Christianities rather than being solely derived from Western Christianity.[21] Supporters of this position are uncomfortable with the term "African independent Christianity," preferring "African initiated/instituted Christianity," because the former implies that Africans were colonially dependent on the West to shape their beliefs.[22]

Secondly, an association is often drawn between colonially complicit historical mission congregations and colonially resistant independent churches. In 1986, Terence Ranger drew attention to how African religious movements were often assumed to represent a developmental state in a later more nationally driven politics of anticolonial resistance. His work points to the need to consider religious movements as sui generis, not as moments in a national teleology.[23]

An elaboration of this last point concerns a widely held distinction between Ethiopianism and Zionism, the former supposedly representative of a radical anticolonialism and the latter an antirevolutionary counterculturalism. The Zionist Christian Church, the largest Zionist church in southern African, is often written about as if complicit in apartheid.[24] A corollary of this view positions mainline churches as irrelevant, institutionally rigid, and theologically homogeneous, at the same time suggesting that only independent churches are worthy of study.

More recently, in reaction to these views, scholars have noted the importance of moving away from a four-fold categorization of African Christianity as either mainline, independent, Zionist, or Pentecostal to an understanding of the practice of faith as denominationally fluid.[25] For example, the current Nigerian Anglican population is around twenty million, a significant number but probably only half the size of its Pentecostal population.[26] However, while the Anglican figure reflects the institutional strength of the former mission churches, it conceals internal variation. Many Nigerian Anglicans are Pentecostal in outlook, many practice polygyny, and almost all oppose homosexuality within the church. However, as Anglicans, they understand themselves to be part of a worldwide communion, even though the Western portion of the church advocates tolerance around sexual preference and orientation.[27] Anglicans in South Africa are split on the issue of offering an LGBTIQ ministry, but in practice, a more divisive issue is the ordination of Black women, because of a combination of patriarchal outlook and fear of sorcery. The point is this: denominational and sectarian allegiances can be fluid; people shift churches frequently, and while institutions and organizations may endure, their congregants are often more faithful to their own relationship to faith than they are to one form of it.[28] They may also hedge their spiritual bets by belonging to different churches simultaneously.

Debating Custom and Tradition in South Africa

If one pole of this book lies in Christianity, the other lies in custom and tradition. In this part of the introduction, I examine some of the tensions inherent in using these terms as well as look more directly at debates about the relationship between Christianity and tradition.

The literature on missions and Christianity in South Africa has usually assumed that cultural innovation and syncretic practices have been the domain of the Ethiopianist and Zionist churches. According to the recent *Cambridge History of South Africa*, "Such churches were prime examples of African cultural reconfiguration, blending Christian practices with a variety of African practices and beliefs (e.g., witchcraft, ancestor worship, polygamy)."[29] For example, the Shembe, or the AmaNazaretha, the subject of Sundkler's work, are widely recognized as sanctioning polygamy and the veneration of ancestors.[30]

However, while Zionists and Ethiopianists are routinely described as being fluid in relation to customary practice, the corollary attributes to mainline Christians a desire to abandon custom. This is a mistaken reading, as I demonstrate in the following chapters. Many of the mainline Protestant denominations tolerated and allowed practices like lobola, polygamy, or, as I discuss in chapter 6, multiple conjugality. Traditional rituals and practices associated with marriage were particularly tenacious, and most mainline Christians found it difficult to abandon them, even if first-generation Christian converts in the nineteenth century attempted to eschew them.

One place to begin the discussion of the role of tradition in mainline Christianity is with a statement about what being modern meant to African Christians.[31] Many Black South Africans, especially those who had converted, viewed Christianity as a route to "civilization," or being modern. T. B. Soga, however, was not convinced that the equation worked in such a neat fashion. "Xosa may be made similar to a whiteman through education & civilization, but he shall never be created a Whiteman for ever & ever." Anyone who argued differently was going against the word of God, or as he wrote, "God created what he has created."[32] He distrusted the teleological narrative that arranged Christianity, civilization, and being modern in the same bouquet. For Soga, Christianity was a claim to modernity that did not require sloughing off his African skin.

At the same time, though, T. B. Soga was an amateur newspaper correspondent firmly attached to the power of literacy, type, and the printing press. His paradoxical view of modernity was shared by many: convenient when it was beneficial, decried when it was not. Indeed, his and others' predicament around modernity should not overshadow the fact that it resonated (and still does) with its users, often precisely because of its orientation to the past.[33] Lynn Thomas describes this as the historicization of modernity, "demonstrating just how diverse and dynamic definitions of the modern have been, and how those definitions have emerged from specific material relations, strategies of rule, and social movements."[34] Her view draws upon Thomas Spear's beautifully succinct description of tradition as "one of the most contentious words in African historiography widely condemned for conveying a timeless, unchanging past and the evil twin of modernity. But it remains critically important in understanding historical processes of social change and representation."[35] Writing about the generation of Black men born around fifty years after T. B. Soga, Daniel Magaziner points to the ways that Steve Biko and other members of the South African Students' Organization grafted their understanding of being Black to the condition of being modern, an intellectual consciousness that considered the past carefully and of a qualified utility. "In their thought the categories of 'African' and 'adult', 'modern' and 'civilized' had been configured and reconfigured time and again."[36]

Part of this reconfiguration included careful attention to tradition, an interest T. B. Soga shared with numerous contemporaries. It was a subject that Soga returned to again and again during the 1920s and 1930s, in an attempt to work out what was distinctive, and modern, about the condition of being African, the "good that should be preserved for any intelligent, progressive people."[37] His exposition of Christianity in *Intlalo xa Xosa* was hybrid. As one of its readers for the Lovedale Press, which was less than enthusiastic about publishing the work, noted, "The writer personally confirms witchcraft to be true and goes on to back up his argument by a Biblical quotation when Eva befriends a serpentine devil."[38]

Despite the concerted efforts of an African elite to link Christianity and tradition—like James Calata, who drew explicit connections between biblical and traditional practice in his early 1920s essay in support of manhood circumcision and lobola—much contemporary academic writing delinks ritual and tradition from the world of Christianity.[39] Take Jacqueline Solway's recent excellent and insightful piece on "slow" versus "fast" *bogadi* (the Tswana word for "lobola") in Botswana.[40] It traces shifts in the tempo of marriage payments after the mid-twentieth century and relates a more contracted payment process to the phenomenon of lavish "white" weddings. Yet the erosion of bogadi is attributed to shifting patterns of consumerism resulting in debt, while Christianity is disregarded as a potential influence on wedding choices.

"Although they may have been Christians," Adam Kuper writes in a recent survey of kinship and marriage in southern Africa, "they often paid bridewealth, but this was not the bridewealth of tradition."[41] This view would not have sat well with T. B. Soga, whose understanding of tradition was capacious, oriented toward past and present. Soga would have felt discomforted by any suggestion that his support for lobola could not simultaneously be both the product of his Christianity and his tradition.

Class, Race, Gender, and Christianity

Between the 1970s and the 1990s, South African history was characterized by race and class as modes of analysis. Social historians wrote about how precolonial societies lost independence as a result of colonialism, urbanization, industrialization, development of migrant labor, and histories of labor protest, in a welcome antidote to Afrikaner nationalist and liberal histories that had shaped history in the preceding decades.[42] This broad school has had a keen imprint on the production of history in South Africa. Among its many effects, a primary one has been to make historical events and processes visible as, and in relation to, Black resistance and state oppression.

A further effect of this work concerns its construction of the migrant laborer and migrant labor as staple subjects of South African history. In the older literature on the history of labor migration in South Africa, the normative labor migrant was a man who first moved temporarily to a city, and later more permanently, in order to work. As a result, a significant portion of South African social history privileges the experience of work over all others in people's lives, although this position has not gone undisputed.[43] Patrick Harries, for instance, has demonstrated the persistence of rural ideologies and practices in how men living in cities and working on the mines conducted their lives.[44]

Several developments helped to shift a focus on race and class and to blur the boundaries between urban and rural. Two are of relevance here. The first lies in the emergence of a significant set of works focusing on women's and gender history, which decentered many of the narratives that privileged men as the agents of history.[45] This includes the work of Belinda Bozzoli and others as part of the development of a literature on female labor migrants and the rise of female-headed households.[46] Deborah Gaitskell's work on Black women in urban areas demonstrated how women used their faith and faith-based networks to negotiate work and family life in hostile urban conditions and under the depersonalized gaze of the white state.[47]

The second development concerns the re-emergence of Christian missions as a significant element in South African history.[48] In 1991, Jean and John Comaroff published *Of Revelation and Revolution: Christianity, Colonialism, and Consciousness in South Africa*, the first in a projected three-volume series on missionaries.[49] The publication of these volumes reflects an important shift from a focus on missions as agents of colonialism to a focus on "the colonization of consciousness" in the "long conversation" between the Tswana and the missionaries.[50]

The most sustained and valid criticism of the first volume of the series lay in its treatment of African agency.[51] It is worthwhile considering this critique, because it represents an ongoing thread in African history.[52] Volume 1 is told mostly from the perspective of the missionaries, and its sources are missionary-produced accounts. The Comaroffs explain this by suggesting that the Tswana lacked narrative accounts of their past for use in the reproduction of their history (a view later tempered in volume 2). This means that the volume is strong in articulating mission agency but much less strong in attributing the shaping of the mission-Tswana encounter to Tswana intention.[53]

While the Comaroffs were completing the first volume, Elizabeth Elbourne was working on evangelical Christianity among the Khoikhoi in the Eastern Cape. Khoi evangelists had appropriated the Christianity impressed upon them by a series of European missionaries and began itinerating through formerly independent Khoi communities as well as among the Xhosa to spread an indigenized Christian spirituality. In the context of growing impoverishment and lack of land, a Khoikhoi—or "pan-Hottentot"— nationalism developed, which drew initially on Christianity and the Bible, and later, on the notion of common land, or blood ground, as sources of authority. Part of the raison d'être of Elbourne's 2002 book was "to incorporate the study of religion more thoroughly into the mainstream of cultural, social and political history."[54]

Elbourne and the Comaroffs were plowing what became a popular furrow. The mid-1990s saw the publication of several edited collections and studies of individual mission societies.[55] Many of these were grounded in and incorporated Black Christian voices and perspectives and considered new thoughts on gendered mission authority and the mission-driven politics of colonialism.

Several of these also grounded African Christianity and African Christians into a politics of transnationalism. In 1995, James Campbell published on African Americans and African evangelical Methodism on different sides of the Atlantic. Working on similar themes, Robert Trent Vinson examined how Christianity infused networks and established political relationships across the world of the diaspora.[56]

One of the more important recent currents in the history of Christianity and the growth of the Black middle class lies in directing attention to intertextual and intergenre literacy mediated through Christianity. In *The Portable Bunyan: A Transnational History of "The Pilgrim's Progress,"* Isabel Hofmeyr explains how Africans and missionaries understood the book as both fetish and parable, its linear narrative making for a translatability that allowed for deft indigenous uses of the text.[57] Joel Cabrita's work has challenged assumptions about the oral nature of African independent churches, showing how the AmaNazaretha in KwaZulu-Natal sustained their Christianity through a remarkable body of self-generated texts, including hymns and autobiographical writing, all carefully attuned to the dynamics of global Christianity.[58]

Together, these works challenge thinking that sees African literary and textual production as less authentically African than oral production and African Christianity as more authentic when steeped and expressed in local idioms and politics. These points relate critically to the context of this book. Denied access to standards of living that most white South Africans considered their right, educated Black Christians used their oratory, their ink, and their pens to channel their frustrations into a range of publications and petitions. In the debates around initiation, lobola, and pernicious urban life that appeared in the Black press, African Christians showed a humorous and dexterous handling of a language few would have learned at their mothers' breast, shifting genres to appeal to wider audiences. These debates extended into fiction, some of which is visible in the quotes that begin many of my chapters. In writing, African Christians could display an intellectual prowess rooted in one of the most confusing yet universal of the Western world's texts, the Bible, to seed intellectual movements like Black consciousness.[59]

The tools provided through the Christian elevation of the self and literacy were equally comfortable in female and male hands, but it seems that men generally felt more comfortable demonstrating them in public. In South Africa, in the outpouring of writing from mission school graduates, in fiction, poetry, and plays, very little work was published by Black women before the late 1950s.[60] The exception is Nontsizi Mgqwetho, quoted elsewhere in this book.[61] The veneration of agency in some recent work has resulted in uneven and selective histories, rendering men more often than women the subjects of action by virtue of their greater literary output and their more prominent public lives.

CHRONOLOGY, SOURCES, AND CONTENT

This book draws from material covering the nineteenth century but is primarily concerned with the period between 1900 and 1950. The chronology that tracks the constitution of Black sexual modernity, or Black intimacy, is roughly bookended by the formation of the Union of South Africa in 1910 and the rise to power of the National Party in 1948. At the turn of the twentieth century, discourses on the African family centered on the negative effects of the movement of men away from their families to South Africa's burgeoning urban areas, a phenomenon referred to at the time as "detribalization." By the 1940s, liberal white and Black attention had shifted firmly to the problems associated with urban family living. Up until sometime in the 1930s, with probably a generational lag of about twenty years, efforts to reverse detribalization were twofold. In urban areas, Christian and liberal concerns focused on demonizing and constraining African women's sexuality and on removing or returning them to rural areas, where they might once again fall under the authority of their male guardians. And in rural areas, magistrates and other officials colluded with senior men to prevent their daughters and female wards from leaving for urban areas. The 1927 Black Administration Act entrenched male authority over daughters and female wards by disallowing independent legal status to Black women.[62]

However, the Great Depression and its effects, coupled with impoverishment in the reserves and domestic labor shortages in urban areas, negated these earlier attempts to keep Black women out of South African cities. The 1932 Native Economic Commission was intended to investigate declining African standards of living and Black impoverishment (even if it did not intend to address them). By the time of its release, the state, liberal white concerns, and Black nationalist organizations, had all recognized the urban African family as fact. From this point onward, attempts to regulate African intimate life, including, for example, attempts geared toward regulating women and the provision of housing, recognized that Black urbanization was irreversible. By the start of World War II, it was generally accepted—certainly by every person who commented publicly about these issues—that African urban life needed to accommodate families, even if only imperfectly (and, in fact, it did so very imperfectly). The 1940 Conference on African Family Life, organized by the Christian Council of South Africa, was an example of this shift in focus; conferences in the first decade of the century had focused on reconstructing rural traditional life. Interest in reconstructing the African family as modern enough to withstand the twentieth century, in comparison with its tribal avatar, was widely held and present across preindependence Africa.[63]

Already mentioned for its role in supporting male authority, the Black Administration Act of 1927 serves as a limiting factor on the shifts covered by this book in relation to older and newer practices of intimacy. By this date, a goodly portion of registered African marriages were under one system of administration instead of the multiple systems inherited from the constituent elements of the Union. Notably, several marriage regimes had prevailed in the Cape. A couple's married life depended on when they married and under which legislation. Some of these recognized women as legal adults, as in the case of Antje Gingxa, discussed later. African Christians in the Cape who had married in the 1890s represented a generation rapidly reducing in size by the 1940s. By simplifying marriage regimes, the Black Administration Act took large swaths of African intimate life out of the eye and from under the attention of the South African state. This move rendered African intimate lives invisible from the official record and allowed for a less complicated legal edifice in relation to customary law. Further, a generational shift in local magistrates, as the men who were the sons of missionaries were replaced by Afrikaner career bureaucrats, made for a much less sympathetic (the term is relative) category of official when it came to the legal resolution of intimate problems.

The shift in the bureaucratic regard for African intimate lives coincides with and is connected to the assumption of power by the National Party. While the introduction of formal apartheid was gradual and patchy,

1948 does mark a line in the sand. Before this date, official racial ideology included some notion of benevolent trusteeship, while official attitudes toward Black urban residents were centered on the control and supply of labor. After 1948, racial discrimination infused the state and white society to an even greater extent. As a result, African family life became more fractured, some of the evidence for which lies in declining rates of marriage or long-term cohabitation legitimized by lobola. By the 1960s, notwithstanding the potentially cohesive effects of Christian thinking, migrant labor, poverty, and increasingly unjust laws had made it extremely difficult for Africans to maintain long-term, dual-parent (or even multiple-parent) families. African family life and Black intimacy had become markedly different.

The narrative behind this chronology makes use of a range of sources drawing on the experiences of Black Christians in South Africa in the first half of the twentieth century. I used a range of archives in my research, noted in the bibliography. The following paragraphs reflect on the politics of archival use, including language and the literal colonial and postcolonial flows of paper.

At the beginning of the period this book covers, Black converts wrote principally in English; by the 1940s, the Black middle class was writing and publishing both in English and a range of indigenous languages, sometimes two or more in the same piece of writing. This language spread is reflected in the sources I used. These are principally written in English but include records in isiXhosa, isiZulu, Setswana, Sesotho, and Afrikaans. A multilingual historicity is not accidental, not just in relation to people's own language fluency but also in the sense that people made choices about the languages in which they wrote. In West Africa, the linguistic politics of the region meant that in the early twentieth century most newspaper publishing was in English; in East Africa, publication was on a smaller scale and often in vernacular-language newspapers; and in southern Africa, newspapers frequently shared space between indigenous languages and English.[64] Newspaper editors chose, or had chosen for them, the languages in which they published in response to complex factors around accessibility and audience. Black reporters often switched between languages to reflect different viewpoints, but before the 1950s, published work more often reflected a bias toward English. Official sources, however, such as court and church records, are exclusively in English, even when many of the meetings they record were conducted in other languages. Black clerks were required to transcribe court proceedings in English, later Afrikaans.

Colonial record flows—the literal movement of pieces of paper via steamship and later aircraft—mean that many of the records used in this book are located in archives far from their place of origin. Several of the collections are located in London at the School of Oriental and African Studies, in New York, or in Edinburgh. There is also a bias toward the records of the historic mission churches; indigenous churches have fewer preserved records. The extent and location of these records speak directly to the power and sway of Protestant ecumenism, not only at the height of mission influence in the nineteenth century but also in the first half of the twentieth century, when almost all Christian aid and Christian services to Africa were channeled through an office in New York or London. "Why North American Christian Forces Should Undertake Now a Programme of Advance in Africa" was the title of a program put forward by the Foreign Missions Conference of North America in 1946. It reflected a common cross-Atlantic fascination with Africa, including consideration of the continent as a destination for future development aid.[65]

The church documents I use speak principally to church life within institutional spaces, like the church itself, local schoolrooms, or diocesan offices in Mthatha and Grahamstown. Minutes and official reports chronicle the meetings that people attended in the course of their church work, the debates that took place, and the proposals that were made. They present the literate face of the church, that part of it and those members within it who felt fluent and confident enough to speak. Sometimes the church records reflect that translation has taken place, but often the fact of translation is concealed. Church events and concerns that happened outside of official meetings must remain the province of speculation. This affects what we know about Black Christians in the early twentieth century, especially Black women in the church.

The church records used in this book reflect a particular style of literacy, one that elevates and values order, form, and the erasure of individual in favor of institutional and collective identity. To counterbalance this, I have used personal writing, including letters.[66] This presents an intermediate and more personal zone of writing, something that would have resonated with T. B. Soga, who fought for many years to have his ideas about history published and who pursued the publication of these ideas across a range of forums. Soga was adept at slipping in and out of genres, his hand equally skilled at writing a minute as it was at recording the speculative history that characterized his amateur ethnography.

I wish to make a final point about many of the archival sources used in this book. They exist still because of a personal tenacity that gifts them with a posthumous agency absent at the time they were produced. For instance, in 1911, John (Gamiso) Kula challenged the occupation of a piece of land by widow Antje Gingxa. Customary law would not have recognized her occupational rights, which came to her via a marriage in community of property, because she and her husband, Moses Kula, had married in church.[67] She appeared in court with a copy of the church register reflecting her marriage. More than one hundred years later, Gingxa's pursuit of justice is relevant to historians like me because of her care of her pieces of paper.

The themes discussed in the first sections of this chapter, as well as the sources I use, ebb and flow through the six chapters that make up this book. Chapter 1 covers two related issues. Firstly, it places church-centered networks in relation to other networks present in South Africa in the early twentieth century. I show how Christianity constituted a significant structuring presence in people's lives that went beyond the weekly rituals of faith, into South African public culture, and even further into a global Christian ecumene. Building on what I call "institutional thickness," I then use the anthropology of texts to outline the different ways that Christianity and literacy allowed for the public convening of a Black intimacy, an expansion on the section "A Convention of Publics" in this introduction.

Chapter 2 is about masculinity, especially older ideas of masculinity transformed and shifted to varying extents within South Africa after 1910. Ethnic differences were critical to the construction of masculinity different from how African women understood their gendered roles. Through an examination of male circumcision and initiation, I show how African Christians brought innovation to the consideration of custom. Some of this centered on relocating both the practice and discussion of custom from the secrecy that cloaked its traditional practice to more public spaces in a context in which African Christians went to great lengths to Christianize initiation. They used a range of arguments based on Christian precedent and the Bible both to defend and to denounce it. The discussion in newspapers, initially about the constitution of Xhosa masculinity, soon developed into a more general discussion about the link between ethnicity and masculinity and what constituted modern masculinity.

Chapter 3 speaks to what happened when African Christians adopted mission-driven moral codes. Through an examination of love letters, church proceedings, and civil court cases from the Eastern Cape, it considers the consequences of love and sex, including the transgression of Christian sexual morality. It also examines the extent to which people's intimate lives were truly ever private, as well as the ways that love affairs were always carried out at least partially in public. Accusations (and proof) of sexual immorality had significant, though different, consequences for men and women, and gendered patterns affected how and whether people attempted to resolve accusations of immorality. The chapter also considers how court cases acted as spaces for the performance of new practices of heterosexual culture, practices given further emphasis when cases were recorded for use as public records.

Marriage is a central concern in the subsequent three chapters. To focus on one of its most important elements—lobola—chapter 4 begins with a description of changing patterns in African marriage. If, before 1915, missionary debates around African marriage in the postwar period usually ended up as a critique of lobola as slavery, this voice became much less audible in favor of African Christian voices. By the 1930s, these opinions were being articulated in ecumenical church forums and national newspapers. Letters to the newspapers helped to give shape and form to the importance of lobola, recreating its status in every literary statement delivered for or against it. Unlike polygamy and initiation, only written about by men, women also wrote about lobola. By the mid-1930s, meaningful church opposition to lobola had virtually ceased, allowing the practice to continue unchallenged as a critical element of modern Black intimacy.

Chapter 5 is about the power and significance of the white wedding in Christian families. By the 1930s, it was clear that most Black Christians were choosing to marry in church. These marriages drew on precolonial gift-giving rituals reconfigured into modern patterns of consumption that favored white wedding gowns, bridesmaids' dresses, wedding cakes, and gifts of cutlery and crockery. Examining these weddings provides insight into how Black families, especially the modernizing elite, created status and cultivated respectability in white-dominated South Africa. Weddings rested in complicated arrangements of gift giving and, as new material forms—such as tea sets and telegrams—entered into gift giving, weddings acted as a nexus for the creation of new types of social relationships.

Polygamy, or its remnants, constitutes chapter 6. The chimera of polygamy is important because it charts the limits of mainline Christianity, certainly the limit to regarding all mainline Christians as cut from the same cloth. Firstly, the Christian fascination with polygamy, at least by World War I, was a fascination with the enduring ghost of marriage past. Polygamy, according to those who opposed it, was a rural practice rooted in the enslavement of women and carnal appetite and needed firm opposition. At the same time, however, when read against people's complicated marital or multipartnered lives, it is apparent that the rural style of polygamy was not as significant as imagined. Instead, African Christians of all denominational affiliations were engaging in a range of multimarried behavior. Moreover, by the late 1930s, it was no longer clear that all African and European clergy in the mainline churches opposed multiple marriage.

1 ~ Convening Christian Publics

Churches, Newspapers, and Customary Courts

> With the exception of the military autocracies established over the Zulus by Tshaka, over the Mndebele bv Umzilikazi, and by the Swazi in Swaziland, the rule of Native Chiefs in South Africa was not so irresponsible as it is generally believed to have been. Their will was tempered and to a very large extent controlled by a Council so weighty and influential that no step of serious tribal importance was taken until the whole matter had been discussed by it at length. This Council consisted of advisers of the Chief commonly spoken of as Councillors. Certainly they were such, but they were much more; they were the direct representatives of the people's wish and in the very considerable freedom of speech permitted to them at their gatherings the popular voice found menus of expression. A Councillor was not formally appointed, simply becoming such as his opinion at the public gatherings increased in weight.[1]

THIS CHAPTER covers how it was that Christian ideals and ideas came to have such an influence on African conceptions and practices of intimacy. It firstly explains the extent to which Christianity wound through African society in South Africa in the early twentieth century. The way Christianity worked in and through people's lives constituted an institutional thickness that allowed Christianity and the knowledge necessary for operating in Christian public life to saturate African society broadly, even into traditional spaces and parts of the country where converts to Christianity were relatively few.

A second phenomenon lies in how education and Christianity fostered new forms of public space for Africans, especially in relation to the circulation of text. Ecclesiastical structures and church forums, where disciplines and practices like debating were critical to participation, built upon earlier traditions of male participation in the *inkundla, legotla,* and, in Xhosaland, the *Bhunga* (*Bunga* in the old orthography), literally "the council of the chief," mentioned in the opening epigraph. The extent of these structures made for a widespread if not extensive African entry into public life. In the late nineteenth and early twentieth centuries, Africans entered the public life of the Cape, Natal, the Free State, and the South African Republic—and, after 1910, South Africa—as Christians, whatever else they also were. This resulted in the creation of public spaces that had a Christian moral imprint that played itself out in thinking, feeling, and behavior around families and couples and how their relationships ought to work and about how people ought to behave in public. Not everyone who engaged in these new public spaces would have advocated for a Christian morality, but everyone who did so was contributing to a wider debate about the relationship between Christianity and tradition.

Chief among the new forms of public spaces were newspapers, novels, and other kinds of writing. While I am interested in all these forms, I am principally concerned in this book with the newspaper, because of its accessibility to a range of audiences and because of the way it transformed orality into text. I am also interested in how newspapers convened audiences of individuals, whatever other corporate identities people may have held and wielded in other spaces. This quality allowed newspapers to address multiple audiences simultaneously, but as individuals as well as parts of collective entities. In southern Africa, this ability effected a critical shift in how audiences had conceived of themselves in the precolonial period. In the late eighteenth century, the spread of print capitalism allowed audiences to conceive of themselves as being constituted by "autonomous, equivalent, interchangeable individuals rather than hierarchically structured great families or specific interest groups" or women and men owing allegiance to the chiefly councils mentioned in the epigraph.[2] In the Black newspapers published from roughly the 1870s onward, in Zulu and Xhosa and English (and other languages not mentioned here), African readers, writers, and interlocutors debated and challenged a range of issues, including the role of traditional male initiation, what constituted masculinity in parts of the country that did not practice circumcision, the importance of lobola, whether polygamy was more immoral than monogamy, and the proper format for relationships between women and men.

However, newspapers and novels were not the only spaces in which Africans remade their ideas about intimacy and marital relations. South African law courts, especially civil law courts dealing with African affairs, were more instrumental in shaping both ideas and practices around marriage than we might realize. Not only did law courts and the hearing of cases clarify how Africans wanted their personal affairs to work out even if the courts did not reach the hoped-for conclusions, but they also built African ideas about marriage and inheritance (if only in a guise that held itself to be more civilized than African practice) into the legal edifice of the racially discriminatory white state. Moreover, court trials built upon forms of accusation and resolution that had local histories, and at the same time capitalized on the way European law allowed women as well as men to plead their cases. Richard Roberts and others working on the social history of law have shown how legal cases reflect and represent not only discrete judicial events but also the instantiation and challenge of social norms and practices.[3] Both performative and socially influential, cases heard in the extensive network of customary courts in South Africa in the early twentieth century helped to shape white and Black perceptions of African marriage.

And lastly, the Christian publics convened by these various forms were cosmopolitan in nature. Ecumenism in South Africa transcended local racial discrimination and was key to opening up a world of transnational associational activity and a religious cosmopolitanism to Black South African Christians. As authors like James Campbell and Joel Cabrita have shown, transnational identities rooted in Christianity were key to how Africans related to and interacted with larger social worlds, in the United States of America and in Europe, in the interwar period.[4]

"A TEXT IS A TISSUE OF WORDS"

The subheading of this section is from scholar Karin Barber's work on the anthropology of texts, where she charts the different contexts in which words and other ways of conveying meaning, including those originally oral, become recognized as texts and gain audiences and public life.[5] Her work points to an ongoing tension in African history between the oral and the written. As many have noted, and as is evident in historical writing that valorizes oral traditions and the spoken voice for being more authentic in the tricky context of reconstructing Africa's largely unwritten past, written documents are often objects of suspicion. However, if we shift our understanding of what constitutes a text, it becomes possible to see continuity as well as disjuncture between oral and textual forms. Writing itself, Barber observes, does not give an object its quality of textuality. "Rather what does is the quality of being joined together and given a recognisable existence as a form."[6] Another quality of texts is their ability to "attract attention and outlast the moment."[7] Barber returns and returns to this idea throughout the book. In her chapter on audiences and publics, she points especially to the role that mission-driven newspapers played in the creation of public discourse and discursive arenas that in turn helped to foster individuals as modern subjects with specific interests.[8] Barber does this by employing the notion that texts can be constitutive of sociality, and she links this idea back to how anthropologists study society. "I take the fundamental subject matter of anthropology to be social relationships, and ask in what ways verbal textuality arises from, and in turn helps to shape, social relationships."[9]

I first encountered this position, that texts or textuality are not only reflective but also constitutive of social relationships, as part of my archaeology curriculum in the early 1990s through the work of scholars like Henry Glassie, Mark Leone, and Ian Hodder. Then, archaeologists, anthropologists, and folklorists had begun more deeply to explore theories of material culture in order to examine what Leone refers to as the interactive or recursive nature of material culture, like some of the ephemera of weddings referred to in chapter 5. "Just as language reflects and in use creates, so things that are made reflect but also substantiate and verify, and thus reproduce the processes that led to making them."[10]

Many historians, however, attuned to using either oral or written texts as sources of evidence, miss the insights offered by the materiality of what they study. This is especially the case with a generation or so of South African historians trained in social history who pay more attention to the consequences of class and race rather than to the ways markers of class and race reproduce social difference. In South Africa, cultural history has a rather unreflective pedigree (which is not necessarily the case elsewhere), located as it has been in a subset of historical work dedicated to studying the architectural styles and objects of early white Afrikaner society. African cultural artifacts, in contrast, were the province of *volkekunde*, the racially derived and essentialist ethnology that characterized the Afrikaans practice of anthropology from the 1940s to the 1980s.[11] As a result, the insights to be gained from studying the material consequences of objects—how forms, genres, and texts impact sociality—are underexplored. In the chapter on weddings, I pay most attention to the point just made, but in this chapter and elsewhere in the book, I want to consider texts as having both social and material consequences, the recursive quality on which Leone wrote.

Some of what I discuss is captured by the phrase "tin trunk literacy," used to refer to everyday styles of literacy in Africa.[12] It refers to how people collected and saved old documents, books, pamphlets, and other paper-based ephemera in tin trunks as a way of preserving them for the future and referencing their own importance. What I have always liked about the metaphor is the "tin trunk" part of it, not because it is a way to include archiving practices in everyday literacy but because tin trunks are physical: they have sharp edges, and they move around, requiring an investment of labor, perhaps on a daily basis, to keep them clean (or not). They reference the form of everyday literacy as much as its content, meaning subsumed into material. Which brings me back to textuality, which percolates through the rest of this chapter. But first, I return to the creation of a Christian public in South Africa.

THE CHURCH

A Brief History of Colonialism and Christianity in the Eastern Cape

To situate my discussion about the institutional thickness of Christianity and its public forms, I begin in the Eastern Cape and among speakers of Xhosa (the language that became the common tongue for different dialect speakers from a range of chiefdoms). While this book is not about Christianity in the Eastern Cape, or even the Xhosa, it does draw examples from this region. This is both because Christianity in South Africa came first to the Xhosa and because this region formed a dense network of mission stations from the early nineteenth century, much more so than any part of what later became South Africa. Moreover, the experience of colonial rule in the Eastern Cape helped to shape post-Union white rule in critical ways, a concept I touch upon further in chapter 2. Developments that occurred at a later date in other parts of the region or that were particular to the Cape Colony, like the vote for African men, meant the Eastern Cape was closely locked into the politics of the Cape Colony, and later, that of the Union of South Africa.

During the nineteenth century, the Eastern Cape region was home to competing and powerful chiefdoms, including the Xhosa, the Thembu, the Mpondomise, and the Mpondo, speaking dialects of a language that later became standardized as Xhosa.[13] Beginning in the late eighteenth century, Dutch and then British colonial forces brought the area under European control. The conflict between the British and various coalitions, of first the Xhosa chiefdoms and subsequently other Xhosa-speaking chiefdoms, spilled out in a series of wars and frontier skirmishes beginning in 1789 and finishing in 1878. Richard Price suggests the British experience in the Eastern Cape constituted a crucible for British imperial rule elsewhere, though his analysis probably ignores to what extent this was more accidental and less intentional.[14] In the decades following the Xhosa loss of independence in the west, especially after the War of the Axe (1846–47), the British experimented with systems of control that ranged from rather more conformity with the then-characteristic liberalism of the Cape Colony to a more coherent style of indirect rule in the Transkeian Territories to the east.

In the nineteenth century, the chieftains across what is today the Eastern Cape ruled via a series of chiefly councils in matters for which an authority higher than the homestead heads was required. In the model of the chiefly council quoted at the start of the chapter, the council was a recognizable but exclusionary oral form. Its pronouncements, however unfair, wise, or otherwise, acted to constitute social reality. Men who gathered at a chiefly council returned to their homesteads to share the deliberations that had occurred at the gathering. The ambiguous model of representative government it introduced was not replicated anywhere else in South Africa, but similar structures were present across the country among the different ethnic groups and chiefdoms.

By the middle of the nineteenth century, in the African territories adjacent to the Cape Colony, the rapacious and anti-African disposition that prevailed among the white settlers on the eastern frontier had given way to a more ostensibly liberal system of rule, often referred to as "Cape liberalism," which held that Africans had the potential to become the equal of Europeans. By the end of the century, African men in the Cape Colony could vote, subject to a property and educational qualification, and own land outside the reserves. Subsequent systems of African control in South Africa would oscillate between this approach to African affairs and the more indirect and paternalist system of rule implemented after the 1860s in the colony of Natal under Theophilus Shepstone. In the early years of the twentieth century, liberalism—coupled with the uneasy familiarity of paternalism—played out in the eastern districts of the Cape.

After 1883, when the Government Commission on Native Law and Custom recommended the introduction of some measure of representative government, and after 1895, when the Mpondo were annexed to the Cape Colony as part of the Transkeian Territories, a local system of representative councils was introduced, which later became known as the Bhunga, until the system was replaced in the 1950s.[15] Representative councils, composed of chiefs and senior male officials, also offered advice to the local government arms of South African state after 1910. It was (and still is) a system based on a territorial ethnic nationalism, its legacy today seen in institutions like the Ingonyama Trust, responsible—through the Zulu king—for the allocation of nearly 30 percent of all land in KwaZulu-Natal. Indirect rule has been written about—and its definition contested—by different historians.[16]

Prior to colonialism, chiefs ruled with the assistance of similar councils, which were able to exercise lesser or greater power in relation to a chief's status and authority. Women could rule as chiefs (or as regents for minor sons), and young chiefs presided over their own chiefly councils.

Convening Christian Publics ~ 27

Colonialism interfered with such arrangements that recognized authority and status in this way, acknowledging only men as chiefs and only senior men as sources of authority in ethnic matters. This manner of indirect rule is known for the convergence it represented between the senior African men and local magistrates. It blocked the access of younger men to positions of authority and their ability to exercise power as chiefly advisers, an obstacle to which the ecumenical nature of Protestant Christianity offered an important solution.[17]

African Christianity in southern Africa was rooted in the entry of evangelical Protestant Christianity in the early nineteenth century, when initial evangelization was undertaken by white missionaries, Khoikhoi, and other Black converts. Itinerant Khoikhoi who had worked on Dutch farms and also as cattle herders learned Christianity from these families and from the evangelical Moravian missionaries who had established mission stations in the west of the Cape Colony from the eighteenth century onward. By the late eighteenth century, many of these Khoikhoi had helped to establish the first community of believers among the Xhosa.[18] In the early 1820s, Presbyterians established their first mission stations. They were followed shortly afterward by the Wesleyans. The first Anglican missions were established just after the mid-nineteenth century, followed later by Moravians from Germany.

The first mission stations were relatively small and attracted few converts but soon grew in number. By the late nineteenth century, Xhosaland had more mission stations than any other corner of the British empire, a churchly thickness which had particular consequences, not only for the shape of Christianity in the region but also for the influence the Eastern Cape was later to exercise over what at the time was referred to as "the native question." Later, this history fed into the strength of anti-apartheid resistance during the 1950s in places like Port Elizabeth.[19]

The Presbyterian imprint on the region deepened after 1841, when it opened a secondary school at Lovedale, an institution that was to become a crucible for South Africa's Black elite until the Bantu Education Act removed mission control of schools in 1953.[20] Lovedale Institution offered an education that went beyond the four or five years of primary schooling provided at most mission stations. Its efforts were soon replicated by the other mainline mission churches. The Wesleyans opened an institution at Healdtown in 1855, and the Anglicans opened their first secondary school, St. Matthew's in Keiskammahoek, in 1856. By the 1860s, the Presbyterians, Methodists, and Anglicans had committed substantial resources to higher education in the Cape Colony. By the end of the century, American

Board, German, Norwegian, and Swiss missionaries had established mission schools across Natal and the two Afrikaner republics, the Orange Free State and the Zuid-Afrikaanse Republiek. The same mission societies also established the region's first hospitals, hospitals prepared to serve African patients as well Europeans. Lovedale, which was the educational choice of southern Africa's Black elite into the 1940s, had a significance and influence in South African ecumenical and educational politics that gave it a status larger than its church's membership would imply.

Especially after the 1860s, and largely as a result of the social destruction caused by the Cattle Killing, Christianity made significant inroads into Xhosa-speaking communities.[21] Its adoption followed colonial penetration, spreading from the west to the east. Many communities remained resolutely traditional and non-Christian into the twentieth century, but few pockets of the region were untouched by either Christianity or mission schooling at the time of Union.

Initially, all African Christians were members of the historic mission churches, a situation that shifted at the end of the nineteenth century as African Christians founded their own independent churches.[22] However, those cleaving to Anglicanism, Presbyterianism, and Methodism constituted the majority of Christians well into the mid-twentieth century. Conversion patterns in the Eastern Cape show that women outnumbered men as converts and that Christian adherence in a family usually developed from an initial female convert before spreading outward.[23] All but the most ardent traditionalists accessed churchly life and practice through their relatives and patronage networks. By the early 1920s, the Xhosa-speaking population to the west of the Kei River was roughly 528,000 people, with around 81,000 or 25 percent—the figures vary—professing a "connection" with the church.[24] In Auckland Location in 1915, most household heads (28 of probably 35) were attached to either the Congregational Church, the African Presbyterian Church (a breakaway from the Presbyterian Church, under Mpambani Mzimba), or the Free Church of Scotland.[25] Figures for adherence decreased from west to east, though they picked up again toward the border between Pondoland and southern Natal.

Christian Publics and Institutional Thickness

In 1932, missionary E. W. Grant traveled throughout the Eastern Cape. He noted subsequently in his report, "During the month under review a distance of 1150 miles has been covered by car. Thirty-two meetings and services have been held in eleven different centres, and there has been opportunity for discussion with a number of missionaries and others."[26]

At one of his services, he notes also "the presence of a large number of 'reds' from the neighbouring kraals."[27] ("Red"—from the red ocher that women and men smeared on their skin—and "school" were terms used, respectively, to refer to traditionalists and Christians.)

At this time, Adolf Hitler was about to come to power in Germany, and the world had been in the grip of the Great Depression for three years. Twenty-two years after Union, the living conditions for Black South Africans, especially those in rural areas, were manifestly worse, and few families were managing to eke out a living from the overgrazed and underfertilized land at their disposal in the reserves. A bad drought in 1924 had only exacerbated the situation.[28]

While many historians would recognize South Africa and the world through these few sentences in the previous paragraph, they would be less likely to see the relevance of Grant's journey to stock farmers struggling to make ends meet or to miners fighting for minimum conditions of service. They certainly would not recognize the extent to which Grant's journey reflected how Christianity had woven itself into the thread of the Eastern Cape, the entire region from its border with Natal in the east to Lovedale in the west. In his car, he had covered an extensive circuit of mission stations and outstations, where his talks attracted not only Christians, aspirant or hesitant, but nonbelievers as well, whose attendance at services demonstrated their curiosity of, if not a conformity with, Christianity.

Grant would have been gratified to discover how far that thinking about Christian practice had permeated among the Xhosa-speaking Mpondomise almost ten years later. One such instance occurred at St. Cuthbert's, a mission station at Tsolo established by the High Church Society of Saint John the Evangelist (SSJE). (The station was also one of the locations of A. C. Jordan's novel *The Wrath of the Ancestors*, an excerpt from which opens chapter 5.) There, in 1941, lay workers and preachers debated male initiation practices during one of their quarterly meetings, which had a routine attendance of between sixty and one hundred people and were a site of regular debate on what constituted proper Christian conduct. The Black lay workers put three different motions before the meeting. In the first, Mr. Maqibela suggested "that Christian headmen be asked to issue no *sutu* [the hut set aside for initiation] sites to Christian parents, who wish to circumcise their boys in the heathen custom." By "heathen custom," he meant the rites and practices that accompanied surgical circumcision. After some discussion, Mr. Maqibela, following tested practice drawn both from experience with Anglican church government and the debating society format, withdrew the motion, which was replaced by another, while a third—eventually passed by the meeting—proposed "that Christian people should put in practice their influence to the entire abandoning of the sutu custom."[29]

The debate was conducted in both Xhosa and English, with two of the clergy interpreting on the fly. We know this because the unnamed secretary recorded the meeting details in a neat and readable longhand. Other quarterly meetings discussed infant and child health, the conduct of marriage parties, whether the wearing of surplices on Good Friday was compulsory, why Anglican women could not marry men of other denominations (women marrying out of their birth denomination was always a provocative topic at church meetings in the Eastern Cape), the shortage of building materials during World War II, and whether a special committee was needed to compose the meetings' agendas.[30] This was a vigorous and engaged Christian life, where lay workers—drawing on older forms of debate used in the chiefly courts but applied in an ecumenically democratized fashion—engaged the SSJE fathers about the content of Christianity.

South African history after the cultural turn in history still struggles with understanding motivations for action and ideology that lie outside of race and class.[31] If, in their work, some South Africanists overprioritize labor issues in people's lives, others underidentify the status of Christianity in the same people's lives. For many humanist or secular academics skeptical of belief, faith is often considered as bound to particular institutional spaces and limited in its possibilities because of this binding. This is despite a wealth of contemporary work on how people are repurposing urban space to fit their rituals of belief.[32] In what follows, I suggest considering the institutional space of the church, here considered not only as literal space but also for what it does to create "a net of social motion" that explains, firstly, the threading of Christianity and its attendant beliefs into African life and, secondly, how Black South Africans practiced and gained skill at being part of a Western-centered public life.[33] Faith is not tied to institutional spaces, but even thin communities of faith can extend beyond institutional spaces, especially when those spaces are thick on the ground.[34]

Glassie's work on the creation of community in Ballymenone in Ireland provides a way to think about how communities are created, for the purposes of this book, the constitution of religious communities in South Africa.

> The landscape displayed no community. Before me, between tall hedges, a road lifted at a flat sky. Across the green, whitewashed houses scattered in no apparent pattern. The map folded in my rucksack had words on it but no clustering of dots to indicate a center of population, but I had to know the community.... To help my

profession and by extension my society, I wanted to study people as they grouped themselves through action, but I was not worried that I did not know where I was. Had there been a village with a name, I could have been misled, for I wanted to construct a community as the people who lived in it did, and there was no reason to assume their arena of action would match a territory on a map. In no hurry, I was confident that one person would lead me to another. Connections would multiply and repeat. Eventually I would be able to drape the net of their social motion over a map of their place.[35]

Two of Glassie's points are relevant here. It is easy to see that first- and second-generation African Christians in South Africa constituted a community, not only within their ethnic categories but also across ethnic categories. This community can be correlated with the numbers of mission-educated Africans at the start of the twentieth century. The restricted size of this constituency meant that many of its members did know one another. This is the Black elite referred to in the introduction. Referring to this group as an elite, however, can be misleading. Unquestionably, this group of Christians was more elite and more educated than the majority of Black South Africans at the start of the twentieth century. Their elite status, however, was in relation to the norms and values of a Western-dominated social system rather than a meaningful material or class comparison to the elite of white society. This is the argument about class status made by so many historians of South Africa: the Black elite lived perilously close to poverty and loss of status, not because of any internal class dynamics but because of a precarity forced upon them by a racist state.[36] Their status was always fragile and subject to erosion, even if in terms of social standing they were vastly—though precariously—better off than most Black South Africans.

As the number of African Christians increased beyond the point of possibility for all of them to know or to know of one another, it becomes more difficult to talk about a Christian public whose values and beliefs could transcend the more sectarian. I need to make an argument that a shared identity as Christians could and did (if not always) trump other identities, like those based on ethnicity. One way to do this is to consider Christians as a community constituted through shared action of a nationwide repetition of social behaviors exercised in relation to the institutions and behaviors of the church. The institutional thickness of Christianity in South Africa eventually created something like Glassie's net of social motion. Moreover, that net of social motion was constituted in person and in text, both spoken text and written text. This way of considering community also means regarding action as actions of the body, including a hand moving a pen across a page or an eye scanning a newspaper.

At the risk of sounding semantically fussy, this is not the same as saying that Africans experienced a construction of communities through an external force, though that is also true. According to John and Jean Comaroff, the refashioning of time and space, bodies, and thoughts that nonconformist missionaries sought was directed toward the incorporation of African converts into the powerful and unified world of capitalism.[37] The process was much more fractured than the Comaroffs initially posit (and as they also subsequently agree), and the relationship of different elements of that conversion were very uneven. If Christianity was a simultaneous making and unmaking, unmaking indigenous understandings of time and concepts like public and private while remaking space, bodies, and thoughts in a template that best suited nineteenth-century industrial capitalism, its form and outcomes were also mediated by the actions and beliefs of individual agents, where agency includes diverse arenas of action.

Regardless of their status, no converts shared one experience of the remodeling that accompanied Christianity. Fractures arose in the intersections of their interests. As they converted in greater numbers through the nineteenth century, their epistemological grasp on faith was not always the same. Some of the Eastern Cape's first converts described experiences almost mystical in outlook, while others understood conversion as a source of self-improvement. Women's experiences of Christianity, of its forces upon their bodies—its somatic effect—of the way Christian modernity reshaped the tempo of their lives, was different from those of men. Men encountered much more closely the institutional arrangements of colonialism, and later, apartheid—the double institutional layering and possibilities for mobility I refer to in this chapter—certainly in the first few decades of the twentieth century.

A recent piece outlines some of the issues with the current uses of the term "agency" in relation to African history. Speaking about a "category of things," Lynn Thomas writes, "Ultimately, though, I am less interested in imbuing things with agency than in using a category of things to construct new—more surprising, more layered—narratives of how and why humans act in the world."[38] Thomas's comments extend to how African Christian belief is often viewed. Much recent writing on African Christianity has viewed agency as an end in itself, sometimes to the extent that any action undertaken by a Christian comes to be viewed as an example of Christian agency. This is a profoundly circular argument in which behaving as a Christian is proof that a person is a Christian, while because a person is Christian, all their actions are necessarily Christian actions. In roughly the same idiom, this is the point that Joel Robbins and others have made concerning the lack of an anthropology of Christianity or sui generis claim. Indeed, to paraphrase, whatever else they are, Africans can also, sometimes simultaneously, be Christians.[39]

Many years ago, I spent far too much time reading histories of Presbyterians and the Scottish disruption, and whenever I try to recall the facts of the Great Disruption, I feel an immanent sense of panic at my lack of recollection. If a sympathetic reader of ecclesiastical history can have this reaction, it is not surprising that the genre of church history is not popular in the early twenty-first century. Many South African church and mission histories, especially ones written prior to the 1990s, are encountered as dense discussions of the shaping of individual denominations on African soil and the internal church arrangements and structures that facilitated this growth. Think instead about Grant's trip through the Eastern Cape or about the quarterly meetings at St. Cuthbert's. The former shows us Christianity as a lattice on the landscape, even if that lattice is fragile. The latter shows us what people who belonged to a church did when they gathered together in the repetitious cycle of meetings that made up church life.

The point about the presbyteries and parishes, then, is to reflect upon what church institutional structures did from the inside out. The Bantu Presbyterian Church (BPC), true to its heritage, organized itself according to a hierarchical but representative system.[40] The individual church—the kirk—was the basic unit of organization. The kirk session, made up of the minister and elders (all men) of an individual mission, was responsible for the spiritual matters of a congregation. Affairs nonspiritual (which in practice meant essentially every other aspect of life) were supervised by a deacons' court, consisting of the minister, deacons, and elders of the congregation, with deacons and elders being lay members. A number of such congregations made up a presbytery. The Ciskeian Presbytery, for instance, included congregations in Port Elizabeth and Cape Town. Each congregation sent its minister and one elder to the presbytery. A number of presbyteries made up a synod, to which each presbytery would send a number of ministers and elders. Sitting above this system and under the guidance of a moderator was the general assembly of the church, which consisted of elders and ministers from the various presbyteries, serving on a rotational system. In practice, the general assembly met only every few years.[41]

Nevertheless, what is significant is that elders and ministers from individual congregations were guaranteed representation in the synod and general assembly of the BPC. Presbyterian church life took both women and men from their homes to their churches in a daily or weekly round of movement; that same round of movement might take men to the diocesan headquarters. Individual congregation members, say, from Pirie Mission, near the foot of Ntaba kaNdoda, might serve on the area's presbytery, traveling roughly sixty kilometers to Lovedale, where most of these meetings were held. For the deacons at Emgwali, the station founded by Tiyo Soga, the journey to Lovedale would have taken considerably more time. If they were deeply involved in the associational life of the church, they traveled to places like Grahamstown, sometimes to Cape Town or Johannesburg, and for a select handful, to the United Kingdom, the United States of America, or India.

South African Presbyterians, whatever their denominational allegiance, were guaranteed a welcome in Scotland, and the mission field (in western, eastern, central, and southern Africa, as well as in India) guaranteed the kind of experience the parent church in Scotland appreciated. South Africa's status as a field of mission for the parent church in Scotland meant that James Stewart, a principal at Lovedale in the late nineteenth century, had sufficient standing to serve as a moderator for the Free Church of Scotland.

The Anglican Church similarly embedded its institutions into daily life. Each parish was represented on the diocesan synod. Parish representatives included the priest-in-charge, assistant priests, deacons, and lay folk. The synod, which met every year, was the highest decision-making body in the diocese, dealing with matters like education, finances, buildings, support funds, and changes to rules. Within a diocese, for instance, St. John's, with its cathedral in Mthatha (formerly Umtata), matters that the synod felt required further investigation, including standing issues, were dealt with by committees and boards, which reported back to the synod. By the 1930s, the diocesan synods coincided with the meetings of the native conference.

Internal migration within South Africa will be familiar to many historians, but its more common aspect is in relation to migrant labor. While many more men traveled to work on mines during this period than traveled because of their faith, what is significant is that Christianity had the potential to take Black South Africans into fields much more extensive than the ones in which they worked.

A Christian Cosmopolitanism

Some of the work referred to so far also demonstrates how a religious cosmopolitanism was present in African Christianity, providing its adherents with the spiritual, the social, and the material tools to move across borders, both within Africa and internationally. David Gordon is concerned with destabilizing the conventional narratives that surround nationhood in Zambia, tracking Christianity in public spaces through twentieth-century political nationalisms and campaigns.[42] Derek Peterson discusses how dissenting Protestants in East Africa advanced a vision of living that transcended and provided an alternative to newly constituted national borders and styles of authority rooted in the past.[43] Both scholars position Christianity as a force linking the personal and the public, daily practice and political life, the past in the present, and the role of the past in the future. Their work weaves disparate African Christianities into more regionally transnational and cosmopolitan forms of political imagining that extend beyond customary and Western-derived understandings of religion rooted in personal spirituality.

Black South Africans increasingly challenged at home by the inequities of a racially discriminatory politics found outlets for their faith and frustrations in spaces more open to their aspirations and talents. While some played out their grievances in print, as I noted earlier, others found a forum for expression in ecumenical interchurch organizations. They were active on committees and across interracial organizations like the joint councils; this was a dense and connected world, referred to by Richard Elphick as a "benevolent empire" spanning Christians of all colors and religious persuasion.[44] They wrote letters to newspapers, ethnographies, praise poems, and novels on the subject, at a slow pace before the 1930s and in an inexhaustible outpouring thereafter. They used intra-Christian forums to bring their economic and social difficulties to an audience of English-speaking white liberals and Afrikaner Calvinist ideologues. Nevertheless, the fraternal experience of ecumenism, the outward and all-embracing disposition of Protestant Christianity after the Edinburgh World Missionary Conference of 1910, suggested that all Christians were part of a larger family (if intensely quarrelsome and prone to fission) and that it was the duty of each member of that family to promote and sustain the bond.

Indeed, African concern around the erosion of tradition and the dissolution of family life in the space of Christianity helped to constitute some of the first Pan-African expressions of African solidarity. As they articulated and debated the relationship between Christianity and tradition, Black Christians used a variety of Christian forums to express their concerns. These included the International Missionary Council (IMC), a body that became the evangelical wing of the World Council of Churches in the 1960s. Associational linkages propelled Africans (and their writing) into a transnational circulatory practice, where African Christians from across the continent defended custom—especially polygamy from the predation of Protestant monogamy. In 1910, the year of South Africa's Union, Western-based Protestant mission churches held the first of several international conferences to discuss and further Protestant ecumenism. At the Le Zoute Conference in Belgium in 1926, the draft resolutions recognized that in "all questions regarding indigenous custom the counsel of mature well-instructed African Christians should be sought; and care should be taken not to create artificial sins.[45] It is our hope that the African Christians will build up a body of Christian custom, true to their genius, and covering the whole of their life."[46]

Notwithstanding this sanctimonious pronouncement, by the 1930s, African Christians were pointing out with alacrity the failure of missionary Christianity to recognize the importance of local practice, critiquing it for moving too quickly to the abandonment of practices central to maintaining the fabric of African society. In 1938, at the IMC conference in Madras, India, Black South African Christians joined a continent-wide debate about the essential tenets of Christianity and whether monogamy was a critical and nonnegotiable element of Christian faith. While some of the international socialist movements went to similar lengths to include Black South Africans in transnational dialogue, and several Black South Africans visited the Soviet Union in the interwar period, this kind of inclusion occurred on a much more limited scale.

MAGISTRATES AND CUSTOMARY COURTS

In the first few decades of the twentieth century, the regional and district magistrates, native commissioners, chief magistrates, and other government officials, including school inspectors, were often locally born. Many of them were the product of missionary families and had grown up attending one of the mission schools, often, like Walter Stanford mentioned later, fluent in Xhosa (or one of the several different dialects spoken in the mid-nineteenth century). As a category, they were often very paternal in their approach to African affairs, but they might also have a deep familiarity with the region. However, by the 1930s, the old paternalist approach to African affairs was waning, making way for the rise of a new class of technocratic official, often appointed from outside the region. Through the 1930s and into the 1940s, native commissioners gradually became less English and more Afrikaans, a trend easily seen across three decades of magisterial court records.

Ecclesiastical structures and their associational forms constitute an obvious point of entry into the consideration of Black public space. Indeed, it is sometimes easy to miss their multifaceted significance because of their everyday—and every evening and weekend—ubiquity. It is, though, less obvious exactly how it is that law courts, criminal courts, and those that deal with people's personal affairs have constituted spaces for the convening of publics. But, if we consider the textuality—the text as a tissue of words with a longevity and accessibility to numerous audiences—manifested in the activities of courts and the records they produce, then the court cases mentioned in this book are also relevant.

Martin Chanock and Elizabeth Thornberry outline the operation of courts from the mid-nineteenth century, first in the Ciskei and later in regions east of that point.[47] Initially, most African affairs were adjudicated by the white magistrates and their associates (including African clerks and interpreters). By the early twentieth century, the customary courts in the Cape Colony were multiracial and allowed participation for both African women and men. In chapter 3, I spend some time outlining how the customary courts worked; for the moment, I aim to consider the context of participation in the courts, more a social than a procedural account of their working.

In the late 1880s, Walter Stanford, then chief magistrate of East Griqualand, wrote about his engagement with "chiefs, headmen, and leading councillors" who were in frequent contact with him at his office, appearing frequently to discuss the news of the day.[48] Stanford's writing, both in his personal reminiscences and in letters he wrote in his capacity as magistrate, is full of references to interactions like those just described. Stanford, the grandson of English settlers, spent his early childhood in Alice, and by age thirteen, was working as a clerk to his uncle, the government agent J. C. Warner, in Glen Grey among the Thembu. His experience of working among Xhosa speakers (he was himself fluent) was extensive and sympathetic.

In 1888, he described a visit to Emfundisweni in Pondoland over a succession issue, a new chief needing to be appointed. "In such an important tribal issue natives responsible for the decision always aim at final unanimity and usually attain it. Delays which would be most irritating to the Europeans are accepted as necessary in the interests of the people.... An elder sister of the late chief was sent for, no doubt to elucidate some fact connected with the order of the 'Houses' to which the young chief belonged."[49] As Stanford himself recognized, a continuity existed between the chiefly deliberations that in theory governed important chiefly matters prior to colonization and European-introduced judicial proceedings. Clearly, important distinctions existed also between the two sets of practices, but sufficient continuity between them allowed magisterial court proceedings to accrete the status and consequences of text, acquiring a form constituted through both audience and longevity. Both the chiefly courts and the European court proceedings were performances, though not perhaps in the manner of popular culture. When Stanford, in 1893, attempted to secure cooperation from Thembu chiefs on scab prevention measures, he was told the following by a Qumbu headman: "The magistrates . . . have made a rule that native men attending at the seat of a magistracy must at the very least wear a pair of trousers besides having a blanket which is our ordinary attire. Well, sir, that rule is being obeyed but I notice that a good many of our men come into the presence of the magistrate wearing their trousers hind part before. This shows that while we are willing to learn the habits of civilization we need time fully to adapt ourselves to them."[50]

As oral court cases became transcribed onto paper, their publics expanded to include not only those initially present and their followers but a white (and later Black) legal profession. Further, the record of any case brought to an appeal was taken out of local context and into the highest courts of the South African state, moving from a physical beginning in a record book in a magistrate's court in the Eastern Cape to Bloemfontein, the judicial capital of South Africa. Once at the level of the nation, these records allowed the personal lives of Africans to become fodder for the institution of precedent in South African's system of Roman-Dutch law.

By the early twentieth century, the imposition of a colonial legal framework in the Eastern Cape had brought interpersonal disputes into a new resolutory framework located in a legal pluralism that considered these cases civil matters. The bulk of the interpersonal cases that came before the magistrates centered on seduction or irregularities around lobola. Stanford described the following: "Two headmen appeared at the offices, each attended by followers and witnesses. No summons had been issued as no complaint had been made to any officer of the court. They had come, they said, to submit a dispute between them to my judgment. It was a case of restoration of dowry and the points involved were soon clearly stated to me. I gave judgment and immediately afterward the snuff box passed between the two headmen and after this friendly action they rode off together good friends."[51] While Stanford's observation says nothing about the women involved in the case, or whether husband and wife left on good terms, his description does reveal the quintessential importance of audience to the resolution of conflict.

Customary litigation practices around seduction depended on the payment of fines to the father or male guardian of the seduced woman. The imposition of fines in relation to seduction formed part of precolonial punishment regimes. As Thornberry has noted, this approach to punishment did not readily conform to how colonial legal regimes understood judicial matters to be either civil or criminal and allocated offenses to either its civil (offenses against an individual) or its criminal (offenses against the state) courts.[52] Before the extension of colonial control over Xhosaland, reparations and fines were also common in cases of nonconsensual sex (rape), which the colonial state would have considered a criminal issue. Because of difficulties with determining consent, cases of nonconsensual sex could make their way into the colonial courts as civil seduction cases, or—more seldom—criminal rape cases.[53] However, because criminal courts used imprisonment as a punishment, local litigants sometimes brought their cases to the civil courts, through which reparation in the form of the payment of fines to individuals was possible. These different routes complicate our understanding of how, why, and under what circumstances cases of seduction arrived in the civil courts.

What did need to happen, though, for Africans to bring a case about land or seduction to a white South African magistrate? Black South Africans living in rural areas routinely tried to resolve disputes involving their kin through recourse to the long-standing practice in which senior men debated a situation's merits and dispensed justice according to precedent. Under segregation, this system became formalized through the institution of village courts, where headmen and subheadmen debated cases involving land and succession. While village courts may have imposed novel roles on people, the courts did continue with the performativity enmeshed in dispensing justice. Previously, the chiefly courts had allowed drawn-out and poetic disquisitions on matters ranging from the smelling out of witchcraft to elaborate cattle genealogies as senior men attempted to understand exactly whom, among litigants, should have rights to the offspring of a cow loaned to a friend twenty years previously. Both the village and customary courts continued with this form of practice. Differences between these courts, however, included the ability for women to appear and for all Africans to enjoy representation by white lawyers. "With the advent of lawyers procedure soon approximated more closely to that of the magistrates in the Cape Colony proper. . . . The natives, while complaining of attorneys and agents-at-law, naming them Ama-Gqweta (perverters), employed them all the same."[54]

The most important distinction, however, lay in how the colonial law courts could take seduction cases directly from the family into an official forum, bypassing the headmen's courts and making public the dispensation of what would previously have been the private adjudication of family matters. The term "private" here is relative, though. A family could be large, and any case of sexual misconduct involved two families at least. To be effective, family resolution had to be seen and participated in by family members. Without an audience, there could be no satisfactory outcome. This may help to explain why kirk justice issued by the Church was adopted with relative alacrity by Christian families on mission stations, as discussed in chapter 3. The choice of court in such cases was important; Thornberry discusses "black women's greater willingness to bring public charges of sexual assault," where sexual assault and seduction were often the same.[55] Thornberry explains this through reference to the acceptance of rape charges as valid charges in customary society, but it also goes to greater openness about sexual issues than was present in white society. For example, if a young African woman lost her virginity and had a child before marrying, her father or senior male relative could sue for damages. This action was possible both in the customary and European civil law courts. Cases involving damages for seduction, with precedent in both African and European law, met in the space of the European court in South Africa by the end of the nineteenth century.

Much of the work studying colonial law courts has also considered the use of court cases as sources. Historians and legal anthropologists, as Roberts has noted, have often approached using court cases in different ways, depending on whether they consider individual cases or the "aggregate data" (Roberts's phrase) to arrive at conclusions.[56] In his work on the colonial Soudan, Roberts notes the need to analyze the context of a legal case—what happens before a case comes to court—as much as the event of the case itself. Further, Roberts speaks to how cases are sociologically meaningful when they cluster around trouble spots.

In the Eastern Cape, in the districts of Alice and King William's Town, two or three cases of seduction came before the customary law courts every year in the period from roughly 1900 to 1940. During this same period, the number of civil cases appearing before the courts each year ranged between 46 and 143.[57] While this total may seem low, it should be noted that the majority of cases that brought Africans to the civil law courts were those involving debt, often to the lawyers they had contracted to act for them in cases of seduction. Before 1929, magistrates' courts heard three principal kinds of civil cases involving Africans—those of seduction, inheritance (centering on how marriage had affected a child or children's rights to inheritance), or land. Thornberry's work similarly documents the prevalence of rape and seduction cases appearing before magistrates in the nineteenth century. These kinds of cases are the trouble spots to which Roberts referred.

While the court documents reveal the importance of lobola and seduction, it is necessary to consider how accurate they may be. An issue surrounding the use of court documents concerns their reliability. Roberts and others have also considered the veracity of individual cases, which extends not only to how litigants present themselves in court but also to whether what they are presenting is accurately reflected in the bureaucratic records,

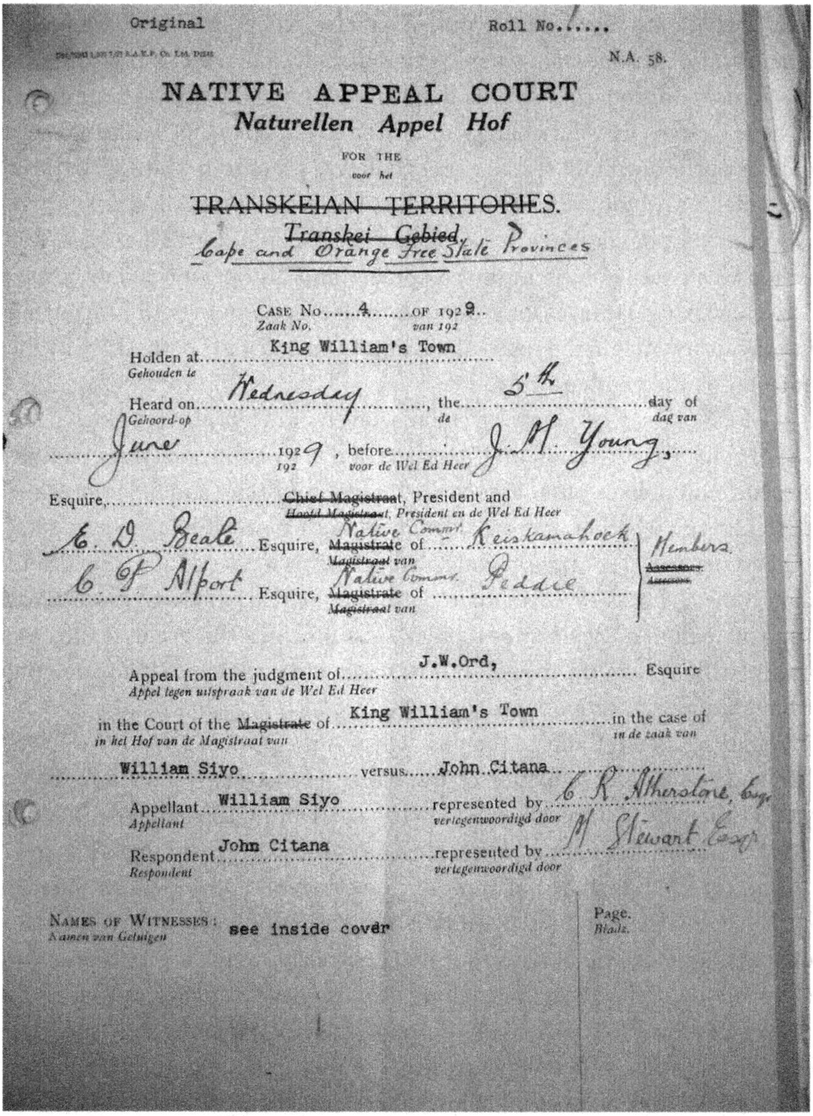

Original Roll No. 1 .....

N.A. 58.

NATIVE APPEAL COURT
Naturellen Appel Hof

FOR THE
voor het

~~TRANSKEIAN TERRITORIES.~~
~~*Transkei Gebied.*~~
Cape and Orange Free State Provinces

CASE No. 4 OF 1929.
Zaak No. van 192

Holden at King William's Town
Gehouden te

Heard on Wednesday, the 5th day of June 1929, before J. M. Young,
Gehoord op de dag van 192 voor de Wel Ed Heer

Esquire, ~~Chief Magistraat~~, President and
~~Hoofd Magistraat~~, President en de Wel Ed Heer

E. D. Beale Esquire, Native Commr. ~~Magistrate~~ of Keiskamahoek
~~Magistraat~~ van

C. P. Alport Esquire, Native Commr. ~~Magistrate~~ of Peddie
~~Magistraat~~ van

Members ~~Assessors.~~ ~~Assessors~~

Appeal from the judgment of J.W.Ord, Esquire
Appel tegen uitspraak van de Wel Ed Heer

in the Court of the ~~Magistrate~~ of King William's Town in the case of
in het Hof van de Magistraat van in de zaak van

William Siyo versus John Citana

Appellant William Siyo represented by C. R. Atherstone, Esq.
Appellant vertegenwoordigd door

Respondent John Citana represented by M. Stewart Esq.
Respondent vertegenwoordigd door

NAMES OF WITNESSES: see inside cover
Namen van Getuigen

Page.
Bladz.

FIGURE 1.1. The front page of a 1929 case lodged in the Native Appeal Court in the Cape. Notice the changes in the titles of the officials and the change from the Transkeian Territories to the Cape, introduced in part as a result of the Black Administration Act of 1927. The case involved a lobola dispute. Siyo's sister had married Citana, but the lobola was not paid in full. Citana disputed the case because, he said, he had married his wife in church. 1/ KWT 2/1/2/1 Civil Cases Bantu Appeal Court 1929–1933. Reproduced courtesy of the Western Cape Archives and Record Service (WCARS).

which are what remain after a case is concluded.[58] While using court records is fraught with difficulty, when read carefully, they provide access to areas of life not covered in other sources.[59]

In many of the cases mentioned in this book, plaintiffs, and defendants, as well as their witnesses, would have testified in Xhosa. The clerk of the court, usually a Xhosa intermediary, would have taken notes and translated their evidence for the legal file that he was compiling. Thornberry has demonstrated how court clerks and interpreters played a significant role in inducing magistrates to take on cases, and this may have been true also of some civil cases.[60] However, it is clear the twentieth-century civil cases I have examined reflect much more a conscious decision by litigants to take a case to the civil law courts.

So far, I have addressed how local cases around seduction found their way into the Eastern Cape magisterial courts, dispensing judgments that had local audiences in performances that would have had their proceedings and outcomes repeated to family members—both those near and those far away—and repeated at the end of each year when migrants to Johannesburg or one of the other cities returned from work at the end of a contract.

However, as these cases moved into text, captured in official proceedings, they gained additional lives and additional, more authoritative audiences. Roman-Dutch law relied heavily on precedent, and so any record of court proceedings from the early twentieth century is full of references to previous judgments. Every year, one of the legal publishers in the country would issue a volume with summaries of cases that had appeared before the Black appeal courts.[61] Magistrates, lawyers, and inquiring litigants and plaintiffs used these to determine how to plead cases, both in their initial appearance and in appeal. Case records from the 1910s onward often included references to previous cases of a similar nature, so a case referencing seduction would refer to previous judgments in similar cases.

Union in 1910 did not simplify matters, as one might imagine. It only meant that court officers often had to refer to several reference books to ascertain which legislation ought to apply in a ruling. References to the law of the Cape Colony and the Transkeian Territories were more frequent in appeal cases because this region of the country had many pieces of legislation on which to draw for precedent. With several matrimonial regimes successively placed in the Cape, appeal court judges often had difficulty establishing which piece of legislation ought to determine the disposition of property. In the legal literature on Black marriage in South Africa, much has been written about the impact of the Natal Code on African marriage and on the 1927 Black Administration Act. However, adjudicating cases arising as a result of this legislation required fewer legal hours and was less complicated than adjudicating cases arising from the legislation emanating from the Cape. Because of the proliferation of legal regimes in the Cape, the research and investigation needed to determine, for instance, the distribution of property was much more extensive. The possibility for a case to be differently adjudicated also meant that these cases were more prone to appeal. As a result, legal rulings from the Cape made before 1927 and for African families whose marriages had concluded before 1927 appeared more frequently before the appeal courts. Their records appeared at the appeal courts and were incorporated into the appeal court cases, giving these cases an extensive textual presence that accumulated as the records proceeded through three levels of court. For these reasons, the Eastern Province's customary court rulings reached a larger white audience than those of Natal, the only other province with a similar number of customary court cases. Natal cases, relatively easy to adjudicate, made it to the appeal court less frequently. These features mean that proceedings from the customary courts in the Cape satisfy Barber's requirements for textuality: they have a recognizable shape and form that continues with their transfer into written format; their format makes their content recognizable to a wide and especially white audience; and they have undoubtedly outlasted the moment.

NEWSPAPERS AND NEWS OF THE DAY

Newspapers are a critical element in the extended discussion about the convening of Black intimacy that constitutes this book. They gather together news items, editorials, letters, advertisements, images, and all the other items that regularly feature within their pages. They are fragile, can be ephemeral, often end up as toilet paper, are used to light fires, to line shoes, and when women give birth. They are a bit like the Swiss Army knife of the text-on-paper world.

Among the different types of work that newspapers have historically performed, they have often been used to give substance to people's social imaginaries and social aspirations, sometimes quite tangibly. As newsprint, they circulate and change hands. Their ink smears the fingers of those who set their type and fold them, the same ink touched by the people who read them. Figure 1.2 shows a page of the newspaper *Umteteli wa Bantu* devoted to "town and country news." Much of the page consists of names, the names of people who are joined together, not only because they were all part of the Bantu Social Institute executive (or attended the same Orange Free State African Teachers' Association meeting) but because they literally appear together on the page.

FIGURE 1.2. "Town and Country News," *Umteteli wa Bantu*, 30 October 1937. This page of newsprint includes advertisements for boot polish, cigarettes, and patent medicine; a letter by Dr. Pixley ka Isake Seme (a founder of the ANC); a report of happenings in Bloemfontein; a header about a football trophy not directly tied to most of the column's content; and the Tshange-Gumede list of wedding presents, discussed in chapter 5. Reproduced courtesy of the University of Johannesburg, http://hdl.handle.net/10210/261050.

This quality of joining people together in a two-dimensional format is readily evident in looking at the newspaper page. It is surprising how research on African newspapers has managed to overlook their multidexterousness. African newspapers (including the Black press in South Africa) have often been written about in relation to their status as vehicles for Black nationalist and anti-apartheid struggle. However, the situation has changed substantially in the last two decades. Recent work in the field of public culture and history points to the hybridity and innovation present, not only in what people wrote or in the personas they assumed when writing but also in their choice of writing language. The work is a reminder to move away from viewing the press only as a reflection of the role of the fourth estate in territories colonized by European powers but also as maps of social aspiration and intent, artistic production, artful avoidance of censorship, and hybrid borrowing in the fashioning of new identities. The chapters in the recent volume *African Print Cultures: Newspapers and Their Publics in the Twentieth Century* show the different ways Africans across the continent have explored ideas about authorship, point of view, and censorship, among others, to show newspapers as much more dynamic than a reduction of their content to anticolonial protest.[62] Similar work has been done in relation to South Africa, with most of the work revisioning the role of the press in its earliest history and covering newspapers published up until the 1960s.[63]

Before the twentieth century, Africans across southern Africa had few opportunities to be part of a shared space. Christianity and mission education provided the language and the institutional forms to convene a shared public rooted in a common set of beliefs. "Through reading and writing, the missionaries fostered a new community, based not on kinship or indigenous hierarchies but on coparticipation in a discursive sphere."[64] However, educated African communities had few ways to interact prior to urbanization and the cheap transport necessary for moving both bodies and paper around. Although these developments set the stage for the emergence of new social communities, a more galvanic effect lay in the emergence of the first Black newspapers.

Early on, Black South Africans realized the potential offered by newsprint for articulating individual aspirations. The printing press Noyi Balfour helped the Scots to transport to the Eastern Cape in 1823 was first used to print copies of portions of the New Testament translated into isiXhosa. By the 1840s, the press was printing sheets of news and opinion. In 1862, Lovedale began to issue a monthly called *Indaba,* later the *Kaffir Express.* The same items, often somewhat changed, were also printed in Xhosa in the sister publication, *Isigidimi sama Xosa.* Other mission presses across the southern African region, from Kimberley to KwaZulu-Natal, were also preparing and printing news sheets, some of which never went beyond a first issue.[65]

In the 1880s, around the time John Tengo Jabavu left the mission-run *Isigidimi* to begin the newspaper *Imvo Zabantsundu,* Africans began to exercise more control over the functions connected to and writing presented in the Black press. Generally, in the smaller newspapers like *Izwi laBantu,* half the content consisted of advertisements. The remainder took the form of news digests, often from other newspapers. Many from this period were newspapers in aspiration rather than reality, because of their infrequency of publication.

More regular and substantial, the lengthier publications were the product of the mission presses, like Lovedale. The 2 January 1911 issue of *Christian Express* included several pieces of news but also a report from a speech by Booker T. Washington from the *Tuskegee Student,* an example of religious cosmopolitanism in action, and a condensed version of a speech given to the students at Lovedale by Dutch Reformed Church missionary Dr. Andrew Murray.[66] This issue also contained several letters on lobola, some of which are quoted in chapter 4.

By the second decade of the twentieth century, Black newspapers like *Ilanga lase Natal* and *Imvo Zabantsundu* were beginning to share social news, including news about peoples' movements, meetings of church associations, and sports clubs, in addition to the news digests that made up their principal content. By a point coinciding roughly with World War I, newspapers were actively creating (and re-creating) networks of social motion among Black South Africans.

As the mission presses and, thereafter, non-mission-funded Black publishing initiatives moved into the arena of newspaper publication, new (and news) spaces were convened for the sharing and constitution of new socialities. One of the early subjects to engage readers was Black masculinity, discussed in chapter 2. As men wrote about their concerns, they created texts "detachable from the flow of conversation, so that they can be repeated, quoted and commented upon— . . . whether written or oral, [they] are accorded a kind of independent and privileged existence."[67] As Barber notes, these texts become forms of action, social facts with the power to engender further action.

One of the best examples of this, though it drew heavily on newspapers for its content, was T. D. Mweli Skota's *The African Yearly Register,* published in 1931.[68] Alas, Skota's "Who's Who" undertaking produced only one substantive version (there was a 1962 reprint with minor details added), but it was widely used, both at the time and subsequently, as a map of the African middle class that plotted out the relationships of people to one another.[69] Its entries not only included biographical detail but also drew attention directly to the connections that existed between people. It was a social map of literate Africa and the connections of its daughters and sons.

As newspapers and their content worked toward the creation of Black sociality, they did so in different way. It is important to remember that African newspapers were generative sources of and for new identities, drawing on writing as the positioning of self in relation to a wider world. These identities were shaped in a context in which literate Africans, especially men, considered themselves part of a print-driven public sphere modeled and partially derived from older oral patterns located in discussion and challenge but adapted to local circumstances. Visible in Black newspapers from the 1870s into the early twentieth century are utterances making the transition from oral to written text through a dual mechanism. This mechanism established newspapers as text through a repetition of form. If, previously, an oral performance or instance had shared news with an immediate audience, now newspapers shared news to a much wider audience. In this way, newspapers are embedded with constitutive social power.

At the same time, though, mission-imparted literacy and ecumenical Christianity's democratic impulses meant that newspapers were much more accessible to ordinary Africans, women and men, than the chiefly councils had ever been. For a second generation of Christians, those who shared a sense of themselves as Christians through a shared net of social motion, the chiefly councils might not, in a previous generation, have heard their voices. But the newspaper and writing acted as a concertina on differences of status to provide spaces for all sufficiently dogged viewpoints to be articulated. The exercise of letter-based debates, discussed in this book in relation to arguments about masculinity, lobola, marriage, and polygamy, is a quintessential example of this. These letters show a remarkable tenacity for the articulation of different viewpoints. Although writers might be separated by distance and income, this was a world where they could contribute through reading and writing to collective discussions about the nature of tradition in modern African life.

Newspapers, in this context, were critical to the production of sociality, or what Harri Englund and others (also following Barber) describe as the constituent elements of the religious life centered on a public, where "the public is an audience whose members are not known to those who address it in order to make claims."[70] When Margaret Wrong of the International Committee on Christian Literature for Africa visited South Africa in 1936, she questioned her interlocutors closely on their reading habits. She found that more and more Africans were reading newspapers. "In Cape Town, I found all read one or more papers and that the literate were being asked to read the news to the illiterate and that school children were not infrequently pressed into this service."[71]

This chapter has been about the convening of African publics, across three distinct spaces. These include the church; the civil law courts where Africans presented their own affairs to court officials and a broader, European legal audience; and South Africa's first Black newspapers. The different spaces helped to convene an African public that spanned both urban and rural areas, with the latter covered more extensively. Importantly, this was a particular kind of public, one consisting of individuals who shared an identity as Christians. Whatever differences existed between Black South Africans, the way the church penetrated people's lives in the late nineteenth and early twentieth centuries meant that Christianity served to bind lives through social motion. When a case went to court, it drew in spectators, lawyers, magistrates, court clerks, and the families of those concerned. These people took news of what they experienced further afield into the various other small and official spaces of the regions where they lived to discuss how the courts worked and what the courts had resolved. But court cases also took African affairs to Cape Town, to Bloemfontein, and to Pretoria, as the state formulated and debated African customary law. Law created a network of sort through which ideas about appropriate African behavior spread far and wide. These courts also brought women into public spaces as actors in ways that the newspapers and Christian associations did not. And newspapers opened up opportunities to people to imagine futures, futures either based on the past or rooted in the kinds of languages of being, like Christianity, newly available to them. Across these three arenas, and through the new forms open to literate Africans for the forging of new subjectivities, African women and men—the former often present only in arduously sought-out corners of public space—used text and voice to defend, deny, create, and sustain ideas about a moral economy of relationships fast undergoing change.

2 ~ Modern Masculinity

> It seems as though in fact, this custom of Circumcision is an African one. A thinking man might as well consider this point because this custom of Circumcision is necessary in a warm country. That is why the majority of the African nations do it; in them as well it is taken as a custom of bringing a person into Manhood.... The other question met by a person is this: "Where is sin in the Custom of Circumcision?"[1]

CHRISTIANITY, CULTURAL nationalism, and tradition feature prominently in these words written by the Reverend James Calata in the early 1920s. They also reference manhood. When Calata wrote them, he was fresh out of his training at St. Matthew's in Keiskammahoek in the Eastern Cape, a deacon in the Anglican Church but not yet an ordained minister, probably not yet long past his own circumcision. Later a prominent member of the African National Congress, known mostly in association with his work in Cradock, he is regarded as part of a more conservative generation of nationalist leaders. The words are from an essay that Calata wrote in isiXhosa about the need to promote and protect circumcision, later published as part of an edited book. While he wrote about the custom as an African one, he was also a Xhosa nationalist, or as Mandy Goedhals described him in her work, a Xhosa cultural loyalist.[2]

At roughly the same time that Calata was writing about circumcision, Umboneli Wezinto (which translates to "Brilliant Observer") wrote a letter in isiXhosa to *Umteteli wa Bantu*. Describing circumcision as part of the "The National Custom" to his imagined community of decidedly masculine African readers, he wrote, "This matter was set up by God. Circumcision is a sacrament that God gave to mankind."[3]

For Umboneli Wezinto and many of the writers who participated in an extended *Umteteli* conversation about foreskin circumcision in the early 1920s, however, the debate about circumcision and its relationship to being Xhosa referenced a much larger, national debate about manhood.[4] The unofficial battle lines regulating much of the discussion lay between Christianity—and the alternative repertoire it offered for understanding masculinity—and more traditional, ethnically determined assertions of *ubudoda* (in both isiZulu and isiXhosa, "manhood"). For instance, not all agreed about the links that Calata, Umboneli Wezinto, and others drew between Christianity and circumcision (where circumcision was a shorthand for being Xhosa) in relation to masculinity. The pseudonymous X. Y. Z., who wrote three long "chapters" on the issue for *Umteteli*, put his finger on the crux of the matter. "What is manhood? It is intelligence, patience, respect, hard work, diligence, avoidance of shameful behaviour, trustworthiness, education, bravery, and love for the nation."[5]

When Black men, newly constituted as an imagined community of the literate, engaged in defining masculinity in the Black press, they were taking public a process already occurring within the institutional spaces of their new faith. In southern Africa, between the mid-nineteenth and early twentieth centuries, contests over circumcision evolved from complete missionary condemnation to substantial accommodation within Protestant Christianity. This change was the result of African Christians engaging their missionary counterparts in a series of debates that continually reiterated the importance of manhood initiation. This process was a delicate one, since it also brought African Christians into conflict with their traditional communities.

Examining contests over initiation shows much more clearly than the other customs examined in this book the extent to which African churchmen were able to direct how traditional practices were made part of Christianity. Taken apart from the practices surrounding marriage and intimacy that appear in subsequent chapters, the inclusion of circumcision (the most obvious way that manhood initiation showed itself), notwithstanding biblical precedent, reveals most clearly the democratic face of Protestant Christianity and its attempts at cooperation and inclusivity about which authors like Alec Ryrie have written.[6] However, when considered against the ways that Christianity worked to affect relations between men and women, it raises important questions about the relationship of that democratic ideal to a homosocial world, in this case in South Africa but also evident more globally.

Through a discussion of the nature of circumcision in the Eastern Cape after the arrival of European missionaries, this chapter examines its centrality as a rite conferring masculinity for Xhosa men. It then looks at the development debates around masculinity that began with Xhosa traditional circumcision, followed by an examination of how masculinity was constructed as an ethnic category. This occurred within both Christian public space and, more crucially, in the Black newspapers and other publications of the early twentieth century.

MANHOOD INITIATION IN THE EASTERN CAPE AND BEYOND

Traditional initiation, now known as traditional male circumcision and initiation (TMCI), has been practiced by the Xhosa since at least the eighteenth century, and likely earlier.[7] Currently, the rite is common to most Xhosa speakers, including the Xhosa, the Thembu, the Mfengu, and the Mpondomise. Although most South Africans would typically associate initiation with the Xhosa, its practice is relatively extensive among other ethnic groups. Outside of the Xhosa, it is more typically associated with the Sotho and the Venda. Female and male initiation rituals are found in all these groups, though more prominence is usually given to male initiation rituals.

While colonial contests over bridewealth, polygamy, and female initiation have a large presence in African history, male initiation has seldom been viewed as contentious. Discussions of female initiation have tended toward viewing genital cutting as a site of anticolonial politics or in relation to women's rights.[8] Discussions of male initiation have focused on its role during periods of conflict or heightened social change, connecting it also to the creation of age-grades and the renewal of intra-African structures of authority.[9]

Recently, Corrie Decker has emphasized the importance of thinking more carefully about age-grades as ways for women as well as men to assert authority, rather than placing emphasis on age-grades as sources of generational authority.[10] Certainly, research into the relevance and status of women's age-grades in South African societies is lacking, though it is clear that at points they were of considerably greater importance than male age-grades.[11] Among the Xhosa and the other Xhosa-speaking chiefdoms, initiation rites also existed for girls, although the female initiation rite, the *intonjane*, was seldom practiced by the early twentieth century.[12] Female initiation rituals were much more complex among, for instance, the Sotho and Venda communities.[13] However, initiation rituals for women in southern Africa did not play the same role or fulfill the same function as did male initiation rituals, and, indeed, it would be more appropriate to compare processes centered on the acquisition of masculinity when considering circumcision than to compare male and female initiation practices.

In what follows, I discuss male initiation—particularly circumcision—in relation to how masculinity is cultivated. It should not still need saying, but it does, that all masculinities (and there are many) are shaped by the societies that produce them. From work in the late 1990s to more recent writing on

African masculinity, a number of scholars have demonstrated the historically and socially contingent nature of the various types of South African manhood.[14] Both historical and more contemporary work has highlighted the extent to which populist constructions of masculinity that link manhood only to violence, warfare, or the warrior are only partially—if at all—accurate.[15] In southern Africa, irrespective of ethnicity, being a man meant having attained the ability to support and sustain a rural homestead—at the risk of simplification, this was true for precolonial societies and is to some extent still true. Even second- and third-generation, city-born Africans, including men who were not interested in supporting rural homesteads, shared the view that being able to support a homestead was the best way to respect the ancestors.[16]

In the past, among South-Eastern Bantu speakers, this journey toward manhood began with initiation centered on circumcision. Today, however, apart from the groups already mentioned, other South-Eastern Bantu speakers, including the Mpondo, the Bhaca, and the Zulu, have not circumcised since some time in the early nineteenth century.[17] But this does not mean that other groups, most notably the Zulu, have abandoned the idea of an initiation into manhood. "Unlike their neighbouring Xhosa and Sotho counterparts, Zulu boys did not enter manhood after a painful rite of teenage circumcision. Instead, they crossed another 'ceremonial' threshold over a longer period of time through cohort-based, rule-bound competitions like stick fighting."[18] Conventionally, the reason for this was Shaka's desire to avoid having to do without the labor and efforts of his youthful *amabutho* recruits during lengthy circumcision seclusion, but it is also likely that he wanted to avoid the potential of initiation ceremonies cementing the recruits' allegiance to particular clans and chiefs.[19] Subsequently, when circumcision is written about in relation to South Africa, it carries on a ghostly life in Zulu constructions of masculinity because of its status as the thing that Zulu men do not do to become men. By this token, through circumcision's conspicuous absence, it has become a characteristic of Zulu masculinity, minor but sufficient enough to feature in early twentieth-century debates about the practice. And while circumcision was a common practice in Sotho-Tswana communities, it is more frequently written about as something Xhosa men had done.

The rite was first described in the late eighteenth century, though most of what we currently know about the practice in the nineteenth century derives from early twentieth-century ethnographic writing (much of it written by missionary ethnographers).[20] Some of the earliest African testimony on initiation is found in the 1883 Commission on Native Law and Custom. The commission, which conducted a large investigation into African laws and customs, questioned its informants carefully about a range of practices, from cattle-tracking to the handling of the succession of family property. Its informants, senior men who belonged to the different Xhosa, Thembu, Mpondo, Mpondomise, and Mfengu chiefdoms, presented their knowledge in a variety of sittings at different locations across the Eastern Cape. Probably the earliest widely available and African-authored account of circumcision is Tiyo Burnside Soga's *Intlalo xa Xosa*, which I discuss later. *Intlalo xa Xosa* was hand copied several times and shared locally in the Eastern Cape before being published by Lovedale Press. Available to a wider and more ethnologically interested audience than *Intlalo xa Xosa* was the volume *Ama-Xosa: Life and Customs*, written by John Henderson Soga, the son of T. B. Soga's father's brother.[21] The two men—both of whom had been through circumcision school—based their accounts on detail collected from other men over a period of time covering the late nineteenth and early twentieth centuries.

T. B. Soga spent two decades spanning the turn of the nineteenth century compiling a manuscript on Xhosa customs and practices, based on material collected from older Xhosa men.[22] Both he and his cousin J. H. Soga were part of the Xhosa proper, and their comments about being Xhosa reflect a real ethnic chauvinism. This partiality was derived from the perceived lesser status of former Xhosa client groups like the Mfengu and from the dominance of the amaXhosa dialect over other Xhosa dialects, but it also extended to a view that—under certain circumstances—Xhosa men were morally superior to men of other ethnicities.[23]

T. B. Soga wrote his manuscript as part of a lifelong effort to stave off the loss of customary knowledge. "Boys were circumcised as a rule, and it was stated that 'today they were brought into manhood'. This was one of the natural customs to the Xosas so much that it would be difficult for anyone to trace it." A boy's father and his senior male relatives decided when he was ready for circumcision—usually between fifteen and twenty-one years old—often waiting so that a group of boys could be initiated together. After the sacrifice of a beast for the *abakhwetha* (initiates), the boys would undergo ritual cleansing before their foreskins were excised by a ritual surgeon. In the words of Soga, "This was the origin & the cause of circumcision custom. To circumcise is to cut the fore-skin with an assegai & the wound was tied & untied with a herb; until it was healed up."[24]

While their wounds healed, they remained apart from their families in purpose-built huts where they were subject to food and language restrictions, the latter similar in purpose to the rules of respectful speech, *hlonipha*, which governed married women. In seclusion, they were attended by a guardian (*ikhankatha*), who made sure the boys observed proper custom and learned the knowledge and behavior expected of them as Xhosa men.

This knowledge included learning chiefly genealogies, those located in fact and those located in myth. As part of their reintroduction into Xhosa society as men, the initiates would practice dances they then performed at neighboring homesteads. Late nineteenth-century and early twentieth-century photographs show striking images of youth, their skin covered entirely in white clay, faces hidden by straw masks, waists encircled by grass skirts, standing in lines to dance in front of seated groups of spectators.

FIGURES 2.1 AND 2.2. Initiates dancing during the circumcision ceremony, ca. late nineteenth century. The first photograph shows an extensive audience clearly aware of the photographer. In the second photograph, note the clay on the young men's bodies, used to indicate the change of status. Joan Broster's *Red Blanket Valley* includes a chapter on traditional initiation ceremonies among the Thembu, and she describes in detail the meaning of the abakhwetha costumes. She also describes her negotiation of taking photographs of various parts of the ceremony. These photographs are from the Stewart Collection BC106 at the University of Cape Town, courtesy of UCT.

Modern Masculinity ~ 55

This instruction and ritual dancing at local homesteads occupied the abakhwetha's time in seclusion, which, by the start of the twentieth century, lasted between one and three months. In the nineteenth century, initiates were notionally at initiation camp for up to a year. The end of initiation was marked by feasting and festivities for the newly made young men, usually at the homestead of one of the senior-ranked fathers.[25]

In the nineteenth century, initiation rituals for boys were different among the various chiefdoms in the Eastern Cape, although much of this difference was owing to issues such as the timing of a chief-in-waiting's coming of age.[26] Before the advent of migrant labor and mission schooling, which disrupted the annual temporality of initiation cycles, the complexity and length of an initiation ceremony were determined by the number of boys circumcised with a chief. The images in this chapter show a relatively small initiation ceremony, based on the number of dancers. The amount of time available for a ceremony and the number of boys attending, as well as the status of parents hosting the ceremony, were some of the factors that accounted for variation in practice. Contemporary and current ethnic partisanship would maintain that there are critical differences to, for instance, initiation among the Xhosa and initiation among the Mfengu. The differences, however, relate more to how masculinity is bound up in ethnicity, rather than material differences. While practitioners of initiation would consider their rituals ethnically specific and defend their ethnic specificity, from what we know of the early twentieth century and what we now know, most practical differences were minor.[27]

There are many ways to consider and understand initiation, and it remains a topic of considerable contemporary significance. In this book, I focus on three aspects. In the first, I consider the way that initiation often served as a space for sexual experimentation, the feature that brought its practice into conflict with Christianity; this collision of values tied Christian sexual codes even more firmly into discussions of traditions. Secondly, I examine the way that its public presence linked it directly to secrecy, the kind of public intimacy mentioned in the previous chapter. Thirdly, I look at the link between pain and properly experienced initiation. Inherent to all these is a central tension between senior men, who controlled the practice and the initiates.

Initiation and Sexual Adulthood

In 2002, Peter Delius and Clive Glaser discussed the importance of initiation and other practices of sexual socialization in South African society.[28] In the Eastern Cape, circumcision rituals were closely linked to the induction of young men into adult sexual behavior. During the nineteenth century, guardians were responsible for instructing their charges in becoming warriors able to fight for their chiefs in times of need, in the duties of men to their chiefs, and in the duties to the homestead and the ancestors, including proper sexual conduct. This was similar to what young Zulu men would have encountered as they grew up and joined amabutho, a more drawn-out process than what occurred in the Eastern Cape. Control of sex was synonymous with control of virility. By the 1930s, instruction during initiation in proper sexual conduct had virtually disappeared.[29]

Initiates were instructed in how and with whom to have sex since the Xhosa stigmatized sex based on the categories of people who engaged in sex, as well as whether sexual activity resulted in pregnancy.[30] Xhosa moral codes preferred young women to be virgins (though not sexually inexperienced) at marriage, but practices like *ukumetsha*, nonpenetrative or thigh sex (in isiZulu, *ukusoma*), were encouraged for boys and girls in similar age groups, which I discuss further in chapter 3. After circumcision, the newly initiated looked down upon *metsha* relationships as childish, while senior men did not think abakhwetha mature enough for fully penetrative relationships.

Initiates, therefore, existed in a space of sexual liminality. To exit this status, they needed to have penetrative sex with a woman, whether an authorized custom or not. Metsha sex would not satisfy this need. There are several hints that during seclusion initiates practiced mutual masturbation, or the kinds of sex acts characteristic of mine marriages, but this is fiercely denied by those who consider themselves authoritative about the practice.[31] For all that the Congress of Traditional Leaders of South Africa and its supporting bodies identify initiation with sexual purity for men, it is evident that it is not, nor likely ever has been, the case.[32] The Sogas and Calata were adamant that sexually licentious behavior was not a traditionally sanctioned part of initiation but were ambivalent on this issue like many others, tying themselves in verbal knots in an effort to be faithful to the practice but to dissociate it from their vision of sin.

In the newspaper dialogue discussed later, some of the anxieties around manhood relate to young men growing up without a proper sense of sexual responsibility. This anxiety featured in other writing, including in James Calata's essay on initiation.

> THE CLEANING OF THE CLAY—This is a very unclean custom. However, it is very new among the XHOSAS: they got it from other nations with which they intermingle. The young man is taken to a certain woman whom he meets once and never meets her again. This makes the whole custom of Circumcision to be degraded

almost entirely because in the course of time it bore a bad fruit in the behaviour of young men. However it is not the custom of Circumcision. This is a new thing.[33]

Calata's description of the "cleaning of the clay" may not have been as new as he suggested. It resonates with another practice, described by J. H. Soga, where Soga links the phrase with the informal name given to a chief's first wife: "The first wife of a chief is invariably an early fancy, just after his circumcision period.... She is called *um-sul'-udaka*—'one who wipes off the mud.' The reference concerns the fact that the young man having emerged from the 'white clay' stage of circumcision, has washed it off, and become a real man by his marriage to the woman. She has helped him to manhood, not to chieftainship."[34]

While Calata and the Sogas were deeply perturbed at the sin they saw attached to circumcision, their concern did not take them as far as addressing some of the more problematic aspects of sexual conduct used to emphasize manhood. For example, often, the sex the initiates had with their metsha partners was coercive and nonconsensual. Xhosa opinion on this nonconsensual sex was divided; some tolerated the latter instance as irresponsible, boyish behavior, but others found these sexual encounters morally reprehensible.

The comments of the Sogas and Calata on this issue, of course, were more general statements on sexual morality and reflect the discomfort of three senior men with more traditional Xhosa sexual mores. Interestingly, they all attempted to dissociate sexual immorality from circumcision, attributing it either to practices outside of circumcision, to influences outside of the Xhosa nation, or to a more modern youth who had no reverence for the moral continence of the past.

CONTESTING PATHS TO UBUDODA (MANHOOD)[35]

As the British extended their power over the Cape Colony and Natal in the nineteenth century, first informally and later through formal conquest, the South-Eastern chiefdoms gradually lost their autonomy. Deprived of the ability to expand land holding as a result of British power and guns, and needing to accommodate themselves to a fiscal yoking in service of a white state, the chiefdoms of the region had to compete not only against each other but also internally within clans and lineages, with household heads seeking to retain access to power. Generational conflicts, always present in the fissiparous and polygynous society of the region, became even more intense. Restricting access to adulthood was one way, in a context of diminished political and other resources, that senior men used to hold on to their authority. One approach was to withhold the cattle needed for lobola, preventing young men from marrying and re-establishing household allegiances, both those in the past to the ancestors and those in the future.

Another way to restrict access to adulthood was to control rites of passage and processes of initiation, not with the aim of preventing initiation but rather with the aim of ensuring that senior men retained the power to decide when initiation was complete. In Zululand, the transition to manhood was already too drawn out to make intervention in this process by senior men overly heavy handed, but in the Eastern Cape, circumcision was a much more definitive point to mark the start of the passage to full adulthood. From at least the early nineteenth century, likely much earlier, Xhosa men referenced their age according to the year of their circumcision: "'I was circumcised in Sigcawu's year' (*Ndaluka ngo nyaka ka-Sigcawu*)."[36]

While attention to generational politics is key in South African history, especially to the allocation of lobola cattle, much of the work concerning generational politics is around contestation among Zulu men.[37] Benedict Carton has pointed to the importance of gerontocratic power in relation to masculinity. In his work with Zulu modes of masculinity, Carton shows how older and younger men were involved in complex negotiations of power, referencing the increasing incorporation of Zulu men into an industrializing economy and the attempt by younger and older men to negotiate status in a new context.[38]

However, the possibility for intergenerational tension attendant upon initiation is less well understood. Control of circumcision served a similar function to what Carton outlines. While most elements of the initiation ceremony were well-known outside traditional society by the early twentieth century, its supporters still spoke as if all its elements should remain secret. Senior men controlled the knowledge of initiation by surrounding it with secrecy, what J. H. Soga referred to as "the mysteries of manhood."[39] What happened during circumcision was something only senior, initiated men were supposed to discuss in private among themselves. Women were excluded from any knowledge of initiation, and wider discussions of initiation were considered transgressive of the proper custom. Outside of the Xhosa, while initiation into manhood occurred in homosocial contexts, manhood initiation itself was not as bound by injunctions to secrecy.

Senior manhood, the masculine culmination of initiation, required a man to be in touch with the spirits of the ancestors and to engage in debate and discussion in almost exclusively homosocial contexts.[40] Initiation set Xhosa men on a path to gaining what John Lonsdale calls "moral authority," a sense of ethnically rooted and lineage-linked social responsibility.[41]

Lonsdale discusses ethnicity as a common moral debate, more about determining who is included in the community of men and less concerned about those excluded. Among the Xhosa, initiation inducted Xhosa boys into a broader community of Xhosa men. "Other black nations do not circumcise at all, and they are disregarded by the Xhosa, taken to be unreliable and incomplete persons. When a person comes back from initiation he comes back prepared to abandon a careless life and intends to live a new life as a responsible member of society."[42] Among the Zulu, *ukubuthwa* (recruitment into a regiment), understood as a Zulu practice and a signifying practice of Zulu masculinity, acted similarly to draw men into a common moral debate.[43] One informant of Eileen Krige distinguished between Zulu and other customs, and customs as a matter of nationhood, in this way: "If a different nation, ignorant of the Zulu customs ... were to take over this country, the proceedings would be carried out in full."[44]

Earlier I wrote about the extent to which Xhosa manhood was associated directly with circumcision, a knowledge present not only among the Xhosa but more broadly within Black South Africa. With the advent of Christianity, contests over generational masculine authority grew to encompass contests between Christianity and custom. In the Eastern Cape, the importance of manhood initiation, though, meant that contests were not around the abandonment of the custom. Instead, they arose in relation to whether it had been performed properly.[45]

One of the points of difference lay in how circumcision was performed. Although few men in the early twentieth century needed the art of the spear, replacing assegai with pen, the toleration of pain remained central to the proper practice of circumcision.[46] Calata was of the view that "a man must tolerate pains."[47] This sentiment was repeated in the research that contributed toward the 1952 *Social Survey* volume of the *Keiskammahoek Rural Survey*. A boy circumcised with anesthetic in hospital "does not feel the pain and thus does not become a man in the true way ... *Alilo siko elo*—that is not the custom."[48] Such men were considered cowardly. Louise Vincent's research similarly shows twenty-first-century connections between initiation and discourses around masculinity and power.[49] "If you are not circumcised through custom in the mountain, you are not regarded as a man. You are a social outcast."[50]

For senior men, a circumcision that had occurred without pain was not a proper circumcision. The *Keiskammahoek* volume reported on the dialogue at coming-out ceremonies, where older men volubly debated fidelity to tradition. "What sort of custom is this? You people are like children, you do not know the customs."[51] As softer forms of masculinity arose among a modern, educated, and Christian African society in the early twentieth century, senior men became increasingly vehement about the need to endure pain.[52] In Tanzania, Anne Marie Stoner-Eby's analysis shows how African clergy cemented their status as "big men in their communities" through the control of initiation.[53] The Masasi case makes clear the link between male power and the control of processes like initiation. In Zululand, men were kept from marriage by their length of service in the amabutho, a move usually seen in terms of its impact on marriage. But initiation also regulated access to adulthood.[54] Thus, converted men had to negotiate their positions on initiation in the messy space determined by the conflictual requirements of Christianity and custom. Christianity complicated these dynamics, pitting traditional chief against white missionary in a struggle for control of African Christians. T. B. Soga's description of initiation referred directly to this customary dilemma faced by Christian men: "The raw Xosas still carry on circumcision and some school natives do it on strictly private lines, because by doing this custom, they are contravening certain rules."[55]

Clerical Support for Circumcision

I began this chapter by referring to the way that Christian men used their writing, both in essays and other academic pieces but more especially within the press, to debate the importance of circumcision and masculinity. However, before circumcision could become an issue in the press, it needed to be disassociated from the secrecy associated with it and established as a subject of public discussion. Missionary condemnation was the catalyst for this separation. The first white missionaries in the Eastern Cape were united in their opposition to the practice, a position that had been adopted by some of their congregants by the middle of the century. However, by the late nineteenth century and certainly by the Great War, Xhosa support of the suppression of circumcision had largely vanished to be replaced by attempts to win white mission approval for Christianized initiation.[56] By roughly 1910, attitudes toward the support for circumcision were heterodox, varied from congregation to congregation, and resisted central attempts to pin down a unified church position.

In the Eastern Cape, within the formal structures of the Anglican Church, anxiety over circumcision is reflected by the fact that it surfaced repeatedly as a source of concern. Resolution did not characterize the ongoing conversation. In 1911, the Diocese of St. John's, which covered an area equivalent to the former Transkei, heard from a report of the Committee on Cooperation in Discipline in Other Religious Bodies, which had investigated how different churches regulated various practices, including the circumcision of boys.[57] The denominations surveyed claimed institutional positions that ranged from a complete ban to partial acceptance (with more observed in the breach). In 1923, the Anglican St. John's debated an amendment to its acts so that circumcision, "provided it is practiced without any accompanying improper rites, should not be treated as in itself immoral."[58] Its own constituent parishes could not reach unanimity on the issue. Boys at St. Cuthbert's, and Anglican mission outside Tsolo, were allowed to attend Christian initiation schools, while boys at St. John's School in Umtata were expelled if they attended (or were discovered to have attended).[59] The 1926 Rules and Regulations of the Grahamstown Diocese, a white settler stronghold, held more equivocation. "Circumcision with any anti-Christian rite should not merely be discouraged but should render all who take part in it liable to censure or exclusion from the Communion of the church. When and if Christian boys are circumcised the practice should be carried out under Christian influence and supervision."[60] By 1950, the same diocese de facto had recognized initiation.

A concern for all the missions among isiXhosa speakers was how to keep up church membership when young men left school, since (according to the missions) attendance at initiation schools almost inevitably resulted in lost souls. Initiation led to lapsed Christians. The conflict over how to proceed on the matter of initiation schools lay at the heart of the discussion at the St. Cuthbert's Workers' Quarterly Meeting, quoted in chapter 1. Church elders were thinking in terms of their available powers, not only in relation to the church, but more especially in relation to headmen and others, only some of whom were Christian. In neither exchange was the fact of circumcision up for debate; rather, it was the format that preoccupied the Christian elders. Moreover, without their intervention, circumcision would not have become an issue for debate in the way that it did in the Black press that gave space to literate Africans. Black Christians wanted a reformed initiation to replace the ritual in its traditional format. Like Calata and the two Sogas, they objected to its moral transgressions, specifically initiation's reference to sex both as part of the practice and for its teaching about traditional sexual responsibilities. Rather than initiation itself having come to encompass "new" immoral behavior, Black clergy had taken on a Christian and post-Victorian sexual morality, which saw premarital sex as a sin. What might formerly have constituted acceptable sexual play for initiates had become, under the influence of the post-Victorian moral climate, a publicly expressed disapprobation.[61] Both Black and white church men were concerned at the extent of sexual immorality that was often coupled with initiation; both had their own reasons for thinking this to be true.

The debate around initiation as part of Christian practice was not limited to the Eastern Cape. In other parts of the country, similar discussions were taking place between white and Black clergy, with the Black clergy advising against prohibiting African boys from attending the initiation schools.[62] A clear call for a Christianized initiation is evident in the proceedings of an Anglican commission in the late 1930s. In 1938, the Anglican Native Conference (the body representing Black evangelical work across the entire province, which included Bechuanaland and Mozambique) appointed a special commission "to explore the possibility of the Church being able to provide some form of missionary activity to displace the African tribal Initiation rites."

CONVENING MANHOOD IN *UMTETELI* AND OTHER PUBLICATIONS

All the early Black newspapers, including *Imvo Zabantsundu, Ilanga lase Natal,* and *Izwi laBantu,* raised issues of masculinity. Some of the earliest references to masculinity took the form of patent medicine advertisements.

THE FREED PILLS THAT CAUSE A FIRM ERECTION

THESE PILLS are certainly capable of restoring a man's sexual prowess. No matter how depleted a man's strength is, these pills restore it within a short space of time. The ingredients of these pills include "DAMIANA" and "NUX VOMICA" as well as "FREE PHOSPHOROUS". These herbs come highly recommended in restoring man's strength, they produce an effective blood tonic that has never failed. Directions for use—Take one three times a day. Prices are 3/6 per bottle, 3/10 via mail; six bottles cost 18/- and 1/- for postage.[63]

In above-the-fold front page advertisements, choice real estate in a newspaper, these medicines promised to restore virility.[64] Some were to be rubbed on, some were to be swallowed. I am not sure how one would write a history of how people used patent medicines (and whether they did), but the appearance of nostrum advertisements for erectile dysfunction is not surprising. Advertisements like these point to anxieties about masculinity that were multilayered and also responsive to a nascent commodification. With the launch of newspapers with national circulation, issues like masculinity could be related directly to issues of concern to the nation and could be discussed as such.

In 1920, *Umteteli wa Bantu* launched with national circulation (*Ilanga* still had further reach in Natal), publishing in three, sometimes four, languages. It heralded a truly nationwide space for debate, whatever else it did. Early on, some of its readers raised the issue of Xhosa circumcision, using a call-and-response format invoking the participation of an audience that would have been familiar with oral genres. The debate centered on the extent to which Christianity should or could modulate ways of being a man.

Until the 1920s, initiation mostly remained the subject of debate in regional and mission-oriented newspapers. One of the earliest examples of a defense of circumcision lies in a series of essays in *Imvo Zabantsundu* in 1901 by Reverend Isaac Wauchope, who defended circumcision through reference to its Old Testament origins.[65] Initiation as a national (Xhosa) custom was "founded upon some real or supposed moral ideas, and are the result of the human mind's search after the greatest good." Wauchope's essays on custom are also significant, showing how initiation was moving from the relatively circumscribed world of internal church debate to a broader forum in the widely circulated and bilingual *Imvo*.[66] Wauchope, who often wrote for *Imvo*, preferred to write in Xhosa, and this piece in English was undoubtedly intended to constitute circumcision as a subject worthy of national discussion.

In an early correspondence in *Umteteli*, initiated in February 1922 and lasting until October, the subject of circumcision was tracked through at least twelve opinion pieces and letters. It is clear that the format of the conversation, in first-person-authored pieces mostly taking the form of a letter, facilitated people's participation. The extended conversation occurred in Xhosa, although the physical location of respondents and their self-identification indicate that not all were Xhosa men.

The first indication of a more than general interest in the subject took place in February, against the backdrop of the Rand Revolt, a subject that otherwise was preoccupying the newspaper. Moses Bandela, writing from Nancefield (today Klipspruit in Soweto), reported on a meeting he had organized to discuss establishing a local circumcision school.

"I called this meeting to look into ways of encouraging amaXhosa to go back to their roots, especially their first and foremost custom which was practiced by our forefathers. We know that an UmXhosa's life can never be successful without this custom."[67] The innovations planned for the practice included a car owned by the ikhankatha, for transport of recruits to a "health facility" if necessary. His anxiety around the loss of roots was palpable and helped to establish one of the threads in the letters that followed.

Mr. Bandela's letter resembled an account of ethnic- and male-centered organizing to promote cultural rights and came out in the same issue of *Umteteli* as a report by the Conference of the Independent Ethiopian Congress Mission, which was calling for an investigation into the decay of custom. Together, the letter and the report sparked the conversation that followed, bringing Calata's threefold interest in Christianity, custom, and ethnic nationalism to national attention. In the discussion of ethnic patriotism in East Africa in the twentieth century, Derek Peterson points to the proliferation of morally conservative associations based on ethnic welfare, all concerned with regulating the terms of engagement with the twentieth century.[68] The debate in *Umteteli* reflects both the existence of ethnic particularities like those Peterson mentions as well as the connection between tradition and innovation that such associations created. These connections centered on a rather paradoxical insistence on a national manhood, paradoxical because when people like T. B. Soga called on a national masculine identity, he meant that all men should make themselves more like Xhosa men. However, Christianity and its ecumenical outlook allowed for challenges to this ethnic particularism.

Umteteli contributor G. G. Nqhini began his questions in a typical opening gambit that brought the paper, its unnamed (and ethnically unidentifiable) interlocutory editor, and all its readers into the same conversation. Indeed, he addressed his comments to all Africans, an expansive and imagined audience. In his message, he stressed lines of communication, both horizontal but also vertical. "Even the Almighty Qamata [God] loves His traditional customs because He designed them as a means of facilitating your communication with Him."[69]

Later the same month, writing from East London in the Eastern Cape, Umboneli Wezinto asked the editors of *Umteteli* to "address the nation on this important issue."[70] His understanding of the nation was both restricted by his ethnicity, assuming the benefit of circumcision to all, and expansive, viewing circumcision as a sacrament that "God gave to mankind" and claiming it for all Christian men.

The comments raised by Umboneli Wezinto, Bandela, and others were not only neutral comments about loss, nor were they statements only about the past. They directly addressed the dislocation that men were feeling in 1922. Bandela's letter advocated the circumcision of grown men because of what he viewed as the negative consequences of "boyish behaviour." "When a Xhosa boy is past circumcision age, no good can come from him.... This has created problems because a boy remains a boy even when he tries to become a leader."[71] This was not an isolated incident; Bandela was referred to the "circumcising [of] old boys" in East London. Forced circumcision was generally viewed as a last resort for men who behaved like irresponsible boys, an antisocial behavior. Bandela was suggesting a serious intervention. His comments reveal a combination of anxieties around masculinity and authority explicitly linked to being Xhosa, but he was writing from Johannesburg in a month that had seen *Umteteli* filled with news about the white miners' uprising and clampdowns on union organization among Black labor. "There are many problems facing us, so many that we do not know where to start talking about them. There are many stock thieves, shops that are broken into, corruption is rife, so are problems of circumcision. The traditional school is coming to an end, people kill one another for no reason, people are plunged into debt by the educated ones, alcoholism is a problem."[72]

The 1922 contributions that elicited the most response were written by X. Y. Z. from Nancefield, a frequent *Umteteli* contributor to news from the area, who viewed circumcision as anti-Christian. X. Y. Z.'s three lengthy "chapters" (*Ulwaluko—Isiqendu I, II, and III*) described how some established churches had fallen into moral laxity through a recommitment to circumcision. He challenged the view that educated Xhosa needed to be circumcised to be considered men: "Back home in the land of the amaXhosa it has been accepted that the educated and the Christians do not circumcise. Many of them have been fighting and maintaining that they will not circumcise.... That battle is still being fought today and we are told to go back to our traditions which is against the word of God."[73]

Perhaps the most intriguing aspect of his correspondence was its transgression of the secrecy that was supposed to surround circumcision. In the letters, he named several men who had not experienced initiation. This gesture showed a contempt for the conventions of respect surrounding the practice, something that would have been evident to all who read his words and which, in turn, greatly angered several of the papers' readers.[74]

X. Y. Z.'s writing was, at heart, a comparison of two understandings of masculinity. In the first, circumcision was the route to manhood. In the second, Christian moral behavior was sufficient to secure the status of a man. "What is manhood? It is intelligence, patience, respect, hard work, diligence, avoidance of shameful behavior, trustworthiness, education, bravery, and love for the nation." Here, the ecumenical possibilities of Protestant Christianity appeared to offer a route out of the rather narrow ethnic particularism some of the debate suggested. Here, the role of faith was potentially transformative of older ways of thinking about Black intimacy.

X. Y. Z.'s responses fell into several camps. In the first of these, non-Xhosa readers generally disagreed with circumcision as a route to manhood. J. P. from Makapane was anti-initiation. "We, the abaKwena tribesmen do not circumcise yet we are far more well behaved than you circumcised men.... We, the uncircumcised BaKwena fear nothing, not even flying machines. We are perfect gentlemen who are constantly improving their standard of education."[75]

A second category of response targeted X. Y. Z.'s repudiation of the importance of custom. A rebuttal by contributor W. S. D. targeted a vital issue, that of the role of white disapprobation in the debate about custom. "The case of X. Y. Z. is a sad one because he still holds on to what a white man once said when he first arrived here, when he said that black people are stupid, that they practice heathen customs."[76] Indeed, W. S. D.'s answer was only the outward manifestation of a latent concern in the correspondence, centered on the need to repudiate white opinion both of custom and of its African practitioners. The point was put even more forcefully fifteen years later, showing how part of the local arsenal in the defense of circumcision included a keen eye for theological finesse, in a disagreement over how Christianity and the Bible should be interpreted.[77] "We learn about circumcision in the Bible because this is a commandment that was given to the Jews by God. That alone indicates that circumcision is not a sin, because God would never have led his people to sin."[78]

In defending custom, African Christians challenged not only the European heterodoxy that being Christian meant being modern but also each other on their interpretations of what it meant to be Christian. Umboneli Wezinto noted parallels between traditional practice, like the anointment of initiates, and what happened in the Bible; he also drew a direct analogy between the Ten Commandments and the advice given to initiates by their guardians. "This matter was set up by God. Circumcision is a sacrament that God gave to mankind."[79] Yet Vazidlule, translated from the Xhosa as "they who have passed," contradicted him two months later through a counter reference to Abraham and his acceptance of faith.[80]

Almost all the *Umteteli* letters dealing directly with circumcision drew parallels with Jewish practice.[81] "Even among the Jews this was a powerful custom, but according to their forefather's (Abraham's) system infants were circumcised."[82] Most commentary drew on the Old Testament, unlike in Kenya, where contributors to the debate on female circumcision might quote Apostle Paul's ambiguous discourse on circumcision.[83] In the relatively rare commentary on circumcision in *Ilanga lase Natal,* discussion of it was generally directly related to where and how it appeared in the Bible, as part of larger biblical discussions.[84]

What the newspaper debates briefly covered received more in-depth treatment in other genres. In *Ama-Xosa: Life and Customs,* J. H. Soga suggested that African circumcision was initially from ancient Israel, theorizing that Africans adopted the practice via an East African Arab influence.[85] Calata in "Bantu Custom" reflected collective thinking on circumcision, first citing a genealogy rooted in Solomon's links with Abyssinia, then quoting Joshua and, finally, Genesis.[86] Their work emphasized Africa's ancient connection to Christianity, placing circumcision parenthetically into the pool of biblical references to Africa, most famously Psalm 68:31.[87] This reference, of course, found fertile ground in Christian arguments legitimating Pan-Africanism.

In writing about Hebrew practice and quoting the Bible, Africans were demonstrating two things. Firstly, their recourse to biblical quotation shows a facility at navigating chapter and verse that matched, if not outperformed, that of white Christians. Secondly, Africans were also engaging with biblical theology. The debates foreground their intellectual acumen, an ability to take on missionary criticism within its own terrain, like the debating students at Lovedale. In his 1922 letter, Vazidlule contradicted both Umboneli Wezinto and standard biblical interpretation to challenge Moses' statements about circumcision. His point was that the Bible needed to be interpreted as a set of context-dependent statements.[88]

In her work on the Lovedale Literary Society, Isabel Hofmeyr has examined the rhetoric and form of the debates that occurred among Lovedale students. She argues that the society acted as a leadership forum for an aspiring African elite. Working creatively with debate form and content, and taking the principle of discussion and advice advocated in chiefly councils, the pupils challenged the terms of white intellectual imperialism.[89] Letters to the editor, which reached wider audiences and had a greater longevity, went much further than debating societies in constituting ideas about custom and Christianity. Through newspaper debate, African men brought into existence a "complex and multidimensional interpretive community," where circumcision leveraged entry into broader discussions about the value of custom, Christianity, and the relationship of both to white assertions of civilizational superiority.[90]

The 1922 exchange also reveals how men were moving back and forth between meetings, church gatherings, and the newspaper in their arguments and conversations, becoming multidimensional raconteurs of custom. Letters referred to the public nature of the debate in meetings and gatherings from Johannesburg to Mafeking to Uitenhage, from men who were equally comfortable in English, Xhosa, and Sotho-Tswana, but chose—mainly—to have the conversation in isiXhosa. "What is noticeable is that everyone is talking about it in Johannesburg. It is such a heated topic that even those who have not been circumcised say they support circumcision because without it children become troublesome."[91] In the same month, in a report on the Pretoria Diocesan Native Conference, well-known Anglican Church figure Reverend Hazael Maimane referred to circumcision as "one of the most important subjects discussed."[92] In September, when the editors closed the correspondence, interest was still high. "It is clear that this matter is still important to men because even though it has been suggested that we stop debating about it, numerous letters discussing circumcision are still pouring in."[93]

If many of the letters to the editor found common cause in decrying increased moral laxity, they were not always clear on what moral laxity entailed in the context of masculinity. Certainly, some of it was a sexual anxiety, but that is not a sufficient answer. Here it helps to reflect on the social community brought into existence via the pages of newspapers like *Umteteli*, not just on the letters about circumcision. In 1922, newspapers across the country carried news of the Rand Revolt; another newsworthy item was the Bulhoek Massacre of the previous year, where a large number of Israelites, an independent Christian church, had been gunned down by state forces near Queenstown. The events at Bulhoek made all African Christians nervous. But a large number of letters to the editor were concerned with the shortcomings of contemporary life. One of the issues that animated this discussion was that of women living independently of men in places like Johannesburg, an issue which has already received widespread coverage in the academic literature.[94] These are the issues that formed the backdrop to the scrutinization of masculinity occurring in the papers. More generally, masculinity was being scrutinized, but not necessarily in relation to moral laxity. When X. Y. Z. wrote about the need to go back to the customs of the fathers, he was articulating a concern about younger men not respecting older men. The letters about circumcision, about a sundered intergenerational respect, coalesced the larger debate about ethnic patriotism and masculinity.

These were important concerns, but it is worth pointing out what the letters from the early 1920s did not discuss. One way to reflect on them is to consider them about choices not made in respect of Black intimate life. These were not letters that reflected how Silas Molema agonized over a choice of wife, quoted in the introduction to this book, nor about the potentially transformative power of Christianity. They were not letters about respecting women as helpmeets and fellow travelers in a new intimate life modeled on Christian family values. The same authors who wrote about masculinity under threat wrote about the scourge of single Black women in urban areas, who had defied their fathers and guardians to strike out on their own. These authors drew on other parts of Christian thinking, simultaneously of the Old Testament and rooted in Victorian sexual prudery. Women away from the control of their families were the embodiment of even more moral laxity then men who were not circumcised yet nevertheless had multiple sexual partners. Moral laxity in men was not the same as moral laxity in women. The former included disrespect to elders but less often the "sins" of fornication or adultery. Moral laxity in women was about loss of male power and participation in sexual relationships unsanctioned by their kin. The Christian imprint in all of this was one of sexual shame for women, rather than Mgqwetho's understanding of it, which would allow for each man to "give equal respect to the woman he marries for only then will the home be harmonious."[95]

In 1928 and 1929, *Umteteli* again carried several letters on circumcision. In this correspondence, the debate was even more explicitly about Xhosa initiation, and the letters were also in Xhosa. As in the previous exchange, writers eagerly followed and responded to the arguments of their predecessors. Contributor D. D. Ngqeleni advocated a return to customary initiation but emphasized the difference between Testament and traditional circumcision.

While Ngqeleni wrote in Xhosa, he twice used the English phrase "only a procession from boyhood to manhood" to emphasize what for him were the most critical elements of the practice and what he most needed to communicate to his audience.[96] This tactic presaged a shift that would be fully apparent ten years later: the infringement of the secrecy and closed nature of conversations about circumcision. The public discussion of circumcision was taboo for traditionalists, a direct goad to the desire of senior men to keep control of both the discursive terrain of the circumcision and its practice. The newspaper debate took the conversation about circumcision from isiXhosa into English and expanded its audience to incorporate anyone—including women—who read the paper. The 1928–29 discussion in *Umteteli* directly raised the issue of appropriateness. Contributor E. B. Mpalisa was very uncomfortable with the letter exchange. "Our tradition does not allow us to discuss such in public, mainly because the readership of this newspaper includes women as well, who by tradition are not supposed to know what happens regarding initiation."[97] Yet his comments did not shut the exchange, and even in public meetings it was still "top of the agenda."[98]

Public interest in circumcision and initiation was also productive of a greater, generalized interest in African custom through the more academically respectable genre of the book. Stephanie Newell's work on literary culture in Ghana has shown how a variety of genres were responsive to context and reader expectation. Writers moved between letters and books to make different points and address different audiences.[99] In 1930, *Bantu* (later *African*) *Studies*, the University of the Witwatersrand journal, encouraged J. H. Soga to translate his Xhosa monograph *The South-Eastern Bantu* into English for publication. Two years later, a London publisher released his *Ama-Xosa: Life and Customs*. A review of the latter described it as "the first of that series of monographs on the Tribes of South Africa for which students are so eagerly waiting."[100]

The possibility of a wider audience also encouraged T. B. Soga to submit the previously self-published *Intlalo xa Xosa* for a British mission-sponsored competition in African vernacular literature.[101] His winning achievement was celebrated in *Listen*, the magazine of the International Committee for Christian Literature in Africa, distributed throughout the continent.[102] The ICCLA's support spoke to the growing transnational interest in African vernacular writing, a move that seemed to have precipitated Lovedale Press to publish the *Intlalo xa Xosa* manuscript in 1936.[103] Lovedale had initially rejected the manuscript on the grounds that it was obscene and inaccurate in its rendering of the Bible.[104] Its reluctance, though, was soon mollified when the book went through several printings, its unavailability drawing a complaint from a Bethelsdorp lending-library reader in 1938.[105] T. B. Soga's treatment of initiation (he had contributed to the newspaper debates) mirrored those in *Umteteli* and other papers, showing the diverse textual genres and languages that literate Xhosa were using to defend circumcision.

The move to writing in English was echoed over the next few years in the pages of various papers, reflecting both the growing popularity of the letters feature and the desire to make letter-based issues more widely accessible to non-African and other African language speakers. By 1935, letters to *Umteteli* were contained within their own section and were principally written in English. Custom repeatedly appeared as a subject in both editorials and letters. In a solicited correspondence on "Bantu History, Law and Customs," initiation was featured alongside topics like lobola and respect for the elders.[106] These letters directed attention to a contemporary loss of knowledge, a direct critique of "detribalization" hiding a more implied fear of modernity. In a letter to the debate, T. B. Soga emphasized giving "present-day detribalised and urban Bantu natives essential insight into the primitive past [in order to] connect that insight as much as possible with the present semi-civilised Christian era."[107] The majority of contributors were in support of retaining custom and tribalism, quoting scripture in support of their arguments about "bad" Christianity as being at the root of the suppression of custom.[108]

The 1935 exchange was followed two years later by a somewhat different one. The initiatory epistle by E. N. Pule carried the headline "Superstition" and asked when practices like turning a mirror to the wall during lightning would be eradicated.[109] He probably did not intend his brief aside about the paradox of a civilized yet uncircumcised university graduate to evoke the response that followed.

But Mr. Pule was rapidly contradicted, in an exchange numbering at least twelve letters. Some referenced the growing orthodoxy, present in medical journals of the period, that circumcision made for a healthier penis. "Circumcision is but a custom and a healthy one too."[110] Several of the letters dealt with the benefits of circumcision and its role in cultivating a healthy body. Here, the writers were reflecting a very new assessment of physical health. By the 1930s, the modern body was of much concern to Africans, expressed in sources as diverse as beauty contests, soap advertisements, and an endless barrage of information on hygiene.[111]

By the end of the decade, circumcision as a subject had gained a respectability that traversed different genres and textual spaces. In 1940, the renowned Xhosa poet and praise singer S. E. K. Mqhayi submitted a manuscript on circumcision to the Lovedale Press.[112] Mqhayi viewed foreskins as a masculine metonymy for colonialism, including in his praise poetry a reference to the trouble "brought by the races with foreskins."[113] What little we know of the volume comes from the press records, since the manuscript was subsequently lost.

Although Mqhayi followed others in supporting a Christianized circumcision, the timing of his submission is interesting. It is likely that public support for initiation, following both the various newspaper correspondences and the publication of the two Soga volumes, led him to believe that Lovedale would relax its preference for publishing didactic literature or ethnic genealogy. However, the press rejected the manuscript, citing it as too controversial and referring to the lack of Christian (it meant white) unanimity on the subject.[114] Public debate on the matter, largely in support of initiation and via newspapers, had not succeeded in facilitating the entry of the issue (notwithstanding the success of *Ama-Xosa*) into the only press in the country publishing in Xhosa.

~

This chapter, more than those in the rest of this book, utilizes newspaper debates, especially letter-based debates, to show some of the contradictions inherent in Black South African thinking and practice concerning custom and tradition and their place in the constitution of moral discourses of masculinity in South Africa in the first half of the twentieth century. The *Umteteli* conversations reflect a concern among literate men about different ways to honor house and home, or how to be a Black man in a modernizing and racially divided South Africa.

While the chapter is more broadly concerned with the constitution of Black masculinities in the early twentieth century, much of the chapter centers on the practice of circumcision. This is because so many of the public debates about masculinity were ethnically premised and first emerged in relation to an initial conversation about circumcision. These conversations, while ethnically specific, are also about the evolution of Black masculinities in relation to the tension between Christianity and tradition. In this chapter, I showed through an examination of initiation in a wide range of mission and printed sources the innovation that African Christians brought to the consideration of custom. Some of this centered on relocating both the practice and discussion of custom from the secrecy that cloaked its traditional practice to more public spaces. With regard to practice, African Christians went to great lengths either to continue initiation outside the Church or to Christianize it. In published and textual spaces, especially newspapers, they defied customary prohibitions on discussing circumcision, using a range of arguments based on Christian precedent and the Bible both to defend and denounce it. The Xhosa men who wrote publicly about initiation were writing to two audiences, pulling it into a Christian repertoire while emphasizing its role in the constitution of Xhosa masculinity.

For the moment, though, I want to gesture at three points. Firstly, in the *Umteteli* conversations, men linked their more well-worn and comfortable understandings of masculinity—ones from their fathers and brothers—to their ethnic or national identities first and to their identities as Africans second. Christianity complicated for them, sometimes in a welcome fashion, their understandings of masculinity.

Secondly, in the nationwide moral community that participated in constituting manhood as a subject of interest, almost all the conversations about how different ethnic groups understood masculinity also included references to Xhosa circumcision. Circumcision for Xhosa men acted then (and still does) as an organizational conceit for conversations about masculinity. While other practices and customs may have been linked to ethnic masculinities, circumcision possessed a public prominence as a rite of manhood not shared by other rites.

Thirdly, it is so obvious that conversations about masculinity took place among men that it is easy to miss what men discussed much less frequently. The public conversations about masculinity seldom gestured to what several generations of missionaries had preached, with a spectacular lack of success, regarding the duties of a husband in a companionate and monogamous marriage. In the construction of Black intimacy in the early twentieth century, in all the attention to marriage and how and whether it could and should be reshaped by Christianity, Old Testament ideas about how men should behave trumped more modern understandings of masculinity.

Modern Masculinity

3 ~ Love, Sex, and Consequence

> It was only yesterday that it dawned to me how impossible it really was for me to go home.... As Wesleyan minister [her father] if I go home in this state & say I stay there without telling anybody and then get married & then they find out from calculating afterward (if they do not notice @ once which they are sure to) Mama can be disqualified or brought forward in the Manyano for hiding her daughter. If I go, the proper & expected thing for her to do is to go & report it to the Women's Manyano. then they come & see me to see if it is true & ask where it happened & all sorts of mad questions—then she'll be safe and remain in her position. Of course it is all ridiculous—you know the women for gossip.[1]

> Ndiyayazi into yokuba [I know very well that] you have never loved me. I know all your aims & objects in making love to me. Kodwake andi zokuyi teta ngoku.[But I won't talk about that now] Kodwa akunditshateli kuba ubuyaku nditshata [You are marrying me because you have no choice, it is not] for love. I know everything ngoku [now]. Kodwa sobona.[But we'll see] We are bound to marry now.[2]

THE EXTRACTS from these letters, two in a correspondence that had been taking place since March 1933, show a love affair in the process of unraveling. Selbourne Bokwe wrote to his lover, Dorothy Kabane, "Wena [You] will not be marrying me for love but for merely to blot off shame & disgrace which you have fallen in," referencing the pregnancy she had just revealed to him. Further on in the same letter, he wrote, "Well coming straight to business immediate marriage is absolutely impossible, there's no need to hide that fact from you."

Distraught at Selbourne's refusal to marry her, Dorothy, daughter of a Wesleyan minister and herself a teacher at Lovedale Infant School, took

Selbourne to the local magistrate's court, or civil court, for breach of promise.[3] She and Selbourne were both members of the African Christian elite in the Eastern Cape, and this may explain the extent to which both used the South African legal system to achieve a favorable outcome. A frequent discussion in the social history of law in Africa concerns whether non-elite Africans felt able or could afford to use colonial law. In South Africa, this discussion does not address the extent to which an oral appeal—a rhetorical presentation and contestation of evidence—was a familiar practice; debates in civil cases were similar in form to debates held before chiefly councils. However, the suite of actions that Dorothy Kabane and Selbourne Bokwe brought, including a civil case at the magistrate's level, its appeal, and a further appeal in front of the Native Appeals Court (NAC) of the Cape and the Orange Free State, resonate with other, similar civil actions that Africans in the Cape brought to the courts in the early twentieth century.

The text of the case consists of the original record from Dorothy Kabane's case against Selbourne Bokwe, as well as the record of his appeal in the NAC, both in 1933. In fact, there is a third record of the case, in the record of decisions in Black appeal cases, "Selected Decisions of the Native Appeal Court, Cape and OFS." Because of its status and the judgment awarded in the NAC, the case forms part of a series of South African Law Reports used by attorneys, native commissioners, and magistrates following the Roman-Dutch tradition of precedent to help reach decisions in African civil cases. All three hearings focus on different aspects of the case, the case becoming more abstract as its hearing moved from the physical presence of the magistrate's court to the appeal court. In editing the appeal case for use as precedent, it was also abbreviated, so that the NAC record presents its findings in a very different manner than the first court event. The various courts' actions, including those of a racially biased white legal profession which heard the iterations of their affair, performed and contested new understandings of intimacy to audiences in ways that unequivocally outlasted the moment. The various court levels and corresponding set of records were a cavalier replication of the intimate details of African lives. This repetition was a textual entrenchment of African lives that successive generations of bureaucrats and administrators needed only to consider in relation to the legal precedent shown in particular cases without considering the very real lives involved.

Some strands of anthropological thinking would suggest that Africans transacted their sex and love affairs without affection, or that people did not fall in love before they learned from missionaries about falling into intimate love. But love affairs that went wrong do not need any historicity attached to them, under any circumstances. In South Africa, young men and women exchanged love tokens in the form of beaded fancies, using colors and patterns to express their feelings.[4] Girls' age-grades sang frankly about the benefits and disadvantages of penises in lovemaking.[5] African fathers and guardians relished displaying their facility with language that allowed them to dispute sundered relationships and bring about their public resolution. But in a context in which Black South Africans were testing out new ways of being moral citizens in private and public, and in instances where a clearly new moral code rooted in a Christian sexual ethic drove a skewed understanding of female sexual agency, the potentiation that occurred when all these elements coincided made for significant changes in Black intimacy.

Dorothy Kabane and Selbourne Bokwe's case and the other examples of love and sex in this chapter, many of them known to us only because they involved some form of judicial event, speak to what happened as Africans adopted mission-driven moral codes as part of their repertoire of intimate practices. By the early twentieth century, it had become clear that as African women and men embraced modern ideas about love and sexuality, they found themselves set adrift from traditional protections for love affairs gone awry. Women who transgressed moral codes around female sexual purity experienced severe consequences, which extended to their mothers. Although Christian fathers were deeply invested in the sexual piety of their daughters, the women endured the repercussions for moral transgression.[6] The sequencing of an accusation of sexual misconduct and its subsequent response, for instance, helped to shape outcomes for men and women. Gendered patterns also affected how and whether people attempted to resolve accusations of immorality.

SEX: PRIVATE AND PUBLIC KNOWLEDGE AND BEHAVIOR

In what follows, I understand sexuality broadly to encompass how people felt and thought about sex, the kinds of erotic and intimate behaviors they practiced (including celibacy as a sexual choice), and that sexual identity includes and references a broader self-identification.[7] It also bears saying that ideas about sexuality are generated between people in relation to the concepts of private and public, themselves historically contingent. Further, sexual morality includes a valuing of these different aspects as part of the social codes that govern and regulate sexuality. As a corollary, it is evident then that sexuality is historically variable.

It is challenging to reconstruct precolonial African ideas and practices around sexuality, including what was private, when it should be public, and who could talk or sing about it. Early accounts of African sexuality, before firstly European and later African anthropologists began their catalog of African sexual practice, were generally filtered through the perceptions of European missionaries or African male converts. They carry both the imprint of a Christian sexual morality and masculine ideas about erotic appetite and appropriate sexuality.[8]

Drawing from a range of historical and contemporary sources in an attempt to overcome the difficulty of working with some of these sources, a few things are readily evident. In southern Africa societies prior to colonialism, a generational temporality determined both the discussion of sex and its practice. What was appropriate for youth (e.g., orgasms were acceptable but vaginal penetration was not) was not the same as what was appropriate for married adults. Similar gendered and generational conventions governed the conditions under which people might talk about sex, so that sex talk between the members of one age-grade was common, but parents seldom talked to their own children about sex. Song and dance were forms particularly suited to explicit sexual content, but regular conversation was not. Private letters sent through the post between literate lovers might express ardent feelings and specify a wish for a lover's particular action, but in daily life Black southern Africans were not willing to comment publicly about other people's sex lives in the interests of research. At least not in interwar period.[9] The puberty songs that Eileen Krige collected from Zulu women are both frank and graphic in their words and actions about sexual enjoyment, but they were created and performed under definite circumstances.[10]

In spite of that candor, a range of avoidances surrounded the discussion of sex, which therefore affected what anthropologists heard about sex. Still, sexual encounters themselves were not necessarily conducted in private. In general, neither secrecy—which would mean that no one else would know about an affair—nor physical privacy were characteristic of love affairs carried out among, for instance, Zulu or Xhosa speakers. Married men and women might have steamy love affairs, as long as they were both discreet but also open about these, although sexual latitude did extend more readily to men than to women. In fact, love affairs almost always had some public component—the publicly contested sexual affairs discussed in this chapter all included defenses that rested on someone else knowing what was happening (or not). Private domestic space did not exist in precolonial African society in the same way it existed in Victorian Britain. Isaac Schapera's *Married Life in an African Tribe* is unusually explicit in relation to other contemporary sources, not so much because people did not talk in that way but because generally the sex talk that Schapera collected was solicited as part of his research and his status as a researcher gave him access to details not usually shared.

"K"
                                    c/o Nurse Hutchinson
                                    The Grey Hospital
                                    Kingwilliams town
                                    3rd Jan. 33

Darling,
    I have just been talking to Bert Bar thro'
the phone. On Friday he wired home & they haven't
answered him up to now he says.
    Well! I asked him what he thinks & suggests
now. He tells me he must see Mr Hain & if you &
mean to get married @ once it is [between]
ourselves.
    Bou darling we must get married immediately
I've been telling him I'm now back from Bells &
they've gone for their New Year to E.L. and I
shouldn't stop here in town 'cause I've
used all my money to the last tickey now
and it is very foolish sticking here maan
consider it. Fancy I have been here from the
9th last month. Shame dear! Darling come
down @ your very earliest chance — you
could even ride maan if the train will
take you long. There is no running away from
it now we have got to & must get married.
    Bert Bar told me to come to the phone

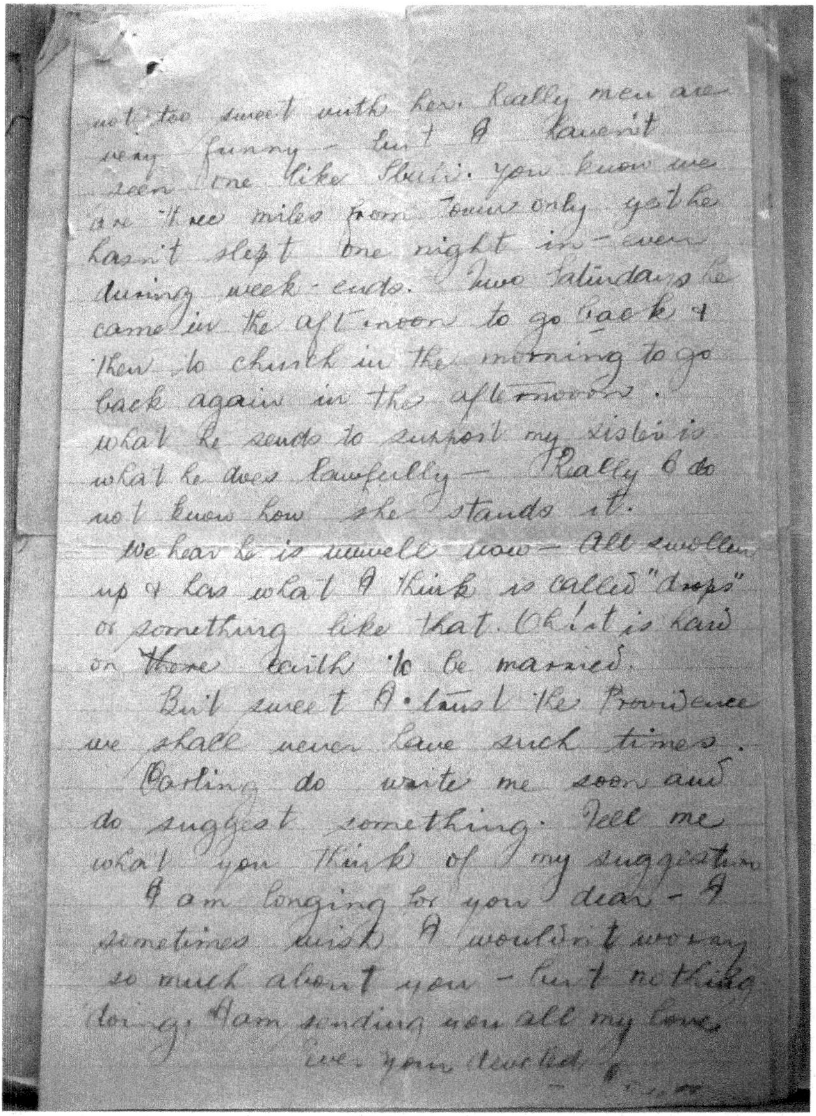

FIGURE 3.1A AND 3.1B. Letter "K," Dorothy Kabane to Selbourne Bokwe, 3 January 1933. Reproduced by permission of the Western Cape Archives and Record Service (WCARS).

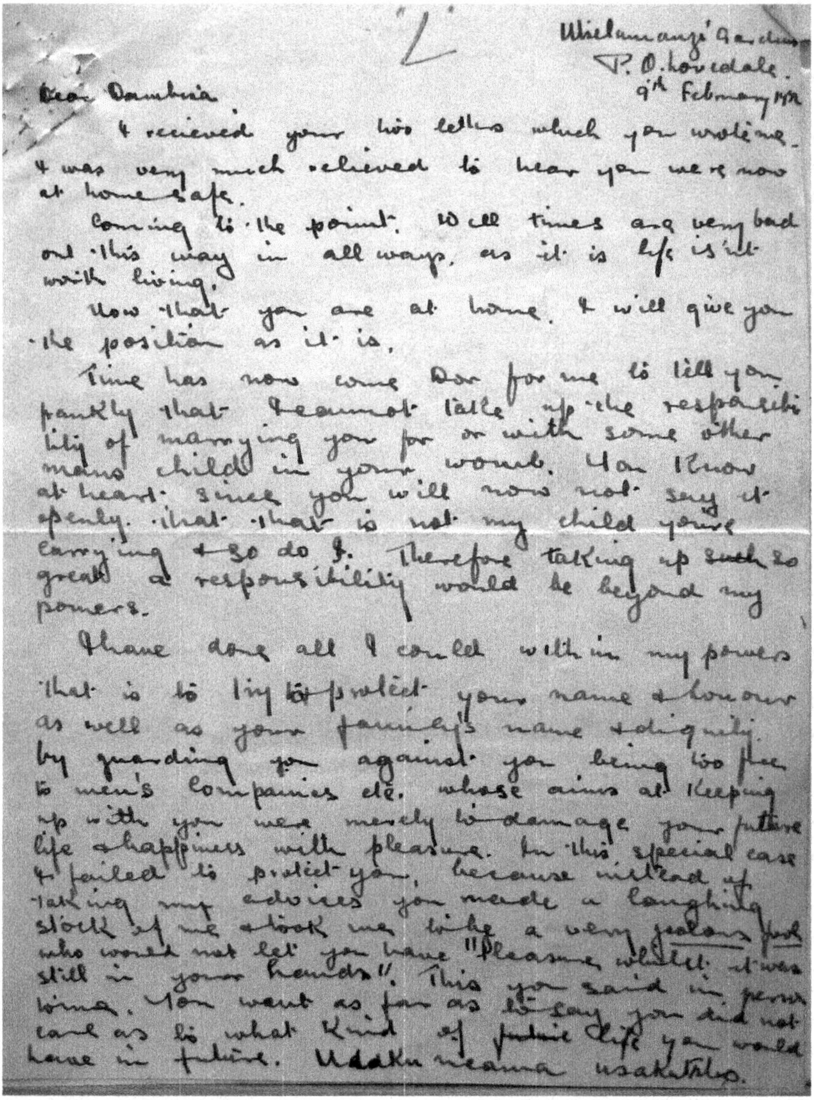

FIGURE 3.2. Letter "L," Selbourne Bokwe to Dorothy Kabane, 9 February 1933. Reproduced by permission of the Western Cape Archives and Record Service (WCARS).

The letters between Dorothy and Selbourne are explicit in a different way from Schapera's book, because their explicit content was the result of new forms of secrecy. Anne Mager suggests much of this shift to secret love affairs occurred toward the middle of the century, but it was in place much earlier. Love letters allowed Africans to be private and secret, a result not only of changing sexual ideology but of the availability of a form, the letter, whose content delivery could potentially evade attention from others.

Selbourne's feelings escape the page in a letter sometime before December 1932, when he advises Dorothy on moisturizing her lips. "Uze nontombise uthambise umlomo ithuba ndifithkile otherwise uyathkutyabauka with kisses. [I warn you, you must moisturize your lips very well otherwise they will be full of blisters from kisses] Hah! Your own, own, Bon."[11] Joel Cabrita's life history of Regina Twala contains references to the love letters between Regina and Dan, some of which were extremely frank about their sex life.[12] While Dorothy employed a go-between to deliver her letters, the messengers denied knowledge of the letters' contents in their court testimony.

Most African love letters, though, that have filtered down to the present are not frank in this way. The letters, about which Keith Breckenridge has written, were more often about daily business and domestic continuity than about the ardent business of the heart.[13] This is also the case with the letters that appear frequently as addenda to Eastern Cape court cases involving seduction. However, in a way, Selbourne Bokwe's letter to Dorothy about moisturizing her lips proves my point about how we reconstruct intimate lives. It is one piece of a more extensive collection of letters submitted as part of the evidence for the case of seduction Dorothy brought against Selbourne. The letters became public via necessity. A relationship collapsed, and the letters entered the public record—not as love letters but as tools with which to contest reputation. So although these letters chart a love affair, their becoming public is part of the process of a love affair entering into the punitive arena of either the church or the state.

HISTORICAL PERSPECTIVES ON AFRICAN SEXUALITY

In precolonial South Africa, sexual activity was generally viewed as necessary and pleasurable.[14] Differences in the perception of appropriate behavior were affected by the age and gender of participants. Young, unmarried women were expected to behave differently from older women; and widows, who had already discharged any familial duties around children and marriage, were permitted a fair degree of license when it came to having lovers. Young men not yet initiated were part of age-grades that practiced ukumetsha (see later), and the same was true for young women.[15]

Sex acts themselves, as long as they took place within a heterosexual matrix, were not considered deviant or immoral.[16] However, because women's reproductive capacities were destined for marriage, socially unsanctioned sexual relationships (generally those that transgressed the rights of fathers) were viewed unfavorably. Premarital pregnancy was especially frowned upon, but sex that avoided pregnancy (usually for girls this meant nonpenetrative sex) was considered acceptable. For unmarried sweethearts, local sex practices included what Victorian Britons would have understood as the nonpenetrative practice of mutual masturbation. Indeed, thigh sex (in isiXhosa, *ukumetsha;* in isiZulu, *ukusoma*), or nonpenetrative sex, was a common activity among Black youth, because it allowed sexual play without the possibility of pregnancy. Once a girl had reached the age of puberty, she was permitted to have male sweethearts or metsha partners who were not known to her female relatives. When women and men married, mostly to partners chosen by their parents to cement ties between lineages, it was commonly understood that both partners might take lovers. As long as a woman was discreet and performed her lineage responsibilities, she could take a lover outside her marriage.

All of this is not to suggest that sex in this period was always consensual or that individuals found their personal sexual choices respected. In a recent book, Elizabeth Thornberry pays particular attention to the shape and form of sexual consent in Xhosaland in the nineteenth century.[17] Thornberry describes the slippage that occurred in civil and criminal cases that involved either seduction, marriage by abduction, or instances of sex that were discernible, both by Xhosa speakers and white magistrates, as acts lacking consent.[18] It is very difficult to distinguish between seduction and rape in the historical record. If anything, recent research on marriage by abduction, *ukuthwala,* possibly underestimates the extent to which it had long been a source of concern for women. Nonconsensual sex is the subject of song and oral performances, but historians do not always consider these to be reliable sources and so they are underutilized in historical reconstructions of sexual activity.[19]

Perhaps the most crucial change in African sexual practice toward the end of the nineteenth century, for the purposes of this chapter, was a relative increase in the rate of premarital pregnancy and, associated with this, a decrease in the practice of ukumetsha.[20] The common refrain across the whole of the region that became South Africa was that unmarried Christian women were more immoral than their traditional counterparts and that a higher rate of premarital pregnancy existed among mission converts.[21]

While it is not possible to verify this observation, it was a frequent one and likely had some relation to truth. However, the truth it represented is not necessarily a truth about sexual activity. Rather, as I and others have indicated, this assertion is probably related to the ability of fathers and male kin to claim compensation in the form of cattle for daughters and wards who had fallen pregnant. Before European colonization, fathers could claim compensation in the form of fines in cattle for daughters who fell pregnant before marriage. This reflected the understanding that a daughter represented value to her parents, value that could be compromised by a pregnancy outside of marriage. Because this was a socially sanctioned remedy, and because the relationship often existed in a context in which it was known to the family, these cases were often resolved relatively smoothly between the male relatives of the two lovers concerned.

One of the ironies of mission Christianity was that young women and men were introduced to notions of Christian sexual morality at the same time they became exposed to nineteenth-century romantic love and individual consent as the basis for marriage. Freed from what they saw as their obligation to marry the husband chosen by their parents, young women embarked upon love affairs without familial approval. Influenced by mission thinking, which viewed ukumetsha and ukusoma as the sin of Onan, these women became pregnant under circumstances in which it was more difficult for fathers to receive compensation for their daughters. The truth referred to previously was about how families managed the consequences of a pregnancy rather than about its incidence.

MODERN LOVE AFFAIRS

In 1931, Dorothy Kabane and Selbourne Bokwe began courting. Their love affair ended sadly for both of them, in a court case that attempted to allocate paternity for the child born to Dorothy in 1933. The record of the case includes testimony from the various parties involved in its first appearance, the appeal, and a further appeal in the NAC. It also includes a series of love letters. The sentiments and feelings expressed in these letters index a wider world in which literate identities, Christianity, love, status, and respectability circumscribe and reinforce each other's effects while calling for an examination of these effects more broadly. Before I discuss the case, which reveals much about love and its peculiar effect at the intersection of sexual morality and Christianity for Africans, love and romance need a moment's consideration.

There is a rich history on the changing meaning of *love* in the Western world, some of which examines what happened to Victorian standards of romantic love in the twentieth century.[22] In the US, as Peter Stearns and Mark Knapp have written, a "new love" had taken over from the transcendental nature of Victorian love by the 1920s.[23] Masculine emotional culture had moved toward stressing compatibility in interests and sexual proclivity while ironically reflecting a misogynistic bent located in male fears of growing female independence. Some of this work is echoed in the recent studies on love in Africa.[24]

The difference between true love, romantic love, and modern love was one that deeply engaged the minds of Africans in the 1930s. In popular writing across the continent, "such discussions engaged conceptions of love promoted by mission Christianity and English fiction to contrast the affective ideals and courtship practices of school-educated young people with those of previous generations."[25] Letters to *Bantu World* contrasted the difference between true love, which resulted in respectful and Christian companionate marriages, and modern love, which was morally weak.[26] Young women were excoriated for their attachment to modern love, in which modern and sexual love were the same and equated with multiple sexual partners.[27]

However, women and men having multiple lovers and having love affairs based on affection was not a new phenomenon. Several of the seduction cases brought to the courts in the Eastern Cape detail relationships of great affection. In a 1908 case, Mxokozeli Batyi described Ngqam Fatyi, the woman he had been in a romantic relationship with for ten years, as "my sweetheart—I am much attached to her." Indeed, his attachment was such that he deliberately (his words, though translated and likely bowdlerized) "had connection with her, or order to get her to be my wife."[28]

While court testimony, as in Batyi's case, hints at enduring relationships, a greater weight to these relationships was presented in the letters clutched in the hands of their doubtless nervous participants as they prepared for court. In 1921, Louisa Nokele was taken back to her father's home from the kraal of Richard Mnci, with whom she lived and who had promised to marry her. In a letter she wrote, she declared her intention never to leave the man with whom she lived as wife, writing that she would "absolutely refuse to discard him." If not a true reflection of her feelings toward her husband, it was at least a simulacrum of them, put forward in a letter expressing her concern for her partner in relation to her father's behavior in seizing her from his kraal.[29] Another letter from a different case concluded with the salutation, "An abundance of love and 320 kisses," a much more ardent closing than the standard "I remain" generally used by letter writers.[30] Constance Magogo, the daughter of King Dinizulu, recorded a love poem in which a woman wept in her mother's arms for her departed lover: "When he looked at me I loved him! / When he laughed, I loved him! / When he spoke, I loved him!," only one of several similar she recorded.[31]

Love letters have recently become the subject of renewed scholarly attention for South Africa.[32] In his work, Breckenridge examines the multiple-authored nature of working-class private lives, with letter writing representing a collective effort on the part of scribes, lovers, and their compound comrades. He was concerned to account for the rise of a private sphere "simultaneously personal and collaborative" among working-class Africans.[33] While letter writing was extensive among Africans in the early twentieth century, including among the working class, it was often constrained. A limited privacy enveloped the letters flowing between the city and the countryside as a result of a combination of censorship and an inability of recipients to read. Breckenridge refers to this as the "ephemerality of the private letter" in Black South African history.[34]

It would perhaps be more accurate to say that letters were without precedent, or without a preceding traditional form, which allowed their easy adoption. Africans who went to court to sue for seduction slipped into an oral form familiar to them; the ease with which they shifted to arguing cases flowed over into the textualization of those cases. The oral genres people used for the exchange of sentiment were public genres. However, love letters lacked a prior form onto which Africans could attach themselves.

One of the few places where it is possible to find letters between couples lies in the court records that tell of splintered relationships. This is where I need to distinguish between patterns of love and love affairs common across Black South Africa, the Eastern Cape particularly. The court records in the archives for the magisterial courts of the Eastern Cape are different in both content and extent than other parts of the country, including Natal and Zululand. The Ciskei and the Transkeian Territories had a much longer history of European conquest and thus longer exposure to practice of magisterial courts than, for instance, Zululand. Magistrates in the Eastern Cape had much more latitude in deciding the outcome of a case, because the legislation was much more diverse and convoluted than the—by comparison—relatively simple legal code instituted by Theophilus Shepstone in Natal, subsequently known as the Natal Native Code.[35] Christianity and mission schooling had a longer history in the Eastern Cape than in other parts of South Africa, so the levels of African literacy were much higher, a factor that translated into how Africans took their cases to court.

In the many court records from the Eastern Cape that I have examined (themselves only a subset of a larger collection of unknown size), letters feature frequently. Some of these letters are like those described by Breckenridge, prosaic and mostly about daily affairs, such as the beast that needed to be slaughtered for a homestead ritual. As a corpus, these letters reference

FIGURES 3.3 AND 3.4. Pieces of paper tendered as evidence from a case about restoration of lobola, Wellington Gwavu v. Henry Lubambo Case 18/1929: Native Appeal Court, King William's Town, 28 February 1930. CAD 1/KWT 2/1/1/36—Civil Court Proceedings 1928–. By kind permission of the Western Cape Archives and Record Service (WCARS). Note the copy of the telegram sent and the returned letter from Elsie Gwavu, who had done her best to escape an arranged marriage with Henry Lubambo. She made herself unavailable for marriage by leaving the Eastern Cape and a succession of employers.

a range of marriage types. If their appearance in court cases is reflective of true life, letters—some rather less and some rather more ardent—were written with relative frequency between husbands and wives and courting couples. Moreover, official questioning often sought out the existence of letters, presenting an assumption on the part of the court that litigants might well present tender epistolary evidence of their ardor. In *The Portable Bunyan*, Isabel Hofmeyr discusses the peculiar materiality of documents.[36] "Pieces of paper can prove troublesome. They change shape and form; they disappear and reappear. They demand different types of attention, behaviour and deportment. At times they must be contemplated as objects. At times they must be carefully carried. Documents, in other words, are dangerous and unpredictable. But, they are also priceless and precious."[37]

In fact, pieces of paper were common in civil cases. In cases of debt or obligation, sales receipts were often produced in evidence, irrespective of their possessors' literacy. In a 1929 case after the court had asked whether the two protagonists could read and had received an answer in the negative, Jilingisa Meva knew to produce a sales receipt. Pieces of paper, either as personal or official documentation, could signify a range of understandings, practices, and relationships, and the trails left by absent and present pieces of paper both reflect and constitute people's sense of themselves in the world. But in this instance, it is the letters of the more literate that are most striking.

When I began reading the Kabane case in the Cape Archives Depot, sneezing from too much dust, I also found, contained within the contents of the pale brown case file, a collection of letters between the two protagonists, though not assembled in the order in which they were written. On different-colored notepaper, some blue, some buff, and envelope-less, were a collection of letters between Dorothy and Selbourne.

While these were not the first love letters I had come across in the civil case records, they are perhaps the most distinctive, both for their number—the fact that they were self-written and without the aid of letter writers—and the language of their writing (English interspersed with isiXhosa). At first, I was struck by the poignancy of Dorothy's rendering up the evidence of her love affair for a dry court record, the pieces of paper that were once both priceless and precious, where evidence of their affair would be permanently shifted to the indifferent hands of the state. I realized later, however, that the collection in the court record is only a subset of Dorothy and Selbourne's correspondence, leaving me to imagine what the other letters might have documented and also what their fate might have been.

TABLE 3.1 KABANE LETTER REGISTER

	From		Place
A	7 March 1932, p.m.	Selbourne Bokwe	Ntselamanzi
B	Thursday, late p.m.	Selbourne Bokwe	Ntselamanzi
B1	9 March 1932, 5:30 a.m.	Selbourne Bokwe	Ntselamanzi
B2	25 Monday, p.m.	Selbourne Bokwe	Ntselamanzi
B3	Tuesday, p.m.	Selbourne Bokwe	Ntselamanzi
B4	10 March 1932, p.m.	Selbourne Bokwe	Ntselamanzi
B5	1 August 1932	Selbourne Bokwe	Ntselamanzi
C	3 December 1932	Selbourne Bokwe	Ntselamanzi
D	27 July 1932	Dorothy Kabane	Lovedale
E	12 October 1932	Dorothy Kabane	Lovedale
F	19 October 1932	Dorothy Kabane	Lovedale
G	6 November 1932	Dorothy Kabane	Umtata
H	15 November 1932	Dorothy Kabane	Umtata
J	18 November 1932	Dorothy Kabane	Umtata
K	3 January 1933	Dorothy Kabane	Grey Hospital, King William's Town
L	9 February 1932	Selbourne Bokwe	Ntselamanzi

Source: Case 13/1933, NAC, KWT, 7 September 1933 (the alphabetical labeling is from the court)

TABLE 3.1. Kabane letter register. A list of the correspondence in CAD ALC 2/1/2/1 Case 13 of 1933, Cape Archive Depot, National Archives, Cape Town.

The letters from this case can be grouped into three categories. The first letters, labeled "A," and "B" by the court, were written by Selbourne in the period immediately following the start of their sexual relationship. These were submitted by Dorothy as evidence of the relationship. The second batch—"D," "E," "F," "G," "H," "J," and "K"—were written by Dorothy after the pregnancy was confirmed and were submitted by Selbourne. The third set, consisting of letters "C" and "L," capture Selbourne responding to Dorothy's request for a speedy marriage and reflect an eye to crafting a possible defense for him.

In his first letters, Selbourne poured his ardor for Dorothy on to the page.

> Darling is there anything sweeter than true, & sincere, love? I am sure darling our hearts met for the first time ever since we made love to one another. All along we've been but strangers to each

other. Is it not true Dor you love me? & that you should love me always! Dor I am dying for your company. I am hopelessly lovesick. I do not know what I shall do with you the day I meet you. I bet I'll be the first to kiss you, & look out I don't crush you darling. I am sure there's something wrong with me, I never meant to love you to this extent. Your very own Bon. Selbourne Bokwe to Dorothy Kabane, 7 March 1932.

This letter, "A," reflects Selbourne's state of mind and his perception of how lovers ought to behave to one another. It was, according to Dorothy, written just after she and Selbourne had first made love. These early letters have much to say about Selbourne's understanding of love, that he still understood that it might be reciprocal and centered on their relationship, regardless of the world outside. In fact, while his letters show Selbourne consistently to have been manipulative in his quest to have Dorothy declare herself for him, mind, body, and soul, they are also a rather fair statement of his perception of the meaning of modern love and his state of emotion. He, as much as Dorothy, did not think through the consequences of modern love. While he does not use the word "modern," it is clear from what he describes as well as how he behaves throughout the case, that he is not writing of more traditional understandings of intimacy. In this letter, as in the next few, Selbourne taxed Dorothy with the strength of her feeling for him, alternating between love as emotion and love as sexual passion.

> So far as I am concerned I am quite sure my love for you is not a mere passing passion as you put it last night.... In the past I have loved you well enough as I did last night, only there was a great deal of doubt as to whether my love for you was of any value to you & whether you cared at all to be loved by me. Only last night did you give me the impression that after all my love could mean something to you.... Why darling do you wish to control your love? Why Dor won't you let your love have its own way where it could if its not in the wrong place?[38]

This was a regular refrain in his first few letters. According to Selbourne, Dorothy's passion and love could never quite match up to his. There are none of Dorothy's letters from this period in the record, so it is unclear how she replied.

The second theme in Selbourne's letters is misunderstanding. "You misinterpret me in all ways. That is, you misinterpreted my love in every way that because you do not understand I love you."[39] "Misinterpretation" was a word he used fairly often—that he spoke at a different register than Dorothy, who did not understand the meaning of his words. While the letters were clearly an attempt to clear up these misunderstandings, Selbourne's somewhat coy allusions lead me to suspect that Dorothy probably understood him fairly well. Dorothy, by her admission furnished in Selbourne's letters, was less trusting and much more reticent. From their declarations, it appears as if both Dorothy and Selbourne were using their letters and the pieces of paper they were written upon to cement something about their relationship, as if writing something down could make it so. While Selbourne was using the letters to create a space for sexual passion, Dorothy—whatever her own thoughts on sexual passion—was using them to will into existence a love affair, with marriage as an outcome.

More instances of ardent love and misinterpretation appear in the letters, closely associated with a third theme, which emphasizes freedom.

> I say I do not know how I stand in your love, because whenever I try to be free in talk & in some other ways you are offended. I have to guard myself in every little act of love I do. Whilst I expect to be at ease whenever I am with you in any way. I had no idea I could have limits in talks, joke & questioning with you. So you have refused me that freedom which means my own happiness.[40]

For Selbourne, freedom appeared to mean the end of any boundary between himself and his lover, a giving up of individual privacy as a token of mutual love. At the same time, though, he viewed his individual happiness as being linked to a state of freedom, a very clear statement of his understanding of the benefits of an individual self.

The final two letters, "C" and "L," were written by Selbourne. In "C," he wrote that he wanted to postpone the marriage, and "L" included his refusal. Selbourne's last letter, perhaps even his last two letters, were written with defense in mind, although it was Dorothy who used his last letter as proof of his breach of promise. Like the letters mentioned by Lynn Thomas in her work on school girl pregnancies in Kenya, some of Selbourne's letters were written with the intention that they later be used as part of his defense. He wrote them as the Bokwes were preparing for a court case, which they started as early as their meeting with the Kabanes in January.

The second batch of letters was written by Dorothy to Selbourne after the pregnancy was confirmed, as she was preparing to leave Lovedale, during a visit to her sister in Lovedale, and a few months before the child was born. Most of these letters were written in a state of considerable emotional and physical distress, the former occasioned by Dorothy's consideration of the consequences of a premarital pregnancy (which resulted in extreme anxiety and insomnia) and the latter by much morning sickness. In several of these letters, Dorothy, in her attempts to get Selbourne to commit to marriage, made vague allusions to herself being to blame. In court, these were used by Selbourne as evidence of her having slept with someone else and become pregnant with this unnamed man's child.

In these letters, Selbourne was operating according to an understanding of love as distinct from marriage. His earlier letters reflect his feelings about having acquired a modern playmate, and at the same time, the letters are clearly an act of love in itself, facilitated by a literacy taught by missionaries. Also, though, he was possessive and jealous of Dorothy's contact with other men. Ultimately, Dorothy proved not to be Selbourne's soul mate, and Selbourne found himself less supportive of the idea of female freedom in love, especially if it impacted his future prospects. At this point, he used more-traditional understandings of relationships gone wrong to extricate himself from their relationship: his brother sent a telegram to break the news of Dorothy's pregnancy to her family. Whether any of Selbourne's relatives would have supported his view, given their definite support for companionate marriage, is questionable. Finally, when faced with what his family considered an unsuitable marriage (we do not know why), Selbourne cleaved to his family's understanding of what was required of him.

Dorothy's first letter, written in late July, contains the following:

> Your yesterdays / Mondays letter crowned by your person gave me the impression of what is in your mind. If there was anything the matter with me—I wouldn't have hesitated to tell you straightaway. Last night you came up with the idea there was, & you were irresponsible (sic), somebody else being responsible—Needless to say how I felt & took it. Well fortunately enough for me—as far as I know the idea is false.[41]

Dorothy's statement in this letter was used by Selbourne to show that he was not responsible for a pregnancy, and he attempted in court to show that she must have got pregnant after this date. However, the issue is not as clear as Dorothy's statement might seem. Dorothy's letters are hesitant about the issue of love, whether it should be companionate or reside in sexual passion. In response to Selbourne's suspicions about her contact with other men, Dorothy's replies consisted of apologies for giving him such an idea. Her apologies relate to matters of emotion rather than matters of the body, although her later letters are filled with the corporeal as she struggled through a difficult and anxiety-laden pregnancy. She was continually fearful, both of Selbourne leaving her and of how she and her behavior would appear to others. In November, she wrote to Selbourne, "Darling I am blue," though at the time she still hoped for marriage.[42] Three days later, she laid out carefully the reasons for their getting married, quoted at the opening to this chapter.[43]

Dorothy's letters show much more of a concern for the community in which she was located, as the comment about her mother reveals. She was preoccupied with Christian respectability, recognizing with no difficulty its greater consequences for her than for Selbourne. Selbourne seldom seemed to have thought beyond his own needs, while Dorothy's letters were all about her needs in relation to the needs of her family. Dorothy's letters convey an understanding of love very different from that conveyed by Selbourne's. Her fearfulness at what other people would say contrasts sharply with Selbourne's stated disregard for them. She saw herself much more as needing to be anchored in a community. This was a different sense of selfhood from Selbourne's, which is possible to ascribe to the nature of her character, but it may also say more about the ability of African women particularly to take up modern notions of selfhood. Ironically, her going to court was an action that challenged prevailing social norms much more than Selbourne's use of his family and traditional forms of seduction resolution to tie up the matter.

Lynn Thomas has described schoolgirl pregnancies and their relationship to love letters in late colonial East Africa in a matter similar to the circumstances around Dorothy and Selbourne's letters.[44] While three decades separate Dorothy's pregnancy from some of those mentioned in Thomas's work, there are marked convergences between the contexts surrounding our cases. As Thomas has shown, letter writing between young people was at the nexus of a set of practices around self-creation, self-promotion, and defense of reputation. Thomas writes of this as evidence of a hybrid and school-learning-centered modernity. School-educated young women in search of suitable husbands would write letters that both displayed their learning and represented them as modern in the eyes of their potential suitors. Letters were a way to advertise the writers' "up-to-dateness," because letters and relationships were linked into other forms of popular culture like detective novels. At the same time, the letters produced within a relationship could serve to confirm the nature of that relationship. In pregnancy compensation cases, letters were often submitted as evidence to prove dates of conception and sexual encounters. Much of this is evident in the Kabane-Bokwe correspondence, both parties submitting letters as evidence of their different claims.

CONSTITUTING SELFHOOD AND MORALITY IN THE CIVIL COURTS

Literally enfolding the letters contained in the archival folder of the Kabane Case in the Cape Archives Depot are the records of the various court cases that chart Selbourne and Dorothy's love affair. These records, both as evidence of a particular kind of public action in court and the textualization of that action, represent some of the other levels at which this case acts as both an example of and a creative force for the constitution of Black intimacy.

One reason this case is so compelling has to do with the extent of the inclusion of love letters given into evidence. These letters present an alternative and parallel record to that of the case as it manifested in the native commissioner's court. They also embed the case in the social world of young Christian converts, emphasizing the importance of seeing cases as the outcome of pre-existing social relationships, some of which would continue after the conclusion of a case, as much as an opportunity to examine the deliberation of colonial legal systems. This case exemplifies Roberts's description of cases as needing to consider both what happens before and after an appearance in court as well as how they provide a crucible through which to discern the "trouble" that arose when one party in a social relationship maintained following custom and the other claimed status as a Christian.

Dorothy was a teacher at one of the children's schools attached to Lovedale. Her father was minister of a Wesleyan church in Butterworth, and her mother was a member of that church's mothers' association. Her brother, Milner, was also a teacher at Lovedale and was a prominent All-African Convention and African National Congress member during the 1930s. Selbourne was also of a prominent Black Christian family. His father was John Knox Bokwe, a minister in the Presbyterian Church, and his siblings included Frieda, Balfour, and Roseberry. Selbourne was an agricultural demonstrator, first near Lovedale and later in the Western Cape.

Roughly a month after Dorothy gave birth, she and her lawyer, Edward Burl, appeared before the Alice Native Commissioner's Court, seeking a judgment of one hundred pounds in compensation for breach of promise, and a second one hundred pounds in damages for seduction and pregnancy. The breach of promise charge related to Selbourne's failure to follow through with a marriage, and the second charge to the financial and emotional damages as a result of her losing her virginity and giving birth.

Most cases of this kind named a woman's guardian as the litigant. It is significant that Dorothy appeared for herself, even if prompted to do so by her family. She also requested to have the case tried under South African civil law. After the Black Administration Act of 1927, seduction cases

Love, Sex, and Consequence

between Africans were a matter for customary law, but because she and Selbourne had "adopted the European standard of living," as the court put it, and were publicly known to be practicing Christians, she was eligible to have the case tried under common law because of a provision in law called the repugnancy clause. The entirely hypothetical instance of a Black woman claiming damages from a white man would automatically have been tried under civil law. A claim for damages (the fine or compensation referred to) under customary law usually carried a penalty of between fifteen and twenty-five pounds, the equivalent then of between three and five head of cattle. The claim under the civil law of the union was substantially greater.

Selbourne's plea, which he prepared together with his attorney, Mr. Welsh, attempted to answer Dorothy's charges in two ways. In the first, he gave reasons why the case should be tried under African customary law, one being because "although both parties to this action are Christians and educated natives, nevertheless both parties adhere to their native law and customs." This plea was disregarded by the court with little or no hesitation. Although this disingenuous ploy must have been clear to all, given the status of his family, it was also an accurate statement about how some African Christians did not see a discrepancy between tradition and faith. When Frieda Bokwe, his sister, married Z. K. Matthews, she wrote in her memoir that "my mother had warned my brother that his father had been one of those . . . who had opposed *Lobola* for the Christians and that she wanted no *Bogadi* for her daughters."[45] Three years later, Selbourne's brother, Roseberry, was to marry in an elaborate wedding in Grahamstown (see chapter 5), which included the transfer of lobola and a traditional ceremony. Unfortunately for Selbourne, the civil court was prepared to accept only a defense that rested on either European or customary law and not both.

Selbourne's second defense rested on the fact that, although he had promised to marry Dorothy, he had not seduced her—or if he had seduced her, she had also had other lovers. As a result, he was not responsible for her pregnancy and was under no obligation to marry her. While this case appears little different to other cases of seduction, certainly in the defense's argument, it is also a lens into how and under what circumstances claiming Christianity could simultaneously benefit and complicate people's lives. In Dorothy's case, her shame arose because she was Christian, but at the same time, because she was Christian, she could argue to have the case tried under civil law.

When the case was heard in court, the initial proceedings taking place just before Dorothy's child was born, Dorothy was first questioned about her claim to be tried according to civil law. She and two other witnesses, her brother Milner and her uncle Michael, stressed their status as Christians and the fact that they did not pay dowry (the transcriber's word) in the traditional manner. The court then questioned Dorothy about how she met and became involved with Selbourne and how he persuaded her to engage in a sexual relationship.

On cross-examination by Selbourne's lawyer, she told the court how her engagement with Selbourne had been secret, even from her parents, despite them knowing that Selbourne was courting her (the transcript's word). From the questions, it is evident the Bokwe defense rested on the fact that they had not really been engaged and that Dorothy had had previous boyfriends. She spoke about having been twice engaged before.[46]

After establishing the initial detail, Dorothy's tale became complex as she recounted under examination her relationship with Selbourne. She had apparently become pregnant in July 1932. Her final testimony concerned the length of her pregnancy and the fact that her baby was not born prematurely.

Following Dorothy's testimony, her brother and uncle were called upon first to confirm that their family did not participate in lobola transactions. Thereafter, Milner recounted how he had found out about the pregnancy in January 1933, when Selbourne's brother, Barbour, had sent Milner a telegram explaining that Dorothy "was in trouble" and that Milner and Barbour should meet. As Milner stressed in his testimony, "the idea of the meeting was not to observe native custom." According to Milner and Michael Kabane, Selbourne waited outside during most of the meeting. When questioned, he did not deny his responsibility for the pregnancy. Rather, his male relatives asked for more time to consider the matter. At the end of February, almost two months later, the Bokwes announced their belief in Selbourne's innocence.

Dorothy herself, Milner, and Michael were the only witnesses for Dorothy's case. The first defense witness was the doctor, Malcolm Macvicar, who had treated Dorothy when she first suspected she was pregnant in August 1932. Macvicar's testimony was necessary to Selbourne's case, because Selbourne hoped to prove that he and Dorothy had been in different locations on her possible date of conception. Among other findings, Macvicar's "medical evidence" was that Dorothy's length of pregnancy was consistent with the average.[47]

Selbourne's own testimony stressed the fact that he never had "intercourse" with Dorothy. While acknowledging that he had not denied responsibility for Dorothy's pregnancy in the January meeting, according to him, a denial did not constitute confirmation.

The magistrate did not have much trouble reaching a decision in Dorothy's favor; similar cases constituted almost the bulk of civil cases appearing

Love, Sex, and Consequence

in front of the native commissioners. One possibility is that he felt sympathetic toward Dorothy. The other is that, failing financial support, Dorothy and her newborn child might become a burden on the state. He based his finding on Selbourne's failure to deny responsibility for the pregnancy.

With too much at stake in terms of his status and his family's finances, Selbourne appealed the decision in September that year.[48] The same month, Judge Barry, Judge President of the Cape and Orange Free State NAC, denied Selbourne Bokwe's appeal for a reversal of the decision. Barry, in his judgment, upheld the decision of Assistant Commissioner Nel to award Dorothy fifty-five pounds in damages—five pounds for Selbourne's breach of promise and fifty pounds for the damages as a result of a pregnancy that had occurred during their relationship. It is important to remember that an appeal consisted of the original judgment—the one captured on paper—being assessed for its adherence to law, along with an additional panel of assessors who examined the evidence of the case—the paper transcript—and not the case itself. In the appeal, Dorothy and Selbourne did not speak to Judge Barry from their own mouths, but from the papers laid before him.

At least two different understandings of Christianity insert themselves into the Kabane case, both drawing very much on ideas in existence before the case and from aspirations for the future. Colonial understandings about African women as oppressed by African men, which derive from views steeped in Christian social morality, saw Dorothy as worthy of the court's care. This meant the court could reward her for her moral character in remaining steadfast in her accusation, notwithstanding her potential loss of virginity (which the record described as "misconduct"). Indeed, the magistrate was at pains to emphasize her respectability. "The plaintiff appears to me to be a very respectable native girl. She gave her evidence in a very straightforward manner ... nor ... has evidence of any description been led to show her to be of a shady character." Possibly her status as the daughter of a minister lent credibility to her statements, but Selbourne was also a minister's child. It is more likely that support from the European missionaries and doctors around Lovedale contributed to this perception. This is despite a court transcript, which—if rendered accurately—showed Miss Kabane's testimony to be full of inconsistencies, something which my rendition of her twelve pages of testimony probably disguises. Elsewhere in his judgment, Nel did refer to the inconsistencies in her testimony, but these were not considered consequential. In fact, Dorothy Kabane's evidence appears to have been of little importance to the case, since Malcolm Macvicar supplied the important details about her condition. Although the court described the letters she and Selbourne supplied as evidence of a "hectic" relationship, the letters were not used as a form of evidence (or, if they were, the court was careful to disguise this fact). The letters acted as additional, rather than confirmatory, proof of her case. Selbourne's guilt was established by the rather convoluted proof supplied by, according to the Kabane male relatives, Selbourne's failure to deny he was responsible for Dorothy's pregnancy in the January meeting. Even Selbourne's male relatives confirmed that he failed then to deny his responsibility for the pregnancy.

Although the courts might have been favorable to Dorothy, they did not take her testimony seriously. The courts were active in upholding ideas about differences between male and female agency, crediting African men with more agency than women.

Historians Sean Redding and Tapiwa Zimudzi have both emphasized the importance of not seeing African women as victims on court cases, either when they were under prosecution in criminal cases or when they were litigants or held other roles in civil cases. Their work stresses the importance of examining women as active participants in such instances.[49] Ironically, in Dorothy's case, her construction as a victim of male perfidy resulted in her preferred court outcome. Stephen Robertson's work on statutory rape in New York in the early twentieth century has shown that the construction of women as passive before the court was not just an attempt to rewrite and constrain their sexual agency but an effort to provide women protection that courts would be otherwise unwilling to accord.[50] The court records needed to write women as passive in order to offer them support. While Dorothy was an active participant in her case, the white lawyers viewed her not as a modern woman in a consensual sexual relationship but rather as a defenseless woman taken in by Selbourne's declarations of love. The courts' view upheld a conventional sexual division of power. While their ultimate judgment cast the mantle of the court over Dorothy, their deliberations more generally confirmed but also re-created ideas about social status and the division of power between men and women.

At the same time, though, the court also reconfirmed Dorothy's status as a Black woman. Not once did any of the courts prevent the case being tried according to European civil law, but Dorothy was still only a "native girl" who could be awarded damages on the European scale but not at the top of it. She qualified for greater than the usual scale of damages in similar cases, but the court awarded her roughly a quarter of what she requested. Selbourne, too, seems to have suffered at the hands of the courts. The courts were not resolved as to what kind of colonial subjects Dorothy and Selbourne represented. The two were neither "natives," since they conducted themselves in fact "according to European standards of living," nor were they the same as Europeans. Their public and visible links with Christianity made their case complex to administer in ways that did not trouble cases involving non-Christians. For this reason, commissioners in the customary courts (called "native commissioners") and magistrates were continually alert to the possibility of Christian status or Christian marriages in cases such as these, a practice that added to the colonial understanding that distinctions existed between Christian and non-Christian subjects. Moreover, the civil court in Alice had allowed Selbourne and Dorothy to act out their status as morally suspect Christians in matters of intimacy to a rather limited audience, but the appeal case decision took that status and broadcast it to a nationwide audience—a white audience who could regard the record of the case as confirmation of the moral shortcomings of Africans, including, if not especially, Christian Africans.

THE PUBLIC CONSEQUENCES OF SEX

While Dorothy and Selbourne's love produced a case that was unique in terms of its detail, it combined sexual morality and public consequence in a manner that is also evident elsewhere.

In 1939, a Lovedale pupil was tried for culpable homicide in the Grahamstown Supreme Court following the discovery of the body of her newborn child within the fences of the institution.[51] Hers was one of seven similar disciplinary cases involving girls in the boarding school. The school's response was to plan an annual medical examination of female pupils, as well as to raise the fence around the girls' section of the school. Although the minutes describe most of the misdemeanors as not connected with the school, the building of a fence indicates a definite sense of an institution under siege. The minutes of the meeting that recorded this incident are not especially sympathetic toward their charges nor show concern for the men responsible for these pregnancies.

While cases like this one may seldom have made it to court, from a host of sources, it is clear that school may have been liberating for young women, but it was also often dangerous. At school, especially at boarding school, young women were removed from the social embrace and sexual scrutiny of their families and were encouraged by their teachers to adopt new ways of thinking about sex and marriage. While what girls learned at school emphasized marriage, young women and men also sought out romantic fiction for pleasure. This, rather than Christian didactic literature, was a form of reading criticized heavily by those same teachers. Christianity may not have been directly responsible for the consequences that ensued, but it certainly intervened to structure ideas about appropriate behavior, and it operated to give structure to the public consequences of sexual activity. Lovedale and the other large mission institutions of the Eastern Cape separated their male and female pupils, both in class and in locating their boarding houses at opposite ends of the school grounds, but there is no doubt that schoolboys and schoolgirls were able to develop relationships very different from those they would have had at home.

Not only the higher mission institutions but also the regular mission schools were potential sources of danger as much as they were sources of learning. In 1948, in what appears to be a standard seduction case, the father of Maziswe (who also went by Euvinah) Mqomboti took her former teacher to the civil court in King William's Town for being responsible for Maziswe's pregnancy and resulting child.[52] His case was successful, including on the appeal of the teacher, Daniel Mzwakali. More troubling than the details of the case, though, is the fact that at the time the couple first began to be intimate, Maziswe was fourteen. Masizwe testified as follows:

> I did not know what was going to happen at Defendant's hut.
> I did not know what Defdt meant when he proposed love to me.
> Defdt told me I should accept him and he would tell me later why he proposed to me. I had no idea what Defdt meant. I used to hear other women speak about these things. I had some idea of what it was all about. When I accepted Defdt. I did not know what was going to happen. I did not know anything about the practice of metsha.

The relationship appears to have continued on and off between 1945 and 1947, at some point leading to a pregnancy. Masizwe's testimony further described how, upon finding out she was pregnant, Daniel beat her and attempted to make her drink some "medicine," presumably to induce an abortion.

While this case has many features in common with other seduction cases, including that Masizwe likely did not consent to a full sexual relationship, it is also troubling because Daniel Mzwakali was a teacher when he set up a relationship with a pupil, and used another pupil, Masizwe's sister, to carry messages between the two of them. One of the pieces of evidence in the case included a postcard calling Daniel's attention to the fee to be paid at St. Matthew's College, Keiskammahoek, for his Junior Certificate Exam.

Anne Mager has written about the redefining of masculinity in the Eastern Cape in the 1950s and 1960s. Pointing to the existence of a "thwarted masculinity," she examines how "masculinities were constructed around a desire to assert control not only over male rivals but also over young females."[53] In the Eastern Cape by the 1960s, about half the adult men were absent at any one point on continuing work contracts, with many women also absent. This resulted in a social context quite different from that of previous generations. In her examination of youth organizations, Mager describes how "youth organisations were rendered less stable" by reshaped behavioral codes that included reinvented traditional practices, importantly pointing to how "secret love affairs and private erotic spaces beyond the purview of associations both enabled new forms of organization and encouraged individualizing practices."[54]

As Mager has noted, secret love affairs had become common by the 1950s, a fact recognized by both schoolgirls and schoolboys.[55] "Love affairs between male teachers and their female students were common."[56] It is possible, at a stretch, to understand these relationships as companionate and reciprocal. Another understanding, though, requires the reading I have just given of the relationship between Masizwe and Daniel. Their relationship may have involved passion and reciprocity but it also involved physical abuse and coercion.

Later material makes the case stronger, and it is difficult to remain unshocked by the casual admissions of rape that this material reveals. In the late 1960s, an educated and respected thirty-six-year-old male teacher from a well-known Christian family in Grahamstown had the following to say about one of his teenage lovers: "If she should become pregnant—why worry if I can escape responsibility. She allowed me to make the child—I do not feel sorry for her therefore."[57] Another Christian teacher, from the same interview collection, described trying to have penetrative sex with one of his girlfriends. "When we 'slept' together for the first time she showed some reluctance to have full sexual relations with me but when I exerted some pressure she stopped struggling."[58] Other interviews given by women to researcher Percy Qayiso also described forced sexual encounters.

While the youthful aggression Mager describes was a concern for all in the Eastern Cape, especially as much of it spilled over into violent fights between competing youth associations, it also encompassed a set of concerns particular to church folk. Private relationships and disquiet about the particular nature of these private relationships between teachers and pupils had become a concern after World War I. In 1935, in the same letter to *Bantu World* quoted in the previous chapter, the author pointed to the Christian equivalent of the *imitshotsho* dances.

> Sir—the "Dance Fever" has seized the youth of these parts whole sale. It has now become a weekly entertainment corresponding to the Friday gathering of the "red" youth which takes place at

our country stores. In these dancing entertainments are commingled without distinction, children, street boys and girls and people worthy of being called ladies and gentlemen. Will those who are thoroughly conversant with this recreation and exercise which has been introduced by modern civilisation, kindly enlighten us as to whether we are on the right lines to be admitting into these entertainments without distinction, drunkards and gentlemen. Is the atmosphere of such an entertainment healthy and conducive to mentle [sic] ease and rest?[59]

According to H. B. Z. Ndidndwa, who wrote the letter, teachers danced with their pupils on these occasions, turning the world upside down and inverting a social order centered on Christianity. He was quite clear that his comments referred to male teachers dancing with female pupils, a move he asserted intended to disrupt natural relations of respect that girls held for their superiors. While male teachers were castigated for their predatory relationships, it was their female and Christian partners who were more generally blamed for the rise in secret relationships and pregnancies.[60]

In the mid-1930s, the South African state convened a series of committees to investigate the prospect of moving African education to the control of the state. While African opinion was generally against the move, many did support removing "the arbitrary powers of missionaries in respect of disciplining teachers for moral offences."[61] As the next section indicates, the disciplining of teachers for immorality was a regular feature of church deliberation. However, what the missionaries themselves and their male converts failed to recognize is that many of these moral offenses were for relationships between teachers and preachers and their pupils, often facilitated by the proximity afforded by being at school. The young women who suffered as a result of disciplinary cases were subject not only to a sexual double standard that damaged them even more through each retelling of an offense (where men did not experience similar damage) but also to the sexual violence that had crept in under the protection of the church and its institutions of learning.

In the two cases I now discuss, the church acting as an arena of censure is an important element. Cases of sexual misconduct heard before the church courts performed and reinforced the civil court cases that performed morality—the church doing so for a literate African audience, the courts (in addition to showcasing Christian morality) doing so for a local, and later to a white, legal audience. Cases became cases because of the Christian status of their protagonists, linking particular understandings of morality and intimacy to the status of being an African Christian. Moreover, they often filtered through into the civil courts after initial church proceedings. In the two examples that follow, the instance of so-called sexual immorality was first heard by the Wesleyans and the Presbyterians. Here, the appearance of these cases in the civil court records is likely more to do with the tenacity of the people accused or defending their positions than of the number of cases of this type. Christian sexual sanctions were a definite—and later destructive—feature of the African Christian landscape, certainly from the 1840s, and still today. This is a deeply ingrained mode of censure for behavior, considered censorious only because of Christian intervention.

In 1845, Jan Beck Balfour, one of the first converts to join the Scottish mission station at Pirie, was found guilty of gross misconduct. He had approached a young woman in her hut during the night to persuade her to have sex. The Christians on the mission station, including some of the converts, were unequivocal in expelling him from communion in the church.[62] Throughout the remainder of the nineteenth century, Christian mission stations in the Eastern Cape (and elsewhere in Africa) viewed the disciplining of sexual misconduct as a part of their Christian duty.[63] Indeed, local-level church records from the early twentieth century are full of references to behavior at odds with Christian sexual morality. Charges of sexual immorality were a continuing church concern during the first half of the twentieth century. In 1914, the Diocese of St. John debated the sanctions it should follow with young male converts who committed immorality.[64] In 1925, the Presbyterians were preoccupied with how to sanction divinity students found guilty of immorality; was it necessary to prevent such students from entering the ministry?[65]

This type of concern is evident until the 1940s, when it seems that reportage of such cases (though not their incidence) tapers off. These and the various concerns around sexual morality reported in other chapters in this book point to sexuality having not only a thick, discursive presence but also a material effect on the lives of those Christians who transgressed their faith's sexual norms.

While all the churches were preoccupied with a general concern around sexual immorality, concern shifted to censure and consequence in relation to more specific cases. The one discussed next is like many others similar to it, not only in terms of outcome and the set of expectations brought to bear on the parties involved but also in its public performance and its subsequent record. The evidence for the case is in one folder containing, it would appear, the original record of the case, Ida Magadlela's challenge to its outcome, and Thomas Ngaki's appeal.[66] The paperwork for the case details events that began sometime prior to 1918 and ended in 1919. To give an account of the case, I have taken a nonlinear and nonchronological set of documents and tried to render them in the order in which events occurred.

The first series of events in this extended case concerns John Makabulo's expulsion from the Pirie congregation because of his rumored adultery. No date is attached to this expulsion. It seems that at some point after John's expulsion, Ida Magadlela was accused of committing adultery with John. At the point at which this accusation was made, John was described as Ida's brother-in-law, also her guardian while her husband was absent. If we consider the lack of clear chronology in the accounts of the case, it is clear that Ida and John's tangled relationship—whether lovers or not—had been preoccupying the congregation at the Presbyterian mission station for a while.

Sometime in July 1917, according to her later testimony, Ida and John—the tone is from the court record—concocted a plan that centered on trapping Thomas Ngaki into admitting that he and Ida had slept together. Ida's proof of some relationship with someone, presumably during her husband's absence, lay in the child born in January 1918.

The following year when her husband was back in Pirie, Ida began telling people that Thomas was the father of her child. These accusations, whether true or not, bore fruit in the form of an examination in front of the Pirie church court. Despite the church court's finding no substance in the rumors against Thomas, or more likely because of the lack of a finding, the Scottish mission authorities at Lovedale directed Thomas Ngaki to have his name cleared in the magistrate's court. As the court record noted, "It seems fairly obvious that the claim would never have been brought." Thomas, conscious of his dignity as a candidate for ordination and of the threat the accusation posed to his honor, was equally keen on having his name cleared.

His solution lay in bringing a case of defamation against Ida Magadlela in the resident magistrate's court in King William's Town. At the first hearing, the case found for Thomas. Ida, however, caused the case to be reopened as a result of "bad law" (her lawyer presented the magistrate's finding as invalid in law). After the court found in her favor, Thomas bought the case on appeal and won.

The case has several interesting features that reveal how gender, racial identity, and Christian status influenced people's lives in tightly knit, peri-urban communities in the early twentieth century. Only Thomas and John faced the possibility of financial damage to their status through these claims, and it appears that mostly men, rather than women, were faced with the threat of expulsion in cases of this nature. Ida is presented in the court record as a scheming woman. And her status as someone accused

Love, Sex, and Consequence

of adultery in the Pirie court worked to reduce the value of her accusation against Thomas when the case was heard by the magistrate.

In 1925, Wilson Jabavu was dismissed from his post as principal at a government-aided, Methodist mission school at Mgqakwebe in King William's Town. In the civil suit he brought against the Administrator of the Cape Province, he claimed two hundred pounds as damages for his wrongful dismissal.[67] In November of 1925, he had been called to a meeting of the school board under the chair of the Wesleyan minister Reverend Ncwana and accused of having an affair with Daisy Yekela (or Nexela), who was an assistant teacher at the same school. According to Reverend Ncwana's testimony, he had called a meeting of the school board after receiving information from the headman, Malewana Mcentana, about the affair. After the hearing, both Jabavu and Yekela were dismissed.

The records of the Cape Education Department during this period are full of disputes between African teachers and the state, as teachers struggled to secure access to their rightful pensions and to avoid unfair dismissal.[68] Histories of African education in South Africa focus principally on the larger mission institutions, often showing how African pupils and teachers attempted to resist the imposition of racist conditions of service and inferior conditions of living.[69] Many of these histories deal directly with the role played by African teachers and pupils in resisting first the conditions of segregation, and later, apartheid. In this history, it is usually the mission institutions that feature most prominently—and for good reason—as ambivalent, often conflicted, and complicit agents of a Christian colonialism. But the grip of the mainline churches went further to include the behavior of the ordinary teachers who supplied African schools, mission or otherwise, across the country. The African men and women who staffed the network of schools across the Cape Province, all of which were mission funded or government aided, needed to be Christians in good standing, even to be considered for appointment. Being dismissed was a serious event: not only would teachers lose their salary for several years until they could be re-registered as a teacher, but the perquisites that came with a teacher's salary were also lost. Wilson Jabavu had a house and six acres of land with his appointment. His wife was living in Aliwal North, and it is quite possible that he would have needed to support two households if he did not have the church accommodation. In interviews I conducted with retired ministers in the Eastern Cape, a frequent recollection involved accounts of the years that men had spent apart from their wives, as work requirements took them to different locations.

Teachers in positions like Wilson Jabavu's had much to lose when confronted with sexual impropriety. In Jabavu's case, the record cannot avoid showing that the accusations against him appear to have been trumped up. The witnesses against him were unable, for instance, to avoid revealing that their accusation was unexpected and unprocedural and that the school board's prosecution of him appeared to be the actions of a group of men disaffected with the teacher. From the manner in which Jabavu questioned the processes leading to his dismissal, it is also apparent that he was well versed in his rights as a teacher. It was easier to dismiss a male teacher for sexual impropriety than to dismiss him because he had become a member of a local teachers' association or had become vocal against the indignities suffered by African teachers. As a result, African Christian teachers were frequently found lacking in white eyes because of their failure to measure up to Christian standards of morality. When found lacking, it was not difficult to bring the might of the state—or even in the person of its local-level agents—to bear against them. Fairly sensibly, Wilson Jabavu brought his accusation against the Administrator of the Cape Colony, rather than one of his accusers. Fortunately for him, the court found in his favor, but rather than finding the charges against him unjust, they found that the original hearing had been unprocedural. In calculating the damages awarded to Jabavu, and taking into account the court finding that "the teaching service of the Cape Province had been closed to them," H. Britten, the magistrate, reckoned his loss of income over the remainder of his active life at a figure of just over sixty-four pounds. If Wilson Jabavu's testimony in front of the court was accurate, the charge against him—one that led to concrete and material loss—was the result of the location headman's antagonism for him. Jabavu's case shows both a community vigilant for sexual immorality and the material consequences of straying from a Christian sexual ethic. The consequences were enacted in this case by agents of the church who were also operating as agents of the state. As for Daisy Yekela, we know nothing further of her.

These cases, almost more than the cases of seduction, which I mention further on in this chapter, reveal the vulnerability of Africans faced with mission-imposed codes of behavior and mission-facilitated access to resources. This was not the case just in South Africa but a frequent occurrence in other British colonies. In *Honour in African History,* John Iliffe writes about honor as manifested in male respectability in the early twentieth century. He quotes a Buganda proverb to capture a further element of this link. "One's occupation is one's honour."[70] Respectability was critical for men who were schoolteachers or who wanted to become more involved in their churches; it was both a quality to which they might aspire and a criterion by which they might be judged, as church authorities (most of whom were white) promoted the position that men in senior and public positions within the church needed to be held to a higher standard of behavior than the lay Christian. In 1921, in a case not involving sex, Searle Putu took Tylden Bam to court for defamation. The latter had written to the Cape Department of Education and published a letter in the newspaper alleging that Putu, a teacher at a Mount Coke school, was absenting himself from the school without leave.[71] Both men in the case made frequent reference to their status as church members, Putu describing himself as a "leader and local preacher" and his lawyer emphasizing that as a result of the accusations Putu had "suffered in his reputation and position."

The cases also present a potential link between skin color of its participants, the nature of their indiscretions, and the financial amount of the damages awarded. Thomas Ngaki's claim for one hundred pounds in damages was reduced by the magistrate to an award of fifteen pounds. While cases of seduction or adultery involving white South Africans similarly had the value of damage claims reduced, the reduction was never as severe as the reduction in cases of Africans quite possibly better off and better educated and—after 1927—tried under civil law.[72] If Ngaki is the same man as the headman whose will went to probate in 1950, listing property near the value of three hundred pounds, then the fifteen pounds he received in damages was woefully too little for his accomplishments.[73] The same reduction of value may be seen in Dorothy Kabane's case. However, in the briefly described defamation case, Searle Putu was granted the two hundred pounds requested in damages, a claim upheld it seems because it did not center on sex but so clearly challenged Putu as both a teacher and representative of the Department of Education. Over the next twenty years, the situation with respect to the "value" of African interpersonal cases only deteriorated. In a 1954 case, also for seduction, the court commented as follows: "She is a young girl whose father is a teacher and they are, therefore, people of some standing; yet her conduct falls short of the standard one would expect from people of that class when it is considered that she was a willing party from the initial stage to defendant's amorous suggestions."[74]

The Ngaki and Jabavu cases have other features in common that highlight different aspects of the way they were gendered and the different consequences of going public in addition to the way they highlight the vulnerability of church men to charges of impropriety. In the cases involving the accusation of a church elder or a male teacher, they all generally began with some kind of surveillance. Often, initial attention to a woman's movements would lead to an accusation leveled at a suspected lover. Typically, community residents gossiped about the people suspected of immorality, noting their movements between church and lodging, or schoolroom and house. All the cases involving either so-called sexual immorality or seduction are quite specific about the location of events. Joseph Williams Location, where the Jabavu case took place, must have had networks of observation that rivaled the most sophisticated French panopticon. These previous webs of seeing, well established by the time Christianity intervened in people's lives, were only compounded by the stratigraphy of Christian networks overlaying the whole. Jabavu's accusers, for instance, were very concerned about where he slept and who slept in the same house with him. He was closely questioned about where Daisy Yekela slept at night because she had been observed visiting his house. Daisy was also questioned about where she lived and ate her lunch. The cross-examination of Ida Magadlela revealed that she and her witness, John Makabulo, had spied out Thomas Ngaki's daily movements so they could stage an encounter between Thomas and Ida that John could witness. Ida's adultery was known because of witnesses who had reported her to the church court.

Not only space but time was important in the development of these extended dramas. In his work on the cases of adultery that appeared before church courts in Tanganyika, Derek Peterson importantly points to how African converts adopted the techniques presented to them in the bureaucratic procedures and record keeping practices of missionaries, reading off the kinds of roles they were supposed to play and presenting these back to the missionaries through the medium of the church court.[75] In the Eastern Cape, the elements of drama are all present in Jabavu's confrontation in the school room, but in fact, the staging of the process was already in motion before the case arrived in the church court.

This staging was rooted in older ideas of gendered propriety. When people were called as witnesses to sexual misconduct in the church court, they were being asked to shift behavior from within the confines of two lineages to a more public stage. As I noted earlier, a girl's lovers were generally known to her family because her female relatives learned of them through observation. Also, her young female companions would report on her behavior to her older female relatives. If a girl fell pregnant, her female relatives would share this information with her father (or her guardian), but only at the point of relevance. In the past, people did not concern themselves with the behavior of a man involved in a love affair, but if a young woman fell pregnant, they recalled this surveillance when her relatives visited the male relatives of her lover. Young women, not men, were the object of surveillance.

This older act of witness was a well-established prolegomenon to an accusation of seduction, and it found new expression in front of the church courts. In giving witness in a church or a schoolroom, a venue suffused with the power of Christianity, people were also giving witness to their faith.

Giving witness was a fraught process under these circumstances, as it required a Christian to prove their faith by indicting another of their congregation. In giving witness to the power of God and of faith in their lives, they were understanding the shift of giving witness for God and his power to giving witness against Christian transgression.

John Iliffe argues for the maintenance of older forms of honor culture in his discussion of similar cases in the Eastern Cape in the late nineteenth century, identifying the upholding of honor as a critical factor in how men responded to such accusations. However, he misses the way Christianity and faith also helped, quite literally, to constitute a community-held understanding of transgression.[76] Christians also understood honor as a virtue to be exhibited before their maker through Christian witness, even if they were often confusing their belief with the cultural patterns of Christianity introduced to them by missionaries.

These cases center on the figures of the men suspected of adultery. They foreground male honor and respectability, where honor lay in the reputation and moral character of senior church figures and teachers. Many of these cases, because of the material consequences of a loss of status, also made their way into civil law cases. This kind of case was much less prevalent by the 1940s, which is a comment on how sexual indiscretion was handled rather than on its frequency. By the late 1950s, the Bantu Education Act of 1951 had finally removed church supervision from Black schools, and the South African state was more interested in sedition and protest action than in sex when it came to prosecuting teachers. By the 1960s, the stigma attached to a premarital relationship was less consequential. When Qayiso interviewed church members about their love lives, several of his teacher interviewees discussed the topic quite frankly. "I will only tell you of the instances where I impregnated girls. In 1961 when I was still teaching in of the Secondary Schools when I happened to fall in love with a lady-teacher. She is a very decent woman because I had to propose love to her for a number of weeks before she could say 'yes'. At the time she was teaching at a neighbouring School."[77] While Qayiso's informant was worried about losing his job if his girlfriend's pregnancy was discovered, his own actions do not seem to have been noticed. Rumor did alert the local school inspector to his girlfriend's condition. When the inspector asked her to resign, she ignored him and went back to teaching after the child was born.

The "evidence" in this chapter consists of cases of sexual misconduct that were heard as part of church disciplinary processes or before the customary or civil law courts. It does not use evidence from sexual relationships that evaded public scrutiny. It does not document the deep and endearing relationships between men and women, or the deep and enduring relationships that men had with men, or women with women, that did not end in acrimony. It also does not consider the range of erotic practices that constituted people's sex lives. What it does begin to consider is how and at what points sexual concord begins to break down, as well as the fractures that exist between what is considered acceptable and unacceptable in the sex lives of twentieth-century Christians.

In the precolonial South Africa, African women whose love affairs went wrong found a measure of protection in the ostensibly private but, in reality, very public nature of those love affairs. From a young woman's age-mates' intervention in setting up her relationships with young men, to the role of a woman's peer group in carrying messages and sleeping nearby while young couples had nonpenetrative sex, an unsanctioned pregnancy found easy remedy in a way that satisfied a girl's family (if not her heart). Christianity and literacy changed this state of affairs, however. The uncomplicated public resolution of cases of seduction through the payment of fines was possible because of a love affair's public nature. Secret love affairs made it easy for men to deny responsibility for a pregnancy. The cases of sexual misconduct that I discuss in this chapter all carry this peculiar burden of being simultaneously private and public. Before colonial conquest, African love affairs and sex were simultaneously intimate and public, the knowledge of them by others an essential quality. New ideas about intimacy and love helped to push love affairs into secrecy, and Christian moral ideas "coded" them as wrong. When these affairs became differently public in the church and courts of public opinion, including law courts, discussion of them helped to mold new ideas of the intimate through the public revelation of transgression.

While Christian women generally found their status compromised as a result of premarital pregnancy, men who had extramarital sex experienced consequences in a different set of spaces. If in general the sexual behavior of women was subject to more scrutiny than that of men, and African women found their attempts to assert independence recast as "looseness," in the Eastern Cape the different ways Christian men and women were subject to a sexual double standard becomes apparent when we examine the consequences of their behavior. Men who strayed from the marital bed found their public status as responsible and respectable men compromised within the spaces of Christianity—the school room and the church. Possibly, where churches were able to influence their local magistrates, Christian headmen might have found their positions compromised.

Christian women experienced the consequences of their behavior in relation to what was considered the more private spaces of Christianity—the home and women's prayer groups. They did not have remunerated church positions to lose, and even married pregnant women had to leave their teaching positions. In addition, they found their status in kinship and family exchanges compromised through depreciation in the amount of the lobola their male guardians could claim for them. Christianity in this context acted to regulate status and provided a set of personal beliefs to structure behavior and the evaluation of morality. Furthermore, the status of Christian congregations, caught between a more relaxed customary attitude to sex on the one hand, and the Christian morality of the missionaries on the other, was extremely fragile and needed to be supported at great lengths, in public.

Women who were sexually active and discovered to be so before they were married found themselves caught between two paradoxical currents. Between their experience in mission schools and their reading, they found themselves drawn to a new set of affective dispositions centered on love expressed in sexual and intimate relations while they were subject to a Christian sexual morality that promoted sexually chaste love and individual consent as the route to marriage.

4 ~ Marriage and Lobola and the Imagining of Black Intimate Life

> Two reasons made Robert Zulu leave teaching at Siam Village School. The first was that he wanted to get married to Miss Jane Nhlauzeko as soon as possible. But as Jane's father had asked for a silly huge sum of money and other gifts for Ilobolo Robert felt that he could not raise this sum quick enough while teaching—teachers' salaries being anything but lucrative at that time. So he made up his mind to leave teaching, and go to Johannesburg to look for work. He felt sure that there he could make more money in more ways than one, and that quickly too. The second reason was that he thought, as most foolish young people think now-a-days, that town life is better in every way than country life. . . . His final decision, therefore, to go to Johannesburg at all hazards, was a blow to his people, who had thought highly of him, as a young Christian teacher in the Mission. This blow was felt even more strongly by his future parents-in-law. But as Robert pointed out to his father-in-law that, unless he reduced his Ilobolo, there was no alternative open to him but that of going to Johannesburg to try and raise money quickly, his father-in-law did not argue any further. . . . He had said: "What business has Robert to ask my daughter's hand in marriage if he has no money to pay for her?" This is unfortunately the parrot-cry of many Christian fathers, the costly mistake which, in many cases, results in poor, and financially stranded homes, or driving the young lovers to the terrible alternative of a "Special License," running away from their homes with disastrous results all too-well known.[1]

REGINALD DHLOMO'S 1928 English novel, *An African Tragedy*, captures almost too perfectly a conundrum faced by young Christian men in the early twentieth century. Robert Zulu, the Christian teacher, finding he did not earn enough to satisfy the lobola demands of his greedy and prospective father-in-law, decided to take a chance at earning in Johannesburg. Miss Jane Nhlauzeko is almost an afterthought in the paragraph, though the excerpt does hint at the position and relative dependency of young women caught between a father and potential lover over the issue of lobola. There can be no doubt that Reginald (R. R. R.) Dhlomo, later to become a senior editor at *Bantu World*, and thereafter editor at *Ilanga lase Natal*, was no fan of lobola, which—in his editorial voice—opened up gulfs between young men and their elders, encouraged avarice, and led those who sought money for its acquisition into the Stygian depths of urban life. Dhlomo returned to this subject several times after 1928 in his persona as editress of the women's pages in *Bantu World*, the most cosmopolitan African newspaper of the 1930s.[2]

Dhlomo, of course, was not the only writer of his generation to comment upon either lobola or marriage. African marriage and lobola preoccupied Africans and Europeans, though for different reasons. In fact, of all aspects of intimate life discussed in public and in text, lobola was the most frequently mentioned. In oral genres, references to cattle were often references to lobola, and cattle were mentioned often.[3] Already a subject of contestation in Christian circles and gatherings since the nineteenth century, by the 1930s, lobola had become a staple of the Black press, as articles and letters to the editor expressed what people, both men and women, felt were either the benefits or disadvantages of the practice.

Shifts in the practice of lobola and marriage are relatively easily tracked through the historical and anthropological literature. These shifts show that lobola was a practice challenged from different directions: authority-threatened fathers, independently earning sons, cattle epizootics, the impact of migrant labor, and the moral teachings of Christianity. Less frequently, these discussions are tied back to the significant rise in the incidence of Christian marriage for Black South Africans over the same period. Changes in both lobola and Christian marriage, however, should be linked, firstly to each other, and secondly, to the interdependent relationship between public discussions of lobola and marriage (particularly the former) and the tenacity of lobola's hold on Black imaginations of intimate life. In this chapter, I examine shifts in African marriage in the early twentieth century to frame the subsequent discussion of Christian marriage practices, including lobola, over the next few decades.

AFRICAN MARRIAGE AND LOBOLA

In a recent piece, Aninka Claassens and Dee Smythe speculate that lobola-marriage became a norm within South Africa only since the late nineteenth century.[4] The historical record, however, disputes this. A reading of the Cape and Natal archive shows that lobola-marriage has had a strong and persistent showing as the central feature of marriage (whatever other forms of cohabitation people may have engaged in) from well before the nineteenth century. Lobola-marriage was not only the ideal of how families married but was and continues to be ubiquitous.[5] However, Claassens and Smythe's work is important for encouraging us to think about how marriage might look if not always viewed through the lens of lobola. Indeed, its ubiquity tends to create the impression that the practice has remained unchanged in its materiality and meaning since the precolonial period. Alternatively, any change that has occurred is viewed as a linear response to South African industrialization and the development of a migrant labor market.[6] With respect to the latter, changes in lobola are linked to its commodification, as bridewealth exchanges began to include cash and goods as substitutes for cattle. Still, neither commodification nor custom encompasses the entirety of lobola's meanings, its status in constituting marriage, and its complicated relation with Christianity. Moreover, examining lobola in Christian marriages is important for countering the persistent bias in anthropological work toward a dissociation of faith and custom.

In precolonial southern Africa, a marriage bore little relationship to what first Dutch and then British settlers would have understood by the term. It eschewed a single definitive ceremony to mark the start of a couple's relationship, instead of as an unfolding as the result of an often-complex process not always intelligible to people viewing from the outside.[7] For Sotho-Tswana and Ndebele chiefdoms, a marriage almost always began with the transfer of cattle from the groom's family to the bride's family according to rules of endogamy or exogamy. Often, the transfer of cattle was ongoing, since it could still occur after a wedding ceremony had taken place. Fathers and male guardians could and did demand more cattle for their daughters. The point at which an African marriage was finalized was difficult to distinguish, often deliberately so, because a finalized marriage meant the cessation of cattle transfer.[8]

The part of a traditional marriage that most resembled a definable ceremony involved the process of a bride taking up residence in her husband's family's homestead or village. This constituted the general pattern of customary, or traditional, marriage. In isiXhosa, the term is *umtshato*, which by the early twentieth century was distinguished from a "church marriage," often known as *umtshato wesilungu*. In addition, a couple could also contract a civil marriage, known both as *umtshato wespeshili*, "marriage by special license," and *umtshato wase-ofisini*, "marriage at the office."[9] Everyday use of these terms was also loose and interchangeable, so that sometimes *umtshato wesilungu* might be translated as "civil marriage."

More generally, marriage was about the iterative joining of the social lives of generations of kin, beginning with the first lobola transaction and continuing throughout a married couple's lifetime. Sometimes a marriage continued after the death of one of the partners, if it was considered the lobola transfers were incomplete. Lobola-marriage linked living kin to those who had already passed to the space of the ancestors, the latter's approval of a union following consequently on the transfer of *ikazi* (the lobola cattle). When the ancestors were unhappy with a marriage, they could and did express their disapproval in measures affecting female fertility, indicated, or so it was thought, by baldness (which afflicted women who did not respect their husband's male ancestors). The ancestors might also indicate disapproval through lack of conception and, sadly, stillbirth.

Lobola represented a recompense to kin for the loss of a daughter. And it safeguarded her status in her marital home. A man who mistreated his wife had no right to complain if she left him to return home and also no right to expect the return of the lobola he or his family had transferred for her. In the early twentieth century, newspaper articles and letters referred to this as the "African woman's charter of liberty." Lobola meant that a wife was treated with respect. However, while these principles were widely recognized as constituting a woman's rights through tradition, they often worked in theory more than they did in practice. The Eastern Cape civil court records are full of references to families leaving their daughters in abusive marriages because they did not want to return the lobola cattle. Women's songs and poetry from the twentieth century, as well as other collected testimony, also refer to how women suffered in marriage.[10]

Before European colonization, lobola was transferred in the preferred form as cattle, or ikazi, but it could also be supplied using sheep, goats, and iron, especially iron tools and implements. In southern Africa, by the early nineteenth century, a much stronger association existed between pastoral domestic animals and bridewealth compared to other parts of the continent. By the late nineteenth century, observers were remarking upon the substitution of part of the lobola, still reckoned in cattle, for its worth in cash. Oblivious of their role in encouraging this shift to cash, early twentieth-century missionary commentators and state officials all referred, many disparagingly, to the commercialization of lobola. By this, they meant the substitution from cattle to cash, as young men either on their own behalf paid cash for a bride or tendered cash to their fathers either in exchange for their fathers' support in providing cattle or to give her kin for a bride.

Lobola-marriage was central to the constitution of African social life, or what early twentieth-century liberals rather scathingly referred to as "primitive

African communalism," nevertheless containing within itself the ability to govern power in relationships between individuals. As scholars have noted, the lobola, or the ability to give the ikazi, was a crucial element of a father's or father figure's relationship with his son.[11]

Older men could and did govern their sons' access to wives. During the later nineteenth century, a frequent lament (so frequent it was probably common even earlier) was that a son was unable to marry because his father would not—or could not—supply cattle for their lobola. Dhlomo described this as "the parrot-cry of many Christian fathers, the costly mistake" blocking the creation of new and respectable Christian families.[12] Robert Zulu's solution lay in a move to the city to earn his lobola, a bypassing of gerontocratic power, the power of older men over younger. By the 1930s, though, with cattle ownership ranging from seven to nine head per adult male in Natal and the Cape, few men were able to supply their son's lobola.[13]

However, a less-often considered effect of the funding of lobola through wage labor is the concomitant drop in status of older men; men who might otherwise have enjoyed respect in their elder days as the supplier of the cattle for their sons' marriages instead became financially dependent on their sons, signaling a shift in household power relations. This is especially evidenced among homestead heads in KwaZulu-Natal, where the emphasis placed on the importance to masculinity of younger men respecting older men diminished.[14] In the Eastern Cape, one of Percy Qayiso's informants shared with him how "young men do not care for the old people these days."[15]

FROM SLAVERY TO LABOR

During most of the nineteenth century, European missionaries opposed lobola for several interrelated reasons. Protestant missionaries arriving in the dusty and treeless space of the Eastern Cape in the early nineteenth century were the humanitarian idealists of their age, the equivalent of students from the West who joined the Peace Corps after the 1960s. Well versed in the literature on the subject, like the London Missionary Society Superintendent John Phillip's manifesto published as *Researches in South Africa,* they were paradoxically better inclined toward Africans than most white settlers while zealously opposed to lobola-marriage, perceived as slavery.[16] It was inevitable that missionaries encountered Xhosa marriage as problematic. While it was yet unclear for many missionaries whether marriage was a sacrament, it represented for them the pinnacle of Christian life. Still, local marriage diverged from missionaries' belief in the sanctity of marriage, in that African unions were potentially plural and dissoluble. Marriage also conflicted with their antislavery liberalism, in that it rested on an exchange of cattle for women. These opinions were the product of several contexts. Many missionaries would have been well aware of the market value of a head of cattle, as they might have come from cattle-farming families or from families who had experienced the Highland clearances, leaving no fond thoughts of cattle. Whether or not they themselves were from farming stock, they came from European nations transitioning from agrarian modes of production to industrialization. They had no frame through which to see Xhosa women as anything but the equivalent of sale items.

While missionary families had a theoretical and theological framework for interpreting the kinds of marriages they heard about, in the early to mid-nineteenth century, most of their daily contact with African marriage was through the presence on their stations of young women fleeing a forced marriage.[17] This phenomenon was not a missionary fiction; as I noted in the previous chapter, women's poetry suggests that trying to escape a forced marriage happened often enough before the arrival of Christian missionaries for it to have entered oral production as a distinct trope. As a result, Protestant mission efforts across southern Africa—not only in the more settled and established colonies of the Cape and Natal but also in the interior (including in what later became the High Commission Territories)—viewed lobola with repugnance, even prior to industrialization.

Although lobola, unlike polygamy, did not necessarily involve adultery or other practices European missionaries associated with sexual immorality, for many, the two practices were intimately connected. Many of the missionary figures of the nineteenth century were convinced that lobola was an incentive leading directly to polygamy. Some of the most vocal discussion of this came from Natal, where a settler population found rhetorical purchase for its deepening racism in comparing lobola to the buying and selling of women. As an 1862 memorial from British Kaffraria noted,

> while the Government is not, as they think, called upon to put down the custom, it at least ought not to countenance or sanction it. Which is manifestly done, when Magistrates, in their judicial proceedings go upon the assumption that the Sale of the Woman is a legitimate Commercial transaction, so that when She, the article of Sale, is withdrawn or withheld, the price paid for her may be recovered by ordinary [courts of law] ... For it seems a strange anomaly that the authority of the British Government should be put forth to support and legalize one and that not the least revolting, form of slavery, while, by the same act it is holding up one of the main props of polygamy.[18]

While almost all contemporary sources from the early twentieth century remark upon what they term the commercialization of lobola, their comments were often disingenuous, the antipathy they felt for the practice revealed in their conflation of lobola and slavery. Dhlomo felt much the same, his novel expounding the popular view that the existence of lobola meant that fathers would sell their daughters to the highest bidder, as Robert Zulu felt was the case with Jane Nhlauzeko's father. In this understanding, which differed little from the view of lobola as promoting slavery, a daughter was a commodity that could be freely exchanged.

However, this view ignored the realities of South Africa's migrant labor economy, which by the 1950s, saw most able-bodied men from the reserves in Natal and the Cape spending extended periods, sometimes up to 90 percent of their time, away from home on labor contracts. "At the heart of the political economy of intimacy during the early period of colonialism was a fundamental shift: the movement of the hitherto self-sufficient rural homestead into dependence on wage labour."[19] While this book suggests that Christian thinking about sex and the public convening of it was perhaps equally consequential (if in a different way), migrant labor was and still is profoundly destructive of Black intimacy. It split and destabilized families, encouraged the proliferation of different and often temporary styles of cohabitation in South African cities, and diverted wages away from the support of original families who remained in the reserves across South Africa. Together with the social and financial inflation of lobola, migrant labor was responsible for the declining rates of long-term cohabitation between men and women, as both found marriage beyond their grasp and as women began to find that female-headed households, however precarious their resource bases, were often preferable to difficult marriages.

Contrary to the thinking that conflates mission opinions of lobola with slavery, at some time in the last decade of the nineteenth century and in relation to the labor requirements of the mineral revolution and urbanization, missionary concern around lobola had shifted to African men. Rather than making victims out of women, the practice and its acquisition or lack thereof (never mind that these positions contradicted one another) became implicated in the growth of a modern and docile industrial labor force. The Swiss missionary Reverend Guye wrote a set of articles in the mission periodical *Christian Express*. Working among Tsonga-speakers in the northern Transvaal, he explained that while lobola as cattle-for-women was not acceptable, he was in support of a "present" from the groom to the bride's father. Opposed to lobola, he nevertheless recognized that it was useful as a goad to waged work; verbal sophistry allowed him to condemn lobola while supporting a groom's employment in the formal labor market. "It is both normal and moral that the said young man should by his own work procure the necessary sum in order to get his wife."[20] Intergenerational transfers, however, were to be avoided because they might keep younger men out of the labor force; fathers who supported sons were subverting labor recruitment for the Witwatersrand mines and other labor centers.

Although it would be exceedingly inaccurate to view the interests of white missionaries and the South African state as aligned, Protestant missionaries exalted in the virtues of labor. Labor as a calling, according to Max Weber, was central to the "fundamental religious ideas of ascetic Protestantism and its maxims for everyday economic conduct."[21] As Weber further notes, "The emphasis on the ascetic importance of a fixed calling provided an ethical justification of the modern specialized division of labour."[22] For Protestant missionaries, work in and of itself was a virtue, even more so if it drew African men away from what missionaries understood as the heathendom of a tribal and cattle-bound existence. Protestant missionaries held this view despite their firsthand knowledge, which was more direct than that of any other white audience in South Africa, of the reserve impoverishment already apparent by 1910.

Most missionaries would not have considered their outlook on labor as being in direct support of how the colonial state and mining capital approached this particular issue, however, the views of the three groups were indeed aligned. In 1902, the *Blue Book on Native Affairs* in Natal expressed its thinking on "Native Questions, principally upon matters connected with education, labour, polygamy and lobola."

> Natives of today may be divided into three classes—(1) those who have adopted Christianity; (2) the dressed town native; and (3) the 'raw' Native. The first mentioned are industrious, honest, and trustworthy. They conform to European customs as regards wearing clothing and living in upright houses. They are generally orderly and law-abiding.... The second class is too well known to require description. They (men and women) have lost all the virtues of the Native, and acquired most of the vices of the white man. Among their ranks are found the prostitute, the thief and the housebreaker.[23]

The central point of difference between the two classes rested on a perception of their relationship to labor in an urban setting.

Attacks on lobola had partially ceased to be about its implications for women and had become more about the status of African men in relation to the South African state. If colonial concerns over land influenced state tolerance of African customs in the nineteenth century, the supply of labor was the preeminent concern of the early twentieth century. In this way, conversations about lobola were framed by the question of labor.[24]

The relationship of lobola to labor and idle men is not a new point. The lazy African was a staple of nineteenth-century mission discourse, a racist trope that reinvented itself across the colonial world and across the twentieth century, most obviously across the subcontinent but also in South Asia. T. B. Soga could not openly and publicly contradict his white colleagues (he was a reader of the *Christian Express*), but he used his manuscript to dispute the stereotype of the lazy African. His comments in *Intlalo xa Xosa* were a response to both missionaries like Guye and to the labor market shifts of the first decade of the twentieth century. "According to the statements of today, laziness was at its height among our people in the olden days. Let us now refute such statements & show how it is misleading & foolish in its appearance."[25]

For most of the Protestant Christian establishment then, lobola was seen as keeping young men from working. However, a significantly different thinking had the opposite view, approving of the custom: "Another feature of this custom which deserves mention is the incentive it affords to native youths, heathen as well as Christian, to seek employment and to engage in regular work."[26] This view from 1911 was still present in 1921. "Lobola ... may also be called 'The backbone of the Labour Question'. It encourages the otherwise indolent Native to proceed to Labour centres to support in the maintenance of the Industries thereby to bring him within easy reach of the missionary."[27]

CHURCH MARRIAGES

Before I begin to discuss how Christianity shaped African marriage and Black intimate practices, we need some understanding of the legal framework in which Christian marriage existed. When the Union of South Africa was created in 1910, it inherited multiple pieces of legislation and ordinances regulating African marriage. The magnitude of confusion this created was apparent in civil and customary cases, where the legal establishment engaged in considerable effort to identify which ordinance or piece of legislation had governed a couple's marriage. In his presentation of a rather dry formulation, which understates the difficulty of the task, Jack Simons describes, "South African legislatures, considered collectively, cannot be accused of indifference or inflexibility in their approach to African marriage. Almost all possible variations were tried out in different territories before Union."[28] The approaches he refers to were all in regular use until the Black Administration Act of 1927. Thereafter, one piece of legislation governed African marriage until the 1980s, but couples married before 1927 still needed to have divorce and succession issues resolved by the law under which they married.

Marriage and Lobola and the Imagining of Black Intimate Life ⁓ 119

Most of the variance, however, occurred with Africans married in the area represented by the former Cape Colony and Eastern Cape reserves. The Cape had the most liberal—in the political sense of the term—marriage regimes, in which African Christians who married in the church received rights equivalent to those accorded European marriages in the Cape. Less liberal regimes characterized British Kaffraria and later the Transkeian Territories, in a roughly thirty-year period between 1865 and 1894, which coincided with their annexation to the Cape. These regimes included the possibility of marriage in community of property, for instance, for those married in the former Cape Colony.

The two Boer colonies and Natal had significantly fewer pieces, over their histories collectively, of legislation under which Africans could marry. The Transvaal and the Orange Free State had separate marriage regulations for Africans. Natal had a system for regulating and registering customary marriages, with Christian marriages also regulated in ways that gave more precedence to custom rather than to Roman-Dutch law.

Until the passage of the Black Administration Act of 1927, African customary marriages had little or no official status in law, except in Natal, and perhaps in the Transkei. If any of the partners in a customary marriage needed to approach a law court about the marriage, hoping to be granted the rights and recognition accorded white South Africans under civil law, the law would treat the individual as if he or she were unmarried. Customary marriages did not have the same legal consequences as civil marriages.

In the Cape Colony, where British law considered customary marriages immoral, a widow had little recourse to the estates of her deceased husband when the male heir under customary law was not willing to support her. Even women married in the church in community of property might find courts refusing to acknowledge the legitimate legal consequences in the event of a divorce. This position was captured in a 1929 amendment to the Black Administration Act, which clearly distinguished between a marriage contracted in civil law in front of a magistrate or Christian marriage officer, and a customary union, since—as legal historian Martin Chanock has noted—the Union government was not willing to do anything that might imply that Black marriages were equal to white marriages.[29]

The proliferation of marriage regimes is, in some respects, a red herring in this book. There is very elegant and able scholarship that describes them, both in their historical evolution and in their consequences.[30] The point I want to make here is that discussions of legal regimes draw the eye away from marriage as an issue for married people and toward marriage as an issue for the law. The law, in this way, has the potential to turn any marriage inside out, to reveal its interior facets to public scrutiny. This is one reason why it is important not to restrict discussions of intimacy to the sphere of interpersonal relations carried out in the notional privacy of the home. This book intersects with marriage and law in other ways, including when marriages ran into trouble or when issues of succession arose, both of which form a significant portion of the civil cases that Africans brought against each other. These cases were points at which family and morality became points of public contestation. I look now at how Christian marriage had become, by the 1930s, the most common and visible way for Africans to marry.

With the arrival of Christianity in South Africa, Africans, who had married according to traditional practice, gained additional ways to marry. While very few African marriages in the nineteenth century were contracted in the church, by the early twentieth century, the incidence of church marriage was on the increase. In the Keiskammahoek valley in the Eastern Cape, church marriages constituted 16.5 percent of all marriages before 1890, increasing to nearly 65 percent by the 1930s. Christian marriage was more common than any other form of marriage for the Keiskammahoek by the late 1940s.[31] By then, only 10 percent of marriages were customary, without any Christian rite attached.[32]

By the mid-1940s, most couples surveyed in Langa, a Black location outside Cape Town, were married according to Christian rite.[33] These figures are supported by trends across the country.[34] In Orlando in 1935, the location superintendent reported to Dr. Ray Phillips, a prominent churchman and a highly public advocate of respectability and morality for African Christians, that approximately 38 percent of Africans applying for family housing were married in church. Regardless of whether this figure is accurate (Phillips and the superintendent disbelieved people's statements about the type of marriage contracted because only 12.5 percent could produce marriage certificates), people were self-identifying as having married in church.[35] In Western Native Township, adjacent to Sophiatown and on the city edge, just under 50 percent of families in residence claimed either civil or Christian marriage.[36] The Union of South Africa Census of 1951 appears to have counted only Christian or civil marriage as marriage (it shows a very large African population of "never married"), recording a figure of approximately 35 percent.[37]

In contrast to the anthropological literature on marriage, which tends to elide the fact that African marriages were often also Christian marriages, these figures reveal that a significant portion of Africans in both rural and urban locations across the country were married in church by the mid-1930s.[38] The actual figure likely varied from between 35 percent to 70 percent, depending on the location and age of those married. Simons, quoted in Mark Hunter, provides figures of 33 percent for Christian and civil (mostly Christian marriage) for South Africa's urban areas in 1951, while 18 percent of rural marriages were Christian.[39] These figures do not make sense as an average, however, because African population distribution was concentrated in Cape Town, Port Elizabeth, the reserves of the Ciskei and Transkei, the greater Johannesburg area, and both urban and rural Natal. It is probable the national figures are skewed by Natal, for which it is difficult to find disaggregated figures for civil and Christian versus customary marriage because of the particular history of African marriage in Natal. Keiskammahoek had a higher rate of Christian marriage, but this was the result of its history of missionization. In 1960, Simons added to his observations and also noted the trend toward more marriages in church, though his figures are more conservative. According to him, many Christian marriages would have been discounted in national censuses because they were performed within the independent churches, which had few licensed marriage officers. He refers to an "appreciable and growing number" of African families established through religious and civil rites.[40]

The extent of African marriage in the church, especially given Simons's comments, highlights the institutional thickness of Christianity in South Africa in a very real way. It also needs to be viewed against the continuing practice of lobola, which accompanied almost every marriage in church during this period. Black South Africans were choosing to have their intimate lives in marriage governed by a church ritual while they were also choosing to marry with lobola. Most of the marriages contracted in the church were accompanied by an exchange of cattle—where possible—or cash, where cattle were not possible or practical. Ellen Hellman, who studied inner-city African life, listed a total of fifty-six out of eighty couples who had married with both a religious ceremony and lobola in Rooiyard in Johannesburg in 1933.[41] In Pretoria in 1936, 59 percent of relationships in the area studied had included lobola; of the total number of relationships, 38 percent were through church marriage or civil rite and lobola; and in Pretoria in 1952, 59.2 percent of marriages were through lobola and the church.[42] The same study documents that 64.9 percent of marriages were constituted through both lobola and the church in Cape Town in 1947 (presumably Ruth Levin's study). Indeed, these figures are likely an underestimation of how often lobola accompanied church marriage, because they disregard the incomplete, partial, or disrupted transfers that were historically, and still are, common in lobola-marriage with or without the church.

Among elite African Christians, the population we know most about, Christian marriage with lobola was the norm and so ubiquitous as to be unremarkable. In 1940, in a paper on marriage among the Baralong, Z. K. Matthews remarked upon the extent of lobola's support, describing it as the "institution which is most resistant to foreign influences and the principles underlying them are found to pervade even Christian and civil marriages."[43] He would have known: His wedding to Frieda Bokwe in 1928 had involved a very "knotty point" around lobola negotiations.[44] The marriages of the children of John Knox Bokwe, a prominent figure at the turn of the century, track through a range of documents and records, including in the relationship between Selbourne Bokwe and Dorothy Kabane. The public record and commentary from Dr. Roseberry Bokwe's wedding, discussed in the following chapter, establishes firmly not only the practice of church marriage with lobola but also its public acceptance. Indeed, lobola alongside a church wedding—even if only one beast in the hope of more—was so prevalent in Christian and civil marriages that it did not need public explanation (in newspapers, for instance). By the interwar period, debates about lobola were not about whether it should accompany a Christian marriage but about how and whether it should become more modern.

Moreover, its ubiquity was apparent outside of African marriages. Despite lobola's inconsequence in civil and Christian marriages, the Native Appeals Courts (NAC), which heard divorce proceedings, often gave judgments that addressed the return, or nonreturn, of the ikazi and any issue of the cattle transferred as part of a marriage. Contractually, the courts considered lobola outside of their purview and an ancillary matter to the civil or Christian rite, but especially before 1948 and in the Cape and Free State circuit, magistrates often did make rulings that considered that lobola had been exchanged. Simons's point about the efforts taken with respect to identifying the appropriate marriage regime for each union applies here, because an unresolved lobola issue quite often came back to haunt the courts, in the ultimate instance, in succession disputes after a father's death. Sometimes, though not frequently, Christian couples' families protected the lobola transaction through the drawing up of a contract under common European or civil law.[45] In fact, the South African law courts were responsible for much of the public convening and legitimation of lobola in the first half of the twentieth century through the frequency that they allowed discussion of lobola to enter into court proceedings.

Lobola transactions often took place in anticipation of a church wedding. Families might begin to transfer lobola and a wife might take up residence at her husband's homestead before a church marriage, which might be able to take place only later. Indeed, it is likely that most marriages that included both lobola and a church wedding unfolded in a manner more reminiscent of traditional and customary marriages than of the single jurally defined moment common to the Western wedding. The NAC records and local-level court records are full of accounts that describe first a customary marriage, followed later by a wedding in the church, followed—at least in the cases reported—by the acquisition of a second wife and the repudiation of the first. Even today, lobola has such an impact that it pulls Western-style marriages contracted in the church into patterns more reminiscent of the unfolding processes described by anthropologists.

But what did it mean to get married in church? What was meant by marrying in church while still holding on to the practice of lobola? And how easy was it to get married in church?

Until the 1940s, Africans who wanted to marry in the church usually needed to approach their minister for permission to do so (after this, it seems that the practice became difficult to enforce because of absolute growth in the numbers of people marrying in church and also because of increasing geographical mobility). Ministers and other church officials regularly refused to allow couples to marry in church, usually citing an out-of-marriage pregnancy. It is worth a reminder that this was a sexual double standard; Black men who had sex before marriage did not catch the church's gaze in the same way that the public stickiness of a bad reputation or pregnant belly did.

Before 1910, the incidence of African church marriage was relatively low, so issues arising from a lack of licensed marriage officers were relatively few. As the incidence of church marriage increased after the Great War, and more especially after the new marriage regulations of 1927 that regularized African marriage, a minister could refuse to marry couples if he did not consider them devout enough. This power was frequently exercised, if public discussion of the issue is any indication. For a couple to get married, one or both partners needed to give evidence of being a practicing Christian and show preference for the minister's own denomination. Interdenominational fighting resulted in ministers refusing to marry noncongregants. The reluctance of the South African state to license African ministers as marriage officers was a continual and repeated sore point with African ministers, not only in the independent churches, where marriage officer licenses were routinely refused, but also in the mainline churches.

At the start of the twentieth century, a time when African ministers were scarce, some ministers took pity on couples who wanted to marry in church and who belonged to another denomination and married them. Even until well into the 1930s, the remoteness of some rural areas combined with few available licensed marriage officers meant that a couple living on the fringes of a parish or presbytery might have to wait for the priest or pastor to visit on an itinerating circuit. Under such circumstances, licensed clergy sometimes married couples they did not know.

Before a couple could get married, the banns needed to be read, preferably in the prospective husband's church. After marriage, a woman always joined her husband's church. The practice of a wife joining her husband's church (even when it was different from her own) was universal (and still is in some places). "In the Langa churches the banns of marriage are called in public at the Sunday services for three consecutive Sundays before the marriage, and the news of the impending marriage soon spreads all around the location."[46] Marriage after the calling of banns was common through most of the mainline churches. In contrast, marriage by license was a speedier affair, as it obviated the need for banns and also avoided a couple's embarrassment at having their intentions known, especially if the woman was already pregnant. It was, however, more expensive than marrying by banns, and both were more expensive than a civil marriage, which had its own benefits. Civil marriage required answering fewer inconvenient bureaucratic and administrative questions. Deborah Posel has shown in her work on civil marriage in the 1950s that the choice of civil marriage was connected to the purpose of securing urban family accommodation for couples who otherwise would not have been able to access it.[47]

Well into the 1950s, and possibly well into the 1960s, the South African state remained reluctant to appoint ministers in independent churches as marriage officers, so most Christian marriages were contracted within the mainline churches (irrespective of how a couple practiced their Christianity after marriage). As noted by Jack Simons, the state did not recognize couples wed in independent churches as married, a situation that impacted official rates of African marriage.

Several conclusions can be drawn from the difficulties, both personal and official, related to marrying in church. Couples who contracted Christian marriage had to invest both time and money in church weddings. White weddings were expensive; couples had to invest time in devotional activities, including attending church services, marriage preparation classes, church festivals, and also a young men's or young women's guild; and the responsibilities of the marriage officer included explaining the legal consequences of a marriage. Africans who chose to marry in church were doing so intentionally. They were choosing a church rite over the less expensive civil marriage. Africans, whether Christian or not, were deeply aware of the significance of their church marriages. For many, their preference reflected the legal, financial, and other benefits that accompanied a Christian marriage—better access to housing and family housing in urban areas and to positions of authority.

For example, in Keiskammahoek, resident magistrates preferred to appoint Christians rather than traditionalists as headmen. The provincial education department and the mission churches appointed only teachers married in the church to the mission schools, and by far, most Black schools in the Cape before the Bantu Education Act of 1953 were mixed church-state affairs. Married men had access to Christian networks of patronage and Christian status, as well as the respectability that accompanied this status. While de jure the legal status that devolved on Christians married in the church was the same as that afforded Africans who married in a civil service, the former carried with it a weight of respectability not attached to the latter. A man who could refer to good standing in a mainline church was afforded more respect (although more respect did not equate complete respect) than someone unattached to a church. Although the courts' view on Christian status shifted after 1948, in that Christianity was no longer the call to respect that it once had been and the consequences of the Black Administration Act were well entrenched for all Africans, the status difference had been significant in the period before.

A generational difference existed between Africans around civil marriage. Before roughly the 1930s civil marriage was not at all respectable for most Christian Africans; some younger Christians, though, viewed civil marriage as more convenient. The first view is articulated in Dhlomo's evocation of it as "the terrible alternative" of a marriage by "Special License," as mentioned in the quote at the opening of this chapter. Levin explains both views in her work on marriage in Langa.[48] Couples who could not marry in the church married in front of a magistrate before requesting a church blessing, a cheaper affair.[49] There is some reason to view Dhlomo's assessment as accurate. Because a civil marriage was cheap at two shillings and six pence (cheaper than marriage in church), and because divorce was also relatively inexpensive (a divorce in the late 1930s could be had for as little as five pounds), civil marriages often failed, whereas customary marriages and those conducted in Church lasted much longer.[50] Almost all the available data for marriage in the 1930s record Christian marriage rates higher than that for civil marriage.

In Natal and the Transvaal provinces of South Africa both before and after 1927, Africans were required to obtain an "enabling certificate" to marry. Sometimes this was supplied by a local magistrate, sometimes by the minister in question. The certificate was to show that a couple had been questioned about already-existing customary marriages and that they had been alerted to the consequences of monogamy, which might be more restrictive than those for customary polygamous marriages. The prospective bridegroom was also questioned about whether he wanted to marry in community of property, via antenuptial contract, or in the absence of either. In a study conducted in the late 1930s, Denys Shropshire gathered information on the changing circumstances of African marriage. Shropshire, an Anglican minister in Natal, had secured funding and support from the South African Institute of Race Relations (SAIRR) for his study. He speculated that the obstacles described in the previous paragraph made Africans reluctant to marry in church or in front of a magistrate, though his comments would not have applied to the Cape.[51] His *Primitive Marriage and European Law: A South African Investigation* was eventually published by the Society for Promoting Christian Knowledge in 1946. Regardless of whether enabling certificates were produced as often as the law required, the rather patronizing questioning required made very clear to African men that they were undertaking a Christian marriage, which would have consequences for their marital relationships and the disposition of their property thereafter. Often churches appear to have followed a parallel process of their own making, especially by the latter half of the period under consideration in this book. By the 1940s, marriage counseling was common in many of the mainline churches, though its intent was principally to instruct couples in their proper duties as a modern, Christian vanguard for all Africans in the nation.

When Shropshire conducted his investigation into African marriage, he held meetings on the subject across the country. At meetings in both Randfontein and Germiston, the audience—all African men—was unable (according to Shropshire) to understand the nature of civil marriage.[52] For them, it was neither customary nor Christian, neither fish nor fowl. However, Christian marriage, with its emphasis on ritual, ceremony, and patriarchal authority (before the admission of women as clergy), was in tune with many aspects of umtshato. And the calling of the banns and the declaration before a minister, who was potentially able to counsel a couple in marital trouble, had some resemblance to a customary marriage contract. Still, one African interlocutor told Shropshire or one of the location officials working with Shropshire that "it is the custom of our people when married people quarrel to first seek for a way of settling the dispute. They look first for conciliation by conference between the families and, if that fails, then with the assistance of the Headman and even the Chief.... But when they go to the magistrate he has no time for conciliation."[53]

Parents, especially male guardians, disliked civil marriage also because it allowed their daughters and wards to marry without their parents' consent. Although minors could not marry without parental consent in Natal and the Transvaal, officials of the Native Affairs Department in the Transvaal's urban locations were less than scrupulous about this requirement.[54] In urban areas, ministers in the mainline churches generally required certificates of good standing from newly arrived congregants. The certificates were often part of the patriarchal bargain struck at home in places like Tsolo among the Mpondomise, Matatiele on the border of eastern Pondoland and Natal, and most of Zululand. Ministers certainly expected women to marry in their husband's church and sought certificates of membership and letters of approval from the wife's church of origin. Ministers, themselves potentially fathers, were keen to assert parental authority from the pulpit and disliked the latitude civil marriages gave couples. In 1911, the Anglican Diocese of Umtata declared that civil marriages lead to immorality. In 1926, the diocese voted to censure six of their communicants who had married in front of the magistrate rather than in church.[55]

THE PUBLIC LIVES OF LOBOLA

What people did in their marriages, their choice about whether to exchange lobola, their decision of whether to marry in church—these actions act as one backdrop to the period between 1910 and 1948. The trend toward increasing numbers of church marriages still accompanied by lobola are relatively easy to discern. The trend was present at the start of this period and only became more so by the end.

A more tangled situation existed, though, in relation to how people thought about and contested lobola and African marriage and in how African marriage was convened in the public life of lobola. Here I am referring to how the public life of lobola was a text in the sense that a text is a tissue of words. It is also important to note that the public life of lobola, even as it shifted during this period, was apparent because of that public's Christianity and literacy. Public debates around lobola were always conducted in relation to Christianity, even if their protagonists did not identify as Christian. Ideas about marriage were created, contested, and defended in the Christian publics at work in church institutions, church publications, scholarly legal work, and the Black press.

Institutional Church Publics

During the first few decades of the twentieth century, as the formerly white-dominated mainline churches relaxed their attitude toward Black ordination and the employment of Black lay clergy, and as more publication forums for literate Africans became available, Black voices began to challenge the white grip on public pronouncements about lobola and marriage.

As a result, the relatively uniform position of viewing lobola as either slavery or a labor issue became increasingly complicated as new viewpoints began to challenge older orthodoxies.

Some of the first volleys in the struggle for lobola were the most obvious and represented gradual church accommodation with the practice. There are several reasons for this. The first and most obvious—which I discuss later—occurred as Black clergy began to challenge the white position that lobola was slavery and was proof of a lack of civilization. Consider again the Reverend Guye's comments against lobola in 1911: "Would there be members of our churches who would not mind dispensing with the nuptial benediction? Perhaps. Of course, such cases would be regrettable in so far as the interested parties would have then given a proof that they were not yet sufficiently liberated from heathen customs, though they called themselves converted."[56] Reverend Guye, who was part of a generation of missionaries who had seen most of their service in the late nineteenth century, drew a clear line in the sand between a blinkered morality and Christianity on one side and all else on the other. To say a man was not a Christian was to say that he was an uncivilized heathen. Conservative white Christians, alarmed at the growing political consciousness and assertiveness of their congregants, used the issue of lobola as an index for savagery. "The writer, Rev. Makubalo must be . . . a married man who bought his wife; I also presume that he has some daughters to sell."[57] This Matatiele-based author's letter to the *Christian Express* was followed by another, written from Natal. "From the Christian viewpoint the lobola custom has a monstrous head with the sharp teeth of avarice and greed and a stinging tail of grief and disappointment. . . . Can a Christian native harbour greed in his heart and still be a Christian?"[58]

Articles, opinion pieces, and letters on lobola were regular features of the monthly. While the *Christian Express* was only one public forum for conversations about lobola, the publication punched above its weight because of its long history and its close association with the Christian and education networks centered on Lovedale Institution.

Not all white clergy bought into the kind of position advocated by missionaries like Guye. Racist optics were not the only thing that drove concern around lobola. In 1911, Brownlee J. Ross, a third-generation Scots missionary in the Eastern Cape, himself a Scottish-African patriarch, wrote to *Christian Express*. Ross was one of a small but vocal group of local white missionaries and clergy who supported lobola.

> Strange as it may seem, marriage is to the native a far more important thing than to many Europeans, Christians though they

be. When he thinks of marriage the native looks behind and ahead. The family history of both sides has to be considered, and those to be born of the marriage have to be considered and well-considered. Marriage is the establishing of a family. It is more the joining of two families to produce a third than the joining of a man and a woman.[59]

His rating of the importance of marriage and the centrality of lobola to marriage was not only accurate but also obsolete. Ross, who had grown up on a mission station before training in Edinburgh in the late 1800s, benefited from speaking fluent Xhosa and belonging to one of the most idiosyncratic mission families of the Eastern Cape. His grandparents were first-generation Scottish missionaries to the Eastern Cape, his father a contemporary and friend to Tiyo Soga. His own close colleagues included Tiyo Burnside Soga ("Burnside" a reference to B. J. Ross's grandmother). From an early age, he had encountered African friends marrying with lobola, both Christian and non-Christian. His description of marriage captures the generational implications of marriage and its links to past and future temporalities in ways few other descriptions of marriage from the period do. In one letter to *Christian Express*, he described the slums of Glasgow, reflecting his familiarity with urban living conditions. Yet his description of African marriage was removed from the changes wrought by urbanization and, in many respects, was a paean to an institution changed from how he had encountered it over his forty-six years. In letters like that written by B. J. Ross in 1911, missionaries who defended the practice rested their defense upon a conservative and retrospective assessment of the practice. Ironically, those who condemned lobola were more in touch with the twentieth century, their ideas revealing modern ideas about Africans as a laboring class. Inversely, missionaries like Ross defended lobola as a result of their experience based on a practice already much changed from their own view of it.

The urbanization and industrialization that characterized the South African region in the first decade of the twentieth century created new issues in how missionaries and church folk considered their work. Indeed, after Union in 1910, most white missionaries in South Africa had become salaried employees—the clergy—of the local mainline churches and were missionaries only in the sense of a calling rather than a profession. In the face of urbanization, church folk who worked with Black congregations grew concerned with the changing nature of the African family in what they referred to as the "detribalization of African society." These concerns became more prominent after World War I, both because general Black impoverishment had become more evident and because generational shifts had occurred in the supply and replacement of clergy—all clergy, though most significantly, white clergy. It is unclear, for instance, how World War I affected the generational configuration of European missionaries to Africa. By the early 1920s, many more church folk from Europe and the US working in Africa had university degrees. Similarly, influential Black clergy had received training either in the US at higher education institutions like Wilberforce College or had received medical and other training in the UK.

These different currents of change meant that many white clergy who worked in the historic mission churches in the early twentieth century were no longer concerned with the eradication of lobola. Some administrators in the US, UK, Scandinavian, German, and Swiss evangelical wings of the South African mainline Protestant churches or in international spaces linked to evangelical and theological research (especially Germany or Switzerland) were more concerned with the reformation of African marriage for the new conditions of the twentieth century rather than with the elimination of lobola. Many of them were located outside Africa and not working as practicing missionaries. As administrators in their mission networks, they had a bird's-eye view of developments in Africa not possible for church personnel on the ground. This view provided them with almost unparalleled access to the pervasiveness of lobola in Africa, a practice that had support throughout most of the continent. As they began to debate the terms of African marriage, their efforts found resonance in the attitude of some of the European clergy in South Africa.

In 1915, following a similar commission in Southern Rhodesia two years previously, the General Missionary Conference (GMC) commissioned a study into lobola and similar practices. While the commission replies are missing, the questions themselves reveal how the interest in lobola was changing. Language alone indicated a change of view, the term "cattle-marriage" reflecting how the relatively new science of anthropology was affecting Western understandings of African custom and practice. It also reflected a more accommodating attitude toward lobola. "With the present ideal of marriage and present social conditions, is the transference of cattle an unmitigated evil; or does it serve a good purpose till the ideal of marriage can be raised by Christian influence?"[60] In the Rhodesian survey, when respondents were asked, "Should Church members be allowed to pay 'lobola', if marrying daughters of heathen parents?," the consensus was that a Christian ought to pay lobola when marrying a daughter of parents who had not converted.

Two years later, the Anglican Diocese of Umtata took a vote declaring that, in and of itself, the transfer of ikazi was not an improper practice.

Similar declarations took place in most mainline churches across the country during the later 1910s, where the move toward acceptance seemed to have been at the level of individual congregations, although quite often official denominational pronouncements were more circumspect.

By the early 1920s, lobola was a standard item on GMC meeting agendas. In 1925, its members resolved that "in view of the many disabilities under which Christian and civilized natives labour with regard to the law of lobola in the Natal Province, and having regard to the failure of the Native Christian Marriage Act of Natal No. 46 of 1887 to afford protection to native women married under its incidence this Conference hereby appoints a committee to investigate."[61]

But by the next meeting, the committee was more concerned with what it termed "the realignment of native life" in response to the growing pressures of urban life than with the practice of lobola. At this and subsequent meetings, lobola gradually became subsumed under discussions of African family life, although—even into the 1940s—pronouncements on proper family life was still dominated by whites. In 1940, at a Christian Council meeting devoted to "African family life," Samuel Samson Tema, who had attended as one of the African delegates at the Tambaram Conference of the International Missionary Council (IMC) in 1938, spoke forcefully enough for the minutes to record that he was unhappy at being the only African speaker on the subject.[62]

African Public Support for Lobola

If one support for lobola's public life was a general acceptance in the mission-oriented Christian churches, where Black voices were present though often not audible, another support lay in secular public life. Although the Black press offered only a relatively circumscribed forum for articulating support in the late nineteenth century, it provided a much greater space in the twentieth century. During the first decade, Black public support for lobola circulated within mostly regional audiences, some of them institutional and some of them living in the limited circulations of regional and mostly vernacular-language newspapers like *Izwi laBantu, Ilanga lase Natal,* and *Tsala ea Becoana*. Initially, public support for lobola was expressed, often quite diffidently, in Xhosa or Zulu, in news and letters to papers like the three just mentioned.[63] As African men gained confidence in their views, they moved their commentary into English. It is difficult to precisely pin some of these shifts because the public discussion of lobola spanned several publications, not all published at the same time or for the same length of time. By the 1910s, African men had harnessed their epistolary talents to the defense of lobola in *Christian Express*, for them both a daunting but familiar space. When *Umteteli* began publishing in 1920, its correspondents took on the challenge of lobola soon after.

After roughly the 1870s, when Black South Africans gained *Isigidimi sama Xosa* as a forum for their autographic talent, Black opinion on lobola tended toward congruence with white opinion as much as it did not. By the 1910s (possibly earlier, but the criterion here is access to published commentary), support for the practice characterized most writing. Perhaps the most common feature of these early discussions is their form; by far, the majority of commentary took the form of letters, and all the public discussion buttressed itself against the formidable bulwark of Christianity. In addition, though, they also drew on international comparisons to justify lobola. By the 1910s, Black South Africans were aware of the extent to which marriages in other parts of the world were different. Local commentators compared practices in South Africa favorably with Hindu dowry practices in India, finding lobola superior. African writers also drew attention to lobola's promotion of sexual fidelity in marriage. British marriages, they thought, were much more susceptible to divorce and infidelity because British women did not have their rights in marriage protected and men did not value their wives because of a lack of lobola transfer. Moreover, because men did not value their wives, they either divorced them easily or engaged in extramarital affairs.

Black commentary also defended the stipulation that lobola was a sale. While this, too, was a feature of nineteenth-century defenses, by the twentieth century, the language of commodification had begun to characterize what people had to say. It was also a response to white criticism of the commoditization of lobola.[64] "Lobola is not like buying a tin of condensed milk and likewise is not made on a materialistic basis."[65] In the previously mentioned 1920 letter to *Christian Express* that sparked off the response from Matatiele, Reverend Makubalo made the following remark, criticizing those who maintained that lobola was a "commercial transaction": "If A sells a commodity to B, the latter has the legal and moral right to sell this same commodity to C. Therefore if lobola is buying and selling, a man shall have the right to sell his wife."[66]

That white condemnation of lobola disguised a raging and critical debate concerning labor and commodity production did not escape the eye of Black commentators. In a letter its writers requested *Christian Express* to publish, the writers—African Christians from Southern Rhodesia—expressed a genuine outrage at white sexual mores. The group, which styled itself as the "Union of South Africa Native Association in Bulawayo," was responding to a request for its opinion of sexual assault by African men, the so-called Black

Peril of the 1910s. The opinion here brings together lobola, immorality, and the sale of sex.

> That Europeans in this country have disgraced themselves by having illicit intercourse with the natives. That in some instances Europeans have not only paid lobola, but are polygamists.... It has also become a frequent custom among white men to send boys to the location to procure prostitutes. This association is of the opinion that white men of that type have to a very great extent taught natives immorality.[67]

By the 1920s, African men were not only writing in support of lobola but—following the example of their distinctly ungracious white colleagues—criticizing the views of those at odds with them. When A. C. Maseko wrote on the subject in *Ilanga* in 1922, he roundly condemned two of the European repeat offenders on the subject, denouncing them as shortsighted on the matter and poking fun at the endless "horrible cases" quoted to support the missionary viewpoint.[68] However, the support given to the practice in the 1920s is more significant than the kinds of individual challenges to lobola that had been the staple of newspaper articles thus far.

Lobola and Urban Anxieties in the 1920s and 1930s

The newspaper discussion of the 1910s, where African interlocutors almost hesitantly took on their white counterparts, had shifted by the 1920s into a more direct attack on the white condemnation of the practice. Newspaper opinion pieces also joined the letter-based, call-and-response-style conversations around the practice. Beginning in August 1922, Henry Selby-Msimang began to battle on behalf of African marriage. Selby-Msimang, aghast at the independence of the modern African woman that he felt led directly to immorality and divorce, published two articles in August and September. In the first, "Native Marriages," he discussed the growing phenomenon of a first Christian marriage followed by a second customary marriage to a different woman.[69] Husbands who married twice—once according to civil law and again in customary law—were becoming not only a trial for their wives but the subject of bigamy prosecution (bigamy was possible in Natal). Selby-Msimang blamed these tangles of intimate married life on not transferring lobola in the first marriage, which meant that either the husband or the wife had not sufficiently valued their union. In an especially convoluted set of thinking around cause and effect designed to show a deterioration in both male and female sexual morality, he continued the theme in a four-part spread, "The Religion and Civilization of the Bantu." "It is my honest conviction," he wrote on 9 September, "that ukulobola should be encouraged."[70]

Selby-Msimang's arguments are interesting because they reflect a shift in public writing about lobola. Rather than noting the binding of families in rural and traditional settings that earlier supporters of lobola like B. J. Ross had done, his defense was a neo-traditional one centered on the African city. It is not so much the point he made, a defense of lobola as an aspect of "Bantu socialism," but rather that his defense of tradition was located in the urban setting of an African township, where Africans on low wages shared resources so they could maintain a standard of living and houses "better than many houses occupied by Europeans in Johannesburg."[71]

Selby-Msimang was not the only person to be concerned about African marriage. By the early 1920s, it was clear that African marriage had become the nexus of a set of expectations about control and mobility that had very little to do with marriage and everything to do with white anxiety, urban control, and the supply of labor. As Posel has written, "It was during the 1920s and 1930s that the issue of marriage in urban African communities became politically prominent, both within the white polity and on the agenda of debate among urban African community leaders. The vitriolic—sometimes alarmist—debate then lingered into the 1940s, as the pace of African urbanization accelerated, but with state actors doing little to shift or ameliorate the problems which they identified."[72]

This is largely correct, although by the start of the Second World War, a variety of state actors, mostly urban and municipal officials, were trying to regularize African marriage, especially customary marriage, because of the problems around housing it occasioned.[73] There is an unwritten history of African marriage, the state, and legal regimes that lies in continual, concerted, and failed attempts to regularize African marriage.

Because marriage constituted the discursive focus of this concern, it is easy to overlook lobola's status as a silent partner in these arenas. Unlike initiation, which was largely tangential to city living, and polygamy, the formal incidence of which was both low and theoretically confined to the reserves, lobola was a source for concern for multiple, differently powerful audiences, including national and local-level state officials, the white church establishment, white liberals, and literate Black men. By the 1930s, this audience included Black women. Selby-Msimang's comments need to be understood in the context not just of industrialization, which tore men from the reserves and their families, but also of urbanization, which brought women to the cities and confirmed the loss of patriarchal control.

Selby-Msimang was not alone in his views nor in the avenues through which he chose to express them. As mentioned, both local and international mission and Christian agencies had by the 1920s turned their attention to African, or "native," marriage. The result was an efflorescence of scholarly work that continued into the 1940s. However, not only did mission and anthropological interests coincide but missionaries and ethnographers across Africa often joined forces to investigate the matter of marriage. In South Africa, this was evident in a conjunction of interests represented by the SAIRR, anthropologists, academics, and officials who served on the SAIRR board, and clergymen across the major churches who were concerned with the changing nature of African marriage.

By the 1930s, the Black press's active support of lobola had led to growing official church acceptance of the practice. This support and the conditions of urban life, coupled with reserve poverty, had created a discourse around the condition of "native marriage," one that called for shoring it up against the disasters of detribalization and required a reorientation to city life. Most of the writing on Black Johannesburg during this period saw support for the African family as an administrative solution to problems with housing and the control of women, all of which would be "solved," or so well-meaning writers hoped, by more effective husbands and proper families. This position seems evident in retrospect, but there was no particular emphasis at the time on making suitably behaved urban families out of Christian families. Still, the model that came to dominate urban administration for Africans was a Christian one. Christianity, both in the shape of the liberals and mission patriarchs and in the form of a vocal class of letter writers, was key in this process to save the urban African family.

Kathy Eales has written about the 1925 attempt to impose curfews on African women in Johannesburg as a shared response by African men and the state to the growing independence of African women. Between 1911 and 1921, the number of African women in Johannesburg had increased from 4,357 to 12,160.[74] But the increase in no way warranted the anxiety and vilification that their presence in the city drew forth. Men like Selby-Msimang, who worried about control over African women, found that their concerns were shared by the urban authorities and other organizations, including the Johannesburg Joint Council. During the 1920s, the council made various attempts to curb the mobility and independence of African women, including suggesting that women be issued night passes. Johannesburg's male African elite provided some of the most vocal support for this suggestion.

"The native man is himself the arbiter of his women's conduct and is resentful of any interference in his matters marital. The native woman has not progressed so far in public affairs as her British prototype," went an *Umteteli* editorial in 1925.[75] The untruth of this assertion may have been apparent to men in private, but its public utterance was a convenient way to assert declining masculine authority in the face of economic and racist vicissitude. While African men had been resident in South Africa's cities since the late nineteenth century, either as members of an elite or as laborers, the presence of larger numbers of African women was a new feature of urban life in the 1920s.

Although the loss of Black masculine authority is often and correctly cited as the reason for this panic about women, the issue of troublesome—and independent—women in urban areas is not often traced back to the issue of lobola. However, Selby-Msimang's and others' writing shows that the issue of marriage in urban areas should not be viewed apart from how urban families negotiated lobola. In the first part of this chapter, I looked at how lobola continued to accompany church marriage for Africans, despite any attempt at missionary prohibition. Here I turn to the issue of what happens when it is not possible to transfer lobola. Women working away from their families in Johannesburg and other urban centers were difficult to arrange marriages for, so parents went without lobola for their daughters. The issue here was not one of aspiration; most of the women concerned, as well as their families, likely aspired to transfer lobola. Rather, the issue was the difficulty of exchanging cattle or even cash for families living some distance apart, not only from the city but also from each other. How did the temporality of city life, which increasingly kept people in cities, allow for the chronology of a lobola exchange? In some instances, though it is unclear how often this occurred, young women in towns could earn their own lobola to present to their parents on behalf of their lovers. But these kinds of unions had a difficulty attached. Couples who married in town without lobola faced a high chance of separation or the husband contracting a subsequent customary marriage. Marriages without lobola were less enduring than those that included it.

African Women and Lobola

Amidst the rather pious and self-important concern around African families expressed by organizations like the joint councils after the 1920s in the epistolary war for lobola, not much evidence exists on what women, literate and otherwise, thought about lobola. Women wrote in support of and against lobola, though not in great numbers, and male correspondents often liked to cite women as supporting lobola. However, more generally it is difficult to detect how women felt about it. As already noted, African women were largely absent in the burgeoning public sphere that accompanied print culture, both literary and newspaper based, in the first two decades of the early twentieth century. Instead, for this period, it is easier to see Black women as either directing their efforts toward oral genres, like song—especially song accompanied by dance—or toward much more personal forms of writing, like letters.[76]

By the early 1930s, though, African women's writing had started appearing in newspapers like *Umteteli, Ilanga,* and *Bantu World*. Marijke du Toit and Palesa Nzuza have noted how women writers began to use the pages of *Ilanga* to debate their concerns from the middle of the decade onward.[77] Among the various subjects that drew women's attention, one of the first was lobola. As both Lynn Thomas and Meghan Healy-Clancy have written, *Bantu World* created a self-consciously public space through which educated African women could express opinions.[78] While Reginald Dhlomo was instrumental in initiating *Bantu World*'s "Pages of Interest to the Women of the Race" and also served as its first "editress," his views on African family life, reflected in the quote from his novel at the start of this chapter, were conservative. He was opposed to the idea of modern, independent women and scathing about women who used cosmetics. Nevertheless, the pages allowed men and women with catholic views to debate their particular and domestic concerns.

In September 1933, just one year after the publication of *Bantu World*'s first issue, a heated exchange was initiated by Dora Msomi's letter, which criticized female nurses and teachers for neglecting their families in favor of their work. A letter from "Anxious" from Ermelo was published under the subheading "Bantu Women Must Tackle the Big Question Confronting Them."[79]

> Sir, I have been constrained to pen these lines by the remarkable letters from your women readers about Miss Dora Msomi's letter. This correspondence served to prove that my sisters are, following their sisters of progressive races in defending themselves and their callings when necessary. So I took the courage to write about the subject that has been worrying me for a long time. The question of 'ukulobola', 'bogadi' has been discussed in the press and on the platforms for many years, but very few Bantu women have voiced their feelings on this very grave matter. I ask them to do so now.

Two weeks later she had her first responses. Mrs. R. E. Masole of Brakpan, writing on what she termed "a delicate subject," was moved to clarify misunderstandings around lobola. Her letter emphasized the mutual respect engendered as a result of lobola.[80] The letter by "No-Civil," a punning pseudonym that could mean that its writer was uncivilized or that referred to her married name, thanked "Anxious" for opening up the matter for "all thinking women" to discuss, though No-Civil herself was not in favor of lobola.[81]

A week later, Nurse Beth Lebele, laying out her professional credentials very carefully, explained that both men and women benefited from lobola.[82] "Ukolobola for the wife is the only thing decent." Both her letter and the one by A. M. M. Phashe in the same edition stressed the importance of lobola to morality and respectability. Mr. Phashe (according to the next edition of the paper) further explained that "there is not the slightest difference between Christian marriage and Bantu marriage," which was also described in the Bible, or as she styled it, the "Book of Books."[83]

The following week, an "Unmarried Lady" wrote in support of lobola, as did Miss L. E. R. Maditse. "Unmarried" emphasized the self-respect that lobola brought forth in married women, while Miss Maditse's letter carried the header "Duty of Every Boy and Girl to Respect the Lobolo Custom." Many other letters in late 1933—and there were many—also emphasized the codependence of respect in marriage and lobola. Lobola created status for women, a status otherwise under threat by African and white men seeking to curtail the movement and independence of women.

Such assertions could not go unchallenged, however. As much as it is a condemnation of lobola itself, the nature of that challenge is interesting for what it reveals about modern power disparities in gender. On 21 October, P. D. S. wrote a stinging critique to the women's pages, of both the discussion and the practice.[84] His targets, in addition to the antiquated practice of lobola, also included misinformed and backward female readers and writers like "Anxious," with whom—he magnanimously informed them—he was willing to share his greater insight into the practice. A week later, he was joined by a Christian minister, who offered his status rather than his name, in condemning the practice.

The placement of their letters in the women's pages and the situation of their debate is significant and potentially puzzling. A summary of male views in the 4 November edition wrote about "foolish, half-witted daughters who encourage the practice," also referring to the supposedly inaccurate content of Miss Maditse's letter. It is difficult to escape the impression that these men were more opposed to women's support of lobola and women's assertion of its importance than to lobola itself. Notwithstanding their support of modernity, they did not want modern wives challenging their views. While using their practice of Christianity to support their opposition to lobola, their words associate them more with the men who preferred to contract "special marriages," or the civil marriage contracted for convenience's sake. "Many men failing to pay this ilobolo resort to special marriages which are ruinous," because they allow for the possibility of easy, and civil, divorce.[85] Whatever the case, women continued to write letters to the newspaper, either supporting or challenging lobola. It is difficult to escape the conclusion that this was one arena in which they felt supremely qualified to comment.

～

The span of years covered by this chapter includes some very real and dramatic shifts in factors related to African marriage. For various reasons, more and more Africans began to marry in church, most Christian marriages taking place within the mainline churches. Despite this shift, which might at one point have been accompanied by a growing opposition to lobola, lobola transfers and Christian marriage were closely associated. Still, by 1940, fewer marriages were being contracted with lobola, the cause of which may be found in urbanization, housing policy, and African women's growing affinity for independent urban life. If by the 1940s these changes were not yet apparent to any great extent, the anxiety around marriage that characterized the 1920s and 1930s clearly shows what white and Black liberals and educated African men and women feared was to come.

By the 1940s, lobola remained as a subject of concern to a relatively small group of people, missionaries included. Neither the IMC nor the Christian Council as a body nor African Christians viewed the practice as inimical to the practice of their faith. Instead, as will become further evident in chapter 5, attention had shifted to the problems surrounding marriage that concerned Africa in general: the ability of urban Africans to craft families that would suit a continent of independent African nations. By 1911, while marriage still retained its importance as the central social institution of African life, it was changing rapidly. The collective impact of colonialism and market capitalism—which viewed African marriage as an impediment to the securing of labor—was dissolving the delicate balance between men and women in marriage, between fathers and sons, and between cattle and women. More specifically, the rise of migrant labor in South Africa, which required a distinctly non-free market supply of workers, coupled with increasing reserve poverty, meant that almost every African marriage by the 1930s had one leg in an urban center and one leg in a rural area. Distance rather than proximity governed people's intimate and conjugal lives, affecting the ability to conduct lobola transactions, to resolve marriage disputes easily, and to establish ties of affection that recognized the status of wife and husband as commensurate in a marriage.

5 ～ Weddings and Status, Consumption and Reciprocity

So grand a wedding... had never been seen in Mpondomiseland before and was never likely to be seen again. In accordance with an old custom, the wedding-feast was held at the bridegroom's home. The bridal party came from Mjika accompanied by a huge band of young horsemen.... The marriage ceremony was held at St. Cuthbert's church which was filled to overflowing with crowds of people—White as well as Black—who had come in cars and on horseback. As for Mphuthumi, he had his hands full that day. In the mkhwelo he was standard bearer, while after the marriage ceremony, when the register was being signed, it was his business to conduct the school choir singing an anthem. And of course he was best man, since Nomvuyo was chief bridesmaid.... As soon as the marriage ceremony was over, the bridal party went to St Mary's Hostel where they had been invited to tea by Sister Monica.... There were so many wedding presents that the bridal couple did not know what to do with them. Piles of congratulatory telegrams—some in English, some in Xhosa—were received at the Royal Place from well-wishers from all walks of life.... The messages that many of them contained added to the jollity of the occasion because they were from old school friends at Fort Hare, Lovedale, and St Matthew's. The day's celebrations were rounded off with a grand dance at St. Cuthbert's.[1]

IN THE A. C. Jordan novel *Wrath of the Ancestors,* first published in Xhosa in 1940, Chief Zwelinzima and Thembeka married, surrounded by the symbols of old and new. Their wedding included motor cars, telegrams, a tea with the nuns at St. Cuthbert's and, later, a grand dance. While some of these items were indisputably modern, others were evocative of a range of duties and responsibilities long associated with traditional Black South African wedding ceremonies.

Jordan's novel is usually viewed as a contest, a vignette into the conflicted feelings evoked by those who felt tradition was unprogressive and those who agonized over the loss of practices that enacted respect for the ancestors. The novel, while focusing directly on the conundrum faced by Black South Africans in relation to the dense categories of meaning rendered here as tradition and modernity, also demonstrates how Christianity had come to have, by the 1940s, such an institutional thickness in the lives of Black South Africans. Christian forms and institutions saturate the novel. One of these lies in processes of courtship and marriage, including grand weddings. Thembeka and Zwelinzima met at Lovedale and began courting when both were at University of Fort Hare, which in the 1930s, was the only African university south of the equator.[2] After completing her studies at Fort Hare, Thembeka had taken up a position as a teacher at St. Cuthbert's, where Zwelinzima proposed to her. Their courting was done partly through telephone call and letter and was stamped with respectability by the mission staff who acted as go-betweens to help arrange their encounters.

While literary analyses of the novel usually focus on its central theme, the novel is also notable for how Jordan captures the progression of a twentieth-century love affair. Thembeka does not have a happily ever after, but until the birth of her first child, the relationship between her and Zwelinzima resembled the companionate marriage that missionary teaching, Christian literature, and the women's pages of the Black press had been promoting for some time. Their relationship initially had an outcome very different from the kind of relationship shared by Dorothy Kabane and Selbourne Bokwe.

Novels like these provide a rare window into the courtship processes of the Black elite in the period after World War I (even if the novels overemphasized sexual tragedy and disappointment). Unfortunately, sources that depict uneventful and successful church marriages are not easy to locate for this period. Paraphrasing Jennifer Cole and Lynn Thomas, work that reduces African intimacy to sex—and nonconsensual sex moreover—without taking emotional attachments seriously is overrepresented in the scholarly literature on Africa.[3] Lauren Berlant suggests that an important area of contemporary research lies in how "the utopian, optimism-sustaining versions of intimacy meet the normative practices, fantasies, institutions, and ideologies that organize people's worlds."[4] In reflecting on weddings in postapartheid South Africa, Danai Mupotsa foregrounds an intent to understand weddings and wedding photographs in relation to "happiness as an affect."[5]

In the previous chapter, I detailed the rising incidence of church marriages in Black South Africa, especially from the 1930s onward. Many of these marriages were accompanied by weddings that drew for precedent

FIGURE 5.1. Photographs of church weddings, ca. 1925 (the image is of a board of photographs). The board shows ten photographs and is emphatic about the photographs being of a Christian wedding, though these are not all of the same wedding. Note the wedding cake in the central photo. No further details are included. University of the Witwatersrand, Historical Papers, AC1971- H- H12. Reproduced courtesy of the Uniting Presbyterian Church in Southern Africa.

on weddings conducted in the West. An ideal African Christian wedding included things—things like wedding rings, white wedding gowns, social announcements in the newspaper, jazz bands, tea services, photographers, cars, and ceremonies conducted under roofs in churches. Paying attention to how weddings were focused on material culture provides insight into how Black families—initially those of the modernizing elite—experienced, staged, and created status through respectability in white-dominated South Africa. Material culture in this sense includes but is not restricted to a consumer culture located in commodification.

These weddings were different from Black traditional wedding ceremonies that involved lobola and patrilocality. In Zulu and Xhosa, these are known as the *umtshato*.[6] This was the name given to the extended rite that marked a bride's move to her husband's home and that was part of a lobola marriage (although the term is currently and popularly used to refer to both the traditional and Christian wedding ceremony). A deeper reading of the weddings, referred to in this chapter as "white weddings" to distinguish them from the umtshato, shows how older forms of social capital put to work in the context of industrialization, urbanization, and political disempowerment were re-created and created anew through a new economy of affect centered on both families and friends. Weddings were the glue that allowed families to hold on to whatever fractured version of Black intimate life was possible under modern conditions. Against the centrifugal tendencies of migrant labor, they worked to convene social networks that went outside of the family in an era of familial disintegration. Weddings, I argue, should be understood as statements about status and respectability, about commodification and modern life, about intimate life showcased to wider audiences, and as performances of sexual morality.

WRITING ABOUT WEDDINGS

While white weddings were frequently featured in novels and in the Black press in popular accounts of married life in the early twentieth century, they are far from standard in academic accounts of African marriage during that same period.[7] In *African Marriage in Southern Africa,* the Christian wedding receives little discussion as a mechanism leading to marriage, a position repeated in a number of anthologies.[8] The comprehensive and underappreciated *Survey of African Marriage and Family Life,* part 3 concerning itself solely with "Christian Marriage in African Society," also has little to say about church weddings. Moreover, while marriage is a prominent element of study on Christian Africa, weddings receive comparatively little attention.[9] The wedding is more present in historical work on African elites[10] and, importantly for this book, work by Monica Hunter, Isaac Schapera, and John and Jean Comaroff.[11]

In contrast to the lack of discussion elsewhere, weddings run like a vein through Monica Hunter's work. Her discussion of weddings, first present in *Reaction to Conquest* after research conducted in the early 1930s, was subsequently elaborated upon and revised as a result of her own Christianity and later development in anthropological theory (specifically the shift in thinking from acculturation and culture clash to a more hybrid model of historical contact). The first image in this chapter is from this volume, a copy of the photograph held in the Monica and Godfrey Wilson Papers at the University of Cape Town. Hunter (later Wilson) wrote about the church wedding in her work on the impact of the European conquest on the Mpondo, although her discussion of marriage rites is dominated by the umtshato.[12] In later work, Wilson described how Xhosa Christians incorporated elements of both European and traditional practices into their weddings.[13]

FIGURES 5.2 AND 5.3. A church wedding in the Eastern Cape in the 1920s. A photograph similar to the first photograph appeared in the first edition of Monica Hunter's *Reaction to Conquest*. Note the bride is wearing what look likes an orange-blossom coronet. Several of the bridal party are dressed in white. In the second photograph, the couple are processing through an audience of adults and children, who likely were not all members of the party. The images are part of the Monica and Godfrey Wilson Collection BC880 in the African Studies Library at the University of Cape Town. Reproduced courtesy of the UCT Libraries.

By the 1930s, anthropologists and others working in South Africa had begun to turn their attention to developments in urban as well as rural areas to comment on the social changes taking place in the former. Through their focus on family life, often but not always its disintegration, Hunter, Schapera, Eileen Krige, Ruth Levin, and Laura Longmore all encountered discussion about marriage, including commentary on the financial cost of the white wedding. Levin's work, completed in the late 1940s, followed the married lives of couples living in Langa, a Cape township, including those who had married in the rural Eastern Cape.[14] Her work, especially in charting the movement of couples or one partner of a married couple between the Ciskei and Transkei reserves, shows how, despite material differences, both urban and rural Black Christians aspired to middle-class status.

As Jordan's novel notes and as the epigraph of the previous chapter corroborates, weddings and marriage also were a staple of personal writing, novels, and drama, whether in the theater or later on the radio. Phyllis Ntantala's memoir described several weddings, as well as her mother's wedding gown sewing and the "piles and piles of bridal material in one corner of the room."[15] Frieda Matthews described her wedding to Z. K. Matthews at Lovedale Mission Institute in 1928 in her memoir, *Remembrances*.[16] Sindiwe Magona, in her published letter/memoir, *To My Children's Children*, comments on the disappointment of her civil marriage compared to the festive and white church weddings of her childhood (ca. 1940).[17] Herbert Dhlomo and Ellen Kuzwayo both described disaster-struck weddings in their short stories, including dramatic tales of jilting at the altar.[18] In Liz Gunner's recent work on the station Radio Bantu, white weddings constitute a staple trope of Zulu radio dramas from the 1960s onward.[19]

WEDDINGS AND MATERIAL CULTURE

By the end of the nineteenth century, mission Christians in the historic mainstream churches (Anglicans, Presbyterians, Methodists, and others) routinely had church weddings. Photographs from the late nineteenth century show African Christians marrying in European clothing, the bride in white and the groom in a suit and gloves.[20] Clothing, though, was not the only element African couples adopted from Europe when marrying via the church; they also had wedding cakes, wedding rings, going-away outfits, speeches, dances, and honeymoons. While some of these elements had indigenous equivalents, like the distribution of cost between the bride's and groom's families, others did not. A three-tiered wedding cake had become standard fare at wedding feasts by the late nineteenth century, representing what Wilson referred to as "ritual change."[21]

Literature on Black consumer culture for the early twentieth century is scant. Most of it emerges from scholarly work on the Black press, which has examined the role and status of advertisements in early papers like *Bantu World* and the publications that came later, like *Drum* and *Golden City Post*. According to Irwin Manoim, a more fully developed consumer culture had emerged only by the 1950s (and, indeed, that Black buying power emerged as a significant factor only by the 1970s).[22] However, this date is too late for the limited if burgeoning African consumer culture already evident by the end of the nineteenth century.[23] Literate and Christianized South Africans, the Black elite, were largely instrumental in the creation of this culture, as they altered their lives and their daily habits to include the square houses, ceilings, and dinner sets that white missionaries held up as emblematic of civilized life. Black men were recruited to the gold mines and other labor centers by the end of the nineteenth century through requiring them to pay taxes, and it did not escape local retailers and merchants that the working-class men who earned wages in this way were also men with potentially disposable income to spend on consumer products.

All of this required money to be spent and things to be acquired so that by the early twentieth century church weddings fed off of and into a growing consumer culture among Black South Africans. These efforts mirrored wedding trends abroad. Accompanying the growing popularity of the wedding in the West, feeding into and off it, was a celebration-directed consumer culture. Silverware merchants and jewelers turned their attention to weddings to produce "a powerful alliance between weddings and the growing market economy."[24] In Britain, from the mid-nineteenth century on, the commodification of weddings was good business for merchants advertising a range of services.[25]

From the late nineteenth century, this trend was also evident in South Africa. Missionary institutions trained African women to sew wedding dresses as evidence of their skill for future employment and had their talent demonstrated at annual exhibitions.[26] Treadle sewing machines were often gifted to young women among their wedding gifts. Bolts of fabric from other parts of the colonial world that had traveled to South Africa on the steamers that crossed the Indian and Atlantic Oceans made their way to trading stations across South Africa's rural areas, where they served as standard items in the exchange of wedding gifts.

People's habits of material consumption were both constituted by and linked back to a print-based advertising industry. By the late nineteenth century, especially after the 1880s, Black newspapers regularly devoted their front pages (and sometimes their back) to advertising. Advertisements for gold wedding rings appeared among ones for patent medicine. General merchants advertised the goods needed to make "i-Wedding Cake."[27] By 1900, these kinds of advertisements were ubiquitous, if not frequent. Photographers offered their services to couples getting married, and dressmakers advertised their skill in sewing wedding dresses.

Looking at weddings from the perspective of consumption makes it clear they were a modern phenomenon that extended beyond a focus on cattle exchange and the joining of families. But weddings were not a case of either modernity or tradition, either manifestations of capitalism or separate from modern patterns of consumption. Timothy Burke has examined consumption centered on domesticity, hygiene, and soap in modern Zimbabwe. His work points to the interplay between the creation of need, the proliferation of commodities, and the independent world of African values and aspirations that helped to create a consumer market out of modern African subjects.[28] Burke, though, tempers the link to capitalism through his reference to the "intricate emotional and intellectual investments made by individuals in commodity culture."[29] His caveat goes to the heart of my argument. Wedding ceremonies and their attendant investment in specialized commodities were partially a response to the rise of a consumer culture. This is an easy argument to make, but insufficient because they also reflected an intricate investment by individuals into worlds set apart from, but coterminous, with money. Weddings, whatever else they also did, convened Black South Africans as a public for a different kind of economy. This is what Webb Keane terms a "representational economy," drawing on the ideas of reciprocity and people joining that were crucial in traditional marriages involving the transfer of bridewealth, as well as the shift of those relations through contact with the material culture of modern capitalism.[30] Weddings were social motion—Henry Glassie's phrase—draped over a map of place, ways to re-create community through shared social action. Jordan's novel, with its descriptions of travel and of people connecting with telegrams and wedding presents, takes that net of motion and writes it into existence through its pages.

WEDDINGS AND STATUS

From the late nineteenth century, engagement and wedding announcements were common features of the South African press, Black and white.[31] Announcements were common if sporadic by the 1890s in the pages of *Imvo Zabantsundu* and other papers with more regional content. By the 1930s, they were ubiquitous in national papers like *Umteteli* and *Bantu World*. The 30 October 1937 edition of *Umteteli* carries a wedding announcement of the Silgee-Frost wedding, in St. Mary's Church, Soweto; a list of wedding presents (exhausting an entire column on a page of five columns) for the

Tshange-Gumede wedding in Langa, Cape Town, including two glass flower vases from the Progress Tennis Club (see figure 1.2); and announcements of two forthcoming weddings, Mr. Amos Oliphant to Miss Elizabeth Mtshoe, and Mr. Johnson Mofokeng to Miss Vina Bokolo.[32] The adjacent pages include an advertisement by Wolf Brothers of Cape Town for wedding rings.

These newspapers, instrumental in defining modern African sensibility and taste, were widely read and critical to African self-representation that challenged dominant racial and gender norms. *Umteteli* mostly carried wedding announcements on its pages devoted to "Town and Country News," while *Bantu World* carried them either on its women's or social pages. Wedding announcements ranged in length from a few lines to whole columns. The longer announcements typically included detail on the bride and groom, their families, the officiant, and the reception venue, and often included a detailed description of the wedding presents and the bridal party's attire (i.e., the bride, bride's mother, bridesmaids, and flower girls).

Reporters who described weddings gave full reign to whimsy in writing up the wedding announcements. The adjectives used to describe the bride and her entourage are striking and effusive. "The bride was gowned in a gown of white radium matlace giving a peacock effect at the back and the sleeves which were opened from the elbow to the wrist. To add perfection and charm she wore a venetian veil and carried a bouquet of white artificial roses and carnations."[33]

By the 1930s, wedding announcements in *Umteteli* and *Bantu World* had incorporated photographs, some of which were formal studio portraits.[34] But both posed photographs and more amateur shots appeared in the papers, often focusing on the bride's dress. The formal studio portraits commonly staged the groom standing behind the bride, with the bride sitting or to the front of the photograph.[35]

THE WHITE WEDDING DRESS: A TALE IN TWO PARTS

In 1938, Miss Annie Tlale married Mr. Isaac Phillips in the Methodist Church in Bensonvale, near Herschel in the Eastern Cape. "The bride, who was given away by her father, was looking charming in a powder blue brocade with a trimmed bodice. Her veil of silk net was held by a halo of orange blossoms." The two flower girls wore white crepe de chine with pink bonnets. The groom's best man was the bride's brother. A reception was held at the Bhunga Hall, Sterkspruit. After the wedding, Mr. and Mrs. Phillips "went by motor to Port Elizabeth for their honeymoon."[36]

In examining clothing and the "dressed body" in Africa and how dress mapped the boundaries between colonial and colonized populations, it is understandable that clothing could be a contested issue.[37] John and Jean

Comaroff write about the importance of clothing, self-fashioning, and consumption in the second volume of their monumental Tswana mission project.[38] Their work considers fabric and material in the fashioning of identity as statements that extend beyond the consumption of commodities into the mimicry of European behavior. Robert Ross writes about the clothes Christian men wore to marry, in the morning coat that author and novelist Sol Plaatje wore at his Mafeking wedding.[39] Wendy Urban-Mead brings together Christianity, identity, and wedding attire in her study of Christians in Matabeleland in colonial Zimbabwe in the mid-twentieth century.[40] Depending on one's vantage point as missionary or convert, wedding garb symbolized both excess and success. Gendered conventions were created and replicated in the weddings of Brethren in Christ Church, where clothing was a point of contention for both male and female converts. Male converts, in particular, used the missionaries' reluctance to antagonize them for fear of losing converts to push for choice in the matter of lavish wedding attire.

Although less frequently considered—perhaps the result of colonialism's overdetermined effect on African history—it is possible to detect a politics of affect, of aesthetic appreciation, in how people created and wore pieces of fabric as they positioned their social skin toward the world. An appreciation of aesthetic quality is reflected in how Joan Broster described some of the Thembu women she questioned in the 1960s about beadwork and traditional dress. "In tribal dress the skirt is cut on a double flair with all the fullness of the flair falling from the small of the back, giving a magnificent swing of folds over the behind.... A small waist followed by a big well-shaped behind gives the right provocative sway to the skirt and is greatly admired, calling forth the compliment, 'Umva wakhe mhle' (What a beautiful behind). The women and girls are very conscious of this beauty and they carry themselves and walk so as to enhance the sway of their skirts."[41]

Descriptions like this take seriously an aesthetic-based perspective regarding what clothing might have meant to the women wearing it.[42] This kind of appreciation is more readily apparent in work from Europe and the US. More recently, aspirations linked to white dresses have begun to feature in the nonhistorical literature. In an anthology on same-sex marriage, a gay couple, Charles and Hompi, describes their wedding: "When I first realized I [Hompi] that I was gay, I said to myself, 'I want to get into a white wedding dress'. It was my dream and it so happened that God answered my dream, and hence the white dress on my wedding day."[43]

One factor to understanding wedding dresses as an aesthetic choice in South Africa lies in the way that writing on traditional or ethnic dress and writing on clothing based on European patterns (I mean the term literally) are insulated from each other. Juliette Leeb-du Toit's history of the blue fabric known in southern Africa as *shweshwe* is a recent example of how to incorporate a sense of what is aesthetic with an understanding of hybrid and conflicted developments in the clothed body.[44]

Part 1: White Dresses, Status, and Respectability

In July 1936, Irene Kuze married Roseberry Bokwe. The report of the wedding captures the importance of the occasion. Both Roseberry Bokwe and Irene Kuze chose fashionable outfits to match their status. "The bride made a radiant picture in her full white satin beauty dress. Her veil was lined with pearls of coronet orange blossoms, and her train was lined with silver lama [*sic*]." She also carried a large bouquet, which she holds in a photograph published in *Umteteli*. Roseberry wore a gray morning coat.[45]

All these details carefully described through successive editions of *Umteteli* index a world of meaning tied to the couple's wedding. That attempts were made to cultivate and broadcast the event through reporting indicates that the wedding was also about status and prestige. Different elements of the wedding reveal the social power of the Bokwe family and possibly the Kuze family. Grahamstown Cathedral, where the couple married, is a large space and was, in the 1930s, the seat of a white congregation. While the Anglican Church did not officially support separating congregations by race, individual congregations were not nearly so accommodating. The officiating priest, the dean of the cathedral, was an important figure in white Anglican life. In an era where most mainstream church congregations were de facto segregated, the occupation of the white cathedral spoke directly to status.

After the ceremony, the couple took a taxi to the reception at the Municipal Location Hall. The married couple had a tea party and a dinner followed by a dance. A tea was the more frequent and more economical option for weddings; most wedding notices for Black couples during this period describe teas. Only those families with more disposable income stretched their festivities to include an evening dance, which involved hiring a venue and a wedding band. The following day, according to "Bantu Custom," the couple completed the "second stage" of their wedding, an echo of the wedding quoted in the epigraph to this chapter.

The church was filled on the day of the wedding by a multiracial and far-traveled body of visitors, including Essie Robeson, herself an activist and also wife of the renowned African American actor and civil rights activist Paul Robeson. Guests had traveled from Natal and Johannesburg and included judges, ministers, missionaries, and chiefs, a liberal elite that included Black and white South Africans.

In her work on weddings, Monica (Hunter) Wilson has noted that Africans used weddings to demonstrate status in the modern and white-dominated society of the early twentieth century.[46] She may have been thinking of this wedding, or ones similar to it. Wedding reportage repeatedly confirmed the status of those being married, as announcements were, as much as the weddings, "public statements of the social standings of the families being joined."[47] The Kuze-Bokwe wedding write-up occupied space in two columns on one page and continued in a third column on another page, covering more space than any other item on the page. A previous edition of *Umteteli* had published news of the engagement, and a later edition published the newly married couple's word of thanks for their gifts.

Part 2: Pale Blue Dresses and Shame

The popularity of the white wedding dress in Anglo-American and European society is widely ascribed to Queen Victoria, but white as a wedding color has been common in Britain from the early nineteenth century.[48] The color was initially linked to sexual purity and class, but working-class women did not marry in the impractical color until the development of easier laundering techniques.[49] From the early nineteenth century, because of increasing secularization in Britain and America, brides were no longer concerned about tying their sexual status to the color of their gown. However, in less secular and more religious Western Christian communities, white continued to be associated with sexual purity.[50] By the early twentieth century, some English brides had begun to marry in cream and ivory.

Earlier in the book, I wrote about how Christian marriage spoke to the gendered and racial relationship effected by and within the context of early twentieth-century South Africa. At a preachers' meeting at Mcumngco in the Eastern Cape in January 1935, one attendee raised the issue of a "fallen" girl who had been restored to the church and wanted to marry in white. He also told of hearing about some girls who had married their childhood sweethearts in white. "But he had never heard of a case where a girl who had given birth to a child had been allowed to marry in a white dress." The participants at the meeting were unanimous in deciding to ban Christian girls who had become pregnant from getting married in white.

Their deliberations, though, were based on complex formulas. Christian girls who had taken lovers but did not become pregnant, and who had shown signs of penitence, might marry in white. Krige considered this a well-known phenomenon based on her work in and around Pretoria. "Differentiation between the bridal attire and marriage-ceremonies of virgins and those of mothers of illegitimate children, so well-known in native society, is not a general practice of churches in the location, although common in some mission stations."[51] If weddings could elevate the status of those marrying, they did not always do so in a straightforward manner. Weddings, then, while they may have reflected and helped constitute social standing, and while they may have been joyous occasions, were also about the symbolic instantiation of sexual impurity.

In 1938, *Umteteli* reported on the wedding of Dorothy Kabane and Joe Busakwe. Kabane's failed relationship with Selbourne Bokwe has already appeared in this book. Like Thembu beadwork, which contained declarations of love and commentary on a lover's standing without a word needing to be spoken, the description of their wedding said more than the text conveyed.

> A pretty wedding took place at Butterworth Methodist Church on Wednesday, 6th July when Mr Joel Busakwe married Dorothy Kabane, daughter of Rev. W. W. and Mrs. Kabane.... She looked charming in an attire of ice blue dress, with a sweeping train. A wreath of orange blossoms held in position her long tulle veil of ice-blue. She wore dainty silver shoes and carried a bouquet of rose pink carnations. The two flower girls, Nozipho Kabane and Noncebo, were in frilled ice-blue tulle dresses ankle length, and they carried flowers. The bridesmaids Victoria Kabane (bride's sister) and Manaseh Nazo, both of Fort Hare, were in blue georgette dresses, ankle length.... The bride was given away by her father, Rev. W.W. Kabane. Her mother was in a sweet blue costume, and she carried flowers.[52]

The announcement is very similar to other wedding notices carried in *Umteteli*. It includes details of who married and what the bride, bridesmaids, and flower girls wore. It reveals the bridal party's careful attention to dress and the matching of color. But the telltale piece is the reference to the bride's attire of "an ice-blue dress." Anyone attending the wedding or reading the account in the paper would have known that Kabane was not a virgin. A collision of elements, including Christian understandings of inappropriate sexuality leading to gendered shaming as well as an association between the press and social legibility, meant that she had to reenact for the world her former failing, in a shade other than white. Likewise, for Annie Tlale, whose wedding announcement describes the bride in a dress of powder blue.

THE AFFECTIVE ECONOMICS OF THE WEDDING

Church weddings of Black Christians depicted respectability and shame both to wedding guests and to wider audiences through wedding notices, but they also performed other roles. On the surface, it might appear as if Black church weddings reflected principally adoption of white practice, including the lure of a consumer culture aimed at weddings. Culture contact and other models that view weddings as mimicry of European style are only partially correct in their assessments.[53] Weddings were not just about cultural homogenization or appropriation. Commodity capitalism did not produce unthinking subjects.[54]

If weddings had a social life that took them tripping through the pages of South Africa's Black press, their gait had slowed by the time they were deliberated upon in church records and mission periodicals. These records include the diocesan records, the minutes of presbyteries, and the proceedings of inter-Christian groups like the Ciskeian and Transkeian Missionary Councils (regional mission bodies in the Eastern Cape) and the General Missionary Council of South Africa, whose deliberations were often reprinted in Black newspapers. Commentary on the extravagance and cost of Christian weddings was frequent and similar enough to mark a trend in Christian liberal deliberation.

The church records have certain features in common. They are particularly clear in their commentary on the expense of church weddings. This thread of discussion, hinted at before 1900, had become common by the period just after World War I and was frequent even two decades after World War II. In 1895, John Knox Bokwe, father of Roseberry, married Maria Sopotela at Emgwali in the Eastern Cape. The Reverend Isaac Wauchope, one of the guests, was grudgingly approving of its levels of sartorialism. "The Bridal Dress was quite suitable, grey in colour, attractive without being too costly—only three pounds ten shillings! It can be worn for many years to come. This is not the kind of dress that costs seven to ten pounds and can be worn for only one day."[55]

Following a 1917 St. John's Diocese investigation into lobola and the cost of church weddings, the committee delivered a rather scathing commentary condemning its own congregants' weddings. According to findings, grooms incurred a minimum expense of sixteen to twenty-three pounds, fathers from thirty to forty pounds. The maximum expense totaled thirty-five pounds for the groom and seventy pounds for the father. The committee resolved the following:

> 4. All agree that too much is spent and that rivalry is very largely at the root of this extravagance. 5. It is generally thought that the fathers are themselves opposed to such expense but are urged on by wives and daughters. It is thought fathers would welcome help to reduce the expense. 6. All are agreed that the results of such a standard of expense are disastrous and lead to the avoidance of Christian marriage either by ukutwala or by going to office.[56]

An ostensible worry for cost as a disincentive to church marriage disguised a deeper concern, not only about expense but about excess and extravagance. The Transkeian Missionary Conference of 1930, dominated by its white members, also investigated what it viewed as needless expense at weddings and the feasts and parties that followed. In 1938, the same issue preoccupied lay workers and clergy at the real St. Cuthbert's, where the fictitious Chief Zwelinzima and Thembeka got married.[57]

Commentary on the expense of church weddings for Black South Africans reveals several fault lines present in Black intimate life. The commentary was dually gendered in that, firstly, women more often than men were blamed for the excess present in weddings, and secondly, this was largely a masculine commentary. That is, this commentary was gendered and emanated from men.

However, comments about extravagance were about not only gender but also race. The St. John's committee compared African Christian weddings explicitly to the quieter, less expensive ones of Europeans. A frequent judgment from the period was that African weddings were not just expensive, though, but too expensive. However, white women wore gowns as elaborate as any I have seen described in the Black press, and their wedding notices outline elaborate festivities. The racist assumptions behind this become clear in a 1917 article on economic difficulties in the Transkei. "Consider extravagances: remember you are dealing with a semi savage people in whom rivalry in outward display is a dominant passion; remember too, that they are just beginning to go into towns and see white men's dress and customs, and you will realize that almost inevitably they fall into childish and wasteful aping of the European. Marriage feasts, wedding cakes—the bride's people have one so the bridegroom's must do ditto—rings etc. Brides, whose father and mother were red Kafirs ten years ago, appear in full wedding costume."[58]

The article, evidently about the problems for Africans caused by an increased cost of living and a diminishing earning capacity, is a thinly veiled criticism of Xhosa families following white custom in organizing their weddings. Comments about extravagance mix with comments about the childish nature of Black people and their unsophisticated and primitive mimicry of whites. White Zimbabweans made similar comments about Black Zimbabweans dressing in European style.[59] Ross discusses the existence of "private sumptuary laws" in relation to converts as the same tendencies in effect in how German missionaries working in the Transvaal in the late nineteenth century objected to their female converts wearing crinolines.[60] Many of these practices were about maintaining a suitable social distance between the Black and white communities: weddings, so obviously about social and biological reproduction, challenged the white maintenance of these boundaries.

But there is a further point to make about extravagant weddings. While missionary comments about extravagance may have been motivated by anxiety over racial boundaries, contemporary ethnographies from the period around World War II were also remarking upon extravagant weddings. According to Levin, weddings reflected as much "exhibition and display as possible."[61] Longmore came to the same assessment.[62] Certainly, some weddings were extravagant, but there is a difference between extravagance for those like the Bokwe family, who could afford it, and those who could not.

Black weddings could be and often were costly. According to Monica Hunter's writing, at the end of the 1920s, Christian weddings could cost a family of relatively little means up to £40, sending the family into debt.[63] Krige commented specifically on the cost of weddings (£20) versus average monthly wages (£3) in 1936.[64] From data gathered by Levin in the 1940s, a bride's outfit could cost approximately £23, with a total wedding cost of approximately £110.[65] She qualified this by noting that these weddings were exceptional. According to Longmore, Johannesburg weddings cost up to £105 in the 1950s.[66] All agree that weddings were disproportionately expensive compared to income and savings.

There is both a realistic and poignant quality to this fact. As a result of war conditions, by the 1940s the Black middle class was in a temporary respite from the downward economic pull of the previous two decades. During the 1920s and 1930s, as several researchers have noted, a deterioration of living standards had occurred in educated Black South Africans, especially "respectable" Christians.[67] While most work has concentrated on urban areas, the case was no less so for rural South Africa and the Christian peasant class. In the reserves, a combination of government taxes and white farming monopolies made it difficult for Black entrepreneurs to build capital or to maintain a middle-class lifestyle. Black South Africans who earned regular wages and who had been able to afford furniture, dresses, and other kinds of goods for sale in trading stores and urban retailers were finding it very difficult to make ends meet, and debt-free families had become saddled with debt by the late 1930s. African purchasing power had declined substantially over the 1910s and 1920s so that weddings were not only expensive in absolute terms but also were becoming more expensive relative to other costs.[68]

Church weddings, however, did not reckon their costs and advantages only in terms of cash. At the Conference on African Family Life, convened in 1940 by the Christian Council of South Africa in Pretoria, Black and white delegates all stressed the possibility of and the dangers surrounding the disintegration of African family life. This was a moral assessment but also a real one, as families were split apart by migrant labor and as support in kinship and mutuality floundered in the face of increasing hardship. The delegates to the conference identified poverty as the main cause of this disintegration; ironically, their proximity to how Christianity and Christian morality had facilitated a refashioned Black intimacy prevented them from recognizing their role in precipitating the situation.[69] African families themselves were keenly aware of the threat to family life posed by segregationist rule. Mothers especially went to great lengths to hold their families together because of this threat.[70]

I want to suggest that weddings were also an attempt not only to hold on to family life but also to publicize its continued importance. Ultimately, these efforts were not successful, as the work of Mark Hunter and others on declining marriage rates after the 1950s makes clear.[71] Formerly, families had been linked together through marriages. In twentieth-century consumer capitalism, weddings began to assume some of this function within a Christian-influenced associational context. Further, weddings built social relationships that went beyond the families.

There are several indicators that weddings maintained and expanded their function in bringing people together. These are more extensive than (but did not exclude) lobola. They also show how people were starting to move outside the limits of the family to create social capital. The kinds of functions and roles allocated to family members in traditional weddings found their way into church weddings, often under new names, like "groom's man."

Levin tabulated the costs associated with several weddings, listing the item and cost against members of the bridal party. The bridesmaid chosen by the bride was outfitted by the bride's brothers, while the groom was responsible for one of the wedding cakes (there were two) and the bride's bouquet. The bride's brothers were further responsible for items such as "two sheep, 3.18.0" and "one tin of custard, -.2.6." For the photographs, the groom paid £4.10.0.[72]

The wedding dress itself was part of a complicated process of reciprocity involving gifts on the groom's part. The fabric for the wedding dress was part of the groom's gifts to the bride's family and might be purchased while the wedding cattle were still in the process of transfer and before the wedding ceremony had taken place, even a wedding in church. In an Eastern Cape civil case brought for restitution of costs expended for an absent bride in 1921, Richard Mnci described how he had paid for his intended's wedding clothes: "I actually handed the wedding outfit over to defendant. I went from Kings with defdt's wife. Defdt said I must get a dress maker. The dressmaker I found one Maude. I paid £3–10 to make the dresses. I paid this when the work was completed at my kraal. This dressmaker lives in Mejeni's Location. It took Maude three days to make the dresses."[73]

Weddings and Status, Consumption and Reciprocity

In 1937, the women's pages of *Umteteli,* following European practice, gave this wedding advice: "The bride's parents pay for the reception, catering, wedding cake, floral decorations and car to take the bride and her parents to the church. The bridegroom gives the bride and bridesmaid gifts and their wedding bouquets, he pays the fees of the clergyman, organist etc., and the car that conveys him and his wife from the church."[74] The same year, *Bantu World* carried an article on "How to Plan a Happy Wedding." "The bride is expected to arrange for her own wedding dress and for the frocks of the bridesmaids. If the bride intends, as in the Scottish custom, to pay for her bridesmaids' apparel, she may choose what style and colour she prefers, but as is more often the case, if the bridesmaids pay for their own frocks, it is only fair that their choice is considered."[75] These "sensible hints from their European contemporaries," the column reprinted from the *Star* newspaper, was very different from the practice outlined in *Umteteli,* where a complicated—to an external eye—formula, a form readily comprehensible to those part of the process, dictated who would pay for the bridesmaids' dresses. It is worth examining this idea in more detail since it speaks to what I call an "affective economy of weddings."

Gift giving, outlined in descriptions from the nineteenth century, was a critical part of traditional marriages. The giving of gifts, indeed, marked out changes in people's status across their lives, and ritual exchanges were a regular feature of precolonial life. As people converted to Christianity and began to marry in church, they carried elaborate codes of gift giving into these new contexts. Among Zulu and Xhosa speakers, brides still moved to their husband's family home and women still took gifts to their new homesteads. From the nineteenth century, whatever their religious practices, brides already had gifted their husband's mother blankets, iron pots, cups, and saucers.[76] Husbands had gifted their wife bolts of fabric and their wife's mother similarly.

It is easy to overlook some of the continuities that characterized traditional and modern weddings. Part of the reason lies in a different temporality. Processes of exchange that were drawn out in traditional weddings became more concentrated over time in the white wedding. Moreover—and I am generalizing here about a pattern that took shape over several decades from the nineteenth to the twentieth century—the ritual value of a gift was added to by a value linked directly to the nature of the gift as a commodity. Wedding costs expanded to include new, essential items, like photographs and tins of custard, which were allocated to different relatives and friends according to a grammar of roles reminiscent of traditional practices but now also reflecting spending ability. Witness the husband, now an independent financial entity, paying for wedding photographs and paying for items for members of the bride's entourage.

Too much of a focus on commodification obscures some of these equivalencies. African Christians were using the form of the church wedding to continue with older marriage-related patterns of reciprocity. This is obvious when considering practices like lobola. Observations about the changed—and commodified—nature of lobola are common in ethnographical work, but change in the associated reciprocal giving at marriages is seldom highlighted.

Moreover, gift exchanges like this included not only family but friends and other contacts linked as a result of holding a role other than kin. If lobola joined families, gifts joined friends and members of the same church groups. This is what Mark Leone refers to as the "recursive nature" of material culture, where artifacts substantiate, verify, and reproduce the social processes that led to their being.[77] The institutional thickness of the church facilitated this. For instance, women in the same church joined clubs whose members committed to buying gifts for each other's daughters when they married.[78]

I mentioned previously the Tshange-Gumede wedding and the gifts joining their union. In 1922, the Msengana-Maqanda wedding report began as follows: "Miss Pikoli, 2 pictures, Mr [and] Mrs Tshula, 2 glass tumblers, Mrs Lekoma, 2 cups & saucers, Miss Poyana, 2 cups . . ." At the end of the report, the amounts of money that people had given to the couple were also itemized: "Imali:—Mrs Mjoji, 2/6, Mr. S. Jakatyana, 2/6, Mr. J. Makoni, 3/-."[79] Most of the Msengana-Maqanda presents were crockery or housewares. Two-thirds of their wedding notice consisted of the names of those who gave presents and what they gave. By the 1930s, gift giving was different and extended beyond the family. Barbara Cooper's studies on marriage gift exchange in Niger, also in the first half of the twentieth century, shows how such exchanges created ties of reciprocity between those giving each other gifts.[80] Groups and associations, many of them linked to church or school networks, also took part in gift giving. For example, The Prospect Tennis Club gave glass vases to the Tshange-Gumede union.

Following this logic, dresses, cakes, and the car to transport the couple from one wedding venue to another were part of a reconfigured relational economy, instantiated through an exchange of consumer items linked to a nuptial commodity economy. Weddings were spaces where married couples and their families created ties with other families and the associations that Africans belonged to—a practice analogous to that of the past but also one speaking to the reconfigured realities of an African family life under fissiparous circumstances, where the growing importance of friends joined the importance of families.

Weddings were important occasions, the sum of their parts reflecting a greater whole. They were rituals that highlighted and reflected, were both constitutive of and brought about by, the social aspirations and limitations of Black middle-class society. They speak to an economy of affect tying people and things, Christianity, gender, and racial politics together in the South Africa of the 1920s and 1930s.

Christian weddings can be read in different ways. Firstly, it is important to remember that weddings were occasions for festivity. They were opportunities for people, especially the bridal couple, to dress up and to celebrate with their family and friends. But weddings also point to the growing power of commodities to shape people's lives, even if in ways unanticipated. Weddings involved a range of goods and services that reflected an orientation toward a capitalist economy. But they also shed light on the changing meaning of wedding-exchange practices as Black South African Christians worked to incorporate older forms and rituals into the new marriages they contracted. They held on to rituals, which constituted family and kinship through the medium of the commoditized church spectacle. This occurred not only through the distribution of wedding costs but also through gift giving, which created social capital among those participating.

Families also used church weddings to mark and create social position in the literate Christian world that the church wedding referenced. This occurred across a range of spaces: between families, within the social context of the church, within Black society more broadly, and also within the liberal white and church-related spaces of South Africa, which provided one of the few opportunities for Black and white individuals to meet as equals. Because of these many connections, a family's status could be correlated to the kind of wedding it held.

But there is also another way, a disjuncture, in the social work performed by weddings. Wedding dresses conveyed a range of meaning, a concept that cannot necessarily be aggregated. A white dress referenced the reification of sexual purity in a convention that had no direct traditional analog, because transgression of sexual morality before the arrival of Christianity had a preceding set of resolutions. A nonwhite wedding dress did not mark the start of a process of reparations but rather proclaimed itself as a public statement of shame. Black intimacy, as it evolved in the early twentieth century, included ideas about shame and public enactments of sexual double standards that had not previously attached to women in the same way.

6 ~ Polygamy, Multiple Conjugality, and Masihlalisane

"I am now two months with child," Mbata blurted out one day. With her pregnancy Mbata abruptly changed to moods of constant irritation and hatred. "He does this for you, and that for you, and what does he do for me?" There was not a day that she did not complain to Christina. "He does not care for me or my child that is to come. He thinks only of you." The other wives would egg Mbata on. Solomon's hut, which had been a haven of love and harmony, became a place in which Christina moved with lips tightly set, and ears pretending not to hear.... The King saw neither treachery nor meanness in her face. He had noted the sullen faces of the others and he was aware that all was not well between his wives, but he thought it was some passing trivia that would adjust itself.[1]

IN 1915, Christina Sibiya became the first of several wives of Solomon kaDinuzulu, the Zulu king from 1913 to 1933. She shared her life history with Rebecca Reyher in 1934. In it she described her relationship with Solomon kaDinuzulu and his other wives, his problematic sexuality, and her attempts to maintain her independence, first within the royal household, and later, on her own after leaving her husband.[2] Fascinating at many levels, Christina Sibiya's account touches this chapter and this book in several ways. Both her father and her husband flirted with Christianity, but this did not detract from their practice of polygamy. Her father, Hezekiah, had married her mother, Elizabeth, in the church but had subsequently—around 1908—decided to marry two other wives. Elizabeth remained with her children on a mission station when Hezekiah moved away leaving behind his "fowl, goats, and cattle, leaving the cattle kraal to stand empty and grow dry."[3]

Christina Sibiya's story is one of very few to describe both the benefits and challenges of being a wife in a polygamous relationship, as the opening quotation to this chapter conveys. The Zulu king, notionally an Anglican, maintained several wives over the course of his life. When Christina left Solomon kaDinuzulu, she separated herself from the benefits and status attached to being a married woman and experienced the consequences of being a wife set aside, difficulties that attracted much Christian concern. Not only that, but as Marcia Wright notes, Christina Sibiya's position "as a separated woman was equivocal at best": she had to maintain herself and her children mostly without assistance from their father, and her unmarried status often needed explanation for her to avoid accusations of "promiscuity"—a kind of sexual double standard that was ascribed to African women who wished to be on their own.[4] And, irrefutably, letters as textuality—as consequential tissues of words—wind their way through Christina Sibiya and Solomon kaDinuzulu's relationship. He wrote letters to her during their courtship, and later he had a secretary carry out his correspondence for him. Critically, Christina Sibiya's testimony to the 1945 Commission on Zulu Succession included reference to a letter as proof of Solomon's wish that her son succeed as king rather than one of his other sons.[5] Virtually the only aspect of this chapter not covered in Christina Sibiya's account is the theme of multiple relationships I refer to in the third part of this chapter.

History, as an academic discipline, does not often put its acts of introspection onto the page that is held by the reader. I deliberately chose to begin this chapter with an epigraph about polygamy that was written by a woman. There are relatively few public spaces where it is possible to uncover the thoughts and feelings of women in polygamous relationships.[6] In its nonacademic life it is, overwhelmingly, a subject written about by men describing the sutures between masculinity and polygamy. Polygyny (decidedly not polyandry) is still both something that people say they practice and a subject of intense public interest. It was important to begin this chapter with Christina Sibiya's account of how different women experienced a polygamous marriage, as an antidote to what follows.

This chapter has three parts. In the first (drawing on the historical reflection of polygamy and its status as a subject of research), I chronicle historical and mission understandings of polygamy, including how African clergy viewed and reacted to the phenomenon of what they understood to be polygamy over a period when Christianity spread and gained credibility as a faith for the twentieth century. In the second, I look to the public life of polygamy represented in church documents and minutes, in public writing, and in the various deliberations on African marriage that formed part of the international ecumenical movement before the pivotal conference at Tambaram in 1938. Perhaps the most intriguing aspect of polygamy's public life is that—for South African Christians and other South African publics—it resembled a storm in a teacup. In all the ink devoted to the evils of polygamy there is little awareness that over the first half of the twentieth century the incidence of polygamy among Black South Africans was low and becoming a less frequent form of marriage.

But as polygamy as a marriage choice was decreasing, multiple-partner relationships in some ways analogous to polygamy were increasing. In the final section of the chapter, I bring polygamy into conversation with other forms of multiple relationships, both those referred to as *vat en sit* or *masihlalisane* (the first is Afrikaans and the second isiZulu, with both roughly meaning "living together").[7] One of the most extensive shifts in Black intimate practices in the twentieth century, detectable by roughly 1925, relates to the proliferation not only of informal unions between men and women but of different forms of multiple-partner relationships. These arrangements were neither necessarily sanctioned nor legitimated by traditional practice or Christianity but nevertheless bore the deep imprint of both. Moreover, interesting similarities exist between these largely urban relationships, which have never been considered as equivalent to polygamy, and shifts within what people refer to as polygamy. In early twenty-first-century South Africa, for instance, when people refer to polygamous marriages, they describe multiple coexisting relationships that do not necessarily involve lobola; this description is remarkably similar to what has been described for masihlalisane. In the reality television show *Mnakwethu* (I watched all the episodes in the first season), billed as a foray into contemporary polygamy, little distinguishes the relationships described as polygamous from those described as vat en sit.[8] Moreover, both relationship styles include rituals, practices, and self-declared beliefs and show ideas about how Christianity as much as assertions about the importance of tradition play a role in defining the practices of intimacy in these relationships.

CHRISTIAN RESPONSES TO POLYGAMY

Polygamy's imprimatur is throughout the late nineteenth- and much of the twentieth-century European chronicling of African history. For some, polygamy was evidence of African sexual exoticism and social depravity, a shorthand for an unconfined and improper male sexuality. For others, it represented the sexual slavery of women. And for many, it was both. The 1910 Edinburgh Missionary Conference, which marked the start of a Protestant twentieth-century global ecumenical effort, described it as "simply one of the gross evils of heathen society which, like habitual murder or slavery, must at all costs be ended."[9] Researchers in the 1950s described it as the distinguishing feature of African marriage. "If . . . we seek to identify the main distinguishing features of African customary marriage, as compared to 'European marriage', there will no doubt be general agreement that the most obvious of such features is the toleration, and even approval accorded to polygamy."[10]

In the 1950s, the *Survey of African Marriage and Family Life* collated observations on the extent of polygamy on the continent. These reflect a higher incidence in West and East Africa than in southern Africa. A 1909 count showed that 50 percent of Ashanti men had more than one wife, though generally, these were only senior men and chiefs. In 1934 Central Africa, the figure was 4 percent.[11] In South Africa, the incidence of polygamy in the region was low, both in comparison to the rest of the continent and to the previous century.[12]

In the later twentieth century, polygamy is noted approvingly as a functionalist and African solution to contraception and population limitation.[13] John Iliffe, in *Africans: A History of the Continent*, identifies it on page 1 as the quintessential African strategy for maximizing fertility, fueling his assertion that generational conflict is more important than class conflict in African history.[14] In a different direction, T. J. Tallie's excellent analysis of the queering logic of polygamy in colonial KwaZulu-Natal begins with the 2010 British reception of the much-married Jacob Zuma, where the media represented the ruling statesman as a buffoon and a sex-obsessed bigot.[15]

Current academic writing generally presents polygamy as a practice in decline, certainly not ever reaching in the twentieth century the extent its titillated and horrified public envisaged for it. Peter Delius and Clive Glaser note its relatively low incidence during the precolonial period, followed by a decline in the late nineteenth century. Their work centers on examining and refuting, through a study of extramarital sex, "a close connection between the tradition of polygamy and contemporary male 'promiscuity.'"[16] For Delius and Glaser, like others, polygamy's significance lies in its relationship to sexual activity rather than marriage, which overlooks its potential complexity.

Generally, it is possible to distinguish two forms of polygamy, though they are not mutually exclusive. The first includes relationships that Europeans would not necessarily understand as typically conjugal: not all polygamous relationships involved sex, for instance.[17] These were the kinds of relationships contracted by big men—chiefs and others who wanted to cement relationships across political units. A big man's wives might not all be intimate partners. Wives who occasionally were intimate partners might spend large periods of time away from their husbands. Christina Sibiya's narrative is full of comings and goings as Solomon moved between his various residences. By the 1930s, this distinction was apparent to mission societies working in Africa, and African Christian deliberations often centered on the status of polygamous wives past the age of childbearing, who were assumed to be no longer intimate with their husbands.

Overlapping with this style of polygamy were the relationships of more ordinary men, who contracted multiple, colocated marriages in which wives lived alongside each other in homesteads and together provided productive labor to the household. This style of polygamy was geared toward the rural economy and was more characteristic of South Africa toward the end of the nineteenth century. Joan Broster described rural marriages of this nature as not exceeding 20 percent in the 1950s, from her observations of a largely unconverted community in the Transkei.[18]

A history of polygamy in Africa that charts its incidence is one thing, the history of the representation of polygamy in European thinking is another, while how theologians understood polygamy is a third. The British construction of polygamy as a subject of concern was to have far-reaching effects on how first-generation African converts understood both their faith and their conjugal lives and also on how colonial forces and interests constructed their ideas about African marriage. By the mid-nineteenth century, the rise of public philanthropy in Britain had placed ideas about polygamy front and center in popular imaginings of how to effect the redemption of Africa.[19] European and North American reading audiences understood that civilization and Christianity were twin forces separating them from what was no longer the unknown at the edge of the map but the unknown present in the lands under and on the fringes of their own dominion. Copious public ink was drafted into service to confirm to European nations the superiority of their own nationhood. Polygamy was a one-word answer to what was wrong with the parts of the world that had not embraced, thoroughly and for a goodly length of time, Christianity. Beginning around 1850 and reaching its height by the 1870s, Victorian newspapers and periodicals fed a steady diet of "news" about the pernicious effects of polygamy to an ever-widening reading public.

Almost invariably, when people wrote about polygamy, they based their accounts on three locations: British possessions in India, where polygamy was a feature of Islam; the Mormon settlement in Utah after 1848; and Africa, the most barbaric instance of these three locations.[20] In all instances, the practice of polygamy fed into discourses around female subjugation and comparisons between polygamy and slavery for women. Polygamy in Africa had the additional titillating effect (for European audiences) of association with African male hypersexuality. The pages of ladies' periodicals and missionary magazines were replete with accounts of polygamy, chronicling female slavery and the inferior position of the African woman as a measure of the backwardness of the unconverted African mass. Without the inconvenience of actually having to meet a polygamist or his wives, European publications commented at length on the incontinent African patriarch and the subjugated African woman.

Much of the outrage around polygamy was fed through a common view of what constituted civilized behavior and European superiority over Africa. Theologically, though, the issue was more complicated. Polygamy transgressed Protestant theology and practice at several levels. During the nineteenth century, Western-rooted ideas about marriage were changing, one of the most crucial reflected in the shift from marriage as a sacrament to marriage as companionship. Nevertheless, for devout Christians, the sacrament of marriage, like baptism and Communion, still resembled the rituals incorporated during the early modern period.[21] Further, what people thought about polygamy was complicated by what they thought about divorce. Middle-class parlors in Britain, the heart of the British voluntary impulse, were not often the site of the difficult choices that came from being caught between the devil of polygamy and the deep blue sea of divorce. However, missionaries working on stations isolated from other European contact in places like colonial Natal faced this conundrum much more frequently than they encountered middle-class sitting rooms.

The conjugally derived family had central importance in the Christianity of Anglican Bishop of Natal John Colenso.[22] Colenso's 1855 *Remarks on the Proper Treatment of Cases of Polygamy, as Found Already Existing in Converts from Heathenism* reserved his greatest ire for divorce following a marriage contracted via holy sacrament. According to Colenso, "It is the *putting* away of one wife to marry another—the more usual and economical way of practising polygamy—it is this, which is condemned by Him."[23] When Magema Fuze converted to Christianity under the tutelage of Colenso, he retained all his wives.[24] Fuze, a Kholwa intellectual, was among the most well-known figures of an early generation of Zulu converts, later writing extensively in *Ilanga lase Natal*. Colenso's unease around advocating divorce to eradicate polygamy found an echo in other mission and Christian communities in Africa.[25] In fact, Colenso's position (his complex argument reduced to support for polygamy) became a lodestar for Anglican and African communities across the continent who wished to argue theological justification for polygamy.[26]

Between the time Colenso wrote his words quoted in the previous paragraph and the start of the twentieth century, advising converts on how to manage their polygamous relationships was a much larger issue because of both the proliferation of mission activity in South Africa and the rising numbers of converts. Most missions required a polygamist to "put away all his wives except one" after conversion.[27] Polygamy was an unambiguous evil, but a secondary evil lay in the consequences of the dissolution of marriage. The Scylla of polygamy and the Charybdis of divorce resulted in a fair amount of theological hair splitting. "I am thankful to say that our position was sustained at Lambeth. . . . Men with more than one wife cannot be baptised—but that wives may—We will not admit the polygamist to the official position of Catechumen though of course we will teach in the preliminary class all who wish to be taught anything. As to wives—We do not find here anything to mark out one wife's position as sufficiently distinct from that of others for us to choose between them."[28]

It is difficult to convey how much European—and later African Christians—were troubled by polygamous marriages and which wives a polygamist should renounce, not only in respect of their own congregants but also in relation to broader church issues. Church attitudes were also complicated by white settlers' attacks on Colenso's position, many of them published in the colonial press, as well as white outrage at a supposed rash of attacks by Black men on white women. As Jeremy Martens has shown, the colonial press in the 1860s drew links between polygamy, a lack of wives, and the sexual unfulfillment of younger Black men.[29]

The issue was debated at the level of individual congregations; within the hierarchy of individual denominations; in intradenominational and interdenominational communications and forums; at gatherings representing churchmen and colonial officials; at gatherings and conferences between supranational Protestant coalitions and the Catholic Church; and at every major international Christian gathering from 1910 to 1938, as well as beyond into recent ecclesiastical history.

The Edinburgh World Missionary Conference in 1910, as noted previously, was strongly opposed to the practice: "Every Mission within our review refuses admission to the Church in Africa to any man who is actually living with more than one wife."[30] This unanimity among missions was rare, offering a stark contrast to the different shades of opinion that enveloped lobola and initiation.[31] No Africans attended the Edinburgh Conference.

Notwithstanding the Edinburgh position, itself theologically predictable, all the discussion circled uneasily around only one ultimately insoluble question: Which wife or wives ought a man to repudiate—those less senior, those married later, those past childbearing age? In a rare act of theological munificence, sometimes the churchmen at the conference debated whether the choice ought to be left to the man contemplating conversion. In the early twentieth century, a historical moment that thought differently about religious belief and its value and took seriously marriage as a sacrament, advocating the breakup of a marriage—even a polygamous one—was unconscionable for many Christians, irrespective of their skin color. Further, the discomfort of Western Protestants at the theological paradox offered by polygamously married Africans was compounded by social conscience. Some of the churchmen who worked with African converts were genuinely concerned about the fate of so-called discarded wives.

Of course, though, the difficulties experienced by converts wishing to convert were a more significant issue than the confusion of Western churchmen. Converts who desired to be baptized into full church membership could not be baptized before they had brought their marital unions into monogamous conformity. This had potentially greater consequences for women than for men. Women who wished to convert had few real choices. If they abandoned their husbands, severing themselves from both their kin of origin and the families they joined upon marriage, they became socially equivalent to prostitutes. At the same time, they still had to find ways to maintain themselves economically, much as Christina Sibiya experienced. Polygamy could and did create miserable conditions for junior wives in a marriage, but even fewer resources were accessible by a discarded wife.

As just described, polygamy was an issue for those contemplating conversion, but the real challenge for polygamy and Christianity in Africa lay in the polygamous recidivism of the postconverted. Phillips outlined this distinction well, identifying a difference "where a person is already, at the time of conversion, a party to a polygamous union; and where a person who is already a professing Christian commits the offense of contracting a polygamous union."[32] The latter category is what Adrian Hastings identifies as a "long-term post-baptismal problem as polygamy re-emerged within the ranks of otherwise committed Christians."[33]

While Hastings views this mostly as a problem for second-generation Christians, and this is well documented in large parts of Africa, it was also a problem for first-generation Christians. In Paulina Dlamini's recollections of spending time on the mission at Lemgo in northern KwaZulu-Natal, where she worked as an evangelist in the 1920s, she describes an encounter with Ben Sibisi, "who after his conversion to Christianity, took a second wife and as a result came under church discipline." Sibisi, on his deathbed, repented of his sins. "He called his family together, including his second wife and, much to her consternation, he renounced his polygamous marriage."[34] Like most women in her position, Ben Sibisi's unnamed second spouse had no choice in being made a discarded wife.

POLYGAMY AND THE TRANSNATIONAL IMAGINATION

In the period between the end of the South African War and Union, as administrators and politicians grappled with how to rule a future South Africa, one step was the convening of a commission into "native affairs" and administration, the South African Native Affairs Commission 1903–5 (SANAC). Saul Dubow and others have discussed how many of the practices and ideas that went into the creation of segregation were first discussed at SANAC, as bureaucrats and administrators from the four colonies debated ways to rule Africans in a future South Africa.[35] Part of the commission's remit was to investigate African customary law, with a view to incorporating it into the South African system as part of a legal pluralism. SANAC collected evidence from across the region, including from chiefs and headmen. Its questioning, intended to elicit information on African administration, also collected information on practices like polygamy. In fact, it included extensive questioning on polygamy, lobola, and the registration of customary marriages.[36] In pronouncing upon the issue of polygamy, the commission found that

> On analysis, the objections resolve themselves into the undeniable charge that the custom is essentially material and unchristian. The Commission has no wish to defend it and looks forward to the time when it shall have passed into oblivion. But no attempt to Christianise the heathen by compulsory legislation can be advised. To destroy the remnants of a recognised and in the temporal sense a healthy polygamous system without having the power to check the licentious inclinations by which it is still sustained, or to extinguish the influence of the traditional associations which cling around it, might lead to a last state far worse than the first; and, seeing that all the signs of the times point to the steady decadence of polygamy, the Commission is of opinion not only that sufficient need for legislative intervention has not been established, but that in all the circumstances such intervention would be unwise and more harmful in its effects than the dying evil it sought prematurely to demolish.[37]

Although the commission decided not to interfere with polygamy, its workings helped to establish the practice both as un-Christian and as an object of public interest. As a result, Christian ideas about polygamy acted as a constitutive force on the ideas both Black and white South Africans had about marriage. Most white magistrates and lawyers working outside of South Africa's urban areas would have applied an understanding that assumed all customary marriages had the potential to become polygamous. The laws governing succession in customary marriages for men who had only one wife were the same as those for men who had several wives. It is the greatest irony that the white legal profession, influenced by a legal discourse that found polygamy profoundly distasteful, in fact, legislated its continued legal existence.

In the early twentieth century, according to many white South Africans, apart from the rather unlikely phenomenon of the never-married African, any marriage that was not demonstrably monogamous had the potential to be polygamous. In 1910, Chief Justice Innes of the Transvaal Supreme Court made this quite clear, in what Martin Chanock describes as the case with the period's most racist outcome. "But it appears to me the better principal that when a man marries under a system which allows polygamy, his marriage is polygamous, and therefore not recognised by this Court, whether he is married to one wife or two."[38] Sixty years later, as noted by Jack Simons, this was still the position. "The common law courts refuse to acknowledge that tribal marriage is a legally binding relationship because they say, it is potentially, if not actually, polygynous."[39]

Polygamy's Christian Publics

In 1903, and again in 1911, the Anglican Church collected views and pronounced upon a practice visibly undergoing change.[40] Driven by a concern to determine whether the different Anglican mission bodies could unite in their positions on polygamy, the church conducted surveys asking questions about which wife a polygamist ought to dispense with; whether he could dispense with all his wives and marry a new one in Christ; whether a great wife (the first or principal wife) beyond childbearing age ought to be retained; and whether a man ought to wait until all but one of his wives had died before he sought baptism.

A range of questions also addressed the obligations of wives: Could wives decide among themselves who should stay and who should go? Would wives who had been given up become sexually promiscuous ("tempted into sin")—to which the unanimous answer of Black and white Christian clergy and magistrates was yes—and did a polygamist have a moral right to leave his wives if they objected to being discarded?[41] Already, in 1903, the questions showed awareness of the new kinds of polygamous relationships.

While all the mainline churches working in South Africa used polygamy as a criterion to judge access to baptism, the Anglicans were the most assiduous in attempting to effect and standardize church policy on polygamy. Anglican deliberations in this respect reflected the hold of the greater

Anglican Church on African policy and the efficiency of its institutional apparatus in facilitating exchange between its doctrinal center at Lambeth and its global foothold throughout its various provinces.

In another Anglican questionnaire completed between 1908 and 1911, directed this time at all mission denominations, the questions were similar and focused still on the perception that polygamy was a phenomenon present only in rurally located and physically contiguous households. None of the denominations presented a uniform position. For example, twenty-six Methodist circuits responded that a man ought to choose which wife he wanted to retain, while forty-seven stipulated that he ought to choose the wife first married.[42] The Anglican pronouncements on the subject, also reflecting the views of the other mainline churches, spoke to a range of anxieties as much about race as religion.

Taken in conjunction with SANAC's position, the continued attempts in the period before World War I to put the issue to bed reveal polygamy's status as a surface wound on the body politic of South African morality. Even though the practice was a comparatively minor issue, it had a distinctive social footprint. Moreover, compared to some other concerns that rose to the status of national sexual anxiety, polygamy and its practice were indisputably real and—as both the Anglican community's anger at Colenso's support for polygamy, and the linking of rape and polygamy in the Natal press show—it already had a history linked to national sexual anxiety.[43] Black and white Christians alike considered polygamy morally reprehensible irrespective of race. However, South African reactions to specifics of the immorality of polygamy were racially affected and differentiated. For instance, most white settlers considered polygamy evidence of uncontrolled lust.

The public comments made by Africans, therefore, including in their institutional and church locations, need to be considered against these different strands of thinking. What emerges is a strange mathematics of morality. The *Christian Express* was horrified in 1913 at a report about the link between monogamy and marital infidelity that appeared in the newspaper *Abantu-Batho*. "There are very few men," wrote *Abantu*, "who have contracted a monogamous marriage who are not guilty of adultery." According to the *Abantu* writers, the high rate of divorce among white South Africans demonstrated that monogamy was "impracticable." "As far as we are concerned, polygamy is the only institution in life which serves as a preventative against the increase of moral sins."[44]

Like all the men who wrote for Black newspapers, the *Abantu* writers, influenced by if not practicing Christianity, had acquired their literacy through mission schools. The comment about polygamy was not an abnegation of moral sin, but it was about placing immorality in a monogamous marriage on one side of the scale and marital fidelity within a polygamous marriage on the other. According to several commentators, sexual promiscuity among the monogamous was more immoral than stability in a polygamous union.

But not all African Christians viewed polygamy the way the writers in *Abantu* did. Its gravity, as T. B. Soga noted, lay in the way it gave reign to "the lust of the flesh." Indeed, Soga, like many others, drew a circular argument between polygamy and sex. In fact, one consequence of Victorian sexual morality for Black South Africans is that it made polygamy partly an issue of sex rather than an issue of status or wealth in people. However, "even today there are polygamists although diminishing, owing to scarcity of cattle." In any case, Soga further observed, polygamy was nonexistent among the educated because "The Tax Laws, and new Marriage Laws which allows a man to marry only one wife classifies all other wives as concubines." In expressing his views, T. B. Soga was reflecting what most of his Christian contemporaries understood about polygamy, which is that it was mostly rurally located and in decline.[45]

Judging by the *Christian Express* reaction to the *Abantu-Batho* piece, the Black commentary about the increasing incidence of white divorce hit a collective white nerve, as if polygamy might cross a racial barrier and infect white South Africans. In this way, discussions about polygamy, at least partly, fed into concerns about a deterioration in white social health as a result of interracial sex.

In addition to race, polygamy was also about belief. Many devout Christians were torn between Colenso's position that previously contracted polygamy was less immoral than divorce and the manifest hardship faced by discarded wives. Polygamy, in this way, was not the same as lobola, according to standards of faith. While lobola was—in terms of its community of practice and the people it united in its net of social motion—a much larger issue, polygamy was a more serious issue. Lobola represented uncivilized behavior, but it did not open a soul up to sin and its consequences in the same way that polygamy did.

Whatever local debate may have said about polygamy, it is important to remember that the size of the issue in South Africa, where the incidence of polygamy was never proportionally high, was much less than that elsewhere in Africa, especially West Africa. West African agitation around polygamy had become clear toward the end of the nineteenth century and, by the 1920s, had formed a key point of contention between African nationalists and the colonial state. In 1918, when the United African Methodist Church formed in Lagos in Nigeria, it recommended there be no discrimination between polygamists and monogamists or between the children born of either polygamous or monogamous unions with respect to baptism. In Nigeria, both educated Africans and many missionaries viewed with approval polygamy's effect on infant health and child spacing through postpartum abstinence from penetrative sex during lactation. The *Times of Nigeria* reflected on this issue in one of its editorials: "Is there anything in the teachings of Christ which forbids polygamy? Did he ever teach anything which would result in race deterioration? ... Do not the missionaries encourage deceit by disregard or ignorance of simple eugenic considerations?"[46] Few mainline Christians in South Africa would have felt comfortable in 1918 expressing these sorts of views openly, although they were common for independent churches like the AmaNazaretha.

The real heart-searching that polygamy prompted in both white clergy and Black converts meant that it had a significant purchase on the national Christian imagination, prompting reflection that occurred both separate from but in tandem with more judicially located conversations about how to legislate African marriage. Polygamy was a minor item on the agenda of the General Missionary Council (GMC) before 1915, but in that year, the conference decided to conduct inquiries into policies for regulating the behavior of church members within the mission and mainline churches. Covering a range of issues in a widely administered questionnaire on the "Uniformity of Discipline," the GMC asked questions about the verses of the Bible and biblical figures that converts quoted in support of polygamy, "David, Abraham, etc," as well as the more critical question about the central necessity of monogamy to Christianity. "Does your experience lead you to conclude that monogamy is an essential condition of social progress ... ?"[47] While the name of the survey reflected the established Christian view that polygamy was a disciplinary issue, the questions asked showed a growing awareness that the repudiation of polygamy had significant social effects. The issue reappeared at almost every subsequent missionary conference (including at a special panel at the sixth GMC in 1925).[48]

These deliberations threw out few solutions, but they did begin to reflect a changing context. The inability of different parishes to respond to instances of polygamy in a uniform manner (there were great differences in position) led the Anglicans in 1926 to propose referring to the diocesan bishop for adjudication all cases where the ruling on the status of a polygamist or his wife was not clear. The rules upheld the predominant view that only men could be polygamists.[49] Moreover, the missionary conference recommended the formation of a "guild for polygamists," where polygamists seeking baptism could meet together, a sort of Christian polygamists' club. This kind of solution reflected an understanding that polygamy was a complex issue, a view much more accommodating than anything that had come of out of the church at the start of the century.

It is possible that Africans' beginning to express their guarded support of polygamy in the Black press contributed to a more generalized relaxation in attitude. As Henry Selby-Msimang explained in an opinion piece in *Umteteli* in 1922, one of the same pieces in which he expounded on lobola, few Black men had ever been able to or could still afford to be married polygamously. His comments echoed those of T. B. Soga and John Dube, editor of *Ilanga lase Natal* and the first president of the ANC: "I am not quite sure that there could be found today more than one out of a hundred among educated Bantu who would dare to marry two wives. The economic pressure which has made monogamy tolerable has made polygamy a thing out of reach."[50] Although Selby-Msimang focused much of his attention on urban social ills, and many of his newspaper contributions concerned the degeneration of African social systems and morality in the country's urban centers, like most of his contemporaries he continued to view polygamy as a phenomenon of the countryside.

If the GMC understood polygamy as an issue of discipline in 1915, ten years later it was clear that polygamy had settled into place as a key feature of a growing transnational Christian focus on the African family. By the 1920s, officials and researchers employed by the International Missionary Council (IMC) and similar bodies in Britain and North America had turned their attention to African marriage, an interest that would only expand over the next fifty years. The South African influence in this grouping was strong; in more recent work, Andrew Bank and others have pointed to the importance of South African anthropology in the international anthropological community in the interwar period.[51] By the late 1930s, Monica Wilson, Hilda Kuper, and Eileen Krige had become regular sources of authority on African cultural practice, including in its shifted urban forms (they were also key sources in Denys Shropshire's African marriage research). The Christian Council of South Africa (CCSA), which succeeded the GMC, regularly quoted their work.[52]

While it is possible to detect in the rather unusual generation of South African female anthropologists a willingness to engage with indigenous African practices on their own terms, an older generation of missionaries remained steadfastly opposed to polygamy. At the special session of the IMC organized in Belgium in 1926 on Christian missions in Africa (the Le Zoute Conference), most attendees cleaved to a more conservative view of ideal

African family life. The bulk of the 250 delegates represented societies based in the US and the UK. Some suggested a compromise between Christianity and custom, but many presented opinions that showed they believed new entrants to the mission field had lost sight of the time-proven approaches of older generations. A general condemnation of polygamy prevailed, though some of the delegates expressed sympathy for women in polygamous relations who wished to convert.

The South African delegation at the conference included representatives of the GMC and also John Dube and Zaccheus Mahabane, who were invited by the IMC as part of its special quota of delegates. Dube was a Congregationalist minister in addition to his other roles, while Mahabane, a Wesleyan minister, was then president of the ANC.[53] Mahabane's public address to the conference addressed what had already become one of the broader points of contention surrounding polygamy: "Western civilisation did not represent Christianity, and so arose in the native mind the inconsistency between the word of the missionary and the life of the irreligious European. This was a stumbling block to Christian progress." Although not in direct support of polygamy, both men advocated a partial acceptance of custom.[54]

Mahabane and Dube, together with other influential African Christians, reflected a guarded and conditional tolerance, just one strand of African thinking concerning polygamy. Another strand, which had more in common with the reactionary views of African culture expressed at Le Zoute, preferred to condemn it outright. But views had become less fixed by the 1930s. With two different but stable sets of opinions on polygamy circulating in ecumenical circles, it is not surprising that polygamy moved into the 1930s as a favorite subject of African debating teams active in South Africa. "Polygamy versus Monogamy" featured on the bill of debating society meetings, like those hosted by the various Gamma Sigma Clubs on the Witwatersrand, including in Johannesburg.[55] Young mission school graduates would happily debate the merits of modern versus traditional marriage, the force of their argument determining the winner of the debate.

This debate carried over into the Black press. In *Umteteli* and *Bantu World*, polygamy was often featured parenthetically in letters to the editor pondering the virtues of marriage. Modern marriage, a "badge of civilisation and Christianity," was compared favorably with the polygamous unions of old.[56] But usually more central to these discussions were unfavorable comparisons of the behavior of men and women in marriage. Men often wrote critically about married women going out to dances, while the fewer women who wrote to newspapers commented upon the lack of respect from their husbands brought about because of the absence of lobola. In most of these letters, polygamy was almost an afterthought—a shorthand for change—addressing the shift from more traditional practices historically located to more modern practices relevant to the present. If only the horrified observers of African polygamy had known how much of a relic it actually was, at least for Black South Africans. In these discussions, which ebbed and flowed through the newspaper pages at regular intervals, people tended to write about polygamy as an example of retrogression and superstition. Moreover, concern over polygamy was usually a subject of the Christian periodicals rather than the mainstream Black press.

Despite the mainline churches' attempts at Le Zoute to reach closure on issues like polygamy, continued discussion of the practice across the African continent, including in letters to newspapers, shows that any appearance of Black and white unanimity on the subject was just that. Certainly, as widely reported in South Africa via *Christian Express* and other publications, Le Zoute had little effect on the ongoing discussion on the matter during the deliberations of the GMC and the CCSA. This irresoluteness continued to be a feature of internal South African debate. The 1937 CCSA debate on the baptism and reception of secondary wives was unable to resolve differences of opinion.[57]

At a ministers' retreat held at Lovedale Bible School in early 1938, in preparation for the following year's IMC conference, the one hundred delegates discussed the Christian home, reflecting on how the topic had been considered at the World Missionary Conference in Edinburgh in 1910 and subsequently.[58] In a rather pithy statement, the CCSA report on the gathering commented on the discussion around polygamy. "The attitude of the Church toward a converted polygamist and his wives was not considered by us, since the view of the different churches varies and the settlement of the issue, if it ever will be settled, would require a treatise in itself."

The following year a report written by a lay correspondent for the CCSA publication, *Et Alias,* discussed the impact that the condemnation of polygamy had on women, realizing that "these women form the backbone of the church."[59] The same report compared practices in the mainline churches to those of the independent churches, suggesting that the mainline churches follow the "separatist" practice of not distinguishing between more and less "moral" converts because of their polygamy.

These views, though, should not necessarily be taken as widespread. For every comment in favor of polygamy, there was at least one against it. Devout Christians felt deeply the importance of cultivating a proper Christian home life, the centerpiece of which was the monogamous and companionate marriage.

By 1939, both these views—that Christianity could not accommodate polygamy and that it should accommodate polygamy—had equal traction in African Christianity. The second view was most famously expressed at the IMC world meeting at Tambaram in India in 1938, where African delegates, especially those from West Africa, asked the larger gathering whether monogamy was central to Christianity or merely a facet of Western civilization.[60]

There is little indication of how Albert Luthuli, S. S. Thema, and Mina Soga spoke to the issue of polygamy at the IMC conference at Madras in 1938, if at all. While delegates from West and East Africa pushed the members of their breakaway session to consider whether polygamy was a bar to conversion, many of the IMC's African supporters felt the conference itself did not go far enough in deliberating the question. The African delegates from the Gold Coast asked directly about the connection between monogamy and a life of faith: the subsequent heart-searching that this question raised presented an unequivocal challenge to polygamy, as evident in the general sentiment of the IMC and its constituents.

In the years after Tambaram, the African Christian lobby in favor of polygamy gained more prominence. Shortly after the meeting, the churches of the Gold Coast called for more discussion.[61] In East Africa, the Methodist Church announced its decision to admit all Christians to Communion, regardless of their status as monogamists or polygamists.[62] In a conference on African marriage called in the wake of Tambaram, the delegates—many of them anthropologists or part of the mission fraternity—addressed the matter with some new concerns. "The relegation of large numbers of women to sexual frustration is an evil of our civilization, an evil against which many women rebel who maintain a women's right to bear children. Under polygamy, African society is free of that evil."[63] This increased concern in Africa is evident in research collected as part of the *Survey of African Marriage and Family Life*, which showed in 1950 no recognizable decline in polygamy among Christians; in fact, it showed quite the opposite.

However, in South Africa, where rural polygamy was on the decline and marriage itself under threat, polygamy ceased to be a major factor of concern for mainline Christian constituencies. At the Conference on African Marriage and Family Life, hosted by the CCSA in Pretoria in June 1940, the focus was on combating the destruction of African family life in urban areas, and polygamy received reflection only in passing.

"IRREGULAR UNIONS" AND A SHIFTED POLYGAMY

In the 1920s and 1930s, public commentary on polygamy largely described it as a moral evil but also considered it a practice in decline. Several of those who wrote about polygamy also wrote about what they variously described as illegitimate and immoral relationships, more specifically the rising incidence of semipermanent relationships between African men and women in South African cities.

These "irregular unions" are detailed in Shropshire's *Primitive Marriage and European Law: A South African Investigation*.[64] "These informal unions sometimes last for years, but they are essentially unstable and often end in the desertion of the woman with children dependent upon her."[65] Shropshire collected his material from most of the anthropologists mentioned in this and other chapters (the only women he spoke to as part of his research), state officials, and senior African men and in so doing replicated either their or his preoccupation with the dissolution of African family life. In the first chapter, titled "Present Urban and Rural Disintegration," he quoted municipal and location officials on the kinds of relationships that existed between African men and women in urban areas. According to the municipal superintendent at Orlando location, "Out of the 200 cases of domestic dispute brought before me during 1939, in 129 cases the persons were merely living together," and the average period of such relationships was two years, "showing the essentially temporary nature of such unions."[66] Shropshire's observations may have been patronizing and sexist, but they were broadly accurate in their description of the proliferating styles of cohabitation.

Over the next forty years (from roughly 1940 until 1980) and until the apartheid state relaxed influx control in its final decade, numerically speaking, polymorphic urban relationships were much more common than polygamous unions. They were also a frequent focus of government reports and sociological and other academic analyses. The emergence of these kinds of relationships is one of the most significant developments in Black intimacy in the post–World War II period. Many of the discussions about new urban relationships were front-loaded by racist understanding that Black family life was in an irretrievable decline, so much so that the stable marital relationship modeled on Christian, heterosexual culture was thought to be the exception rather than the rule. There are some exceptions to this. For instance, Jack Simons's sympathetic portrayal of short-lived urban relationships recognizes that limits to stability arose from external forces, such as forced removals from urban areas or the high rate of mortality for men working underground. By the 1980s, sympathetic discussion of this issue was much more frequent. Mamphela Ramphele, one of South Africa's first Black, female anthropologists, provides an excellent and insightful description of these types of relationships from the late 1980s to the early 1990s in her discussion of hostel life in Cape Town.[67]

These relationships are linked to the inevitable declines in the marriage rate of Black South Africans. Often, what Shropshire and others viewed with disapproval were in fact attempts at living together in ways that existed at the limits of what was possible in urban areas. In a case from Johannesburg in 1939, Kate Dula reported her living arrangements to the Native Affairs Department. Her first husband had died in 1927, after which she took a lover, Phillip Mbomezulu, who stayed with her for four years. When he left, he took their furniture. She was five months pregnant. He also left her with the rent on their joint house, four pounds in arrears.[68] She had applied to the municipal Native Affairs Department for the title on the house and to be allowed to share it with another woman, her anxiety about urban accommodation a result of the Johannesburg policies that linked housing to married status. This account, in its lack of detail, can only hint at the poignancy of her situation and what she must have realized was the futility of attempting to secure the right to occupy a house in her own name. In the same set of reports, a similarly affecting account is given of the occupants of house No. 971. Samuel Legoale had been living in the house for some time, taking only "temporary wives," but at the time of investigation was living with his wife, Maria Mogatini. Unfortunately for the two of them, it turned out that Maria had recently been living with another man at house No. 586, but he had thrown her out. Maria was advised to return with her six children to her father in Rustenberg, and even though she and Samuel declared an intention to marry, both were ordered to vacate the house.

We do not know whether these two couples were married, or whether they planned to marry, as might have been the case with Maria and Samuel. Belinda Bozzoli has noted in her work on female migrant labor that many couples lived together who still planned to get married but had not yet had the opportunity to do so.[69] While the women Bozzoli wrote about were Christian and were concerned about the stigma attached to having children before marriage, the point is that many of these relationships were neither temporary nor unstable, even if they did not include a formal marriage.

In chapters 4 and 5, I wrote about lobola and its continued presence as a feature of Black intimacy, one so widely recognized that lobola's textual life was as extensive as its actual practice. It was widely accepted in Black society that lobola had existed, that it had not disappeared, and that it would continue to exist. This was in contrast to what people thought about masihlalisane, or vat en sit, which they did not recognize as having precedent in polygamy. None of the wide range of people writing about Black intimacy in the 1920s and 1930s would have understood the proliferation of relationships that emerged from the 1920s onward as polygamy. This was despite the fact that many of the relationships described lasted for up to twenty years, spanned city and country, and likely included incomplete attempts to transfer lobola.

Indeed, Philip Mayer is quite clear that masihlalisane was not a form of polygamy. Rural migrants to the cities of the Eastern Cape in the 1950s and 1960s were frequently in long relationships called *ukushweshwa,* or "staying together."[70] "*Ukushweshwa* is on no account to be confused with polygamous secondary marriage," because it involved the establishment of a relationship without the involvement of kin.[71] In contrast, Laura Longmore did consider that cohabiting relationships provided "the mechanism which permits the polygynous tradition to remain a living one," but I have not seen the two practices conflated in other sources.[72]

Mayer's description of ukushweshwa, however, hides as much as it reveals through its overemphasis on the differences between the rural and urban areas, ascribing changes to intimate practices as having occurred in urban areas only. But Black intimate relationships, whether medium-term or long-term, were all experiencing change, irrespective of their location. What the various accounts reveal is a multiplicity of African cohabitation practices that defies description as polygamy, monogamy, or a more casual living together.

In the 1940s, H. I. E. Dhlomo, not usually in favor of independence in women, provided a fairly accurate account of what I have just described: "Some of the younger people who worked in Durban and returned home at weekly, monthly or longer intervals, adhered strictly neither to tribal nor to Christian morals especially in their sex relations. It was not that they were corrupt and decadent. They were proud of their family and personal reputations, afraid of being disgraced, and to all appearances lived a decent life. Unfortunately most of them had succumbed to the practice of free love."[73]

The finer detail of these changes, however, is lost because of a tendency to describe what Dhlomo calls "free love" through a moralizing vocabulary given shape through Christianity. When people referenced sexual morality in the 1930s, they did so in relation to either "tribal" or "Christian morals," Dhlomo's evocation of Christianity compared to tradition echoing every other piece of newspaper commentary referred to in this chapter. Even for non-Christians, the same socially constructed language of morality was used to define African practices of cohabitation.

Another feature of Dhlomo's account, however, also requires our attention. The same feature is present in Mayer's description of ukushweshwa. Both authors linked the changes in intimate practice to urban areas. This link, however, is misleading There is evidence that intimate practices in rural areas were shifting as well, including within polygamous relationships and within relationships where polygamy and Christianity coexisted. Moreover, several of the relationships I shall now describe predate the limited churchly acceptance of polygamy discussed previously but also the masihlalisane relationships described from the 1930s onward.

The abbreviated entries that stand in for people's personal lives in the records of the Native Appeals Court (NAC) provide detail on these shifts. "The Plaintiff sues Defendant for restoration of dowry which according to Native Custom he paid to Defendant for his daughter to whom he was married in 1912 according to Christian rites. Subsequently in 1913 Plaintiff took a Native wife to live with him whom he married according to Native custom. The wife married in accordance with Christian rites thereupon sued Plaintiff for divorce and a divorce was granted."[74]

The terse summary of Welton Sicence's marital history describes how he first married in church and subsequently contracted a customary marriage. The same happened in the marriages of Sibisi earlier described by Dlamini. It also happened to Maggie Resha's grandfather, who married her grandmother in the late 1800s or early 1900s on the advice of his first wife, although he was subsequently excommunicated from the Anglican Church.[75] Women interviewed by Belinda Bozzoli and Mmantho Nkotsoe for their research described relatives whose marriages led them into a similar conundrum of faith.[76] We do not know how the wives of Welton Sicence felt about being part of a de facto polygamous marriage, but we do know that his first wife divorced him in the NAC. After the divorce, Welton Sicence lodged a civil claim for the return of the lobola transferred for her.

A 1914 case relating to a succession dispute reported on Paulus Panyeko's three marriages. His first wife married him via "civil rites" (the term used in the record), but she died. His second wife, Jane, married him via custom. While still married to Jane, he married his third wife, Annie, in church.[77] Paulus Panyeko's marriage to Annie would possibly have been considered a monogamous one by his church, but because he was married to Jane by custom, both women had standing as wives. His type of marriage arrangement was fairly common. Although South African law would not have considered Paulus Panyeko a polygamist because his customary marriage preceded his Christian marriage, he appears to have been party to two simultaneous marriages. It is unknown whether he continued to support and maintain both wives after his Christian wedding.

In a 1930 case heard in King Williams Town, the issue in question was the disposal of lobola cattle to a subsequent generation. The son of a marriage contracted according to customary law after a prior marriage in which the father had married in the church was attempting to gain access to some of the lobola cattle from his sister's marriage. The case law is important only in the lives of those it affected, but it does reveal a civil court treating seriously the existence of both marriages, even if the second was customary. In this case, it appears as if both wives remained married to their joint husband, neither detectably objecting to sharing.[78]

In a report in *Umteteli* in 1935, a native commissioner in Ladysmith had to explain to a local man why "polygamy as far as you are concerned, can only be a memory of your forefathers," after first being married in church.[79] "It is good you must realise that once you discarded your motsha and put on trousers, you put your foot on a progressive street: it is against the law to take your trousers off and put on your motsha again."

Maude and Jemima Titi met in the Umtata Native Appeals Court. The circumstances that brought them together are worthy of a soap opera, the dry language of the court hiding the potential heartache behind Maude's case. Note that this case has its origins in the first two decades of the twentieth century but came to court only in 1935.

> It is common cause that the late John Titi was married four times. His first wife, Nomaki, and his second wife, Majam, were married by Native Custom. He subsequently married Nomaki by Christian rites and Majam then left her kraal and never returned. Nomaki's eldest son, born before the Christian marriage, was Samuel. Samuel married one Jemima by Christian rites and had a son Hemming Sonwabu, who is described as the heir of the late John Titi's Great House. After the death of Nomaki, John Titi married successively by Christian rites Emma, who died leaving no male issue, and Maude, the present plaintiff, whose eldest son is admittedly heir to what is termed John Titi's "Right Hand House."[80]

Maude was a widow of the late John Titi, while Jemima was the wife of his son, Samuel, by one of Maude's co-wives. John Titi appears to have been both an astute businessman and fond of marriage. Sometime toward the start of the century, he married his first wife, Nomaki, by custom. He then married a second wife, Majam, also by custom. Following his conversion to Christianity, he then married Nomaki in the church, whereupon Majam left him. Nomaki and John had a son, Samuel, who was born before the church wedding. After Nomaki died, John remarried twice in church, first to Emma (who died) and then to Maude. After John died in 1933, Jemima tried to evict Maude from the kraal where Maude had lived her married life with John. Jemima also threatened Maude by sending armed men to raid Maude's livestock under cover of darkness.

Apart from this particular dispute, which is what brought John Titi's affairs to court, the case is fascinating because it reveals a successful peasant farmer with a goodly knowledge of legal process and the pieces of paper linked to the various stages of a person's life. John Titi made sure to leave a will, and he took the unusual step for the period of placing title deeds in at least two of his wives' names. The discussion of property in the case also reveals that none of John's wives, including the two first, lived on the same site, nor did they live close by. Separated households for different wives do not feature in the historical accounts of polygamy.

Whatever his motivation, it is evident that John Titi's careful choices about marriage and providing for his dependents need to be considered as choices about responsibility and not just as choices about sex. He and Maude kept a Christian household, which she continued to do after his death, apparently not seeing any incongruity between their faith and its treatment of polygamy as a sin. Maude described in passing one of the raids on her stock occurring just after prayers, and her witnesses to this event included two teachers (a shorthand for Christian status), daughters of John by one of the previous marriages. Maude also accepted Jemima's claim that Samuel was John's heir in his great house, her claim relating only to the usufruct of the site of her household for the remainder of her life.

So far, I have discussed a variety of multiple-partner arrangements in this chapter. These include couples living together as man and wife in kin-sanctioned relationships for considerable lengths of time; relationships existing for perhaps five to ten years before either a husband or wife switched partners for a subsequent medium- to long-term relationship in which fines rather than lobola sanctioned the relationship; long-standing relationships that existed between a married man and his female lover, as described by Mayer; and series of overlapping marriages that displayed some of the features of polygamy.

Also, some cases defy all previous analyses. In a 1925 case from Mount Frere, concerning events as far back as the last decade of the nineteenth century, Blyth (or Bly) Mbuto took Xidela Masumpa to court over the custody of two children. The case does not involve Christians, but it is a convoluted case of potential serial conjugality. While Mbuto was away on a work contract, his wife through cattle, Mamqaloti, eloped with Masumpa and had a child with him, an action that was covered by a fine in cattle or possibly by a marriage through cattle. When Bly returned to his home, Mamqaloti came back to him. She became pregnant with him but returned to Masumpa when Blyth returned to the mines. She died in the influenza epidemic in 1918. Whatever the merits of the case, including the fact that the local chief had intervened to force Mamqaloti to return to Blyth on the first occasion, it appears that she was a wife with two husbands for perhaps a few years. If she had lived, the record of this case would have included her evidence. As in so many instances, however, we do not know what she thought. It appears that she exercised some choice in leaving her first marriage and contracting a second. There are, of course, several ways to interpret the events leading to this case, as the plaintiff and defendant argued, but serial marriage seems to have taken place.[81]

At the start of the twentieth century, polygamy was subject to a rhetorical deployment across a range of spaces in South African life, indicative of its status as a moral quandary for all the mainline churches. By the First World War, it had become evident that polygamy was a more complex issue than standard church policy would indicate. White missionaries and African Christians now found it necessary to grapple with converts who progressed from monogamy to polygamy, rather than the converse, which had been the norm only a generation or so before. Both the critique of polygamy as immoral and the view that encouraged accommodation are evident in the workings and deliberations of church bodies over the next few decades.

By the mid-1920s, it had emerged as a central preoccupation linked to the cluster of issues around African marriages and was discussed in a range of venues across the continent but also in Europe and North America. This prominence ensured polygamy's status as a staple of debate in Christian periodicals, publications, conferences, and committees. On these occasions, polygamy was a known and bounded practice, manifestly the antithesis of monogamy. Polygamy, in this space, was either un-Christian and immoral altogether or needing regulation. But it was also on the decline.

It is easy to discount the many ways that African men and women cohabited and shared conjugality if polygamy is understood as one thing only. When the first part of this chapter—the defining and history of polygamy—is read against the complicated marital lives of the men whose marriages were described throughout (along with their sometimes incompletely named or unnamed wives), the weight of evidence is as much about the range of multimarried and multipartnered behaviors that Africans accommodated in their Christianity as it is for a single tale outlining the attrition of a practice.

In marriages occurring among Africans who were not converts, it is possible to describe them without referring to them as polygamous; however, in marriages involving Christians, their ascription as polygamous becomes more complex. According to both the church and traditionalists, Christian wives whose husband remarried under custom, where lobola was transferred for all wives, were polygamously married. A man who married first by custom and subsequently in the church was exercising a long-standing local practice to marry more than one wife. In such cases, if a husband remained with both wives, it is quite likely that he would have been viewed (depending on the eye of the beholder) as either bigamous or polygamous. These examples are what makes it more difficult than one might realize to write about the decline of polygamy. If we consider relationships that flirted with polygamy like the ones just described, it becomes apparent that polygamy is either too narrow or too capacious a construct to describe how people understood themselves to be married. Polygamy in this respect is not at all like lobola, about which both detractors and supporters shared a common set of ideas about what it involved (although their understanding of its moral value differed).

The court records—where these accounts of the multiply, polygamously, and serially polygynous are found—suggest a much more complex situation concerning marriage than the Union census, which recorded only one marriage at a time, might suggest. It is not clear, for instance, how many of those married in church may have found themselves in a subsequent marriage, nor is there any way to know how many couples married first in church only for one of the partners (most likely the male partner) subsequently to marry according to custom. It is also not clear to what extent women who married in church used their ability to sue for divorce to express unhappiness at sharing their husbands with other wives. These are the kinds of partnerships that the binary of polygamy/pagan and monogamy/Christian obscures. Also, these are the relationships that an emphasis on urban conjugal confusion tends to miss.

All of this is to note that, while white and Black clergy debated polygamy in the period between 1910 and 1940, they had their eyes on the wrong ball. They missed the extent to which many Christians, those not linked into the broader, more elite Christian networks, found their married and intimate lives moving in several different directions simultaneously. Some of these directions were new, and some were variations on older practices. They have been overshadowed by a fascination with polygamy understood as a homogeneous practice, always defined by the ideals of the past and carried out in an arena where only men exercised agency. These cases, and others like it, point to some of the parallel lives of polygamy or, more accurately, its ghosts in South Africa in the first half of the twentieth century.

In a new kind of polygamy, men married serially without first freeing themselves, either through custom or through the white courts, of their preceding marriages. It was polygamy of a very uneven, unbalanced sort that usually involved a first marriage contracted formally according to custom or in the church and subsequent marriages involving a lobola exchange. These marriages were different from conventional polygamous marriages in that husbands did not intend to establish traditional polygamous households where they could live in parallel with all their wives. Nevertheless, these were not relationships based on concubinage, because the men who contracted them viewed and represented them as marriage. What women thought of these marriages is unclear, but there are several cases of women taking their husbands to the divorce court once a marriage had grown to include an additional wife. The new kind of polygamy is most easy to detect where kin were in close proximity and lobola was exchanged on more than one wife's behalf. However, it is also possible that such relationships straddled the rural-urban divide (although most commentators are clear that town wives were not formally married with lobola).

In addition, by the second decade of the twentieth century, African men and women, Christian and non-Christian, were involved in multiple different styles of relationships, some involving town and country partners but some involving stable, successive town partners. The existence of these relationships has often been obscured by the prominence accorded polygamy, unfortunately working to erase the legitimacy of relationships of long-term commitment because of a narrow focus on conjugality as either monogamous or polygamous.

Conclusion

Black Intimacy into the Present

IN ALL that has been written about South Africa between 1910 and 1948, in the saddening iteration of African lives undone and forced apart by migrant labor and loss of land, we sometimes disregard the creative responses and spaces from which Africans challenged their manifold dispossession and the loss of their pasts, crafting lives in tune with the twentieth century. One of the most paradoxical of "the means by which Africans have learned to compensate for the impossibility of their everyday lives" was Christianity.[1] Not only was it a source of spiritual comfort but it also provided its adherents with a range of tools and associated dispositions to craft lives geared to the complexities of their situation. It offered guidelines, imperfect and imbricated in their own structures of power, for holding families together in the face of an impersonal state that worked actively or through disinterested neglect to tear them asunder. Confronted with the demands of mining capital and life in the city, which sought to keep families apart, Christianity offered solutions, however flawed, to social reproduction, which made room for the persistence of older ideas and for new configurations of kin. It was not an ideological and spiritual leaning tied to only one kind of space, but it bridged the divide that separated the urban from the rural. Understanding Black social history in the first part of the twentieth century is impossible without considering its relation to Christianity and its complicated and multifaceted relationship to the broader body politic of South Africa. As Africans turned to Christianity for reasons both conservative and emancipatory, in their writing and in their rituals, their efforts revealed a heterogeneous arena that allowed the retention of tradition alongside a commitment to the modern—a space that allowed a focus on the family while it also turned people's gazes outward into the world wrought by literacy.

These possibilities emanate from the emancipatory potential especially resident in Protestant Christianity, which rooted itself in South African life through two qualities: a spirit of free inquiry—an "open-ended, ill-disciplined argument"—and a strong tendency toward democracy, both evident in the spread of Protestant ecumenism after World War I and relevant to how Black South Africans embraced modernity in the first half of the twentieth century.[2]

But this emancipatory potential was just that. At the same time that Christianity in South Africa offered its followers new paths and sources of inspiration, its internal assumptions and priorities limited how it could be shaped. Christianity worked to model Africans' intimate lives in different ways. Through the institutional operations of the church, Christianity linked Black South Africans into a net of social motion that connected all Black South Africans to each other in a manner that transcended ethnicity and other social differences. That movement and that facility was enabled by what I have called the "institutional thickness" of the church. The church infused people's lives at several levels, perhaps difficult to comprehend in what passes for the secular condition of the early twenty-first century. It also built upon previous structures and practices, like chiefly councils and the oratory they utilized, to facilitate entry into other institutional structures, like the state. Within these spaces and utilizing oral and written genres, African Christians articulated a range of ideas about what their married and intimate lives ought to be. Tiyo Burnside Soga, already much discussed in this book, was a minister, but he was connected through his father—brother of Tiyo Soga—to his grandfather, who was one of the senior councillors of the Xhosa chief, Ngqika, and subsequently, Ngqika's son, Sarhili. His entire life was a round of movement between church and what he considered tradition. He moved seamlessly between oral and written forms, customary and modern practice. While his manuscript, *Intlalo xa Xosa,* was concerned with a wide range of subjects, some of its principal preoccupations were gendered behavior and disposition. He found himself torn between his faith and its contrary conjunction with modernity. While he approved of young people's church associations responsible for moral upliftment, he was also deeply suspicious of what he called "Imitshotsho (dance) for the young & Saturday's Festivals." While imitshotsho were common at traditional gatherings, including wedding celebrations, Soga found himself criticizing them. "In the olden days there was no such big gatherings for the young people. These Saturday's gatherings & such customs of today, were unknown in those days. The reason for their coming into existence is darkness in the people themselves. It is bad teaching & kills any good morals in young people." His view of the link between literacy, school, and sexual trysts was very different from that of Nthana Mokale, quoted in the introduction. "We say 'Stop now! This nation is decaying as it has no decent young people!!!'"[3]

Soga may have been a modern archconservative, but he was correct in his view that the night dances, the imitshotsho, facilitated sexual encounters. However, his negative assessment of them arose because he was unable to see his Christianity as separate from late nineteenth- and early twentieth-century patterns of gendered sociality (a link many historians are also unable to draw). As Soga had noticed, some of Christianity's most potent impacts lay in relation to Black intimacy. The package of Christian modernity that took shape in South Africa after 1910 had uneven outcomes for men and women. European Christianity was rooted in a gendered and sexual ethic that operated differently from that of Black society. Premarital sex, for instance, was common under socially sanctioned conditions in precolonial African societies. When couples entered marriage, the relationships they had with their parents, with their natal families, with their new families, and with each other were reconfigured. Many of the gendered practices and customs that Africans sought to accommodate in their Christianity were about negotiating, in a fairly immediate sense, the relationships between men and women. Within this context, Christian belief and statutory Christianity clashed and combined with traditional ideas to affect the distribution of power in relationships in ways that were markedly different from those of the nineteenth century. Practices around marriage were the crucible of much conflict, so much so that customary marriage legislation constituted some of the earliest European attempts to control African society. Such an understanding was inimical to a European, post-Victorian sexual sensibility.

In the grander story of colonialism and apartheid, all Black South Africans were on the losing side. However, a more nuanced gaze, the task of the historians, shows that it was African women who, more often, lost status and power. Black women who converted to Christianity gained significant spiritual comfort from it, but they also experienced significant consternation, sometimes distress, because of its gendered burdens. Female purity before marriage and sex only during marriage became part of a discourse around what made for authentic and proper Christians, causing the maintenance of Christian morality to be much more fraught for Black women than for men. Not only were Christian men and women subjected to a sexual double standard, but the consequences of so-called sexual transgression were much more apparent for women. Dorothy Kabane and her mother were censured for Kabane's becoming pregnant outside of marriage, her actions publicly declaimed in the color of her wedding dress, evident not only to the wedding guests but also detailed in the wedding notice in *Umteteli*. Women's church associations, as Deborah Gaitskell has noted, were centrally preoccupied with female purity because of the consequences for women's status with its loss.[4] Dorothy's brother, Milner, was not affected socially when his sister's transgressions became public. He appeared regularly in *Umteteli* through the remainder of the 1930s, in recognition of his status as a teacher and his growing stature as a respected member of the African National Congress (ANC). Both Milner's elevation and Dorothy's shame were facilitated by their Christian upbringing and the power of mission literacy.

Conceptions of shame had consequences at a personal level and constituted part of the reshaping of Black intimacy. More general shifts, too, were happening, as outlined in the various chapters of this book. While more and more Africans married in church during the period covered by this book, lobola transfers remained relatively constant. Very few of the couples I have mentioned by name married without lobola. The near ubiquity of lobola transfers in Christian marriage indicates a further shift, one having to do with the nature of mainline Christian practice itself. Although in the mid to late nineteenth century, European missionaries had condemned lobola, and a first generation of converts had done likewise, by World War I, literate Christians were adamant in their public defense of it. By the 1930s, this was a dual-gendered debate. Both men and women wrote to *Umteteli* and especially *Bantu World* on the subject of lobola. Lobola, more so than other traditionally gendered practices, was a subject that concerned and led to consternation among both men and women.

At least two processes were in force from about 1910 to 1940 concerning polygamy. African male clergy initially united in condemning polygamy. However, by the 1930s, it was clear that many were becoming less opposed to polygamy. Either African clergy supported polygamy as part of their support for the Africanization of Christianity or they pointed to its declining importance. Nevertheless, polygamy continued to exercise a great hold across a variety of imaginations. But the debate about polygamy that captured the public imagination was often about other issues, especially multiple conjugality, masked by their incorporation into discussion about the practice. The imprint of Christianity on understandings of African marriage has retrospectively wiped out the visibility of the multiple styles of conjugal relationships in precolonial South Africa. These forms of relationships did not disappear with colonialism, but new frameworks of understanding marriage in terms of only polygamy or monogamy made them much less conspicuous. Some of these relationships, both in urban and rural areas, resembled polygamy, even if they were never referred to as such. As legal records from magistrates' courts in the Eastern Cape reveal, Christians and others were contracting successive marriages where the first marriage in the sequence had not necessarily been dissolved. It was quite frequent for a man to marry first according to custom, and then in church. This was neither proscribed according to customary law or to the civil law of South Africa, though it was undoubtedly unfair to the partner thus sundered from their marriage. Black men were contracting simultaneous or successive Christian marriages without entering into formal divorce proceedings.

This book does not cover the second half of the twentieth century, but in what follows, I gesture at the present moment. I do not want to suggest an unbroken continuity of issues but rather to point to the depth and salience of the practices and dispositions just discussed.

In chapter 2, I discuss how traditional male circumcision was linked to debates about the content of masculinity. When initiation shifted in relation to Christianity, it was the practice that shifted rather than understandings of masculinity. These remained tied to masculinity as ethnic patriotism rather than missionaries' hoped-for reshaping of masculinity as a constituent of companionate intimate partnerships. When its interlocutors debated initiation in public, the discussion allowed Xhosa men to engage with other ethnicities, which shifted debates about masculinity out of the moral authority of Xhosadom into a wider conversation about Black masculinity across the whole of South Africa. These conversations in which African men defined masculinity as reverence for the ancestors, for custom, and for tradition, reflect the paradoxical ecumenism of Christianity, because they allowed for the development of an avowedly masculine public sphere.

The subject of initiation is also important because it shows the continual making and remaking of tradition. In South Africa's current system of traditional governance, circumcision and initiation are sites of considerable dispute. Public debate is inevitably accompanied by comments about who has the right to speak for African custom and whether those customs are depicted accurately. One set of contests relates to Xhosa defenses of masculinity, as is evident in the fracas surrounding the forced circumcision of ANC politician Fikile Mbalula in 2008.[5] Current contests also center on the validity of surgical circumcision, which is linked to a reduction in male susceptibility to HIV/AIDS, while Xhosa traditionalists maintain that circumcision clinics funded with donor aid are a corruption of tradition. The grip of tradition is also such that even ethnic groups that have not circumcised in the last century have called for the reintroduction of circumcision.[6]

Even more recently, a public controversy erupted around the film *Inxeba,* released in 2017, which depicts a homosexual relationship between two Black men appointed as guardians during the rites of circumcision.[7] An application, including an appeal, to have the rating on the film raised from sixteen to eighteen years, is informative of contemporary links between sex, power, and manhood—and also, how aspects of the practice have shifted since the early twentieth century. The application was brought by Contralesa, the Congress of Traditional Leaders of South Africa, among a group of amicus curiae including other traditional associations.

> Initiation or circumcision is strongly believed to be sacred not only by the amaXhosa, but by the majority of African people in South Africa and elsewhere in other African countries. Sexual intercourse is a taboo subject in the context of *ulwaluko* which should not even be spoken about, let alone practiced. It contradicts the idea of ritual purity which is a cornerstone of circumcision. Any person associated with the initiates is strictly prohibited from engaging in sexual conduct, more especially the caregivers who have to handle the initiates and treat them to heal.... There are also medical reasons for the above in that sexual stimulation or arousal can have devastating and even deadly consequences for the initiates.[8]

Largely, the objections that the traditional leaders' associations raised about the authenticity of *Inxeba* to traditional circumcision are correct.[9] But, as writers like James Calata showed, initiation and sex were closely linked, so any objections to the linking of initiation to sex as articulated by the *Inxeba* protesters refer to an attitude that has only recently become prevalent. In fact, what we see with the protests around *Inxeba* are arguments in favor of what Dhammamegha Leatt refers to as "re-establishing traditional authority" in South Africa.[10]

Indeed, Leatt's arguments about how democracy is linked to secularism—and about the more general failure of popular support for democratic liberalism separate from religion and tradition in South Africa—point to some of the more useful questions to ask about current understandings of Black intimacy. How are faith and tradition linked in the postcolonial moment? In her argument, Leatt poses the question in relation to the state, but I am more concerned with faith and tradition in relation to the politics of intimacy and the intimate public referenced by Berlant and others, including in the public life of weddings.

South Africans still routinely refer to "traditional weddings" and "white weddings" as if there is a significant difference between them, as if white weddings were secular affairs apart from tradition.[11] This distinction, though, is more discursive than it is a reflection of the extent to which traditional and white weddings are routinely coupled. The South African–produced reality television show *Our Perfect Wedding* is geared toward Black audiences and has aired five hundred episodes since 2017. The episodes run according to a formula in which most couples marry through two ceremonies, first a traditional and then a white wedding. The latter forms "the climax of each episode."[12] The language of weddings that permeates the show recognizes casually a divide between the two ceremonies. In fact, though, the two ceremonies are the wedding. The distinction between ceremonies misses a point critical to the argument of this book, which is that the distinction between tradition and Christianity that many South Africans draw upon routinely to explain everyday life ceased to exist in practice, though not in rhetoric, some time ago. If, for many years, Christianity has responded and accommodated itself to African tradition, a glance at the public life of weddings in contemporary South Africa suggests the two are now irrevocably part of an ongoing mash-up.

Along with weddings, polygamy has seized the public imagination, appearing across novels and reality television shows. In Sue Nyathi's novel *The Polygamist*, set in Zimbabwe, Joyce Gomora finds out her husband has another wife. In the hospital for a tubal ligation, Joyce encounters her partner wife, who is giving birth.

> Four wives later and yes I was still married to Jonasi Gomora. I don't know if I was fortunate or unfortunate to be wife number one. I guess it depends which way you look at it. Anyway the point is I can say with certainty that I was his first wife. I doubt others could so with certainly they would be his last. At 44 my husband was still hurtling along like a rolling stone. He had recently added another wife to the harem. Our own modern version of King Solomon. . . . Marriage is just bullshit.[13]

In the novel, Joyce and her co-wives speak out through different chapters about their experience of being married to the same wealthy man, until his death from AIDS at the age of forty-six. For three of the wives, the co-marriage was not the issue that bothered them most but rather Jonasi's personal failings and inability to communicate fairly with each of them.

Nyathi's novel is a frank discussion of polygamy, more frank about its negative effects on women than many other contemporary depictions of the practice. In the tangle of emotions the novel lays bare, Christianity is an easy but unremarked-upon participant, from Joyce's wedding, where she walked down the aisle under the "white veil of dishonour" (she was pregnant) to Jonasi's funeral at a Catholic church.[14]

Christianity also operates in the background of several reality television shows about polygamy.[15] Both recent series *Uthando Nes'Thembu* ("Love and polygamy") and *Mnakwethu* ("Intimate friend," much like a brother) focus on the interaction between wives and husbands, marital jealousy, and Musa Mseleku, the husband in *Uthando Nes'Thembu* and host of *Mnakwethu*, offering advice to men who are considering a second wife. The subtitled episodes of both have a large following, especially on Twitter, with readers and viewers commenting on the different choices faced by Mseleku's household and the various households he advises in *Mnakwethu*. The shows consciously set out to make polygamy both commonplace and controversial. *Uthando Nes'Thembu* particularly emphasizes the incompatibility between Christianity and tradition, but this is more staged than it is real. After overcoming her religious reservations, MaCele, his first wife, remarried Musa in a traditional ceremony in 2019, after a church wedding in 2012 (and after an earlier transfer of lobola). She spoke about this in an interview at the time of the 2019 ceremony, quoting Ephesians 5:22 about the duty of wives to submit to their husbands.[16]

Not every marriage represented in the two shows speaks as eloquently to the contest between Christianity and tradition as MaCele did. It is also true that *Uthando Nes'Thembu* and *Mnakwethu* would not work half as well as they do if Christianity did not supply a ready antagonist to claims about polygamy. However, just as in *The Polygamist*, Christianity is also part of the backdrop to both programs. In the public discussion of both shows, in what they represent of everyday relationships, Christianity hovers unobtrusively in the background, the quiet dinner guest present in the choices of funeral caskets and what to have for supper after Sunday church service.

Just as these shows and novels produce and stage intimate life in the early twenty-first century, roughly a century back in time, intimate life was also being produced and contested in the church, in courts, and in text, especially across the range of newspapers through which Black South Africans gave shape and content to their future intimate lives. And Christianity, operating at different levels, established a tone affecting the shape of that intimate life. The missionary and Christian origins of literacy and education, both instrumental in the establishment of the Black press, meant that discussions of intimacy were rooted within a matrix of Christian morality. This occurred first among literate Christians and later, as literacy spread, among all South Africans. The debates about whether European marriages were more romantic than African marriages, whether lobola was slavery, whether polygamy was more moral than monogamy, whether masculinity was defined by respect for women or for the ancestors—all were fractured, partial, conflictual, and ambiguous, perhaps to be completely disregarded, but they were irrevocably and indisputably present and definitive. In contemporary reality television, these debates are just as present and just as contested. They also carry, unacknowledged at this point, the thorough imprint of Christianity.

Notes

INTRODUCTION

1. T. B. was the brother's son of the more famous Tiyo Soga. I am working from a contemporary translation of *Intlalo xa Xosa*. All references in this book to *Intlalo xa Xosa* are to this manuscript. For more on this manuscript, see chap. 2. Grahamstown, Cory Library for Historical Research, MS16369b, trans. C. S. Papu. Soga, *Intlalo,* 32. Xosa was the ancestor of the amaXhosa.
2. My thinking about intimacy is influenced by Mark Hunter's work in Mark Hunter, *Love in the Time of AIDS: Inequality, Gender, and Rights in South Africa* (Bloomington: Indiana University Press, 2010).
3. Belinda Bozzoli and Mmantho Nkotsoe, *Women of Phokeng: Consciousness, Life Strategy, and Migrancy in South Africa, 1900–1983* (Johannesburg: Ravan, 1991), 113. Mokale was interviewed in 1982/3.
4. For similar rich detail of the intersection between Christianity and custom, see Phyllis Ntantala, *A Life's Mosaic: The Autobiography of Phyllis Ntantala* (Cape Town: David Philip, 1992). Ntantala's husband was A. C. Jordan, whose writing opens chap. 5.
5. Lauren Berlant and Michael Warner, "Sex in Public," *Critical Inquiry* 24, no. 2 (1998): 552.
6. See also Berlant and Warner, "Sex in Public," 555.
7. For instance, Rebecca Flemming, "The Invention of Infertility in the Classical Greek World: Medicine, Divinity, and Gender," *Bulletin of the History of Medicine* 87, no. 4 (20 December 2013): 565–90; Nick Hopwood, Rebecca Flemming, and Lauren Kassell, "Reproduction in History," in *Reproduction: Antiquity to the Present Day,* ed. Lauren Kassell, Nick Hopwood, and Rebecca Flemming (Cambridge: Cambridge University Press, 2018), 3–18; Moira Donald and Linda Hurcombe, *Gender and Material History in Archaeological Perspective* (New York: St. Martin's, 2000).
8. Leonore Davidoff and Catherine Hall, *Family Fortunes: Men and Women of the English Middle Class 1780–1850* (London: Routledge, 1987), 149.
9. Hlonipha Mokoena, *Magema Fuze: The Making of a Kholwa Intellectual* (Scottsville, South Africa: University of KwaZulu-Natal Press, 2011), 20.

10. South Africa, ed., *Union Statistics for 50 years, 1910-1960* (Pretoria: Bureau of Census and Statistics, 1960), A-29. I also discuss issues with the reliability of these statistics.

11. "Largely" is a generalization, I know, and depends on the extent of the introduction of indirect rule in a particular region. See, for instance, William David Hammond-Tooke, *Command or Consensus: The Development of Transkeian Local Government* (Cape Town: David Philip, 1975); Inneke van Kessel and Barbara Oomen, "One Chief, One Vote: The Revival of Traditional Authorities in Post-apartheid South Africa," *African Affairs* 96, no. 385 (1997): 561–85; J. B. Peires, "Traditional Leaders in Purgatory: Local Government in Tsolo, Qumbu and Port St Johns, 1990–2000," *African Studies* 59, no. 1 (2000): 97–114; Jill E. Kelly, "Bantu Authorities and Betterment in Natal: The Ambiguous Responses of Chiefs and Regents, 1955–1970," *Journal of Southern African Studies* 41, no. 2 (4 March 2015): 273–97, https://doi.org/10.1080/03057070.2015.1012917.

12. Alec Ryrie, *Protestants: The Faith That Made the Modern World* (New York: Viking, 2017).

13. Karin Barber, *The Anthropology of Texts, Persons and Publics: Oral and Written Culture in Africa and Beyond*, New Departures in Anthropology 5 (Cambridge: Cambridge University Press, 2007), 2.

14. Willem J. Schoeman, "South African Religious Demography: The 2013 General Household Survey," *HTS Teologiese Studies/Theological Studies* 73, no. 2 (2017): 2.

15. STATSSA, "General Household Survey 2015" (Pretoria, South Africa: Statistics South Africa, 2015), 27–28, http://www.statssa.gov.za/?page_id=1859.

16. David M. Gordon, *Invisible Agents: Spirits in a Central African History* (Athens: Ohio University Press, 2012), 2. For a similar view in the teaching of African history of religion, see Asonzeh Ukah and Tammy Wilks, "Peter Berger, *The Sacred Canopy*, and Theorizing the African Religious Context," *Journal of the American Academy of Religion* 85, no. 4 (30 December 2017): 1147–54, https://doi.org/10.1093/jaarel/lfx080.

17. Stephen Ellis and Gerrie ter Haar, *Worlds of Power: Religious Thought and Political Practice in Africa* (New York: Oxford University Press, 2004); Gerrie ter Haar and Stephen Ellis, "The Occult Does Not Exist: A Response to Terence Ranger," *Africa* 79, no. 3 (2009): 399–412.

18. For the essentialization of African Christianity, see Maia Green, "Confronting Categorical Assumptions about the Power of Religion in Africa," *Review of African Political Economy* 33, no. 110 (2006): 635–50. For a larger discussion on the motive force of spirits in African life and a distinctive African spirituality, see also Tinyiko Sam Maluleke, "Half a Century of African Christian Theologies: Elements of the Emerging Agenda for the Twenty-First Century," *Journal of Theology for Southern Africa* 99 (1997): 4–23; Tinyiko Sam Maluleke, "Black and African Theologies in the New World Order: A Time to Drink from Our Own Wells," *Journal of Theology for Southern Africa* 96 (1996): 3–19.

19. Ruth Marshall, *Political Spiritualities: The Pentecostal Revolution in Nigeria* (Chicago: University of Chicago Press, 2009), 3.
20. South Africa, *Union Statistics for 50 years, 1910–1960.* The figures in this paragraph are from the opening pages of the census (Population Figures, Race and Sex, A-4–A.5), and the figures on religious affiliation are from Religion, A-26–A-29. Compare these to religious affiliation among white South Africans. In 1951, the white South African population numbered roughly 2.6 million. Of this number, 1.1 million declared themselves to be members of the Dutch Reformed Church; 416,472 were Anglicans; 219,021, Methodists; and 100,739, Presbyterian. While the census figures are open to speculation at various levels, the increase in the self-profession of Christianity is borne out by other sources and is likely accurate. Anthony John Christopher, "The Union of South Africa Censuses 1911–1960: An Incomplete Record," *Historia* 56, no. 2 (2011): 1–18.
21. Mercy Amba Oduyoye, "Re-imagining the World: A Global Perspective," *Church & Society* 84, no. 5 (1994): 82–93; Mercy Amba Oduyoye, "Christianity and African Culture," *International Review of Mission* 84, nos. 332/333 (1995): 77.
22. For a summary of this argument, see Joel E. Tishken and Andreas Heuser, "'Africa Always Brings Us Something New': A Historiography of African Zionist and Pentecostal Christianities," *Religion* 45, no. 2 (2015): 156.
23. Terence Ranger, "Religious Movements and Politics in Sub-Saharan Africa," *African Studies Review* 29, no. 2 (1986): 1–69. See also James T. Campbell, "'Like Locusts in Pharoah's Palace': The Origins and Politics of African Methodism in the Orange Free State, 1895–1914," *African Studies* 53, no. 1 (1994): 39–69; Arianna Lissoni et al., eds., *One Hundred Years of the ANC: Debating Liberation Histories Today* (Johannesburg: Wits University Press, 2012).
24. For more on the phrase "African independent" and a refutation of this position, see Barbara Bompani, "African Independent Churches in Post-apartheid South Africa: New Political Interpretations," *Journal of Southern African Studies* 34, no. 3 (2008): 667. There is an interesting account of Zionist anti-apartheid protest in an interview with Jean Comaroff on her 1980s work on Zion Christianity: "We also had lots of friends in the black community, particularly people in the churches which were always a refuge for politics there. I was working on churches; I left the LSE assuming that I would study 'traditional religion,' because African Christianity was what scholars of comparative religion did at the time. When I got there, Christianity was a major idiom of local life, forms of Christianity made under local conditions, an integrated aspect of Tswana history and life. Several of the leaders of the various local denominations were extraordinary leaders, involved in everything from feeding the hungry to giving asylum to those on the run; one close friend had actually been the priest for Robert Sobukwe, and he took us to be ritually treated by a local healer to protect us against the security police. The most significant thing about all this was that the kind of structural-functionalist methods that we had learned at the LSE

were just totally inadequate when we got to this world, where you couldn't separate religion from politics, 'local' ethnography from the structure of the whole colonial, Apartheid state." Jean and John Comaroff, interview by Kalman Applbaum, *Alan MacFarlane*, 15 November 2008, http://www.alanmacfarlane.com/DO/filmshow/comaroff_fast.htm.

25. Birgit Meyer, "Christianity in Africa: From African Independent to Pentecostal-Charismatic Churches," *Annual Review of Anthropology* 33 (2004): 447–74. Also Joel Cabrita and Natasha Erlank, "New Histories of Christianity in South Africa: Review and Introduction," *South African Historical Journal* 70, no. 2 (3 April 2018): 307–23, https://doi.org/10.1080/02582473.2018.1495753.

26. David Goodhew, "A Story of Growth and Decline," *Church Times*, 6 January 2017, https://www.churchtimes.co.uk/articles/2017/6-january/features/features/a-story-of-growth-and-decline; Marshall, *Political Spiritualities*, 2.

27. Anglican Ink, "Dear Gay Anglicans Letter," press release, 22 February 2021, https://anglican.ink/2021/02/22/dear-gay-anglicans-letter/.

28. Thomas Blom Hansen, Caroline Jeannerat, and Samadia Sadouni, "Introduction: Portable Spirits and Itinerant People: Religion and Migration in South Africa in a Comparative Perspective," *African Studies* 68, no. 2 (2009): 187–96.

29. Philip Bonner, "South African Society and Culture 1910–1948," in *The Cambridge History of South Africa. Volume 2: 1885–1994*, ed. Robert Ross, Anne Kelk Mager, and Bill Nasson (Cambridge: Cambridge University Press, 2011).

30. Bengt Sundkler, *Bantu Prophets in South Africa* (Cape Town: Oxford University Press, 1961).

31. For Africans viewing their Christianity as evidence of a contested modernity, see Paul la Hausse de Lalouviere, *Restless Identities: Signatures of Nationalism, Zulu Ethnicity and History in the Lives of Petros Lamula (c.1881–1948) and Lymon Maling (1889–c.1936)* (Pietermaritzburg: University of Natal Press, 2000); Lize Kriel, *The "Malaboch" Books: Kgaluši in the "Civilization of the Written Word"* (Stuttgart, Germany: Franz Steiner Verlag, 2009); Robert J. Houle, *Making African Christianity: Africans Reimagining Their Faith in Colonial South Africa* (Bethlehem, PA: Lehigh University Press, 2013).

32. Soga, *Intlalo xa Xosa*, 136.

33. Dipesh Chakrabarty, *Habitations of Modernity: Essays in the Wake of Subaltern Studies* (Chicago: University of Chicago Press, 2002); Frederick Cooper, *Colonialism in Question Theory, Knowledge, History* (Berkeley: University of California Press, 2005).

34. Lynn M. Thomas, "Modernity's Failings, Political Claims, and Intermediate Concepts," *The American Historical Review* 116, no. 3 (2011): 734.

35. Thomas Spear, "Neo-traditionalism and the Limits of Invention in British Colonial Africa," *Journal of African History* 44, no. 1 (2003): 5–6. Spear's article is an excellent summary of these trends. Similar overviews, including Derek Peterson's rather exasperated chronicling of the number of book

titles including "The Invention of," may be found in Derek R. Peterson, "Culture And Chronology In African History," *Historical Journal* 50, no. 2 (2007): 483–97; Terence O. Ranger, "The Invention of Tribalism Revisited: The Case of Colonial Africa," in *Inventions and Boundaries: Historical and Anthropological Approaches to the Study of Ethnicity and Nationalism,* ed. Preben Kaarsholm and Jan Hultin, IDS Roskilde Occasional Papers (Denmark: University of Roskilde, 1994), 5–50.

36. Daniel R. Magaziner, "'Black Man, You Are on Your Own!' Making Race Consciousness in South African Thought, 1968–1972," *International Journal of African Historical Studies* 42, no. 2 (2009): 226; Daniel R. Magaziner, *The Law and the Prophets: Black Consciousness in South Africa, 1968–1977,* New African Histories Series (Athens: Ohio University Press, 2010).

37. *Umteteli,* 11 May 1935, 7.

38. Soga, *Intlalo,* 34–36.

39. James Calata, "Ukudlelana kobu-Kristu namasiko olwaluko lwabantu abaNtsundu," in *Inkolo Namasiko A-Bantu: Bantu Beliefs and Customs,* ed. Sydney J. Wallis (London: Society for Promoting Christian Knowledge, 1930), 38–49.

40. Jacqueline Solway, "'Slow Marriage,' 'Fast *Bogadi*': Change and Continuity in Marriage in Botswana," *Anthropology Southern Africa* 39, no. 4 (2016): 309–22.

41. Adam Kuper, "Traditions of Kinship, Marriage and Bridewealth in Southern Africa," *Anthropology Southern Africa* 39, no. 4 (2016): 278.

42. For instance, Colin Bundy, *The Rise and Fall of the South African Peasantry* (London: Heinemann, 1979); André Odendaal, *Vukani Bantu! The Beginnings of Black Protest Politics in South Africa to 1912* (Cape Town: David Philip, 1984). For a discussion of these historiographical divisions, see Christopher Saunders, *The Making of the South African Past: Major Historians on Race and Class* (Cape Town: David Philip, 1988). For a nuanced discussion of the potential of class analysis in this literature, see Keith Breckenridge, "Promiscuous Method: The Historiographical Effects of the Search for the Rural Origins of the Urban Working Class in South Africa," *International Labor and Working-Class History* 65 (2004): 26–49.

43. For the larger debate referenced here, Alan H. Jeeves, "Identity, Culture and Consciousness: Industrial Work and Rural Migration in Southern Africa, 1860–1987," *South African Historical Journal* 33, no. 1 (1 November 1995): 198–99.

44. See Patrick Harries, *Work, Culture and Identity: Migrant Laborers in Mozambique and South Africa, c.1860–1910,* Social History of Africa (Portsmouth, NH: Heinemann, 1991).

45. Some of this history includes Helen Bradford, "'We Are Now the Men': Women's Beer Hall Protests in the Natal Countryside, 1929," in *Class, Community and Conflict: South African Perspectives,* ed. Belinda Bozzoli (Johannesburg: Ravan, 1987); Kathy Eales, "Patriarchs, Passes and Privilege: Johannesburg's African Middle Classes and the Question of Night Passes

for African Women, 1920–1931," in *Holding Their Ground: Class, Locality and Culture in 19th and 20th Century South Africa,* ed. Phillip Bonner et al. (Johannesburg: Wits University Press, 1989); Cherryl Walker, ed., *Women and Gender in Southern Africa to 1945* (Cape Town: David Philip, 1990); Cherryl Walker, "Women and Gender in Southern Africa to 1945: An Overview," in Walker, *Women and Gender;* Linzi Manicom, "Ruling Relations: Rethinking State and Gender in South African History," *Journal of African History* 33, no. 3 (1 January 1992): 441–65.

46. Belinda Bozzoli, "Marxism, Feminism and South African Studies," in *Segregation and Apartheid in Twentieth-Century South Africa,* ed. William Beinart and Saul Dubow, (London: Routledge, 1995), 118–44; Pauline Peters, "Gender, Developmental Cycles and Historical Process: A Critique of Recent Research on Women in Botswana," *Journal of Southern African Studies* 10, no. 1 (1983); Bridget O'Laughlin, "Missing Men? The Debate Over Rural Poverty and Women-Headed Households in Southern Africa," *Journal of Peasant Studies* 25, no. 2 (1998): 1–48.

47. Deborah Gaitskell, "Female Mission Initiatives: Black and White Women in Three Witwatersrand Churches, 1903–1939" (PhD thesis, University of London, 1981); Deborah Gaitskell, "Devout Domesticity? A Century of African Women's Christianity in South Africa," in *Women and Gender in Southern Africa to 1945,* ed. Cherryl Walker (Cape Town: David Philip, 1990); Deborah Gaitskell, "'Praying and Preaching': The Distinctive Spirituality of African Women's Church Organizations," in *Missions and Christianity in South African History,* ed. Henry Bredenkamp and Robert Ross (Johannesburg: Witwatersrand University Press, 1995).

48. Norman Etherington, *Preachers, Peasants, and Politics in Southeast Africa, 1835–1880: African Christian Communities in Natal, Pondoland and Zululand,* Royal Historical Society Studies in History Series, no. 12 (London: Royal Historical Society, 1978). These exceptions include Sheila M. Brock, "James Stewart and Lovedale: A Reappraisal of Missionary Attitudes and African Response in the Eastern Cape, South Africa, 1870–1905" (PhD thesis, University of Edinburgh, 1974); Jane M. Sales, "The Mission Station as an Agency of 'Civilization': The Development of a Christian Coloured Community in the Eastern Cape, 1800–1859" (PhD thesis, University of Chicago, 1972); Jane M. Sales, *Mission Stations and the Coloured Communities of the Eastern Cape, 1800–1852,* vol. 8 (Cape Town: Balkema, 1975); Bridget E. Seton, "Wesleyan Missionaries and the Sixth Frontier War, 1834–1835" (PhD thesis, University of Cape Town, 1962); Donovan Williams, "Social and Economic Aspects of Christian Missions in Caffraria, 1816–1854, Part 1," *Historia* 30 (1985): 33–48 and "Social and Economic Aspects of Christian Missions in Caffraria 1816–1854, Part 2," *Historia* 31 (1986): 25–58. For the missionary interaction with African cosmologies, see Janet Hodgson, *The God of the Xhosa* (Cape Town: Oxford University Press, 1992); and Janet Hodgson, "A Battle for Sacred Power: Christian Beginnings among the Xhosa," in *Christianity*

in *South Africa: A Political, Social, and Cultural History*, ed. Richard Elphick and Rodney Davenport (Cape Town: David Philip, 1997).

49. Jean Comaroff and John L. Comaroff, *Of Revelation and Revolution*, vol. 1, *Christianity, Colonialism and Consciousness in South Africa* (Chicago: Chicago University Press, 1991). An incomplete draft version of the third manuscript, reputedly about the mission-educated elite, is available in the John and Jean Comaroff Papers Collection, Archives and Special Collections, University of Chicago.

50. For some of the commentary and critique of these volumes, see Clifton C. Crais, "South Africa and the Pitfalls of Postmodernism," *South African Historical Journal* 31, no. 1 (1994): 274–79; Leon De Kock, "For and Against the Comaroffs: Postmodernist Puffery and Competing Conceptions of the 'Archive,'" *South African Historical Journal* 31, no. 1 (1994): 280–89; Johannes Du Bruyn, "Of Muffled Southern Tswana and Overwhelming Missionaries: The Comaroffs and the Colonial Encounter," *South African Historical Journal* 31, no. 1 (1994): 294–309.

51. It is difficult to think of a more exemplary and distilled example of comparative African historical scholarship than that produced in the wake of the publication of this volume and its companion, *Ethnography and the Historical Imagination*. See Shula Marks, "From *Of Revelation and Revolution* to *From Revolution to Reconciliation?* A Comment," *Interventions* 3, no. 1 (2001): 55–64; Jan Vansina, review of *Ethnography and the Historical Imagination*, by Jean Comaroff and John Comaroff, *International Journal of African Historical Studies* 26, no. 2 (1993): 417–20; Elizabeth Elbourne, "Word Made Flesh: Christianity, Modernity, and Cultural Colonialism in the Work of Jean and John Comaroff," *American Historical Review* 108, no. 2 (2003): 435–59.

52. For not only African history, see, for instance, Webb Keane, "From Fetishism to Sincerity: On Agency, the Speaking Subject, and Their Historicity in the Context of Religious Conversion," *Comparative Studies in Society and History* 39, no. 4 (1997): 674–93; Sherry B. Ortner, "Resistance and the Problem of Ethnographic Refusal," *Comparative Studies in Society and History* 37, no. 1 (1995): 173–93.

53. In one of the more biting considerations of the volume, John Peel drew a direct link between this failure to attribute narrative to the Tswana and "its consequences for the kind of accounts that can then be given of Tswana historical agency." John D. Y. Peel, "For Who Hath Despised the Day of Small Things? Missionary Narratives and Historical Anthropology," *Comparative Studies in Society and History* 37, no. 3 (1995): 586.

54. Elizabeth Elbourne, "Early Khoisan Uses of Mission Christianity," *Kronos: Journal of Cape History* 19, no. 1 (1992); Elizabeth Elbourne, *Blood Ground: Colonialism, Missions, and the Contest for Christianity in the Cape Colony and Britain, 1799–1853*, ed. Donald Harman Akenson, McGill-Queen's Studies in the History of Religion (Montreal: McGill-Queen's University Press, 2002), 17; Elbourne, "Word Made Flesh." This goal is present also in Les Switzer's

work on the history of the Ciskei, which draws on his work on the Black press in South Africa to examine the way in which educated African Christians used the tools at their disposal, more the pen than the sword, in their political efforts to resist white colonial power. See Les Switzer, *Power and Resistance in an African Society: The Ciskei Xhosa and the Making of South Africa* (Madison: University of Wisconsin Press, 1993).

55. Elphick and Davenport, *Christianity in South Africa;* Henry Bredekamp and Robert Ross, eds., *Missions and Christianity in South African History* (Johannesburg: Wits University Press, 1995).

56. James T. Campbell, *Songs of Zion: The African Methodist Episcopal Church in the United States and South Africa* (Oxford: Oxford University Press, 1995); Amanda D. Kemp and Robert Trent Vinson, "'Poking Holes in the Sky': Professor James Thaele, American Negroes, and Modernity in 1920s Segregationist South Africa," *African Studies Review* 43, no. 1 (2000): 141; Robert Trent Vinson and Robert Edgar, "Zulus Abroad: Cultural Representations and Educational Experiences of Zulus in America, 1880-1945," *Journal of Southern African Studies* 33, no. 1 (1 March 2007): 43–62; Robert Trent Vinson, *The Americans Are Coming! Dreams of African American Liberation in Segregationist South Africa*, New African Histories (Athens: Ohio University Press, 2012).

57. Isabel Hofmeyr, *The Portable Bunyan: A Transnational History of "The Pilgrim's Progress,"* ed. Emily Apter, (Princeton, NJ: Princeton University Press, 2004). In a similar vein, see Derek Peterson's examination of the aspirational, intellectual, and social lives of Christians in mid-twentieth century Kenya, especially their commitment to reading contemporary texts in heterogeneous ways. Derek R. Peterson, *Creative Writing: Translation, Bookkeeping, and the Work of Imagination in Colonial Kenya*, ed. Allen Isaacman and Jean Allman, Social History of Africa (Portsmouth, NH: Heinemann, 2004).

58. Joel Cabrita, *Text and Authority in the South African Nazaretha Church* (London: Cambridge University Press, 2014); Hofmeyr, *The Portable Bunyan*.

59. Magaziner, *The Law and the Prophets*.

60. For some of the earliest published work, see Peter T. Mtuze, "A Preliminary Annotated Bibliography of Xhosa Prose, Drama and Poetry, 1909–1990," *South African Journal of African Languages* 13, no. sup2 (1 January 1993): 14–26; Noni Jabavu, *Drawn in Colour: African Contrasts* (London: Murray, 1960); Miriam Tlali, *Muriel at Metropolitan* (Johannesburg: Ravan, 1975).

61. In addition to her work cited in Opland, see also Nontsizi Mgqwetho, *The Nation's Bounty: The Xhosa Poetry of Nontsizi Mgqwetho*, African Treasury Series 22 (Johannesburg: Wits University Press, 2007).

62. For a closer look at these debates see Katherine Anne Eales, "Gender Politics and the Administration of African Women in Johannesburg, 1903–1939" (master's thesis, University of Witwatersrand, 2009), http://wiredspace.wits.ac.za/handle/10539/7457; Kathy Eales, "'Jezebels', Good Girls and Mine Married Quarters: Johannesburg, 1912" (working paper, African Studies Institute—Seminar Series, 14 September 2010), http://wiredspace.wits.ac.za//handle/10539/8673.

63. For the reconstruction of African family life, see Natasha Erlank, "Strange Bedfellows: The International Missionary Council, the International African Institute, and Research into African Marriage and Family," in *The Spiritual in the Secular: Missionaries and Knowledge about Africa*, ed. Patrick Harries and David Maxwell (Grand Rapids, MI: W. B. Eerdmans, 2012).
64. Derek R. Peterson and Emma Hunter, "Introduction," in *African Print Cultures: Newspapers and Their Publics in the Twentieth Century*, ed. Derek R. Peterson, Emma Hunter, and Stephanie Newell (Ann Arbor: University of Michigan Press, 2016).
65. Foreign Missions Conference, Burke Theological Library, New York MRL 12/ Ecumenical World FMCNA Box 11: 2, Africa Committee, 16 February 1948.
66. Karin Barber, "Introduction : Hidden Innovators in Africa," in *Africa's Hidden Histories: Everyday Literacy and Making the Self* (Bloomington: Indiana University Press, 2006), 18.
67. Native Appeal Court, ed., *Reports of Cases Decided in the Eastern Districts Local Division* (Cape Town: Juta, 1911), 344–51.

CHAPTER 1: CONVENING CHRISTIAN PUBLICS

1. *South African Native Affairs Commission, 1903–5: Report of the Commission* (Cape Town: Cape Times, Govt. Printers, 1905), 90.
2. Karin Barber, *The Anthropology of Texts, Persons and Publics: Oral and Written Culture in Africa and Beyond*, New Departures in Anthropology 5 (Cambridge: Cambridge University Press, 2007), 1.
3. Richard L. Roberts, *Litigants and Households: African Disputes and Colonial Courts in the French Soudan, 1895–1912* (Portsmouth, NH: Heinemann, 2005); Emily S. Burrill, Richard L. Roberts, and Elizabeth Thornberry, eds., *Domestic Violence and the Law in Colonial and Postcolonial Africa* (Athens: Ohio University Press, 2010).
4. James Campbell, *Songs of Zion: The African Methodist Episcopal Church in the United States and South Africa* (Oxford: Oxford University Press, 1995); Joel Cabrita, *Text and Authority in the South African Nazaretha Church*, International African Library 46 (Cambridge: Cambridge University Press, 2014).
5. Barber, *Anthropology of Texts*, 1.
6. Barber, 1.
7. Barber, 2.
8. Barber, 152. However, I do not agree with her assessment of Magema Fuze's impact on the creation of public audiences (155).
9. Barber, 29.
10. Mark P. Leone, "Epilogue: The Productive Nature of Material Culture and Archaeology," *Historical Archaeology* 26, no. 3 (1992): 131. Here Leone is drawing on Anthony Giddens. For a discussion of this duality in structure, see William H. Sewell, *Logics of History: Social Theory and Social Transformation* (Chicago: University of Chicago Press, 2005), chap. 4.
11. "Volkekunde emphasised that humans were members of culturally separate peoples, that each lived according to its culture in a highly integrated

ethnos with clear boundaries into which new generations were enculturated. The emphasis on deep cultural differences between ethnic groups was associated with an essentialist understanding of culture and ethnos." C. S. (Kees) van der Waal, "Long Walk from Volkekunde to Anthropology: Reflections on Representing the Human in South Africa," *Anthropology Southern Africa* 38, nos. 3–4 (7 October 2015): 221.

12. Karin Barber, "Introduction: Hidden Innovators in Africa," in *Africa's Hidden Histories: Everyday Literacy and Making the Self,* ed. Karin Barber (Bloomington: Indiana University Press, 2006), 2.
13. For a compelling discussion of these trends, see Jochen S. Arndt, *Divided by the Word: Colonial Encounters and the Remaking of Zulu and Xhosa Identities,* Reconsiderations in Southern African History (Charlottesville: University of Virginia Press, 2022).
14. Richard Price, *Making Empire: Colonial Encounters and the Creation of Imperial Rule in Nineteenth-Century Africa* (Cambridge: Cambridge University Press, 2008).
15. William David Hammond-Tooke, "The Transkeian Council System 1895–1955: An Appraisal," *Journal of African History* 9, no. 3 (1968): 455–77.
16. Recently and intriguingly by the late Jeff Guy, *Theophilus Shepstone and the Forging of Natal: African Autonomy and Settler Colonialism in the Making of Traditional Authority* (Scottsville, South Africa: University of KwaZulu-Natal Press, 2013). Guy suggests that most people overattribute indirect rule's least palatable features to Shepstone.
17. For more detail on local government arrangements run through the Native Affairs Department in South Africa, see Saul Dubow, "Holding 'a Just Balance between White and Black': The Native Affairs Department in South Africa c.1920–33," *Journal of Southern African Studies* 12, no. 2 (1986): 219; Les Switzer, *Power and Resistance in an African Society: The Ciskei Xhosa and the Making of South Africa* (Madison: University of Wisconsin Press, 1993).
18. Elizabeth Elbourne, *Blood Ground: Colonialism, Missions, and the Contest for Christianity in the Cape Colony and Britain, 1799–1853,* ed. Donald Harman Akenson, McGill-Queen's Studies in the History of Religion (Montreal: McGill-Queen's University Press, 2002); Natasha Erlank, "The Spread of Indigenous Christianity in British Kaffraria after 1850," *Missionalia* 31, no. 1 (2003): 19–41.
19. Tom Lodge, *Black Politics in South Africa since 1945* (London: Longman, 1983).
20. On Lovedale and its educational politics on whether it advocated regular or industrial education for Africans, see Sheila Brock, "James Stewart and Lovedale: A Reappraisal of Missionary Attitudes and African Response in the Eastern Cape, South Africa, 1870–1905" (PhD diss., University of Edinburgh, 1974); Leon De Kock, *Civilising Barbarians: Missionary Narrative and African Textual Response in Nineteenth-Century South Africa* (Johannesburg: Wits University Press, 1996); Natasha Erlank, "'Raising Up the Degraded Daughters of Africa': The Provision of Education

for Xhosa Women in the Mid-nineteenth Century," *South African Historical Journal* 43, no. 1 (2000): 24–38; Robert H. W. Shepherd, *Lovedale, South Africa: The Story of a Century, 1841–1941* (Lovedale, South Africa: Lovedale, 1940).

21. On the Cattle Killing, see Jeff B. Peires, *The Dead Will Arise: Nongqawuse and the Great Xhosa Cattle-Killing Movement of 1856-7* (Johannesburg: Ravan, 1989). On how Christianity spread in relation to it, see Erlank, "Spread of Indigenous Christianity."
22. On African initiated churches, see Hennie Pretorius and Lizo Jafta, "'A Branch Springs Out': African Initiated Churches," in *Christianity in South Africa: A Political, Social, and Cultural History*, ed. Richard Elphick and Rodney Davenport (Cape Town: David Philip, 1997), 211–26, and other sources in this section.
23. Conversion in southern Africa did not always occur first amongst women. See, for instance, Paul Stuart Landau, *The Realm of the Word: Language, Gender, and Christianity in a Southern African Kingdom* (Portsmouth, NH: Heinemann, 1995).
24. Switzer, *Power and Resistance in an African Society*, 235.
25. Cape Archives Depot, Cape Town, CAD 1/ALC Churches and School Sites.
26. National Library of Scotland, Acc. 75486, Part B, Lovedale Bible School, Report of work in the outside areas during the period of 6 August to 4 September of 1932.
27. National Library of Scotland.
28. For an excellent account of an African peasant class facing declining access to resources and cattle epizootics, see Sean Redding, "Peasants and the Creation of an African Middle Class in Umtata, 1880–1950," *International Journal of African Historical Studies* 26, no. 3 (1993): 513–39. This framework holds also in future chapters.
29. University of the Witwatersrand (Wits), Johannesburg, Department of Historical Papers, Church of the Province of South Africa (CPSA) AB799, St. Cuthbert's Mission, Bb, Workers' Quarterly Meeting, 13 December 1941.
30. Wits, CPSA AB799, Bb, Workers' Quarterly Meeting.
31. For some of this debate, see Geoff Eley, "Dilemmas and Challenges of Social History since the 1960s: What Comes after the Cultural Turn?," *South African Historical Journal* 60, no. 3 (1 September 2008): 310–22, https://doi.org/10.1080/02582470802417391.
32. Matthew Wilhelm-Solomon et al., eds., *Routes and Rites to the City: Mobility, Diversity and Religious Space in Johannesburg*, Global Diversities (London: Palgrave Macmillan UK, 2016).
33. Henry Glassie, *Passing the Time in Ballymenone: Culture and History of an Ulster Community* (Bloomington: Indiana University Press, 1995), 13.
34. A similar point is made about how people occupy multiple identities simultaneously, in William Beinart and Colin Bundy, "Introduction: 'Away in the Locations,'" in *Hidden Struggles in Rural South Africa: Politics and Popular*

Movements in the Transkei and Eastern Cape 1890–1930, ed. William Beinart and Colin Bundy (Johannesburg: Ravan, 1987), 1–45.
35. Glassie, *Passing the Time in Ballymenone*, 13.
36. Phillip Bonner, "The Transvaal Native Congress, 1917–1920: The Radicalisation of the Black Petty Bourgeoisie on the Rand," in *Industrialisation and Social Change in South Africa: African Class Formation, Culture, and Consciousness, 1870–1930*, ed. Shula Marks and Richard Rathbone (London: Longman, 1982); David Goodhew, "Working-Class Respectability: The Example of the Western Areas of Johannesburg, 1930–55," *Journal of African History* 41, no. 2 (2000): 241–66.
37. Jean Comaroff and John L. Comaroff, *Of Revelation and Revolution*, vol. 1, *Christianity, Colonialism and Consciousness in South Africa* (Chicago: Chicago University Press, 1991).
38. Lynn M. Thomas, "Historicising Agency," *Gender & History* 28, no. 2 (2016): 330, 335.
39. "A first step toward for an anthropology of Christianity would be to move past this, to have anthropologists who study Christianity be able to say that whatever else they are, they are also anthropologists of Christianity. Only once they take this step can the intellectual work of establishing an anthropology of Christianity for itself begin." Joel Robbins, "What Is a Christian? Notes toward an Anthropology of Christianity," *Religion* 33, no. 3 (2003): 195.
40. Dissenting Presbyterians in Scotland split from the established church in the late 1830s over the principle that each congregation should be able to call its own minister. Calvinist theology made for a conservative church. The church legacy in Africa meant that local churches valued local wishes but within a framework that supported the church. John H. S. Burleigh, *A Church History of Scotland* (London: Oxford University Press, 1960).
41. Shepherd, *Lovedale, South Africa*, 340.
42. David M. Gordon, *Invisible Agents: Spirits in a Central African History* (Athens: Ohio University Press, 2012).
43. Derek R. Peterson, *Ethnic Patriotism and the East African Revival: A History of Dissent, c.1935–1972*, African Studies (Cambridge: Cambridge University Press, 2012).
44. A phrase in his book and in several of his articles. Richard Elphick, "The Benevolent Empire and the Social Gospel: Missionaries and South African Christians in the Age of Segregation," in *Christianity in South Africa: A Political, Social and Cultural History*, ed. Richard Elphick and Rodney Davenport (Cape Town: David Philip, 1997), 347–69; Richard Elphick, *The Equality of Believers: Protestant Missionaries and the Racial Politics of South Africa*, Reconsiderations in Southern African History (Charlottesville: University of Virginia Press, 2012). Elphick focuses on the role that Protestant missionaries played in mediating and shaping racial politics in South African history.
45. For Le Zoute, see Elphick, *The Equality of Believers*, 129. Elphick also includes detail on the various other conferences mentioned here (see chap. 8).

46. School of Oriental and African Studies (SOAS), IMC/CBMS Africa 1, Box 217 Le Zoute, File: Draft Resolutions.
47. Martin Chanock, *The Making of South African Legal Culture 1902–1936: Fear, Favour and Prejudice* (Cambridge: Cambridge University Press, 2001); Elizabeth Thornberry, *Colonizing Consent: Rape and Governance in South Africa's Eastern Cape* (Cambridge: Cambridge University Press, 2018).
48. Walter Ernest Mortimer Stanford, *The Reminiscences of Sir Walter Stanford 1885–1929*, ed. John Macquarrie, vol. 2, Van Riebeeck Society Second Series 43 (Cape Town: Van Riebeeck Society, 1962), 11.
49. Stanford, 109.
50. Stanford, 145.
51. Stanford, 12.
52. Thornberry, *Colonizing Consent*, 182, and elsewhere in the volume.
53. Thornberry discusses meanings and understanding of consent in Xhosaland in the nineteenth century, as well as the difficulty around agreement on the definition of rape according to the Xhosa, the colonial lawmakers, and the historical record. Thornberry, 18.
54. Stanford, *Reminiscences*, 11.
55. Thornberry, *Colonizing Consent*, 305.
56. Roberts, *Litigants and Households*, 2.
57. Compare the list of judgments in the Civil Judgements books with the list of proceedings. The judgments are available, but the latter includes only cases considered worthy of preservation. Cape Archives Depot, 1/ALC 2/4/1 Civil Judgement Book with 1/ALC 2/1/1/35 Civil Proceedings, 1916–1928.
58. Benjamin N. Lawrance, Emily Lynn Osborn, and Richard L. Roberts, "African Intermediaries and the 'Bargain' of Collaboration," SSRN Scholarly Paper (Rochester, NY: Social Science Research Network, 22 August 2006), https://papers.ssrn.com/abstract=1914787; Burrill, Roberts, and Thornberry, *Domestic Violence and the Law*.
59. Thomas V. McClendon, *Genders and Generations Apart: Labor Tenants and Customary Law in Segregation-Era South Africa, 1920s to 1940s* (Portsmouth, NH: Heinemann, 2002), 26.
60. Thornberry, *Colonizing Consent*, 172, 263.
61. For examples, see Native Appeal Courts, ed., *Selection of Cases Decided in the Native Appeal and Divorce Court: Cape and Orange Free State Division . . . with Table of Cases and Alphabetical Index* (Cape Town: Juta, 1914); and Native Appeal Courts, ed., *Selection of Cases Decided in the Native Appeal and Divorce Court: Cape and Orange Free State Division . . . with Table of Cases and Alphabetical Index* (Cape Town: Juta, 1929).
62. Derek R. Peterson, Emma Hunter, and Stephanie Newell, eds., *African Print Cultures: Newspapers and Their Publics in the Twentieth Century* (Ann Arbor: University of Michigan Press, 2016). Also Stephanie Newell, *Literary Culture in Colonial Ghana: "How to Play the Game of Life"* (Manchester: Manchester University Press, 2002); Stephanie Newell, *The Power to Name: A History*

of Anonymity in Colonial West Africa, New African Histories (Athens: Ohio University Press, 2013).

63. For a brief listing of some of this work, see Natasha Erlank, "*Umteteli wa Bantu* and the Constitution of Social Publics in the 1920s and 1930s," *Social Dynamics* 45, no. 1 (2 January 2019): 75–102; Meghan Healy-Clancy, "The Politics of New African Marriage in Segregationist South Africa," *African Studies Review* 57, no. 2 (September 2014): 7–28; Isabel Hofmeyr, *Gandhi's Printing Press: Experiments in Slow Reading* (Cambridge, MA: Harvard University Press, 2013); Athambile Masola, "'Bantu Women on the Move': Black Women and the Politics of Mobility in *The Bantu World*," *Historia* 63, no. 1 (May 2018): 93; Bhekizizwe Peterson, "*The Bantu World* and the World of the Book: Reading, Writing, and 'Enlightenment,'" in *Africa's Hidden Histories: Everyday Literacy and Making the Self*, ed. Karin Barber (Bloomington: Indiana University Press, 2006), 236–57; Corinne Sandwith, "Revolutionaries or Sell-Outs? African Intellectuals and *The Voice of Africa*, 1949–1952," *English in Africa* 33, no. 2 (2006): 67; Corinne Sandwith, *World of Letters: Reading Communities and Cultural Debates in Early Apartheid South Africa* (Pietermaritzburg: University of KwaZulu-Natal Press, 2014).

64. Barber, *The Anthropology of Texts*, 150.

65. For a list of these, see Les Switzer and Donna Switzer, *The Black Press in South Africa and Lesotho: A Descriptive Bibliographic Guide to African, Coloured and Indian Newspapers, Newsletters and Magazines 1836–1976*, Bibliographies and Guides in African Studies (Boston: G. K. Hall, 1979). An online copy may be found here: "Archives and Online Resources," Black Press Research Collective, accessed 31 July 2021, http://blackpressresearchcollective.org/resources/scholarship-archives/.

66. "Dr. Booker T. Washington on the Negro Problem" and "The Gift of the Father," *Christian Express*, 2 January 1911, 8.

67. Barber, *The Anthropology of Texts*, 3.

68. T. D. Mweli Skota, *The African Yearly Register: Being an Illustrated National Biographical Dictionary (Who's Who) of Black Folks in Africa* (Johannesburg: R. L. Esson, 1931).

69. James T. Campbell, "T. D. Mweli Skota and the Making and Unmaking of a Black Elite," (working paper, 14 February 1987), http://wiredspace.wits.ac.za/handle/10539/7732; Herbert I. E. Dhlomo, *H. I. E. Dhlomo: Collected Works*, ed. Tim Couzens and Nick Visser (Johannesburg: Ravan, 1985).

70. Harri Englund, ed., *Christianity and Public Culture in Africa*, Cambridge Centre of African Studies Series (Athens: Ohio University Press, 2011), 8.

71. International Committee for Christian Literature in Africa, School of Oriental and African Studies 509/8, Margaret Wrong, 1 June 1936.

CHAPTER 2: MODERN MASCULINITY

1. James Calata in a manuscript at the University of Cape Town, African Studies Library, Lestrade Collection BC 255 A3.229, hereafter BC 255 A3.229. The

manuscript has no page numbers. Grateful thanks to Jochen Arndt for bringing this to my attention. The text is in English, copied and possibly translated by the eminent linguist Lestrade on his visit to the Eastern Cape sometime in the 1920s. The published piece is available as "Ukudlelana kobu-Kristu namasiko olwaluko lwabantu AbaNtsundu" in *Inkolo Namasiko A-Bantu*, ed. S. J. Wallis (London: Society for Promoting Christian Knowledge, 1930), 38–49. Peter Mtuze comments on the volume in "Hidden Presences in the Spirituality of the AmaXhosa of the Eastern Cape and the Impact of Christianity on Them" (master's thesis, Rhodes University, 1999), 64, https://core.ac.uk/reader/145053771. Lestrade's translation predates this volume.

2. Mandy Goedhals, "African Nationalism and Indigenous Christianity: A Study in the Life of James Calata (1895–1983)," *Journal of Religion in Africa* 33, no. 1 (2003): 72.
3. Umboneli Wezinto, "Isiko Lesizwe," *Umteteli*, 25 March 1922, 7.
4. All the historical and most of the contemporary popular and vernacular literature refers to "circumcision" rather than "initiation." The professional and academic literature more often refers to the practice as "traditional male circumcision and initiation," or "TMCI." I follow popular usage.
5. X. Y. Z., "Ulwaluko-Isiqendu II [Circumcision—Chapter II]," *Umteteli*, 2 September 1922, 7.
6. Alec Ryrie, *Protestants: The Faith That Made the Modern World* (New York: Viking, 2017).
7. John Henderson Soga, *The Ama-Xosa: Life and Customs* (Lovedale, South Africa: Lovedale, 1932), 169; Jeff Peires, *The House of Phalo: A History of the Xhosa People in the Days of Their Independence* (Johannesburg: Ravan, 1981), 199n31.
8. Lynn M. Thomas, "'Ngaitana (I Will Circumcise Myself)': The Gender and Generational Politics of the 1956 Ban on Clitoridectomy in Meru, Kenya," *Gender and History* 8, no. 3 (1996): 338–63; Christine J. Walley, "Searching for 'Voices': Feminism, Anthropology, and the Global Debate over Female Genital Operations," *Cultural Anthropology* 12, no. 3 (1997): 405–38.
9. Charles H. Ambler, "The Renovation of Custom in Colonial Kenya: The 1932 Generation Succession Ceremonies in Embu," *Journal of African History* 30, no. 1 (1989): 139–56; Jan Vansina, *Paths in the Rainforests: Toward a History of Political Tradition in Equatorial Africa* (Madison: University of Wisconsin Press, 1990); John Lonsdale, "Mau Maus of the Mind: Making Mau Mau and Remaking Kenya," *Journal of African History* 31, no. 3 (1990): 393–421; Bruce Berman and John Lonsdale, *Unhappy Valley: Conflict in Kenya and Africa*, Eastern African Studies (London: Ohio University Press, 1992); Jan Jacob de Wolf, "Circumcision and Initiation in Western Kenya and Eastern Uganda: Historical Reconstructions and Ethnographic Evidence," *Anthropos* 78, nos. 3/4 (1983): 369–410.
10. Corrie Decker, "A Feminist Methodology of Age-Grading and History in Africa," *American Historical Review* 125, no. 2 (April 2020): 418–26.

11. For instance, see Henri Alexandre Junod, *The Life of a South African Tribe* (London: Macmillan, 1927); John Blacking, "243. Fictitious Kinship amongst Girls of the Venda of the Northern Transvaal," *Man* 59 (1959): 155–58; Joan A. Broster, *Red Blanket Valley* (Johannesburg: H. Keartland, 1967); Eileen Jensen Krige, "Girls' Puberty Songs and Their Relation to Fertility, Health, Morality and Religion among the Zulu," *Africa* 38, no. 2 (1968): 173–98.
12. Berthold A. Pauw, *Christianity and Xhosa Tradition: Belief and Ritual among Xhosa-Speaking Christians* (Cape Town: Oxford University Press, 1975), 98, 172; Monica Wilson et al., *Keiskammahoek Rural Survey*, vol. 3, *Social Structure* (Pietermaritzburg: Shuter and Shooter, 1952), 111.
13. For instance, Nicholas J. Van Warmelo and Wilfred M. D. Phophi, *Venda Law* (Pretoria: Government Printer, 1948); Alan Kirkaldy, *Capturing the Soul: The Vhavenda and the Missionaries, 1870–1900* (Pretoria: Protea Book House, 2005); Anitra Nettleton, "Ethnic and Gender Identities in Venda *Domba* Statues," *African Studies* 51, no. 2 (1 January 1992): 203–30; Philip Bonner, "'Desirable or Undesirable Basotho Women?' Liquor, Prostitution and the Migration of Basotho Women to the Rand, 1920–1945," in *Women and Gender in Southern Africa to 1945*, ed. Cherryl Walker (Cape Town: David Philip, 1990).
14. Robert Morrell, "Masculinity in South African History: Towards a Gendered Approach to the Past," *South African Historical Journal* 37 (1997): 167–77.
15. Clive Glaser, "Swines, Hazels, and the Dirty Dozen: Masculinity, Territoriality, and the Youth Gangs of Soweto, 1960–1976," *Journal of Southern African Studies* 24, no. 4 (1998): 719–36; Elizabeth Gunner, "Soft Masculinities, *Isicathamiya* and Radio," *Journal of Southern African Studies* 40, no. 2 (2014): 343–60; Mark Hunter, *Love in the Time of AIDS: Inequality, Gender, and Rights in South Africa* (Bloomington: Indiana University Press, 2010); Anne Kelk Mager, *Beer, Sociability, and Masculinity in South Africa* (Bloomington: Indiana University Press, 2010).
16. Including in research done for the state-funded South African Bureau for Racial Affairs, Anna F. Steyn, *Die Bantoe in die Stad: Die Bantoegesin* (Pretoria: Suid-Afrikaanse Buro vir Rasse-Angeleenthede, 1966).
17. William Beinart, *The Political Economy of Pondoland 1860–1930* (Johannesburg: Ravan, 1982); William David Hammond-Tooke, *Bhaca Society: A People of the Transkeian Uplands, South Africa* (Cape Town: Oxford University Press, 1962), 19–22.
18. Benedict Carton and Robert Morrell, "Zulu Masculinities, Warrior Culture and Stick Fighting: Reassessing Male Violence and Virtue in South Africa," *Journal of Southern African Studies* 38, no. 1 (1 March 2012): 40; John Laband, "The Rise and Fall of the Zulu Kingdom," in *Zulu Identities: Being Zulu, Past and Present*, ed. Benedict Carton, John Laband, and Jabulani Sithole (Scottsville, South Africa: University of KwaZulu-Natal Press, 2009), 87–96.
19. Laband, "The Rise and Fall of the Zulu Kingdom," 87; Mxolisi Mchunu, "A Modern Coming of Age: Zulu Manhood, Domestic Work, and the 'Kitchen Suit,'" in *Zulu Identities*, 580.

20. For a fascinating and comprehensive discussion of current debates, including a review of the historiography, see Harriet Deacon and Kirsten Thomson, "The Social Penis: Traditional Male Circumcision and Initiation in Southern Africa, 1800–2000: A Literature Review," (working paper, Centre for Social Science Research, Cape Town, 2012), https://open.uct.ac.za/bitstream/item/22004/Deacon_Social_Penis_2012.pdf?sequence=1. For historical circumcision among isiXhosa speakers, in addition to the sources mentioned in this chapter, see Percy W. Laidler, "Bantu Ritual Circumcision," *Man* 22, nos. 6–7 (1922): 13–14; Frank Brownlee, "248. The Circumcision Ceremony in Fingoland, Transkeian Territories, South Africa," *Man* 31 (1931): 251–54; Barend J. F. Laubscher, *Sex, Custom and Psychopathology: A Study of South African Pagan Natives* (London: George Routledge & Sons, 1937).

21. John Henderson Soga, *The Ama-Xosa: Life and Customs* (Lovedale, South Africa: Lovedale, 1932).

22. Cory Ms16369b: Translation of *Intlalo xa Xosa* 1917 by T. B. Soga. Trans. C. S. Papu (hereafter T. B. Soga, *Intlalo* and page number).

23. For J. H. Soga's comments on Xhosa superiority, see Soga, *The Ama-Xosa: Life and Customs*, 11. For the Mfengu, see Wallace G. Mills, "The Fork in the Road: Religious Separatism versus African Nationalism in the Cape Colony, 1890–1910," *Journal of Religion in Africa* 9, no. 1 (1978): 51–61; Timothy J. Stapleton, "The Expansion of a Pseudo-Ethnicity in the Eastern Cape: Reconsidering the Fingo 'Exodus' of 1865," *International Journal of African Historical Studies* 29, no. 2 (1996): 233–50.

24. Soga, *Intlalo*, 79–81.

25. Laidler, "Bantu Ritual Circumcision"; Brownlee, "The Circumcision Ceremony in Fingoland"; Calata, "Ukudlelana kobu-Kristu."

26. Natasha Erlank, "Gendering Commonality: African Men and the 1883 Commission on Native Law and Custom," *Journal of Southern African Studies* 29, no. 4 (2003): 937–53; Jack Lewis, "An Economic History of the Ciskei, 1848–1900" (PhD thesis, University of Cape Town, 1984).

27. For some account of these differences as emanating from a modern versus a conservative background, see Wilson et al., *Keiskammahoek*, appendix B.

28. Peter Delius and Clive Glaser, "Sexual Socialisation in South Africa: A Historical Perspective," *African Studies* 61, no. 1 (2002): 27–54.

29. Patrick A. McAllister and Dumisani Deliwe, "Youth in Rural Transkei: The Demise of 'Traditional' Youth Associations and the Development of New Forms of Association and Activity: 1975–1993" (working paper, Institute of Social and Economic Research, Rhodes University, 1994).

30. Soga, *Intlalo*, 79. Before the 1950s, the Xhosa masculine ideal centered on the figure of a warrior, with the instruction of initiates reflecting this goal. Anne Kelk Mager, *Gender and the Making of a South African Bantustan: A Social History of the Ciskei 1945–1959*, Social History of Africa, ed. Allan Isaacman and Jean Allman (Cape Town: David Philip, 1999), 128–33.

31. For the practice and a more in-depth discussion of sex as "men having sex with men" (not homosexuality), see T. Dunbar Moodie (with Vivien Ndatshe

and British Sibuye), "Migrancy and Male Sexuality on the South African Gold Mines," *Journal of Southern African Studies* 14, no. 2 (1988): 228–56; Zackie Achmat, "'Apostles of Civilised Vice': 'Immoral Practices' and 'Unnatural Vice' in South African Prisons and Compounds, 1890–1920," *Social Dynamics* 19, no. 2 (1 December 1993): 92–110. For initiation and masturbation, see Joshua Peter Willows, "Shaping the Boys' South African Identity: Suppressed Queer Space in *Spud* and *Inxeba*" (master's thesis, University of the Western Cape, 2020), 66–69, http://etd.uwc.ac.za/xmlui/handle/11394/8143.

32. "Indigenous Film Distribution (Pty) Ltd and Another v Film and Publication Appeal Tribunal and Others (3589/2018) [2018] ZAGPPHC 438; [2018] 3 All SA 783 (GP) (27 June 2018)," http://www.saflii.org/za/cases/ZAGPPHC/2018/438.html. See the conclusion for a discussion of how circumcision was made public in relation to the film *Inxeba*.

33. Calata quoted in Lestrade's translation of his writing. UCT, Lestrade Collection BC 255 A3.229.

34. Soga, *The Ama-Xosa: Life and Customs*, 48.

35. Kropf translates the word thus: "*ubu-Doda, N. 7.* Manhood, manliness, euphem. for the penis; virility." Albert Kropf, *A Kafir-English Dictionary*, 2nd ed. (Stutterheim, South Africa: Lovedale Mission, 1915), 81.

36. Soga, *The Ama-Xosa: Life and Customs*, 99.

37. Benedict Carton, *Blood from Your Children: The Colonial Origins of Generational Conflict in South Africa* (Charlottesville: University of Virginia Press, 2000); Nafisa Essop Sheik, "African Marriage Regulation and the Remaking of Gendered Authority in Colonial Natal, 1843–1875," *African Studies Review* 57, no. 2 (2014): 73–92; Anne Kelk Mager, "Youth Organisations and the Construction of Masculine Identities in the Ciskei and Transkei, 1945–1960," *Journal of Southern African Studies* 24, no. 4 (1998): 653–67.

38. See also Beinart, *The Political Economy of Pondoland*; William Beinart, "The Origins of the *Indlavini*," *African Studies* 50, no. 1 (1991): 103–28. Also, for more specifically on the construction of masculine identity, see Mager, *Gender and the Making of a South African Bantustan*; Mager, "Youth Organisations."

39. Soga, *The Ama-Xosa: Life and Customs*, 253.

40. Soga, 248; Berthold A. Pauw, *The Second Generation: Study of the Family among Urbanized Bantu in East London* (Cape Town: Oxford University Press, 1973), 89.

41. Berman and Lonsdale, *Unhappy Valley*, 317.

42. Pauw, *The Second Generation*, 89–90. Quotation collected from an informant in the 1950s.

43. Deacon and Thomson, "The Social Penis," 43; Eileen Jensen Krige, *The Social System of the Zulus*, 2nd ed. (Pietermaritzburg: Shuter and Shooter, 1950), 106–11.

44. Krige, *The Social System of the Zulus*, 108.

45. For a recent discussion of this, see Andile Mayekiso, "'*Ukuba yindoda kwelixesha*' ('To Be a Man in These Times'): Fatherhood, Marginality and Forms

of Life among Young Men in Gugulethu, Cape Town" (PhD thesis, University of Cape Town, 2017), https://open.uct.ac.za/handle/11427/24447.
46. The association of pain and initiation is well established in the anthropological literature. For example, see Alan Morinis, "The Ritual Experience: Pain and the Transformation of Consciousness in Ordeals of Initiation," *Ethos* 13, no. 2 (1985): 150–74.
47. Calata quoted in BC 255 A3.229.
48. Wilson, Kaplan, and Maki, *Keiskammahoek*, 203; Pauw, *The Second Generation*, 95.
49. Louise Vincent, "Cutting Tradition: The Political Regulation of Traditional Circumcision Rites in South Africa's Liberal Democratic Order," *Journal of Southern African Studies* 34, no. 1 (2008): 77–91; Louise Vincent, "'Boys Will Be Boys': Traditional Xhosa Male Circumcision, HIV and Sexual Socialisation in Contemporary South Africa," *Culture, Health & Sexuality* 10, no. 5 (2008): 431–46. These two excellent articles were very helpful in formulating my thinking in this chapter.
50. Congress of Traditional Leaders quoted in Vincent, "Cutting Tradition," 81.
51. Wilson, Kaplan, and Maki, *Keiskammahoek*, 216–19, including endnotes.
52. For use of the term "soft," see Gunner, "Soft Masculinities, *Isicathamiya* and Radio."
53. Anne Marie Stoner-Eby, "African Clergy, Bishop Lucas and the Christianizing of Local Initiation Rites: Revisiting 'The Masasi Case,'" *Journal of Religion in Africa* 38, no. 2 (May 2008): 185.
54. Jeff Guy, *The Destruction of the Zulu Kingdom: The Civil War in Zululand, 1879–1884*, New History of South Africa (Johannesburg: Ravan, 1982), 11–12.
55. Soga, *Intlalo*, 81.
56. Erlank, "Gendering Commonality."
57. University of the Witwatersrand (Wits), Historical Papers, Wits CPSA AB16539, Minutes of the Diocesan Synod, 13 July 1911, Umtata.
58. Wits, Minutes, 1923.
59. Wits CPSA AB1653, Aa1.5 Minutes 1908–1926: 9–13 July 1911.
60. Cory MS16638 Pamphlet: Rules and Regulations of the Diocese, 1926, p. 2.
61. Natasha Erlank, "Missionary Views on Sexuality in Xhosaland in the 19th Century," *Le Fait Missionaire* 11, no. 1 (2001): 9–44; Deborah Gaitskell, "'Wailing for Purity': Prayer Unions, African Mothers and Adolescent Daughters 1912–1940," in *Industrialization and Social Change in South Africa: African Class Formation, Culture, and Consciousness, 1870–1930*, ed. Shula Marks and Richard Rathbone (London: Longman, 1982); Wallace G. Mills, "Missionaries, Xhosa Clergy and the Suppression of Traditional Customs," in *Missions and Christianity in South African History*, ed. Henry Bredekamp and Robert Ross (Johannesburg: Wits University Press, 1995).
62. Wits, AB769, Diocese of Pretoria, Native Conference Minutes, Potchefstroom 1916, Heidelberg 1917.
63. This is the translated text of the advertisement, which I have laid out in a text box. *Umteteli*, 6 June 1920, 1.

64. For instance, see advertisements for Seana Marena throughout the early 1910s, including in *Ilanga lase Natal* (20 October 1905), 1.
65. Isaac Wauchope, "Primitive Native Customs," in *Isaac Williams Wauchope: Selected Writings 1874–1916* (Cape Town: Van Riebeeck Society, 2008), 321–22.
66. Wauchope, 321–22.
67. Moses Bandela, "Asiwxoleli Amaxosa," *Umteteli*, 18 February 1922, 5.
68. Derek R. Peterson, *Ethnic Patriotism and the East African Revival: A History of Dissent, c.1935–1972*, African Studies (Cambridge: Cambridge University Press, 2012), 4, 16.
69. G. G. Nqhini, *Umteteli*, 4 March 1922, 8.
70. Umboneli Wezinto, "Isiko Lesizwe," 7.
71. Bandela, "Asiwxoleli Amaxosa," 5.
72. X. Y. Z., "Ulwaluko—Isiqendu I," *Umteteli*, 26 August 1922, 7.
73. X. Y. Z., "Ulwaluko—Isiqendu II," *Umteteli*, 2 September 1922, 7.
74. X. Y. Z., "Isiqendu II."
75. J. P. Makapane, "Ulwaluko," *Umteteli*, 16 September 1922, 8.
76. W. S. D., "Ulwaluko e Nancefield," *Umteteli*, 9 September 1922, 9.
77. See R. Nkosie, "About Superstition," *Umteteli*, 14 August 1937, 9, for a list of Bible chapters in favor of circumcision.
78. Nkosie, "About Superstition."
79. Umboneli Wezinto, "Isiko Lesizwe."
80. Vazidlule, "Isakwiti Ekomityini," *Umteteli*, 15 April 1922.
81. Soga, *The Ama-Xosa: Life and Customs*, 247. See also Walter B. Nqini, "About Superstition," *Umteteli*, 1 January 1938, 8. Compare the King James Version, Gen. 17:10–11.
82. Soga, *Intlalo*, 81.
83. Berman and Lonsdale, *Unhappy Valley*, 390. "For in Jesus Christ neither circumcision availeth anything, nor uncircumcision; but faith which worketh by love." Gal. 5:6 (King James Version).
84. For instance, "Umteto Nomteta," *Ilanga lase Natal*, 3 June 1921, 2.
85. Soga, *The Ama-Xosa: Life and Customs*, 247. Ham's son Cush was known as the founder of modern Ethiopia. Many Bible readers have taken this to mean that Ham was the father of the northeastern peoples of Africa. See Gen. 9 (King James Version). On the validity of the Hamitic myth and male circumcision, see de Wolf, "Circumcision and Initiation in Western Kenya and Eastern Uganda."
86. Calata in Lestrade, UCT BC 255 A3.229.
87. Ps. 68:31 (King James Version). "Princes shall come out of Egypt; Ethiopia shall soon stretch out her hands unto God."
88. Vazidlule, "Isakwiti Ekomityini," 7.
89. Isabel Hofmeyr, "Reading Debating/Debating Reading: The Case of the Lovedale Literary Society, or Why Mandela Quotes Shakespeare," in *Africa's Hidden Histories: Everyday Literacy and Making the Self*, ed. Karin Barber (Bloomington: Indiana University Press, 2006), 271.

90. Hofmeyr, "Reading Debating/Debating Reading," 260.
91. H. K. Mahaluba, "Ulwaluko/Impendulo ku X. Y. Z.," *Umteteli*, 16 September 1922, 8. Also, G. M. Matete, "Mafeking," *Umteteli*, 16 September 1922, 9.
92. H. M. M., "Native Conference," *Umteteli*, 23 September 1922, 9.
93. Editor, "Ulwaluko," *Umteteli*, 30 September 1922, 9.
94. Bonner, "'Desirable or Undesirable Basotho Women?'"; Katherine Eales, "Gender Politics and the Administration of African Women in Johannesburg, 1903–1939" (master's thesis, University of the Witwatersrand, 1991), http://wiredspace.wits.ac.za/handle/10539/7457; Katherine Eales, "Patriarchs, Passes and Privilege: Johannesburg's African Middle Classes and the Question of Night Passes for African Women 1920–1931," in *Holding Their Ground: Class, Locality and Culture in 19th and 20th Century South Africa*, ed. Phillip Bonner et al. (Johannesburg: Wits University Press, 1989); Karen Jochelson, *The Colour of Disease: Syphilis and Racism in South Africa, 1880–1950*, St. Antony's Series (Basingstoke, UK: Palgrave, 2001).
95. Mgqwetho quoted in Jeff Opland, *Xhosa Poets and Poetry* (Cape Town: David Philip, 1998), 214.
96. D. D. Ngqeleni, "Ulwaluko," *Umteteli*, 10 November 1928, 8.
97. E. B. Mpalisa, "Amakwenkwe Makoluswe," *Umteteli*, 8 December 1928, 9. See also Nqini, "About Superstition," for the same sentiment.
98. Zangwa, "Ngo Lwaluko," *Umteteli*, 26 January 1929, 10. E. F. J. Fuku, "Ngo Lwaluko," *Umteteli*, 26 January 1929, 10.
99. Stephanie Newell, *Literary Culture in Colonial Ghana: "How to Play the Game of Life"* (Manchester: Manchester University Press, 2002).
100. Alfred Hoernlé, review of *The Ama-Xosa: Life and Customs*, by John Henderson Soga, *American Anthropologist* 35, no. 2 (1933): 369.
101. SOAS, CBMS/ICCLA 541/38 '*Listen*' Bound Copies, Vol 1.1. Jan–Feb 1932, 6.
102. For the impact of *Listen* in Ghana, see Newell, *Literary Culture in Colonial Ghana*, 89.
103. Ruth Compton Brouwer, "Books for Africans: Margaret Wrong and the Gendering of African Writing, 1929–1963," *International Journal of African Historical Studies* 31, no. 1 (1998): 53–71.
104. Jeff Peires, "The Lovedale Press: Literature for the Bantu Revisited," *History in Africa* 6 (1979): 155–75.
105. Cory Ms16369, Tiyo Burnside Soga.
106. Editor, *Umteteli*, 13 April 1935, 1, and 27 April 1935, 2.
107. T. B. Soga, *Umteteli*, 11 May 1935, 7. Also, Ngqeleni, "Ulwaluko."
108. N. T. J. Ncalo, "Mr. Nazo's letter," *Umteteli*, 4 May 1935, 7.
109. E. N. Pule, "Superstition," *Umteteli*, 19 June 1937; A. S. Grootboom, "What a Rustenburg Reader has to Say about Superstition," *Umteteli*, 24 July 1937, 8; R. M. S. Langa, *Umteteli*, 27 November, 1937, 8.
110. Nomeva, "About Superstition," *Umteteli*, 3 July 1937, 8.
111. For bodies and hygiene, see Timothy Burke, *Lifebuoy Men, Lux Women: Commodification, Consumption, and Cleanliness in Modern Zimbabwe* (Durham,

NC: Duke University Press, 1996). The benefits of circumcision for health are discussed in Calata in Lestrade in UCT BC 255 A3.229.
112. Cory Ms16297, Minutes of Press Sub-Committee, 23 September 1940; Opland, *Xhosa Poets and Poetry*, 168–70.
113. Samuel E. K. Mqhayi, *Abantu Besizwe: Historical and Biographical Writings, 1902–1944* (Johannesburg, South Africa: Wits University Press, 2009), 84.
114. Cory Ms16297, Minutes of Press Sub-Committee, 23 September 1940; Mqhayi, *Abantu Besizwe*.

CHAPTER 3: LOVE, SEX, AND CONSEQUENCE

1. Cape Archives Depot, Cape Town, ALC (Alice) CAD ALC 2/1/2/1 Case 13 of 1933. References to this case, including the letters between Dorothy Kabane and Selbourne Bokwe, are to this file in the Cape Archives, unless otherwise specified. Dorothy Kabane to Selbourne Bokwe, Umtata, end Nov/start Dec 1932. In this chapter, Selbourne Bokwe is abbreviated in endnotes to "SB" and Dorothy Kabane to "DK."
2. SB to DK, Ntselemanzi, 3 December 1932.
3. I refer to the magistrates' or native commissioner courts (what they were called in the 1920s) as civil courts to avoid the difficulties from only referring to them as customary courts (not all civil cases between Africans were heard according to so-called customary law). Also, these courts were often referred to by different names in the period under review and depended on the region of the country where the cases were heard.
4. Joan A. Broster, *The Tembu: Their Beadwork, Songs and Dances* (Cape Town: Purnell, 1976).
5. Eileen Jensen Krige, "Girls' Puberty Songs and Their Relation to Fertility, Health, Morality and Religion among the Zulu," *Africa: Journal of the International African Institute* 38, no. 2 (1968): 173–98, https://doi.org/10.2307/1157245; Broster, *The Tembu*.
6. Deborah Gaitskell, "'Wailing for Purity': Prayer Unions, African Mothers and Adolescent Daughters 1912–1940," in *Industrialization and Social Change in South Africa: African Class Formation, Culture, and Consciousness, 1870–1930*, ed. Shula Marks and Richard Rathbone (London: Longman, 1982). Wendy Urban-Mead, "'Girls of the Gate': Questions of Purity and Piety in the Mtshabezi Girls' Primary Boarding School in Colonial Zimbabwe, 1908–1940," *Le Fait Missionaire* 11 (2001): 75–99; Wendy Urban-Mead, *The Gender of Piety: Family, Faith, and Colonial Rule in Matabeleland, Zimbabwe* (Athens: Ohio University Press, 2015), 79.
7. Stevi Jackson and Sue Scott, *Theorizing Sexuality* (Maidenhead: McGraw-Hill International [UK], 2010); Carol S. Vance, "Social Construction Theory and Sexuality," in *Constructing Masculinity*, ed. Maurice Berger, Brian Wallis, and Simon Watson (New York: Routledge, 1995).
8. Isaac Schapera, *Married Life in an African Tribe* (London: Faber and Faber, 1940); Natasha Erlank, "Missionary Views on Sexuality in Xhosaland in the Nineteenth Century," *Le Fait Missionaire:* 11, no. 1 (2001): 9–44.

9. Across several years of teaching a module on gender, fertility, and reproduction at third-year level, students often commented that their parents never talked to them about sex. It took me several years to realize that the question I should have asked was, Who can you talk to about sex?
10. Krige, "Girls' Puberty Songs," 188–89.
11. SB to DK, Ntselemanzi, late Thursday. This is letter "B" in table 3.1.
12. Joel Cabrita, *Written Out: The Life and Work of Regina Gelana Twala* (Athens: Ohio University Press, forthcoming).
13. Keith Breckenridge, "Reasons for Writing: African Working-Class Letter Writing in Early-Twentieth Century South Africa," in *Africa's Hidden Histories: Everyday Literacy and Making the Self*, ed. Karin Barber (Bloomington: Indiana University Press, 2006), 143–63.
14. Catherine Burns, "Sex Lessons from the Post?," *Agenda* 12, no. 29 (1996): 79–91; Natasha Erlank, "'Plain Clean Facts' and Initiation Schools: Christianity, Africans and 'Sex Education' in South Africa, c.1910–1940," *Agenda* 62 (2004): 76–83; Mark Hunter, *Love in the Time of AIDS: Inequality, Gender, and Rights in South Africa* (Bloomington: Indiana University Press, 2010).
15. Krige, "Girls' Puberty Songs"; Monica Wilson et al., *Keiskammahoek Rural Survey*, vol. 3, *Social Structure* (Pietermaritzburg: Shuter and Shooter, 1952).
16. Among Black South Africans, socially sanctioned forms of sex were largely heterosexual. This is not to say that individuals did not participate in same-sex relationships or activities but rather that so many aspects of social reproduction were heteronormative that nonheteronormative acts probably passed relatively unnoticed or were considered erotic practice outside definitions of sex.
17. Elizabeth Thornberry, *Colonizing Consent: Rape and Governance in South Africa's Eastern Cape* (Cambridge: Cambridge University Press, 2018). See also Nyasha Karimakwenda, "Today It Would Be Called Rape: A Historical and Contextual Examination of Forced Marriage and Violence in the Eastern Cape," *Acta Juridica* (2013): 339.
18. Thornberry, *Colonizing Consent*.
19. See many of such love songs and laments in Jeff Opland, *Words That Circle Words: A Choice of South African Oral Poetry* (Parklands, South Africa: Ad. Donker, 1992).
20. These two phenomena may or may not be related. If *metsha* is replaced by penetrative sexual relationships, then it seems logical that pregnancy rates would increase. However, if the rising rate of pregnancy is more about perception, then it is difficult to correlate the two. Peter Delius and Clive Glaser, "Sexual Socialisation in South Africa: A Historical Perspective," *African Studies* 61, no. 1 (2002): 4; Erlank, "Missionary Views on Sexuality."
21. Natasha Erlank, "Gendering Commonality: African Men and the 1883 Commission on Native Law and Custom," *Journal of Southern African Studies* 29, no. 4 (2003): 945.
22. For a discussion of this literature, see Peter N. Stearns and Mark Knapp, "Men and Romantic Love: Pinpointing a 20th-Century Change," *Journal of Social History* 26, no. 4 (1993): 769–95.

23. Stearns and Knapp, "Men and Romantic Love."
24. Jennifer Cole and Lynn M. Thomas, eds., *Love in Africa* (Chicago: The University of Chicago Press, 2009); Jennifer S. Hirsch and Holly Wardlow, eds., *Modern Loves: The Anthropology of Romantic Courtship and Companionate Marriage* (Ann Arbor: University of Michigan Press, 2006); Hunter, *Love in the Time of AIDS*.
25. Cole and Thomas, *Love in Africa*, 17.
26. Lynn M. Thomas, "Love, Sex, and the Modern Girl in 1930s Southern Africa," in *Love in Africa*, ed. Jennifer Cole and Lynn M. Thomas (Chicago: University of Chicago Press, 2009), 46.
27. Thomas, "Love, Sex, and the Modern Girl."
28. CAD 1/ALC 2/1/1/34, Records Civil Proceedings, 1908–1916, Case No. 66 of 1908.
29. CAD 1/KWT 2/1/1/3/2 Civil Cases, Native Magistrates 1918–1928, Case No. 94 of 1921. This letter and the one referenced in the next endnote were written in isiXhosa and translated for the court at the time.
30. CAD 1/KWT 2/1/2/1 Civil Cases BAC 1929–1933, Case No. 10 of 1931.
31. Opland, *Words That Circle Words*, 64.
32. Keith Breckenridge, "Love Letters and Amanuenses: Beginning the Cultural History of the Working Class Private Sphere in Southern Africa, 1900–1933," *Journal of Southern African Studies* 26, no. 2 (June 2000): 337–48; Vukile Khumalo, "Ekukhanyeni Letter-Writers: A Historical Inquiry into Epistolary Network(s) and Political Imagination in KwaZulu-Natal, South Africa," in Barber, *Africa's Hidden Histories*, 113–42.
33. Breckenridge, "Love Letters and Amanuenses," 338, 346.
34. Breckenridge, 343–44. Also, see footnotes 33 and 34 on p. 344.
35. For a discussion of these legal codes, see Martin Chanock, *The Making of South African Legal Culture 1902–1936: Fear, Favour and Prejudice* (Cambridge: Cambridge University Press, 2001); Christopher Saunders, *The Annexation of the Transkeian Territories*, Archives Year Book (Pretoria: Government Printer, 1976); David Welsh, *The Roots of Segregation: Native Policy in Colonial Natal, 1845–1910* (Cape Town: Oxford University Press, 1971).
36. Isabel Hofmeyr, *The Portable Bunyan: A Transnational History of "The Pilgrim's Progress,"* ed. Emily Apter (Princeton, NJ: Princeton University Press, 2004).
37. Isabel Hofmeyr, "Dreams, Documents and 'Fetishes': African Christian Interpretations of *The Pilgrim's Progress*," *Journal of Religion in Africa* 32, no. 2 (2002): 448. This article appears as chap. 6 in Hofmeyr's book. For more on writing and letters, see also Barber, *Africa's Hidden Histories*, which, through a series of pieces covering most of Africa, discusses in detail how letters played a role in self-making.
38. Letter "A."
39. Letter "B1."
40. Letter "B4."
41. Letter "D."

42. Letter "H."
43. Letter "J."
44. Lynn M. Thomas, "Schoolgirl Pregnancies, Letter-Writing and 'Modern' Persons in Late Colonial East Africa," in Barber, *Africa's Hidden Histories*, 180–207.
45. Frieda Bokwe Matthews, *Remembrances*, Mayibuye History and Literature Series, no. 54 (Bellville, South Africa: Mayibuye Books, 1995), 11.
46. It is unclear what the record means by the term "engagement." It could possibly have referred to Dorothy having had previous boyfriends, or it might have been her confusion in front of the court.
47. This is from the record of the appeal, also in the original case folder.
48. *Selection of Cases Decided in the Native Appeal and Divorce Court: Cape and Orange Free State Division . . . with Table of Cases and Alphabetical Index*, vol. 5 (Cape Town: Juta, 1933), 18.
49. Sean Redding, "Deaths in the Family: Domestic Violence, Witchcraft Accusations and Political Militancy in Transkei, South Africa 1904–1965," *Journal of Southern African Studies* 30, no. 3 (2004): 519–37; Tapiwa B. Zimudzi, "African Women, Violent Crime and the Criminal Law in Colonial Zimbabwe, 1900–1952," *Journal of Southern African Studies* 30, no. 3 (2004): 499–517. Brett L. Shadle discusses the interesting ways that women present their agency in court cases centered on adultery in Kenya in *"Girl Cases": Marriage and Colonialism in Gusiiland, Kenya, 1890–1970*, Social History of Africa (Portsmouth, NH: Heinemann, 2006), 120–21.
50. Stephen Robertson, "Age of Consent Law and the Making of Modern Childhood in New York City, 1886–1921," *Journal of Social History* 35, no. 4 (2002): 781–89.
51. National Library of Scotland (NLS), Edinburgh, Acc 75486 Vol B Lovedale Institution Minutes, 7 August 1939.
52. CAD 1/KWT 2/1/2/2 Civil Case, Bantu Affairs Commissioner, 1934–1950, Case No. 28 of 1948.
53. Anne Kelk Mager, "Youth Organisations and the Construction of Masculine Identities in the Ciskei and Transkei, 1945–1960," *Journal of Southern African Studies* 24, no. 4 (1998): 657.
54. Mager, 657.
55. Mager, 661.
56. Mager. The quote is from footnote 53, in which Mager also cites the Mqomboti v. Mzwakali case. I am grateful to this article for the reference to this case.
57. Cory Library for Historical Papers, Rhodes University, Grahamstown, Ms 18691 Qayiso, Interview with Tena, 50.
58. Qayiso, Interview with Qangule, 3. The description at the top of the interview follows: "Name—J. Qangule; Age—32 yrs.; Tribe—Xhosa; Education—matriculation; Church—Methodist church; Occupation—Clerk (R. M. O.); Sex—man; Marital status—unmarried."
59. H. B. Z. Ndidndwa, "Dance Fever in Engcobo District," *Bantu World*, 5 January 1935. Although I have subsequently used *Bantu World* extensively myself,

this letter was first shared with me by the late Phillip Bonner, a generous colleague and researcher in every respect.
60. Mager, "Youth Organisations," 662.
61. NLS Vol B. 369, Native Affairs Commission, Committee on Church and Nation and JD Rheinnalt Jones to Betty Gibson, 11 April 1938.
62. Natasha Erlank, "Sexual Misconduct and Church Power on Scottish Mission Stations in Xhosaland, South Africa, in the 1840s," *Gender & History* 15, no. 1 (2003): 69–84.
63. Thornberry, *Colonizing Consent*, 78.
64. Johannesburg, University of the Witwatersrand, Historical Papers Department, CPSA AB1653 Minutes, 5–11 July 1914, Umtata.
65. NLS, MS7815 "Proceedings of Third General Assembly, BPC, King William's Town July 1925," 189.
66. Cape Town, Cape Archives Depot, Magistrate and Bantu Affairs Commissioner, King William's Town 1/KWT 2/1/1/1/358, No. 436 of 1919.
67. CAD 1/KWT 2/1/1/1/359—Civil Cases 1923–1926 No. 232 of 1926. The defendant was the Cape Province Department of Education.
68. For instance, CAD BEK 1 CE110/Miscellaneous/South African Teachers' Association/ Native Matters 1930–1946, Mrs. E. A. Oliphant to Secretary, Education, CT, 31 Jan 1944.
69. For more about these struggles, see Linda Chisholm, *Between Worlds: German Missionaries and the Transition from Mission to Bantu Education in South Africa* (Johannesburg: Wits University Press, 2018); Jonathan Hyslop, *The Classroom Struggle: Policy and Resistance in South Africa, 1940–1990* (Pietermaritzburg: University of Natal Press, 1999); Sue Krige, "Segregation, Science and Commissions of Enquiry: The Contestation over Native Education Policy in South Africa, 1930–36," *Journal of Southern African Studies* 23, no. 3 (1997): 491–506; Cynthia Kros, *The Seeds of Separate Development: Origins of Bantu Education* (Pretoria: Unisa, 2010).
70. John Iliffe, *Honour in African History*, African Studies (Cambridge: Cambridge University Press, 2005), 248.
71. CAD 1/KWT 2/1/1/1/358—Civil Cases Case no. 1008 of 1921.
72. For instance, see Werner v. Andre, a civil case heard in Grahamstown in 1913, in which Emma Werner sued Victor Andre for £1000 for damages resulting from seduction and pregnancy. The defendant's family had previously offered £250 before the case went to court. The court found the sum sufficient, although the lawyers for Werner argued that there was precedent for "heavy damages." *South African Law Reports, Decisions of the Local Division of the Supreme Court, Eastern Districts, 1913* (Cape Town: Juta, 1913), 532–33.
73. "South Africa, Cape Province, Probate Records of the Master of the High Court, 1834–1989," Thomas Ngaki, 1950, database with images, *FamilySearch*, accessed 28 September 2018, familysearch.org; citing Probate, Grahamstown, Albany, Cape Province, South Africa, 1950, Pietermaritzburg

Archives (Formerly Natal State Archives), South Africa; FHL microfilm 1,670,258.

74. R. Meaker, *Reports of the Native Appeal Courts, Volume III* (Cape Town: Cape Times, 1954), 118, https://repository.up.ac.za/handle/2263/57595.

75. Derek R. Peterson, "Morality Plays: Marriage, Church Courts, and Colonial Agency in Central Tanganyika, ca. 1876–1928," *American Historical Review* 111, no. 4 (October 2006): 983–1010.

76. Iliffe, *Honour in African History,* 257, examines how Black school teachers were accused of immorality in the late nineteenth century in the Cape Colony.

77. Qayiso, "Xhosa Morality—Grahamstown," 46. Note that page numbers in this collection are quite often repeated.

CHAPTER 4: MARRIAGE AND LOBOLA AND THE IMAGINING OF BLACK INTIMATE LIFE

1. Reginald R. R. Dhlomo, *An African Tragedy* (Lovedale, South Africa: Lovedale, 1928), 1.

2. Corinne Sandwith, "Reading and Roaming the Racial City: R. R. R. Dhlomo and *The Bantu World*," *English in Africa* 45, no. 3 (1 November 2018): 17–39.

3. For instance, see Jeff Opland, *Words That Circle Words: A Choice of South African Oral Poetry* (Parklands, South Africa: Ad. Donker, 1992), 58, 62, 63.

4. Aninka Claassens and Dee Smythe, "Marriage, Land and Custom: What's the Law Got to Do with It?," in *Marriage, Land and Custom: Essays on Law and Social Change in South Africa,* ed. Aninka Claassens, Dee Smythe, and Graham Bradfield (Cape Town: Juta, 2013), 1–27.

5. Dorit Posel, "Marriage and Bridewealth (Ilobolo) in Contemporary Zulu Society," *African Studies Review,* no. 2 (2014): 51; Stephanie Rudwick and Dorrit Posel, "Contemporary Functions of Ilobolo (Bridewealth) in Urban South African Zulu Society," *Journal of Contemporary African Studies* 32, no. 1 (2014): 118–36.

6. For an important contribution to its continued relevance, see Michael Yarbrough, "Very Long Engagements: The Persistent Authority of Bridewealth in a Post-apartheid South African Community," *Law & Social Inquiry* 43, no. 4 (2017): 647–77.

7. John L. Comaroff and Jean Comaroff, *Ethnography and the Historical Imagination,* Studies in the Ethnographic Imagination (Boulder, CO: Westview, 1992); Adam Kuper, *Wives for Cattle: Bridewealth and Marriage in Southern Africa* (London: Routledge & Kegan Paul, 1982); John L. Comaroff, "Bridewealth and the Control of Ambiguity in a Tswana Chiefdom," in *The Meaning of Marriage Payments,* ed. John L. Comaroff (London: Academic Press, 1980).

8. The following articles are intriguing discussions of the nonlinear way that chronology, time, and sequencing of events and processes occurred in marriage: Mark Hunter, "Is It Enough to Talk of Marriage as a Process? Legitimate Co-habitation in Umlazi, South Africa," *Anthropology Southern*

Africa 39, no. 4 (2016): 281–96; Julia Pauli and Rijk van Dijk, "Marriage as an End or the End of Marriage? Change and Continuity in Southern African Marriages," *Anthropology Southern Africa* 40, no. V1 (1 January 2017): 257–66; Jacqueline Solway, "'Slow Marriage,' 'Fast *Bogadi*': Change and Continuity in Marriage in Botswana," *Anthropology Southern Africa* 39, no. 4 (2016): 309–22; Hylton White, "The Materiality of Marriage Payments," *Anthropology Southern Africa* 39, no. 4 (2016): 297–308.

9. For *umtshato wase-ofisini,* see Ruth Levin, "Marriage in Langa Native Location" (PhD diss., University of Cape Town, 1946), 89, https://open.uct.ac.za/handle/11427/23447. For *umtshato wesilungu,* see S. G. Melele to Mhleli, *Umteteli wa Bantu,* 25 March 1922, 8.

10. Joan A. Broster, *Red Blanket Valley* (Johannesburg: H. Keartland, 1967), 34.

11. Benedict Carton, *Blood from Your Children: The Colonial Origins of Generational Conflict in South Africa* (Charlottesville: University of Virginia Press, 2000); Patrick Harries, *Work, Culture and Identity: Migrant Laborers in Mozambique and South Africa, c.1860–1910* (Portsmouth, NH: Heinemann, 1991); Anne Kelk Mager, "Youth Organisations and the Construction of Masculine Identities in the Ciskei and Transkei, 1945–1960," *Journal of Southern African Studies* 24, no. 4 (1998): 653–67; Thomas V. McClendon, *Genders and Generations Apart: Labor Tenants and Customary Law in Segregation-Era South Africa, 1920s–1940s* (Oxford: James Currey, 2002).

12. Dhlomo, *An African Tragedy;* Meghan Healy-Clancy, "Women and the Problem of Family in Early African Nationalist History and Historiography," *South African Historical Journal* 64, no. 3 (2012): 450–71.

13. Mark Hunter, *Love in the Time of AIDS: Inequality, Gender, and Rights in South Africa* (Bloomington: Indiana University Press, 2010), 41.

14. Mxolisi Mchunu, "A Modern Coming of Age: Zulu Manhood, Domestic Work and the 'Kitchen Suit,'" in *Zulu Identities: Being Zulu, Past and Present,* ed. Benedict Carton, John Laband, and Jabulani Sithole (Scottsville, South Africa: University of KwaZulu-Natal Press, 2009), 573–83.

15. Cory Library for Historical Research, Rhodes University, Grahamstown, Ms16891, Qayiso, Interview Dikani, St Lukes. For more detail on this collection, see the "Abbreviations" at the start of this book.

16. John Philip, *Researches in South Africa* [. . .] (New York: Negro Universities Press, 1969). For more discussion of this and earlier missionary liberalism, see Elizabeth Elbourne, *Blood Ground: Colonialism, Missions, and the Contest for Christianity in the Cape Colony and Britain, 1799–1853,* ed. Donald Harmon Akenson, McGill-Queen's Studies in the History of Religion (Montreal: McGill-Queen's University Press, 2002); Elizabeth Elbourne, "Concerning Missionaries: The Case of Van Der Kemp," *Journal of Southern African Studies* 17, no. 1 (1991): 153; Greg Cuthbertson, "Van Der Kemp and Philip: The Missionary Debate Revisited," *Missionalia* 17 (1989): 77–94. Jeff Guy has an interesting discussion on changing settler attitudes and pivotal points in the nineteenth century in Jeff Guy, *Theophilus Shepstone and the Forging of Natal:*

African Autonomy and Settler Colonialism in the Making of Traditional Authority (Scottsville, South Africa: University of KwaZulu-Natal Press, 2013), 7–9.

17. Natasha Erlank, "Re-examining Initial Encounters between Christian Missionaries and the Xhosa, 1820–1850," *African Historical Review* 31, no. 1 (1999): 6–32; Norman Etherington, *Preachers, Peasants, and Politics in Southeast Africa, 1835–1880: African Christian Communities in Natal, Pondoland, and Zululand,* Royal Historical Society Studies in History Series, no. 12 (London: Royal Historical Society, 1978).
18. Cape Archives Depot, Cape Town CAD BK92, Records of British Kaffraria, Polygamy, Memorial to the Lieutenant Governor, 12 July 1862.
19. Hunter, *Love in the Time of AIDS*, 37.
20. Reverend Guye, *Christian Express,* 1 February 1911.
21. Max Weber, *Protestant Ethic and the Spirit of Capitalism,* 2nd ed. (London: Harper Collins Academic, 1930), 55.
22. Weber, 163.
23. Extract, Blue Book on Native Affairs, *Christian Express,* 1 December 1902, 179.
24. See also Nafisa Essop Sheik, "African Marriage Regulation and the Remaking of Gendered Authority in Colonial Natal, 1843–1875," *African Studies Review* 57, no. 2 (2014): 73–92; Nafisa Essop Sheik, "Customs in Common: Marriage, Law and the Making of Difference in Colonial Natal," *Gender & History* 29, no. 3 (1 November 2017): 589–604.
25. T. B. Soga, *Intlalo xa Xosa,* 44.
26. *Christian Express,* 1 June 1911, 93.
27. *Ilanga lase Natal,* 12 August 1921, 4.
28. Harold Jack Simons, "Marriage and Succession among Africans," *Acta Juridica,* 1960, 312–33.
29. Martin Chanock, *The Making of South African Legal Culture 1902–1936: Fear, Favour and Prejudice* (Cambridge: Cambridge University Press, 2001), 334.
30. See all the references in this chapter, but for readers interested in pursuing marriage in the European community before the reforms of 1985 and that was coconstitutive of African marriage legislation, see H. R. Hahlo, *South African Law of Husband and Wife,* 5th ed. (Cape Town: Juta, 1985).
31. Change to: Monica Wilson et al., *Keiskammahoek Rural Survey,* vol. 3, *Social Structure* (Pietermaritzburg: Shuter and Shooter, 1952), 82.
32. Monica Wilson et al., 80–85.
33. For her study, Levin interviewed couples living in Langa, but not all the couples had married in Langa. Many had married in the Eastern Cape or other rural areas before moving to Langa. Ruth Levin, "Marriage in Langa Native Location," 46.
34. Arthur Phillips, ed. *Survey of African Marriage and Family Life* (London: Oxford University Press, 1953), 41.
35. Denys William Tinniswood Shropshire, *Primitive Marriage and European Law: A South African Investigation* (London: Society for Promoting Christian Knowledge, 1946), 10.

36. Shropshire, 10.
37. South Africa, ed., *Union Statistics for 50 years, 1910–1960* (Pretoria: Bureau of Census and Statistics, 1960), A.16, A.29; Anthony John Christopher, "The Union of South Africa Censuses 1911–1960: An Incomplete Record," *Historia* 56, no. 2 (November 2011): 1–18. Christopher discusses the limitations of the census volume; my calculation is a relational one assuming even bias across the census.
38. The absence of Christianity is evident (and odd) in what are in other respects an excellent set of papers in a recent special issue of *Anthropology Southern Africa*, cited above with papers by Pauli, van Dijk, Solway, and White.
39. Hunter, *Love in the Time of AIDS*, 45.
40. Simons, "Marriage and Succession among Africans," 313–14.
41. Ellen Hellmann, "Native Life in a Johannesburg Slum Yard," *Africa* 8, no. 1 (1935): 51.
42. Anna F. Steyn and Colin M. Rip, "The Changing Urban Bantu Family," *Journal of Marriage and Family* 30, no. 3 (1968): 507.
43. Zacchariah K. Matthews, "Marriage Customs among the Barolong," *Africa: Journal of the International African Institute* 13, no. 1 (1940): 1–24; Zacchariah K. Matthews, *Freedom for My People* (Cape Town: David Philip, 1981), 6. Also Monica Hunter, *Reaction to Conquest: Effects of Contact with Europeans on the Pondo of South Africa*, 2nd ed. (Cape Town: Oxford University Press, 1961).
44. Frieda Bokwe Matthews, *Remembrances*, Mayibuye History and Literature Series, no. 54 (Bellville, South Africa: Mayibuye Books, 1995), 11.
45. Alistair J. Kerr, *The Customary Law of Immovable Property and Succession*, 2nd ed. (Grahamstown: Rhodes University Press, 1976), 220–21.
46. Levin, "Marriage in Langa Native Location," 90.
47. Deborah Posel, "Marriage at the Drop of a Hat: Housing and Partnership in South Africa's Urban African Townships, 1920s–1960s," *History Workshop Journal*, no. 61 (2006): 57–76. See also Laura Longmore, *The Dispossessed—a Study of the Sex-Life of Bantu Women in and around Johannesburg* (London: Corgi, 1966).
48. Levin, "Marriage in Langa Native Location," 91.
49. Levin, 91.
50. There is very little on the social history of divorce, including and especially in the native divorce courts in South Africa. The native divorce courts emanated from a 1929 amendment of the Black Administration Act. Originally, there were two divorce circuits, the Cape and the Free State, and Natal and the Transvaal, which expanded to three after 1948. The divorce courts, which were presided over by three native commissioners, heard directly from applicants but only heard divorce cases for Christian or civil marriage, as customary marriages were not held to be legal unions. The proceedings of the native divorce courts are fascinating, because often they involved cases of divorce many years—sometimes decades—removed from the physical separation of a couple. I have consulted the records of the Cape and Free State divorce courts. For Natal, see Benedict Carton, "'My

Husband Is No Husband to Me': Divorce, Marriage and Gender Struggles in African Communities of Colonial Natal, 1869–1910," *Journal of Southern African Studies* 46, no. 6 (1 November 2020): 1111–25.
51. University of the Witwatersrand, Historical Papers Department, AD843B 42.1, Preliminary Report Submitted to the Institute of Race Relations by D. W. T. Shropshire, c.1940.
52. Shropshire, *Primitive Marriage and European Law*, 70.
53. Shropshire, 69.
54. Posel, "Marriage at the Drop of a Hat," 58.
55. Historical Papers, University of the Witwatersrand, Church of the Province of South Africa, AB1653.
56. Guye, *Christian Express*, 1 February 1911, 28.
57. Paul Ramseyer, *Christian Express*, 1 June 1921, 97.
58. A. M. Anderson, *Christian Express*, 1 June 1921, 99.
59. Brownlee J. Ross, *Christian Express*, 1 May 1911, 75–6.
60. SOAS, London, CBMS A2 Box 1224, Commission on Uniformity of Discipline.
61. SOAS, London, CBMS A2 Box 1224, Report on 6th General Missionary Conference, Johannesburg, 1925.
62. SOAS, London, ICM CBMS A2 Box 1225, Conference on African Family Life Pretoria June 1940.
63. Wauchope, *Isaac Williams Wauchope*, 323 (from his writing in *Imvo*). See also "Diskolo tsa Bana," *Tsala ea Becoana*, 4 March 1911, 3.
64. For instance, in *Christian Express*, 1 July 1911, 109.
65. *Christian Express*, 1 April 1911, 61.
66. *Christian Express*, 1 November 1920, 174.
67. *Christian Express*, 2 October 1911, 156.
68. A. C. Maseko, *Ilanga*, 7 July 1922.
69. Henry Selby-Msimang, "The Religion and the Civilization of the Bantu," *Umteteli*, 19 August 1922, 2–3. This was part of a series of articles with the same title and on the same subject.
70. Selby-Msimang, "The Religion and the Civilization of the Bantu," *Umteteli*, 9 September 1922, 2–3.
71. Selby Msimang, "The Religion and the Civilization of the Bantu," *Umteteli*, 16 September 1922, 3.
72. Posel, "Marriage at the Drop of a Hat," 58–59.
73. See, for instance, the debates in Wits SAIRR AD843b—where participants were largely in favor of regularizing and licensing customary marriages.
74. Katherine Anne Eales, "Gender Politics and the Administration of African Women in Johannesburg, 1903–1939" (master's thesis, University of the Witwatersrand, 2009), 107, http://wiredspace.wits.ac.za/handle/10539/7457.
75. Quoted in Eales, "Gender Politics," 119.
76. Shula Marks, *Not Either an Experimental Doll: The Separate Worlds of Three South African Women*, Killie Campbell Africana Library Publications (Durban: Killie Campbell Africana Library and University of Natal Press, 1987).

77. Marijke du Toit and Palesa Nzuza, "'Isifazane Sakiti Emadolobheni' (Our Women in the Towns): The Politics of Gender in *Ilanga lase Natal*, 1933–1938," *Journal of Natal and Zulu History* 33, no. 1 (2019): 62–86.

78. Meghan Healy-Clancy, "The Politics of New African Marriage in Segregationist South Africa," *African Studies Review* 57, no. 2 (September 2014): 7–28; Lynn M. Thomas, "The Modern Girl and Racial Respectability in 1930s South Africa," *Journal of African History* 47, no. 3 (2006): 461–90.

79. Anxious, "Bantu Women Must Tackle the Big Questions Confronting Them," *Bantu World*, 16 September 1933, 10.

80. R. E. Masole, *Bantu World*, 30 September 1933, 10.

81. No-Civil, *Bantu World*, 30 September 1933, 10. It is also possible that No-Civil was a man, since—while women used pen names when they wrote—women's pen names at this time were usually fairly descriptive.

82. Beth Lebele, *Bantu World*, 7 October 1933, 10.

83. Lebele, *Bantu World*.

84. P. D. S., *Bantu World*, 21 October 1933, 10.

85. *Bantu World*, 4 November 1933, 10.

CHAPTER 5: WEDDINGS AND STATUS, CONSUMPTION AND RECIPROCITY

1. Archibald C. Jordan, *The Wrath of the Ancestors: A Novel* (Cape Province, South Africa: Lovedale, 1980), 55–56.

2. For a history of Black access to South African universities, see Bruce K. Murray, "Wits as an 'Open' University 1939–1959: Black Admissions to the University of the Witwatersrand," *Journal of Southern African Studies* 16, no. 4 (1 December 1990): 649–76.

3. Jennifer Cole and Lynn M. Thomas, eds., "Introduction," in *Love in Africa* (Chicago: University of Chicago Press, 2009), 3–4.

4. Lauren Berlant, "Intimacy: A Special Issue," *Critical Inquiry* 24, no. 2 (1 January 1998): 282.

5. Danai Mupotsa, "The Promise of Happiness: Desire, Attachment and Freedom in Post/Apartheid South Africa," *Critical Arts: A South-North Journal of Cultural & Media Studies* 29, no. 2 (2015): 184.

6. For Sotho-Tswana wedding processes, see Zachariah K. Matthews, "Marriage Customs among the Barolong," *Africa: Journal of the International African Institute* 13, no. 1 (1940): 1–24.

7. For example, Diana Jeater, *Marriage, Perversion and Power: The Construction of Moral Discourse in Southern Rhodesia 1894–1930* (Oxford: Oxford University Press, 1993); Margot Lovett, "'She Thinks She's Like a Man': Marriage and (De)Constructing Identity in Colonial Buha, Western Tanzania, 1943–1960," *Canadian Journal of African Studies* 30, no. 1 (1996): 52–68; Jeremy Rich, "My Matrimonial Bureau: Masculine Concerns and Presbyterian Mission Evangelization in the Gabon Estuary, c. 1900–1915," *Journal of Religion in Africa* 36, no. 2 (2006): 200–223; Marc Schiltz, "A Yoruba Tale of Marriage, Magic, Misogyny and Love," *Journal of Religion in Africa* 32, no. 3 (2002): 335–65.

8. Eileen Jensen Krige and John L. Comaroff, eds., *Essays on African Marriage in Southern Africa* (Cape Town: Juta, 1981). See also the essays, including the one referenced, in the following special issue. Julia Pauli and Rijk van Dijk, "Marriage as an End or the End of Marriage? Change and Continuity in Southern African Marriages," *Anthropology Southern Africa* 40, no. V1 (1 January 2017): 257–66.
9. David Gitari, "The Church and Polygamy," *Transformation* 1, no. 1 (1984): 3–10; Adrian Hastings, *Christian Marriage in Africa* (London: Society for Promoting Christian Knowledge, 1973).
10. For instance, Kristin Mann, *Marrying Well: Marriage, Status and Social Change among the Educated Elite in Colonial Lagos*, ed. J. Dunn, J. M. Lonsdale, and A. F. Robertson, African Studies Series (Cambridge: Cambridge University Press, 1985); Barbara M. Cooper, *Marriage in Maradi: Gender and Culture in a Hausa Society in Niger, 1900–1989* (Portsmouth, NH: 1997); Barbara M. Cooper, "Women's Worth and Wedding Gift Exchange in Maradi, Niger, 1907–89," *Journal of African History* 36, no. 1 (1 January 1995): 121–40.
11. John L. Comaroff and Jean Comaroff, *Of Revelation and Revolution*, vol. 2, *The Dialectics of Modernity on a South African Frontier* (Chicago: University of Chicago Press, 1997), 22–55; Isaac Schapera, *Married Life in an African Tribe* (London: Faber and Faber, 1940), 73–78.
12. Monica Hunter, *Reaction to Conquest: Effects of Contact with Europeans on the Pondo of South Africa*, 2nd ed. (Cape Town: Oxford University Press, 1961), 213–20.
13. Monica Hunter, "The Effects of Contact with Europeans on the Status of Pondo Women," *Africa: Journal of the International African Institute* 6, no. 3 (1933): 259–76; Monica Wilson, "The Wedding Cakes: A Study of Ritual Change," in *The Interpretation of Ritual: Essays in Honour of AI Richards*, ed. J. S. La Fontaine (London: Tavistock, 1972), 187; Monica Wilson, "Xhosa Marriage in Historical Perspective," in *African Marriage in Southern Africa*, ed. Eileen J. Krige and John L. Comaroff (Cape Town: Juta, 1981). See also William David Hammond-Tooke, *Bhaca Society: The People of the Transkeian Uplands, South Africa* (Cape Town: Oxford University Press, 1962), 129–32, 309–12.
14. Ruth Levin, "Marriage in Langa Native Location" (PhD diss., University of Cape Town, 1946), https://open.uct.ac.za/handle/11427/23447.
15. Phyllis Ntantala, *A Life's Mosaic: The Autobiography of Phyllis Ntantala* (Cape Town: David Philip, 1992).
16. Frieda Bokwe Matthews, *Remembrances*, Mayibuye History and Literature Series, no. 54 (Bellville, South Africa: Mayibuye Books, 1995).
17. Sindiwe Magona, *To My Children's Children* (New York: Interlink Books, 1998).
18. Herbert I. E. Dhlomo, *H. I. E. Dhlomo: Collected Works*, ed. Tim Couzens and Nick Visser (Johannesburg: Ravan, 1985); Ellen Kuzwayo, *Sit Down and Listen* (London: Women's Press, 1990).

19. Elizabeth Gunner, *Radio Soundings: South Africa and the Black Modern*, The International African Library 59 (London: Cambridge University Press, 2019).
20. James Stewart, *Lovedale Missionary Institution, South Africa* (Edinburgh: Andrew Elliot, 1894); Schapera, *Married Life in an African Tribe*, 84; Comaroff and Comaroff, *Of Revelation and Revolution*, 254.
21. Hunter, *Reaction to Conquest*, 71; Wilson, "The Wedding Cakes," 187.
22. Irwin Stanley Manoim, "The Black Press 1945–1963: The Growth of the Black Mass Media and Their Role as Ideological Disseminators" (MA thesis, University of the Witwatersrand, 1983), http://wiredspace.wits.ac.za/handle/10539/7460.
23. See also Timothy Burke, *Lifebuoy Men, Lux Women: Commodification, Consumption, and Cleanliness in Modern Zimbabwe* (Durham, NC: Duke University Press, 1996).
24. Barbara Penner, "'A Vision of Love and Luxury': The Commercialization of Nineteenth-Century American Weddings," *Winterthur Portfolio* 39, no. 1 (2004): 2.
25. Edwina Ehrman, *The Wedding Dress: 300 Years of Bridal Fashions* (London: V&A, 2011), 67.
26. *Christian Express*, 1 January 1885, 8–10; Comaroff and Comaroff, *The Dialectics of Modernity*, 255.
27. Advertisement for Phillips, Mount Fletcher, *Izwi laBantu*, 6 August 1901, 1.
28. Burke, *Lifebuoy Men, Lux Women*, 5; Comaroff and Comaroff, *The Dialectics of Modernity*.
29. Burke, 6.
30. The term "representational economy" is from Webb Keane. Keane examines how words and things are related both to each other and to the lives of the people they serve. Webb Keane, *Christian Moderns: Freedom and Fetish in the Mission Encounter*, The Anthropology of Christianity 1 (Berkeley: University of California Press, 2007), 18.
31. For instance, "The Spurling-Greathead Wedding," *Grahamstown Journal*, 12 June 1913, 4; "An Alexandria Wedding, Miss Gardner of Harvest Vale," *Grahamstown Journal*, 16 December 1913.
32. *Umteteli*, 30 October 1937, 4–5.
33. *Bantu World*, 20 July 1935, 13. The words are possibly "radiant matte lace," which would make a lot more sense. "Matt lace" is a raised lace design on a matte background. "Radium" is sometimes used to refer to a brilliant white color but is not often used to describe clothing.
34. African couples also invented wedding portraits for themselves, as documented in a recent and fascinating piece by John Peffer, "Together in the Picture," *Chimurenga Chronic*, 23 November 2015, https://chimurengachronic.co.za/together-in-the-picture/.
35. "Clifton Studio, Wedding Groups a Speciality," *Umteteli*, 17 May 1934, 16. Lynn Thomas discusses how photo portraiture helps to create and display

the figure of the modern African. Lynn M. Thomas, "The Modern Girl and Racial Respectability in 1930s South Africa," *Journal of African History* 47, no. 3 (2006): 473–74.
36. *Umteteli*, 5 February 1938, 7.
37. Some of this phrasing is from Karen Tranberg Hansen, "The World in Dress: Anthropological Perspectives on Clothing, Fashion, and Culture," *Annual Review of Anthropology* 33 (2004): 374–75. For examples, see also Deborah Durham, "The Predicament of Dress: Polyvalency and the Ironies of Cultural Identity," *American Ethnologist* 26, no. 2 (1 May 1999): 389–411; Kirsten Ruether, "Heated Debates over Crinolines: European Clothing on Nineteenth-Century Lutheran Mission Stations in the Transvaal," *Journal of Southern African Studies* 28, no. 2 (1 June 2002): 359–78; Robert Ross, *Clothing: A Global History* (Cambridge: Polity, 2008).
38. Comaroff and Comaroff, *The Dialectics of Modernity*, 218–73.
39. Ross, *Clothing*, 96.
40. Wendy Urban-Mead, "Religion, Women and Gender in the Brethren in Christ Church, Matabeleland, Zimbabwe 1898–1978" (PhD diss., Columbia University, 2004); Wendy Urban-Mead, "Negotiating 'Plainness' and Gender: Dancing and Apparel at Christian Weddings in Matabeleland, Zimbabwe, 1913–1944," *Journal of Religion in Africa* 38, no. 2 (2008): 209–46.
41. Joan A. Broster, *Red Blanket Valley* (Johannesburg: H. Keartland, 1967), 42.
42. Kathryn Church, "Something Plain and Simple? Unpacking Custom-Made Wedding Dresses from Western Canada (1950–1995)," in *Wedding Dress across Cultures*, ed. Donald Clay Johnson and Helen Bradley Foster (Oxford: Berg, 2003).
43. Melanie Judge, Anthony Manion, and Shaun De Waal, eds., *To Have and to Hold: The Making of Same-Sex Marriage in South Africa* (Auckland Park, South Africa: Fanele, 2008), 318.
44. Juliette Leeb-du Toit, *IsiShweshwe: A History of the Indigenisation of Blueprint in South Africa* (Scottsville, KwaZulu-Natal: University of KwaZulu-Natal Press, 2017).
45. "Wedding Bells in Grahamstown," *Umteteli*, 4 July 1936, 19–20.
46. Wilson, "The Wedding Cakes," 195.
47. Peter Lacey, *The Wedding* (New York: Grosset & Dunlap, 1969), 176.
48. Ehrman, *The Wedding Dress*, 59.
49. Ehrman, 9–11.
50. Church, "Something Plain and Simple?," 13.
51. Eileen Jensen Krige, "Changing Conditions in Marital Relations and Parental Duties among Urbanized Natives," *Africa: Journal of the International African Institute* 9, no. 1 (1 January 1936): 6. For mention of this same phenomenon, see also Deborah Gaitskell, "Wailing for Purity: Prayer Unions, African Mothers and Adolescent Daughters 1912–1940," in *Industrialization and Social Change in South Africa*, ed. Shula Marks and Richard Rathbone (London: Longman, 1982).
52. *Umteteli*, 6 August 1938, 6.

53. Levin, "Marriage in Langa Native Location," 219; Virginia Van der Vliet, "Traditional Husbands, Modern Wives? Constructing Marriages in a South African Township," in *Tradition and Transition in Southern Africa: Fechtschrift for Philip and Iona Mayer*, ed. Andrew D. Spiegel and Patrick McAllister (Johannesburg: Wits University Press, 1991), 46–48.
54. Burke, *Lifebuoy Men, Lux Women*.
55. Isaac Wachope, *Isaac Williams Wauchope: Selected Writings 1874–1916*, Van Riebeeck Society for the Publication of South African Historical Documents, second series, no. 39 (Cape Town: Van Riebeeck Society, 2008), 107. A similar report is in *Christian Express*, 1 July 1911, 109.
56. University of the Witwatersrand, Johannesburg, Department of Historical Papers, CPSA, AB1653, St. John's Diocese, Minutes 8 July 1917.
57. Wits CPSA, AB3154, Transkeian Missionary Conference, 1930; also Wits CPSA AB799, Minutes of Preachers' and Teachers' Meetings, 1 October 1938.
58. *Christian Express*, 1 March 1917, 36.
59. Burke, *Lifebuoy Men, Lux Women*, 102–3.
60. Ross, *Clothing*, 97; Ruether, "Heated Debates over Crinolines"; Urban-Mead, "Negotiating 'Plainness' and Gender."
61. Levin, "Marriage in Langa Native Location," 46.
62. Longmore, *The Dispossessed—a Study of the Sex-Life of Bantu Women in and around Johannesburg* (London: Corgi, 1966), 22; Krige, "Changing Conditions in Marital Relations," 16; Schapera, *Married Life in an African Tribe*.
63. Hunter, *Reaction to Conquest*, 220.
64. Krige, "Changing Conditions in Marital Relations," 15–17.
65. Levin, "Marriage in Langa Native Location," 54–55.
66. Longmore, *The Dispossessed*, 131.
67. Phillip Bonner, "The Transvaal Native Congress, 1917–1920: The Radicalisation of the Black Petty Bourgeoisie on the Rand," in *Industrialisation and Social Change in South Africa*, ed. Shula Marks and Richard Rathbone (London: Longman, 1982); Alan G. Cobley, *Class and Consciousness: The Black Petty Bourgeoisie in South Africa, 1924–1950*, Contributions in Afro-American and African Studies No. 127 (New York: Greenwood, 1990); David Goodhew, "Working-Class Respectability: The Example of the Western Areas of Johannesburg, 1930–55," *Journal of African History* 41, no. 2 (2000): 241–66.
68. This argument—the relative prosperity in the Ciskei at the end of the nineteenth century, followed by a decline in economic conditions—is presented in Colin Bundy's pivotal work and subsequently refuted by Jack Lewis, who takes issue with Bundy's periodization. Bundy, *Rise and Fall of the South African Peasantry* (London: Heinemann, 1979); Jack Lewis, "The Rise and Fall of the South African Peasantry: A Critique and Reassessment," *Journal of Southern African Studies* 11, no. 1 (1984): 1–24.
69. School of Oriental and African Studies, London, SOAS, ICM/CBMS Africa 2, Proceedings, Conference on African Family Life, 26–27 June 1940.
70. Gaitskell, "Wailing for Purity"; Deborah Gaitskell, "Devout Domesticity? A Century of African Women's Christianity in South Africa," in *Women and*

Gender in Southern Africa to 1945, ed. Cherryl Walker (Cape Town: David Philip, 1990).
71. Mark Hunter, *Love in the Time of AIDS: Inequality, Gender, and Rights in South Africa* (Bloomington: Indiana University Press, 2010), 5–6.
72. Levin, "Marriage in Langa Native Location," 55–56.
73. Cape Archives Depot, Cape Town, CAD 1/ KWT 2/1/1/3/2 Civil Cases, Native Magistrates 1918–1928, Case 94 of 1921.
74. "A Marriage Has Been Arranged," *Umteteli*, 1 May 1937, 9.
75. *Bantu World,* 27 February 1937, 11.
76. For instance, Hunter, *Reaction to Conquest*, 193.
77. Mark P. Leone, "Epilogue: The Productive Nature of Material Culture and Archaeology," *Historical Archaeology* 26, no. 3 (1992): 131.
78. Wilson, "The Wedding Cakes."
79. "Umshato e Bhai," *Imvo Zabantsundu*, 25 November 1922, 6.
80. Barbara M. Cooper, "Women's Worth and Wedding Gift Exchange," 122.

CHAPTER 6: POLYGAMY, MULTIPLE CONJUGALITY, AND MASIHLALISANE

1. Rebecca Hourwich Reyher, *Zulu Woman: A Biography of Christina, Wife of Solomon, King of the Zulus. With a Portrait* (New York: Columbia University Press, 1948), 69–70. This is the original edition of the book. The same text is in the 1999 edition of the book, Rebecca Hourwich Reyher and Christina Sibiya, *Zulu Woman: The Life Story of Christina Sibiya* (Pietermaritzburg: University of Natal Press, 1999), 56.
2. The 1999 edition of the book includes a literary afterword by Elizabeth Gunner (also a historical contextualization by Marcia Wright). Gunner writes about not only the double framing of Sibiya's life story through her first-person narrative and Reyher's third-person account but also the often "silenced themes of marriage, sexuality, and domestic violence." Gunner also examines how Sibiya's life account "suggests the need for redefining the domains of the private and the public, for regarding them as densely overlapping." Elizabeth Gunner, "'Let All the Stories Be Told': Zulu Woman, Words and Silence," in *Zulu Woman* (1999), 199.
3. Reyher, *Zulu Woman* (1948), 4–5.
4. Marcia Wright, "Introduction," in *Zulu Woman* (1999), xi.
5. On the succession, see Antony Costa, "Custom and Common Sense," *African Studies* 56, no. 1 (1 January 1997): 19–42. Costa's article is dismissive of Sibiya's account. On letters, see Gunner, "Let All the Stories Be Told," 208–9.
6. Vuyiswa Ndabayakhe and Catherine Addison, "Polygamy in African Fiction," *Current Writing: Text and Reception in Southern Africa* 20, no. 1 (1 January 2008): 89–104.
7. "In urban (especially township) English: Of a relationship between a man and a woman: common-law, unsolemnized, 'live-in'; of a person: in such a relationship; of an attitude or opinion: favouring such a relationship." "Vat En

Sit—Definition of Vat En Sit in A Dictionary of South African English—DSAE," accessed 25 August 2021, https://dsae.co.za/entry/vat-en-sit/e07587.

8. "Mnakwethu Season 2 2021," Facebook, accessed 25 August 2021, https://www.facebook.com/groups/234054868351576. See also MzansiMagicOfficial, "You Are Not Welcome," *Mnakwethu,* Mzansi Magic, 25 August 2021, https://www.youtube.com/watch?v=YxHm3qbAE84.
9. Adrian Hastings, *The Church in Africa 1450–1950,* Oxford History of the Christian Church (Oxford: Clarendon, 1994), 317.
10. Arthur Phillips, ed. *Survey of African Marriage and Family Life* (London: Oxford University Press, 1953), xiv.
11. For these figures, see Lucy Mair, "African Marriage and Social Change," in Phillips, *Survey of African Marriage and Family Life,* 26–27, 59, 153.
12. Monica Hunter, *Reaction to Conquest: Effects of Contact with Europeans on the Pondo of South Africa,* 2nd ed. (Cape Town: Oxford University Press, 1961).
13. John C. Caldwell and Pat Caldwell, "The Cultural Context of High Fertility in Sub-Saharan Africa," *Population and Development Review* 13, no. 3 (1987): 409–37.
14. John Iliffe, *Africans: The History of a Continent* (Cambridge: Cambridge University Press, 1995), 1.
15. T. J. Tallie, "Queering Natal: Settler Logics and the Disruptive Challenge of Zulu Polygamy," *GLQ: A Journal of Lesbian and Gay Studies* 19, no. 2 (2013): 167–89; also T. J. Tallie, *Queering Colonial Natal: Indigeneity and the Violence of Belonging in Southern Africa* (Minneapolis: University of Minnesota Press, 2020).
16. Peter Delius and Clive Glaser, "The Myths of Polygamy: A History of Extra-Marital and Multi-Partnership Sex in South Africa," *South African Historical Journal,* no. 50 (2004): 84. Although, there is also evidence that polygamy increased in the early colonial period before diminishing rapidly in the late nineteenth century under the impact of Christianity (ibid, 48 and 92).
17. For a fascinating example of this, see the controversy about the Fon of Bikom, who apparently had 110 wives, many of whom were inherited from his predecessor. "Wives Total 110, Not 600, Fon Says; Chief of Bikom Tribe Says Any May Go Home—Agrees to Ban Forced Marriage," *New York Times,* 28 January 1949, https://www.nytimes.com/1949/01/28/archives/wives-total-110-not-600-fon-says-chief-of-bikom-tribe-says-any-may.html; M. D. W. Jeffreys, "Some Notes on the Fon of Bikom," *African Affairs* 50, no. 200 (1951): 241–49.
18. Joan A. Broster, *Red Blanket Valley* (Johannesburg: H. Keartland, 1967), 9.
19. Frank Prochaska, *The Voluntary Impulse: Philanthropy in Modern Britain* (London: Faber and Faber, 1988); Susan Thorne, "The Conversion of Englishmen and the Conversion of the World Inseparable," in *Tensions of Empire: Colonial Cultures in a Bourgeois World,* ed. Fred Cooper and Ann Stoler (Berkeley: University of California Press, 1997).
20. For polygamy in the Americas, see Sarah M. Pearsall, *Polygamy: An Early American History* (New Haven, CT: Yale University Press, 2019).

21. Christine Peters, "Gender, Sacrament and Ritual: The Making and Meaning of Marriage in Late Medieval and Early Modern England," *Past & Present*, no. 169 (2000): 63–96.
22. Jeff Guy, *The Heretic: A Study of the Life of John William Colenso, 1814–1883* (Johannesburg: Ravan, 1983), 73–74.
23. John William Colenso, *Remarks on the Proper Treatment of Cases of Polygamy, as Found Already Existing in Converts from Heathenism* (Pietermartizburg: May & Davis, 1855), 6.
24. Hlonipha Mokoena, *Magema Fuze: The Making of a Kholwa Intellectual* (Scottsville, South Africa: University of KwaZulu-Natal Press, 2011).
25. Timothy W. Jones, "The Missionaries' Position: Polygamy and Divorce in the Anglican Communion, 1888–1988," *Journal of Religious History* 35, no. 3 (2011): 396.
26. For evidence of this, see Jones, "The Missionaries' Position."
27. Phillips, *Survey of African Marriage*, xiv.
28. University of Cape Town, Special Collections, Stewart BC106, C.144, Bishop of Zululand to JS, Isanhlwana, 8 January 1888.
29. Jeremy C. Martens, "Settler Homes, Manhood and 'Houseboys': An Analysis of Natal's Rape Scare of 1886," *Journal of Southern African Studies* 28, no. 2 (2002): 379–400; Jeremy Martens, "Polygamy, Sexual Danger, and the Creation of Vagrancy Legislation in Colonial Natal," *Journal of Imperial & Commonwealth History* 31, no. 3 (2003): 24. See also Benedict Carton, "'My Husband Is No Husband to Me': Divorce, Marriage and Gender Struggles in African Communities of Colonial Natal, 1869–1910," *Journal of Southern African Studies* 46, no. 6 (1 November 2020): 1111–25.
30. Hastings, *The Church in Africa 1450–1950*, 317.
31. See Steven Kaplan, "The Africanization of Missionary Christianity: History and Typology," *Journal of Religion in Africa* 16, no. 3 (1986): 166–86, for a more detailed discussion of missions' positions on polygamy—he uses a typology that begins with tolerance and moves through to inculturation to describe these different positions.
32. Phillips, *Survey of African Marriage and Family Life*, xxiv.
33. Hastings, *The Church in Africa 1450–1950*, 321.
34. Heinrich Filter and Sighart Bourquin, eds., *Paulina Dlamini: Servant of Two Kings*, Killie Campbell Africana Library Publications (Durban: University of Natal, 1986), 102.
35. Saul Dubow, *Racial Segregation and the Origins of Apartheid in South Africa, 1919–1936* (Oxford: Macmillan, 1989), 5–6.
36. *South African Native Affairs Commission, 1903–5: Report of the Commission* (Cape Town: Cape Times Limited, Govt. Printers, 1905).
37. *South African Native Affairs Commission, 1903–5*, 57.
38. Martin Chanock, *The Making of South African Legal Culture 1902–1936: Fear, Favour and Prejudice* (Cambridge: Cambridge University Press, 2001), 198–99.
39. Henry Jack Simons, *African Women: Their Legal Status in South Africa* (London: C. Hurst, 1968), 78.

40. University of the Witwatersrand, Historical Papers Research Archive (Wits), Church of the Province of South Africa (CPSA) Pamphlet, BX5700.6.5 CHU, "Polygamy"; Wits CPSA AB1653, Minutes of Diocesan Synod, St Johns, 9–11 July 1911 and Cory Library for Historical Research (Cory), Rhodes University, Grahamstown, Ms 16638, "Rules and Regulations of the Missionary Conference," pp. 1–2, 1926.
41. Wits.
42. Wits.
43. Martens, "Settler Homes, Manhood and 'Houseboys'"; Jock McCulloch, *Black Peril, White Virtue: Sexual Crime in Southern Rhodesia, 1902–1935* (Bloomington: Indiana University Press, 2000).
44. "Report on Abantu-Batho," *Christian Express,* 1 March 1913, 35.
45. T. B. Soga, *Intlalo,* 47; Heather Hughes, "Doubly Elite: Exploring the Life of John Langalibalele Dube," *Journal of Southern African Studies* 27, no. 3 (2001): 445–58.
46. *Times of Nigeria,* 22 March 1922, 3.
47. School of Oriental and African Studies (SOAS), IMC/ CBMS (International Missionary Council/ Conference of British Missionary Societies) Box 1224, 1915 Conference, Uniformity of Discipline Questionnaire Paper G, Polygamy.
48. Cambridge University Library, Royal Commonwealth Society Collection, The Evangelisation of South Africa, Report of the Sixth General Missionary Conference.
49. Cory MS 16638, 'Rules and Regulations of the Missionary Conference, 1–2, 1926.
50. Henry Selby Msimang, *Umteteli,* 30 September 1922, 2–3.
51. Andrew Bank, *Pioneers of the Field: South Africa's Women Anthropologists,* The International African Library (Cambridge: Cambridge University Press, 2016); Andrew Bank, "The 'Intimate Politics' of Fieldwork: Monica Hunter and Her African Assistants, Pondoland and the Eastern Cape, 1931–32," *Journal of Southern African Studies* 34, no. 3 (2008): 557–74; Andrew Bank, "'Bridging the Gap between the Intellectual and the Human': The Awkward Biography of Anthropologist and Scholar-Activist Iona Simon Mayer (1923–)," *African Studies* 78, no. 2 (2019): 267–89.
52. SOAS IMC/CBMS Africa 1: Box 207, Africa Education Group.
53. Natasha Erlank, "'God's Family in the World': Transnational and Local Ecumenism's Impact on Inter-church and Inter-racial Dialogue in South Africa in the 1920s and 1930s," *South African Historical Journal* 61, no. 2 (June 2009): 278–97.
54. SOAS ICM/CBMS AFRICA 1, Box 17 Le Zoute.
55. See *Umteteli,* 18 March 1933, 5.
56. *Umteteli,* 20 October 1934, 6.
57. Wits AC623 (South African Council of Churches) 1.4.1.1 Christian Council Executive Minutes 2 Sept 1937.

58. SOAS, ICM/CBMS Africa 2, Box 1226 SA Missions General File A: Reports, Leaflets etc 1906-1947,—Report on The Younger Church in SA, Ministers' Retreat, 26 Jan—3 Feb, 1938.
59. SOAS, ICM/CBMS Africa 2, Box 1226, 10 September 1938.
60. Phillips, *Survey of African Marriage and Family Life*, 333.
61. IMC 2.31.31.
62. SOAS ICM/CBMS AFRICA 1, Minutes Africa Comm, 8 July 1940.
63. SOAS ICM/CBMS AFRICA 1, Informal Conference consideration of Tambaram 9 Dec 1939.
64. Denys William Tinniswood Shropshire, *Primitive Marriage and European Law: A South African Investigation* (London: Society for Promoting Christian Knowledge, 1946).
65. Shropshire, 2.
66. Shropshire, 1.
67. Mamphela Ramphele, *A Bed Called Home: Life in the Migrant Labour Hostels of Cape Town* (Cape Town: David Philip, 1993).
68. Kate Dula's case, summarized by Mrs. Henderson, in Shropshire, *Primitive Marriage and European Law*, 4. The details in this paragraph are all from the same source, pp. 4-5.
69. Belinda Bozzoli and Mmantho Nkotsoe, *Women of Phokeng: Consciousness, Life Strategy, and Migrancy in South Africa, 1900-1983* (Johannesburg: Ravan, 1991), 113.
70. Philip Mayer, *Townsmen or Tribesmen: Conservatism and the Process of Urbanization in a South African City*, vol. 2 (London: Oxford University Press, 1971), 256. Mayer describes the phenomenon in some detail, over several pages, ascribing the practice to Red migrants in the cities of the then Eastern Cape, rather than to School migrants. The latter, he writes, prefer to keep their extramarital relationships secret, though clearly this is not a statement that applies beyond (or even within) Mayer's own research.
71. Mayer, 260, 265.
72. Laura Longmore, *The Dispossessed—A Study of the Sex-Life of Bantu Women in and around Johannesburg* (London: Corgi, 1966), 354.
73. From a short story by Herbert Dhlomo, "He Forgave Her." The story appears to date to the 1940s. H. I. E. Dhlomo, *H. I. E. Dhlomo: Collected Works*, ed. Tim Couzens and Nick Visser (Johannesburg: Raven, 1985), 483.
74. Sicence v. Sicence, Native Appeals Court, *Selection of Cases Decided in the Native Appeal and Divorce Court: Cape and Orange Free State Division . . . with Table of Cases and Alphabetical Index* (Cape Town: Juta, 1914), 184.
75. Maggie Resha, *'Mangoana Tsoara Thipa Ka Bohaleng: My Life in the Struggle* (London: S. A. Writers, 1991), 4.
76. Bozzoli and Nkotsoe, *Women of Phokeng*, 36-37.
77. Tutuka and Ndela v. Pankeyo, Native Appeals Court, *Selection of Cases Decided in the Native Appeal and Divorce Court* (1914), 194.

78. Sipo Mlumbi and another v. Dodo Salayi, *Selection of Cases Decided in the Native Appeal and Divorce Court: Cape and Orange Free State Division . . . with Table of Cases and Alphabetical Index* (Cape Town: Juta, 1930), 27–28.
79. *Umteteli* 16 Feb 1935, 5. The meaning of *motsha* is unclear; it is possibly a misspelling of a word related to goat skin.
80. Cape Archives Depot (CAD) 1/UTA 2/1/1/136 Case 950 of 1935; also Titi v. Titi, Native Appeals Court, ed., *Selection of Cases Decided in the Native Appeal and Divorce Court: Cape and Orange Free State Division . . . with Table of Cases and Alphabetical Index* (Cape Town: Juta, 1936), 101.
81. CAD 1/MFE 2/1/2/1 Case 293 of 1925. The record contains the records of both the Native Appeals Court ruling and the original case.

CONCLUSION

1. David Hecht and Abdulmalique M. Simone, *Invisible Governance: The Art of African Micro-politics* (Brooklyn, NY: Autonomedia, 1994), 8.
2. Alec Ryrie, *Protestants: The Faith That Made the Modern World* (New York: Viking, 2017), 2–3, 296.
3. Cory Ms16369b: Translation of *Intlalo xa Xosa* 1917 by T. B. Soga. Trans. C. S. Papu 97. Kropf describes the singular of imitshotsho as follows: "um-Tshotsho, N. 6. Night dance of boys and girls, with ejaculations by the boys." Albert Kropf, *A Kafir-English Dictionary*, 2nd ed. (Stutterheim, South Africa: Lovedale Mission Press, 1915), 407.
4. Deborah Gaitskell, "Wailing for Purity: Prayer Unions, African Mothers and Adolescent Daughters 1912–1940," in *Industrialization and Social Change in South Africa*, ed. Shula Marks and Richard Rathbone (London: Longman, 1982).
5. Zenoyisa Madikwa, "Mbalula Goes to the Mountain," Sowetan LIVE, 9 September 2008, http://www.sowetanlive.co.za/sowetan/archive/2008/09/09/mbalula-goes-to-the-mountain.
6. Mia Malan, "Medical Back-Up in Pondo Initiation," *M&G Online*, 28 September 2013, http://mg.co.za/article/2013-09-28-00-medical-back-up-in-pondo-initiation/.
7. "Placing the Film *Inxeba—The Wound* in Historical Review," South African History Online, 14 September 2021, https://www.sahistory.org.za/article/placing-film-inxeba-wound-historical-review; Joshua Peter Willows, "Shaping the Boys' South African Identity: Suppressed Queer Space in *Spud* and *Inxeba*" (master's thesis, University of the Western Cape, 2020), http://etd.uwc.ac.za/xmlui/handle/11394/8143.
8. "Indigenous Film Distribution (Pty) Ltd and Another v Film and Publication Appeal Tribunal and Others (3589/2018) [2018] ZAGPPHC 438; [2018] 3 All SA 783 (GP) (27 June 2018)," http://www.saflii.org/za/cases/ZAGPPHC/2018/438.html.
9. See for instance, "Why *Inxeba* Was Assigned a Classification X18—FPB Appeal Tribunal—DOCUMENTS," Politicsweb, 23 February 2018, https://www

.politicsweb.co.za/documents/why-inxeba-was-assigned-a-classification-x18--fpb-.

10. Dhammamegha Annie Leatt, *The State of Secularism: Religion, Tradition and Democracy in South Africa* (Johannesburg: Wits University Press, 2017), 98–99. Leatt draws some of her thinking from Talal Asad's work on secularism, which has also informed my thinking. Talal Asad, *Formations of the Secular: Christianity, Islam and Modernity,* ed. Mieke Bal and Hent de Vries, Cultural Memory in the Present (Stanford, CA: Stanford University Press, 2003).

11. Michael Yarborough makes a similar point in relation to the flattening out of narratives in relation to gay weddings in Michael W. Yarbrough, "A New Twist on the 'Un-African' Script: Representing Gay and Lesbian African Weddings in Democratic South Africa," *Africa Today* 67, no. 1 (2020): 48–71.

12. Alexia Smit and Tanja Bosch, "Television and Black Twitter in South Africa: Our Perfect Wedding," *Media, Culture & Society* 42, nos. 7–8 (2020): 1115.

13. Sue Nyathi, *The Polygamist* (Cape Town: Logogog Press, 2012), 10–11.

14. Nyathi, 7, 13.

15. "One Man, Four Wives: The New Hit Reality TV Show," *BBC News,* 4 June 2017, https://www.bbc.com/news/blogs-trending-40136391; MzansiMagicOfficial, "You Are Not Welcome—Mnakwethu," Mzansi Magic, 17 March 2020, https://www.youtube.com/watch?v=YxHm3qbAE84.

16. Zama Chutshela, "Inside Uthando NeSthembu's Musa Mseleku's Three Wedding Celebrations," *Drum,* 3 May 2019, https://www.news24.com/drum/advice/inside-uthando-nesthembus-musa-mselekus-three-wedding-celebrations-20190503.

Bibliography

ARCHIVAL SOURCES

Burke Theological Library
   Foreign Missions Conference of North America (FMCNA)
Cambridge University Library
   Royal Commonwealth Society Collection
Cape Archive Depot, National Archives, Cape Town
   Magisterial Court Records / Native Commissioner Court Records
      1/ALC Alice
      1/FBF Fort Beaufort
      1/KNM Kuruman
      1/KWT King Williams Town
      1/MFE Mount Frere
      1/TSO Tsolo
      1/UIT Uitenhage
      1/UTA Umtata
   Other Records
      BEK Regional Director of Bantu Education, King William's Town (1921–57)
      BK92 Records of British Kaffraria
      CCK Chief Commissioner, Eastern Cape (1922–63)
      CMT Chief Magistrates Transkei, 1875–1912
      NA Secretary of Native Affairs

NATIONAL LIBRARY OF SCOTLAND

Acc.75486 Church of Scotland, Minutes of the South African Mission
MS7813–5 Church of Scotland, Letterbooks

NEW COLLEGE, SCOTLAND

Gibs Mss

RHODES UNIVERSITY, CORY LIBRARY FOR HISTORICAL PAPERS, GRAHAMSTOWN,

MS16291—Ms16417 Lovedale Press Records
Ms16436 Bantu Literature
MS16622 Missionary Conferences
MS16638 Diocese of Grahamstown
MS16891 Percival Qayiso.

SCHOOL OF ORIENTAL AND AFRICAN STUDIES, LONDON

International Committee for Christian Literature in Africa (ICCLA)
International Missionary Council (IMC) Microfiche
International Missionary Council / Conference of British Missionary Societies (IMC/CBMS) Africa 1
International Missionary Council / Conference of British Missionary Societies ICM/CBMS Africa 2

UNIVERSITY OF CAPE TOWN SPECIAL COLLECTIONS

BC255 Lestrade Collection
BC106 James Stewart
BC880 Godfrey and Monica Wilson Papers

UNIVERSITY OF THE WITWATERSRAND, HISTORICAL PAPERS COLLECTION

Records of the Anglican Church of South Africa (formerly Church of the Province of South Africa, CPSA)
    AB1653 Records Diocese of St. Johns
    AB234f Gell
    AB3154 Transkeian Missionary Conference
    AB769 Pretoria Native Conference Minutes
    AB787F Initiation
    AB799 St. Cuthbert's Mission

Other Records
    AD843B South African Institute of Race Relations
    AD843 RJ South African Institute of Race Relations
    AC623 South African Christian Council
    AD1433 Joint Council Movement

NEWSPAPERS

Abantu-Batho
Bantu World
Christian Express

Grahamstown Journal
Ilanga lase Natal
Imvo Zabantsundu
Society for Women Missionaries Journal
St John's Chronicle
Times of Nigeria
Umteteli wa Bantu

SECONDARY SOURCES

Achmat, Zackie. "'Apostles of Civilised Vice': 'Immoral Practices' and 'Unnatural Vice' in South African Prisons and Compounds, 1890–1920." *Social Dynamics* 19, no. 2 (1 December 1993): 92–110.

Ambler, Charles H. "The Renovation of Custom in Colonial Kenya: The 1932 Generation Succession Ceremonies in Embu." *Journal of African History* 30, no. 1 (1989): 139–56.

Anglican Ink. "Dear Gay Anglicans Letter." Press release, 22 February 2021. https://anglican.ink/2021/02/22/dear-gay-anglicans-letter/.

"Archives and Online Resources." Black Press Research Collective, accessed 31 July 2021. http://blackpressresearchcollective.org/resources/scholarship-archives/.

Arndt, Jochen S. *Divided by the Word: Colonial Encounters and the Remaking of Zulu and Xhosa Identities.* Reconsiderations in Southern African History. Charlottesville: University of Virginia Press, 2022.

Asad, Talal. *Formations of the Secular: Christianity, Islam and Modernity.* Edited by Mieke Bal and Hent de Vries. Cultural Memory in the Present. Stanford, CA: Stanford University Press, 2003.

Bank, Andrew. "'Bridging the Gap between the Intellectual and the Human': The Awkward Biography of Anthropologist and Scholar-Activist Iona Simon Mayer (1923–)." *African Studies* 78, no. 2 (2019): 267–89.

———. "The 'Intimate Politics' of Fieldwork: Monica Hunter and Her African Assistants, Pondoland and the Eastern Cape, 1931–1932." *Journal of Southern African Studies* 34, no. 3 (2008): 557–74.

———. *Pioneers of the Field: South Africa's Women Anthropologists.* The International African Library. Cambridge: Cambridge University Press, 2016.

Barber, Karin, ed. *Africa's Hidden Histories: Everyday Literacy and Making the Self.* Bloomington: Indiana University Press, 2006.

———. *The Anthropology of Texts, Persons and Publics: Oral and Written Culture in Africa and Beyond.* New Departures in Anthropology 5. Cambridge: Cambridge University Press, 2007.

———. "Introduction: Hidden Innovators in Africa." In Barber, *Africa's Hidden Histories*, 1–24.

Beinart, William. "The Origins of the *Indlavini*." *African Studies* 50, no. 1 (1991): 103–28.

———. *The Political Economy of Pondoland 1860–1930.* Johannesburg: Ravan, 1982.

Beinart, William, and Colin Bundy. "Introduction: 'Away in the Locations.'" In *Hidden Struggles in Rural South Africa: Politics and Popular Movements in* the *Transkei and Eastern Cape 1890–1930,* edited by William Beinart and Colin Bundy, 1–45. Johannesburg: Ravan, 1987.

Berlant, Lauren. "Intimacy: A Special Issue." *Critical Inquiry* 24, no. 2 (1 January 1998): 281–88.

Berlant, Lauren, and Michael Warner. "Sex in Public." *Critical Inquiry* 24, no. 2 (1998): 547–66.

Berman, Bruce, and John Lonsdale. *Unhappy Valley: Conflict in Kenya and Africa.* Eastern African Studies. London: Ohio University Press, 1992.

Blacking, John. "243. Fictitious Kinship Amongst Girls of the Venda of the Northern Transvaal." *Man* 59 (1959): 155–58.

Bompani, Barbara. "African Independent Churches in Post-apartheid South Africa: New Political Interpretations." *Journal of Southern African Studies* 34, no. 3 (2008): 665–77.

Bonner, Philip. "'Desirable or Undesirable Basotho Women?' Liquor, Prostitution and the Migration of Basotho Women to the Rand, 1920–1945." In Walker, *Women and Gender in Southern Africa,* 221–50.

———. "South African Society and Culture 1910–1948." In *The Cambridge History of South Africa. Volume 2: 1885–1994,* edited by Robert Ross, Anne Kelk Mager, and Bill Nasson, 254–318. Cambridge History of South Africa. Cambridge: Cambridge University Press, 2011.

———. "The Transvaal Native Congress, 1917–1920: The Radicalisation of the Black Petty Bourgeoisie on the Rand." In *Industrialisation and Social Change in South Africa,* edited by Shula Marks and Richard Rathbone, 270–313. London: Longman, 1982.

Bozzoli, Belinda. "Marxism, Feminism and South African Studies." In *Segregation and Apartheid in Twentieth-Century South Africa,* edited by William Beinart and Saul Dubow, 118–44. London: Routledge, 1995.

Bozzoli, Belinda, and Mmantho Nkotsoe. "Women and the Beerhall Protests in the Natal Countryside in 1929." In *Class, Community and Conflict,* edited by Belinda Bozzoli, 292–323. Johannesburg: Ravan, 1987.

———. *Women of Phokeng: Consciousness, Life Strategy, and Migrancy in South Africa, 1900–1983.* Johannesburg: Ravan, 1991.

Breckenridge, Keith. "Love Letters and Amanuenses: Beginning the Cultural History of the Working Class Private Sphere in Southern Africa, 1900–1933." *Journal of Southern African Studies* 26, no. 2 (June 2000): 337–48.

———. "Promiscuous Method: The Historiographical Effects of the Search for the Rural Origins of the Urban Working Class in South Africa." *International Labor and Working-Class History,* no. 65 (2004): 26–49.

———. "Reasons for Writing: African Working-Class Letter Writing in Early-Twentieth Century South Africa." In Barber, *Africa's Hidden Histories,* 143–63.

Bredekamp, Henry, and Robert Ross, eds. *Missions and Christianity in South African History.* Johannesburg: Wits University Press, 1995.

Brock, Sheila. "James Stewart and Lovedale: A Reappraisal of Missionary Attitudes and African Response in the Eastern Cape, South Africa." PhD diss., University of Edinburgh, 1974.

Broster, Joan A. *Red Blanket Valley.* Johannesburg: H. Keartland, 1967.
———. *The Tembu: Their Beadwork, Songs, and Dances.* Cape Town: Purnell, 1976.
Brouwer, Ruth Compton. "Books for Africans: Margaret Wrong and the Gendering of African Writing, 1929–1963." *International Journal of African Historical Studies* 31, no. 1 (1998): 53–71.
Brownlee, Frank. "248. The Circumcision Ceremony in Fingoland, Transkeian Territories, South Africa." *Man* 31 (1931): 251–54.
Bundy, Colin. *Rise and Fall of the South African Peasantry.* London: Heinemann, 1979.
Burke, Timothy. *Lifebuoy Men, Lux Women: Commodification, Consumption, and Cleanliness in Modern Zimbabwe.* Durham, NC: Duke University Press, 1996.
Burleigh, John. H. S. *A Church History of Scotland.* London: Oxford University Press, 1960.
Burns, Catherine. "Sex Lessons from the Post?" *Agenda* 12, no. 29 (1996): 79–91.
Burrill, Emily S., Richard L. Roberts, and Elizabeth Thornberry, eds. *Domestic Violence and the Law in Colonial and Postcolonial Africa.* New African Histories Series. Athens: Ohio University Press, 2010.
Cabrita, Joel. *Text and Authority in the South African Nazaretha Church.* International African Library 46. Cambridge: Cambridge University Press, 2014.
———. *Written Out: The Life and Work of Regina Gelana Twala.* Athens: Ohio University Press, forthcoming.
Cabrita, Joel, and Natasha Erlank. "New Histories of Christianity in South Africa: Review and Introduction." *South African Historical Journal* 70, no. 2 (3 April 2018): 307–23.
Calata, James. "Ukudlelana kobu-Kristu namasiko olwaluko lwabantu AbaNtsundu." In *Inkolo Namasiko A-Bantu: Bantu Beliefs and Customs,* edited by Sydney J. Wallis, 38–49. London: Society for Promoting Christian Knowledge (SPCK), 1930.
Caldwell, John C., and Pat Caldwell. "The Cultural Context of High Fertility in Sub-Saharan Africa." *Population and Development Review* 13, no. 3 (1987): 409–37.
Campbell, James T. "'Like Locusts in Pharoah's Palace': The Origins and Politics of African Methodism in the Orange Free State, 1895–1914." *African Studies* 53, no. 1 (1994): 39–69.
———. *Songs of Zion: The African Methodist Episcopal Church in the United States and South Africa.* Oxford: Oxford University Press, 1995.
———. "T. D. Mweli Skota and the Making and Unmaking of a Black Elite." Working Paper, 14 February 1987. http://wiredspace.wits.ac.za/handle/10539/7732.
Carton, Benedict. *Blood from Your Children: The Colonial Origins of Generational Conflict in South Africa.* Charlottesville: University of Virginia Press, 2000.
———. "'My Husband Is No Husband to Me': Divorce, Marriage and Gender Struggles in African Communities of Colonial Natal, 1869–1910." *Journal of Southern African Studies* 46, no. 6 (1 November 2020): 1111–25.
Carton, Benedict, and Robert Morrell. "Zulu Masculinities, Warrior Culture and Stick Fighting: Reassessing Male Violence and Virtue in South Africa." *Journal of Southern African Studies* 38, no. 1 (1 March 2012): 31–53.

Chakrabarty, Dipesh. *Habitations of Modernity: Essays in the Wake of Subaltern Studies*. Chicago: University of Chicago Press, 2002.

Chanock, Martin. *The Making of South African Legal Culture 1902–1936: Fear, Favour and Prejudice*. Cambridge: Cambridge University Press, 2001.

Chisholm, Linda. *Between Worlds: German Missionaries and the Transition from Mission to Bantu Education in South Africa*. Johannesburg: Wits University Press, 2018.

Christopher, Anthony John. "The Union of South Africa Censuses 1911–1960: An Incomplete Record." *Historia* 56, no. 2 (November 2011): 1–18.

Church, Kathryn. "Something Plain and Simple? Unpacking Custom-Made Wedding Dresses from Western Canada (1950–1995)." In *Wedding Dress across Cultures*, edited by Donald Clay Johnson and Helen Bradley Foster, 5–22. Oxford: Berg, 2003.

Chutshela, Zama. "Inside Uthando NeSthembu's Musa Mseleku's Three Wedding Celebrations." *Drum*, 3 May 2019. https://www.news24.com/drum/advice/inside-uthando-nesthembus-musa-mselekus-three-wedding-celebrations-20190503.

Claassens, Aninka, and Dee Smythe. "Marriage, Land and Custom: What's the Law Got to Do with It?" In *Marriage, Land and Custom: Essays on Law and Social Change in South Africa*, edited by Aninka Claassens, Dee Smythe, and Graham Bradfield, 1–27. Cape Town: Juta, 2013.

Cobley, Alan G. *Class and Consciousness: The Black Petty Bourgeoisie in South Africa, 1924–1950*. Contributions in Afro-American and African Studies No. 127. New York: Greenwood Press, 1990.

Cole, Jennifer, and Lynn M. Thomas. "Introduction." In Cole and Thomas, *Love in Africa*, 1–31.

———, eds. *Love in Africa*. Chicago: University of Chicago Press, 2009.

Colenso, John William. *Remarks on the Proper Treatment of Cases of Polygamy, as Found Already Existing in Converts from Heathenism*. Pietermartizburg: Printed by May & Davis, 1855.

Comaroff, Jean, and John L. Comaroff. "Jean and John Comaroff." By Kalman Applbaum. *Alan MacFarlane*. 15 November 2008. http://www.alanmacfarlane.com/DO/filmshow/comaroff_fast.htm.

———. *Of Revelation and Revolution*. Vol. 1, *Christianity, Colonialism and Consciousness in South Africa*. Chicago: Chicago University Press, 1991.

Comaroff, John L. "Bridewealth and the Control of Ambiguity in a Tswana Chiefdom." In *The Meaning of Marriage Payments*, edited by John Comaroff, 161–96. New York: Academic Press, 1980.

Comaroff, John L., and Jean Comaroff. *Ethnography and the Historical Imagination*. Studies in the Ethnographic Imagination. Boulder, CO: Westview, 1992.

———. *Of Revelation and Revolution*. Vol. 2, *The Dialectics of Modernity on a South African Frontier*. Chicago: University of Chicago Press, 1997.

Cooper, Barbara M. *Marriage in Maradi: Gender and Culture in a Hausa Society in Niger, 1900–1989*. Portsmouth, NH: Heinemann; Oxford: J. Currey, 1997.

———. "Women's Worth and Wedding Gift Exchange in Maradi, Niger, 1907–89." *Journal of African History* 36, no. 1 (1 January 1995): 121–40.

Cooper, Frederick. *Colonialism in Question Theory, Knowledge, History.* Berkeley: University of California Press, 2005.

Costa, Antony. "Custom and Common Sense." *African Studies* 56, no. 1 (1 January 1997): 19–42.

Crais, Clifton C. "South Africa and the Pitfalls of Postmodernism." *South African Historical Journal* 31, no. 1 (1994): 274–79.

Cuthbertson, Greg. "Van Der Kemp and Philip: The Missionary Debate Revisited." *Missionalia* 17 (1989): 77–94.

Davidoff, Leonore, and Catherine Hall. *Family Fortunes: Men and Women of the English Middle Class 1780–1850.* London: Routledge, 1987.

Deacon, Harriet, and Kirsten Thomson. "The Social Penis: Traditional Male Circumcision and Initiation in Southern Africa, 1800–2000: A Literature Review." Working Paper. Cape Town: Centre for Social Science Research, 2012. http://www.cssr.uct.ac.za/publications/working-paper/2012/social-penis-traditional-male-circumcision-and.

Decker, Corrie. "A Feminist Methodology of Age-Grading and History in Africa." *American Historical Review* 125, no. 2 (April 2020): 418–26.

De Haas, Mary. "Is There Anything More to Say about Lobolo?" *African Studies* 46, no. 1 (1987): 33–55.

De Kock, Leon. *Civilising Barbarians: Missionary Narrative and African Textual Response in Nineteenth-Century South Africa.* Johannesburg: Wits University Press, 1996.

———. "For and Against the Comaroffs: Postmodernist Puffery and Competing Conceptions of the 'Archive.'" *South African Historical Journal* 31, no. 1 (1994): 280–89.

Delius, Peter, and Clive Glaser. "The Myths of Polygamy: A History of Extra-Marital and Multi-Partnership Sex in South Africa." *South African Historical Journal*, no. 50 (2004): 84–114.

———. "Sexual Socialisation in South Africa: A Historical Perspective." *African Studies* 61, no. 1 (2002): 27–54.

Dhlomo, Herbert I. E. *H. I. E. Dhlomo: Collected Works.* Edited by Tim Couzens and Nick Visser. Johannesburg: Ravan, 1985.

Dhlomo, Reginald R. *An African Tragedy.* Lovedale, South Africa: Lovedale Institution Press, 1928.

Donald, Moira, and Linda Hurcombe. *Gender and Material History in Archaeological Perspective.* New York: St. Martin's, 2000.

Dubow, Saul. "Holding 'a Just Balance between White and Black': The Native Affairs Department in South Africa c.1920–33." *Journal of Southern African Studies* 12, no. 2 (1986): 217–39.

———. *Racial Segregation and the Origins of Apartheid in South Africa, 1919–1936.* Oxford: Macmillan, 1989.

Du Bruyn, Johannes. "Of Muffled Southern Tswana and Overwhelming Missionaries: The Comaroffs and the Colonial Encounter." *South African Historical Journal* 31, no. 1 (1994): 294–309.

Durham, Deborah. "The Predicament of Dress: Polyvalency and the Ironies of Cultural Identity." *American Ethnologist* 26, no. 2 (1 May 1999): 389–411.

du Toit, Marijke, and Palesa Nzuza. "'Isifazane Sakiti Emadolobheni' (Our Women in the Towns): The Politics of Gender in *Ilanga lase Natal*, 1933–1938." *Journal of Natal and Zulu History* 33, no. 1 (2019): 62–86.

Eales, Katherine Anne. "Gender Politics and the Administration of African Women in Johannesburg, 1903–1939." Master's thesis, University of the Witwatersrand, 1991. http://wiredspace.wits.ac.za/handle/10539/7457.

———. "'Jezebels,' Good Girls and Mine Married Quarters: Johannesburg, 1912." African Studies Seminar series, paper presented October 1988. http://wiredspace.wits.ac.za//handle/10539/8673.

———. "Patriarchs, Passes and Privilege: Johannesburg's African Middle Classes and the Question of Night Passes for African Women 1920–1931." In *Holding Their Ground: Class, Locality and Culture in 19th and 20th Century South Africa*, edited by Philip Bonner, Isabel Hofmeyr, Deborah James, and Tom Lodge, 105–40. Johannesburg: Wits University Press, 1989.

Ehrman, Edwina. *The Wedding Dress: 300 Years of Bridal Fashions*. London: V&A, 2011.

Elbourne, Elizabeth. *Blood Ground: Colonialism, Missions, and the Contest for Christianity in the Cape Colony and Britain, 1799–1853*. McGill-Queen's Studies in the History of Religion, edited by Donald Harman Akenson. Montreal: McGill-Queen's University Press, 2002.

———. "Concerning Missionaries: The Case of Van Der Kemp." *Journal of Southern African Studies* 17, no. 1 (1991): 153.

———. "Early Khoisan Uses of Mission Christianity." *Kronos: Journal of Cape History* 19 (1992): 3–27.

———. "Word Made Flesh: Christianity, Modernity, and Cultural Colonialism in the Work of Jean and John Comaroff." *American Historical Review* 108, no. 2 (2003): 435–59.

Eley, Geoff. "Dilemmas and Challenges of Social History since the 1960s: What Comes after the Cultural Turn?" *South African Historical Journal* 60, no. 3 (1 September 2008): 310–22. https://doi.org/10.1080/02582470802417391.

Ellis, Stephen, and Gerrie ter Haar. *Worlds of Power: Religious Thought and Political Practice in Africa*. New York: Oxford University Press, 2004.

Elphick, Richard. "The Benevolent Empire and the Social Gospel: Missionaries and South African Christians in the Age of Segregation." In *Christianity in South Africa: A Political, Social and Cultural History*, edited by Richard Elphick and Rodney Davenport, 347–69. Cape Town: David Philip, 1997.

———. *The Equality of Believers: Protestant Missionaries and the Racial Politics of South Africa*. Reconsiderations in Southern African History. Charlottesville: University of Virginia Press, 2012.

Elphick, Richard, and Rodney Davenport, eds. *Christianity in South Africa: A Political, Social and Cultural History*. Cape Town: David Philip, 1997.

Englund, Harri. *Christianity and Public Culture in Africa*. Cambridge Centre of African Studies Series. Athens: Ohio University Press, 2011.

Erlank, Natasha. "Gendering Commonality: African Men and the 1883 Commission on Native Law and Custom." *Journal of Southern African Studies* 29, no. 4 (2003): 937–53.

———. "'God's Family in the World': Transnational and Local Ecumenism's Impact on Inter-church and Inter-racial Dialogue in South Africa in the 1920s and 1930s." *South African Historical Journal* 61, no. 2 (June 2009): 278–97.

———. "Missionary Views on Sexuality in Xhosaland in the 19th Century." *Le Fait Missionaire* 11, no. 1 (2001): 9–44.

———. "'Plain Clean Facts' and Initiation Schools: Christianity, Africans and 'Sex Education' in South Africa, c.1910–1940." *Agenda* 62 (2004): 76–83.

———. "'Raising Up the Degraded Daughters of Africa': The Provision of Education for Xhosa Women in the Mid-nineteenth Century." *South African Historical Journal* 43, no. 1 (2000): 24–38.

———. "Re-examining Initial Encounters between Christian Missionaries and the Xhosa, 1820–1850." *African Historical Review* 31, no. 1 (1999): 6–32.

———. "Sexual Misconduct and Church Power on Scottish Mission Stations in Xhosaland, South Africa, in the 1840s." *Gender & History* 15, no. 1 (2003): 69–84.

———. "The Spread of Indigenous Christianity in British Kaffraria after 1850." *Missionalia* 31, no. 1 (2003): 19–41.

———. "Strange Bedfellows: The International Missionary Council, the International African Institute, and Research into African Marriage and Family." In *The Spiritual in the Secular: Missionaries and Knowledge about Africa*, edited by Patrick Harries and David Maxwell, 267–92. Grand Rapids, MI: W. B. Eerdmans, 2012.

———. "*Umteteli wa Bantu* and the Constitution of Social Publics in the 1920s and 1930s." *Social Dynamics* 45, no. 1 (2 January 2019): 75–102.

Essop Sheik, Nafisa. "African Marriage Regulation and the Remaking of Gendered Authority in Colonial Natal, 1843–1875." *African Studies Review* 57, no. 2 (2014): 73–92.

———. "Customs in Common: Marriage, Law and the Making of Difference in Colonial Natal." *Gender & History* 29, no. 3 (2017): 589–604.

Etherington, Norman. *Preachers, Peasants, and Politics in Southeast Africa, 1835–1880: African Christian Communities in Natal, Pondoland, and Zululand*. Royal Historical Society Studies in History Series, no. 12. London: Royal Historical Society, 1978.

Filter, Heinrich, and Sighart Bourquin, eds. *Paulina Dlamini: Servant of Two Kings*. Killie Campbell Africana Library Publications. Durban: University of Natal, 1986.

Flemming, Rebecca. "The Invention of Infertility in the Classical Greek World: Medicine, Divinity, and Gender." *Bulletin of the History of Medicine* 87, no. 4 (20 December 2013): 565–90.

Gaitskell, Deborah. "Devout Domesticity? A Century of African Women's Christianity in South Africa." In Walker, *Women and Gender in Southern Africa*, 251–72.

———. "Female Mission Initiatives: Black and White Women in Three Witwatersrand Churches 1901–1939." PhD thesis, University of London School of Oriental and African Studies, 1981.

———. "'Praying and Preaching': The Distinctive Spirituality of African Women's Church Organizations." In Bredekamp and Ross, *Missions and Christianity*, 211–32.

———. "Wailing for Purity: Prayer Unions, African Mothers and Adolescent Daughters 1912–1940." In *Industrialization and Social Change in South Africa: African Class Formation, Culture, and Consciousness, 1870–1930*, edited by Shula Marks and Richard Rathbone, 338–66. London: Longman, 1982.

Gitari, David. "The Church and Polygamy." *Transformation* 1, no. 1 (1984): 3–10.

Glaser, Clive. "Swines, Hazels, and the Dirty Dozen: Masculinity, Territoriality and the Youth Gangs of Soweto, 1960–1976." *Journal of Southern African Studies* 24, no. 4 (1998): 719–36.

Glassie, Henry. *Passing the Time in Ballymenone: Culture and History of an Ulster Community*. Bloomington: Indiana University Press, 1995.

Goedhals, Mandy. "African Nationalism and Indigenous Christianity: A Study in the Life of James Calata (1895–1983)." *Journal of Religion in Africa* 33, no. 1 (2003): 63–82.

Goodhew, David. "A Story of Growth and Decline." *Church Times*, 6 January 2017. https://www.churchtimes.co.uk/articles/2017/6-january/features/features/a-story-of-growth-and-decline.

———. "Working-Class Respectability: The Example of the Western Areas of Johannesburg, 1930–55." *Journal of African History* 41, no. 2 (2000): 241–66.

Gordon, David M. *Invisible Agents: Spirits in a Central African History*. Athens: Ohio University Press, 2012.

Green, Maia. "Confronting Categorical Assumptions about the Power of Religion in Africa." *Review of African Political Economy* 33, no. 110 (2006): 635–50.

Gunner, Elizabeth. "'Let All the Stories Be Told': Zulu Woman, Words and Silence." Afterword to *Zulu Woman: The Life Story of Christina Sibiya*, by Rebecca Hourwich Reyher and Christina Sibiya, 199–210. Pietermaritzburg: University of Natal Press, 1999.

———. *Radio Soundings: South Africa and the Black Modern*. The International African Library 59. London: International African Institute and Cambridge University Press, 2019.

———. "Soft Masculinities, *Isicathamiya* and Radio." *Journal of Southern African Studies* 40, no. 2 (2014): 343–60.

Guy, Jeff. *The Destruction of the Zulu Kingdom: The Civil War in Zululand, 1879–1884*. New History of South Africa. Johannesburg: Ravan, 1982.

———. *The Heretic: A Study of the Life of John William Colenso, 1814–1883*. Johannesburg: Ravan, 1983.

———. *Theophilus Shepstone and the Forging of Natal: African Autonomy and Settler Colonialism in the Making of Traditional Authority*. Scottsville, South Africa: University of KwaZulu-Natal Press, 2013.

Hahlo, Hermann R. *South African Law of Husband and Wife*. 5th ed. Cape Town: Juta, 1985.

Hammond-Tooke, William David. *Bhaca Society: A People of the Transkeian Uplands, South Africa.* Cape Town: Oxford University Press, 1962.

———. *Command or Consensus: The Development of Transkeian Local Government.* Cape Town: David Philip, 1975.

———. "The Transkeian Council System 1895–1955: An Appraisal." *Journal of African History* 9, no. 3 (1968): 455–77.

Hansen, Karen Tranberg. "The World in Dress: Anthropological Perspectives on Clothing, Fashion, and Culture." *Annual Review of Anthropology* 33 (2004): 369–92.

Hansen, Thomas Blom, Caroline Jeannerat, and Samadia Sadouni. "Introduction: Portable Spirits and Itinerant People: Religion and Migration in South Africa in a Comparative Perspective." *African Studies* 68, no. 2 (2009): 187–96.

Harries, Patrick. *Work, Culture and Identity: Migrant Laborers in Mozambique and South Africa, c.1860–1910.* Social History of Africa. Portsmouth, NH: Heinemann, 1991.

Hastings, Adrian. *Christian Marriage in Africa.* London: Society for Promoting Christian Knowledge, 1973.

———. *The Church in Africa 1450–1950.* Oxford History of the Christian Church. Oxford: Clarendon, 1994.

Healy-Clancy, Meghan. "The Politics of New African Marriage in Segregationist South Africa." *African Studies Review* 57, no. 2 (September 2014): 7–28.

———. "Women and the Problem of Family in Early African Nationalist History and Historiography." *South African Historical Journal* 64, no. 3 (2012): 450–71.

Hecht, David, and Abdulmalique M. Simone. *Invisible Governance: The Art of African Micro-Politics.* Brooklyn, NY: Autonomedia, 1994.

Hellmann, Ellen. "Native Life in a Johannesburg Slum Yard." *Africa* 8, no. 1 (1935): 34–62.

Hirsch, Jennifer S., and Holly Wardlow, eds. *Modern Loves: The Anthropology of Romantic Courtship and Companionate Marriage.* Ann Arbor: University of Michigan Press, 2006.

Hodgson, Janet. "A Battle for Sacred Power: Christian Beginnings Among the Xhosa." In Elphick and Davenport, *Christianity in South Africa*, 68–88.

———. *The God of the Xhosa.* Cape Town: Oxford University Press, 1992.

Hoernlé, Alfred. "The Ama-Xosa: Life and Customs by John Henderson Soga." *American Anthropologist* 35, no. 2 (1933): 369–72.

Hofmeyr, Isabel. "Dreams, Documents and 'Fetishes': African Christian Interpretations of *The Pilgrim's Progress.*" *Journal of Religion in Africa* 32, no. 2 (2002): 440–56.

———. *Gandhi's Printing Press: Experiments in Slow Reading.* Cambridge, MA: Harvard University Press, 2013.

———. *The Portable Bunyan: A Transnational History of "The Pilgrim's Progress."* Edited by Emily Apter. Translation/Transnation. Princeton, NJ: Princeton University Press, 2004.

———. "Reading Debating/Debating Reading: The Case of the Lovedale Literary Society, or Why Mandela Quotes Shakespeare." In Barber, *Africa's Hidden Histories*, 258–77.

Hopwood, Nick, Rebecca Flemming, and Lauren Kassell. "Reproduction in History." In *Reproduction: Antiquity to the Present Day,* edited by Lauren Kassell, Nick Hopwood, and Rebecca Flemming, 3–18. Cambridge: Cambridge University Press, 2018.

Houle, Robert J. *Making African Christianity: Africans Reimagining Their Faith in Colonial South Africa.* Bethlehem, PA: Lehigh University Press, 2013.

Hughes, Heather. "Doubly Elite: Exploring the Life of John Langalibalele Dube." *Journal of Southern African Studies* 27, no. 3 (2001): 445–58.

Hunter, Mark. "Is It Enough to Talk of Marriage as a Process? Legitimate Cohabitation in Umlazi, South Africa." *Anthropology Southern Africa* 39, no. 4 (2016): 281–96.

———. *Love in the Time of AIDS: Inequality, Gender, and Rights in South Africa.* Bloomington: Indiana University Press, 2010.

Hunter, Monica. "The Effects of Contact with Europeans on the Status of Pondo Women." *Africa: Journal of the International African Institute* 6, no. 3 (1933): 259–76. https://doi.org/10.2307/1155677.

———. *Reaction to Conquest: Effects of Contact with Europeans on the Pondo of South Africa.* 2nd ed. Cape Town: Oxford University Press, 1961.

Hyslop, Jonathan. *The Classroom Struggle: Policy and Resistance in South Africa, 1940–1990.* Pietermaritzburg: University of Natal Press, 1999.

Iliffe, John. *Africans: The History of a Continent.* Cambridge: Cambridge University Press, 1995.

———. *Honour in African History.* African Studies. Cambridge: Cambridge University Press, 2005.

"Indigenous Film Distribution (Pty) Ltd and Another v Film and Publication Appeal Tribunal and Others (3589/2018) [2018] ZAGPPHC 438; [2018] 3 All SA 783 (GP) (27 June 2018)." http://www.saflii.org/za/cases/ZAGPPHC/2018/438.html.

Jabavu, Noni. *Drawn in Colour: African Contrasts.* London: Murray, 1960.

Jackson, Stevi and Sue Scott, ed. *Theorizing Sexuality.* Maidenhead: McGraw-Hill International (UK), 2010.

Jeater, Diana. *Marriage, Perversion and Power: The Construction of Moral Discourse in Southern Rhodesia 1894–1930.* Oxford: Oxford University Press, 1993.

Jeeves, Alan H. "Identity, Culture and Consciousness: Industrial Work and Rural Migration in Southern Africa, 1860–1987." *South African Historical Journal* 33, no. 1 (1 November 1995): 194–215. https://doi.org/10.1080/02582479508671856.

Jeffreys, M. D. W. "Some Notes on the Fon of Bikom." *African Affairs* 50, no. 200 (1951): 241–49.

Jochelson, Karen. *The Colour of Disease: Syphilis and Racism in South Africa, 1880–1950.* St. Antony's Series. Basingstoke, UK: Palgrave, 2001.

Jones, Timothy W. "The Missionaries' Position: Polygamy and Divorce in the Anglican Communion, 1888–1988." *Journal of Religious History* 35, no. 3 (2011): 393–408.

Jordan, Archibald C. *The Wrath of the Ancestors: A Novel*. Cape Province, South Africa: Lovedale, 1980.

Judge, Melanie, Anthony Manion, and Shaun De Waal, eds. *To Have and to Hold: The Making of Same-Sex Marriage in South Africa*. Auckland Park, South Africa: Fanele, 2008.

Junod, Henri Alexandre. *The Life of a South African Tribe*. London: Macmillan, 1927.

Kaplan, Steven. "The Africanization of Missionary Christianity: History and Typology." *Journal of Religion in Africa* 16, no. 3 (1986): 166–86.

Karimakwenda, Nyasha. "Today It Would Be Called Rape: A Historical and Contextual Examination of Forced Marriage and Violence in the Eastern Cape." *Acta Juridica* (2013), 339.

Keane, Webb. *Christian Moderns: Freedom and Fetish in the Mission Encounter*. The Anthropology of Christianity 1. Berkeley: University of California Press, 2007.

——. "From Fetishism to Sincerity: On Agency, the Speaking Subject, and Their Historicity in the Context of Religious Conversion." *Comparative Studies in Society and History* 39, no. 4 (1997): 674–93.

Kelly, Jill E. "Bantu Authorities and Betterment in Natal: The Ambiguous Responses of Chiefs and Regents, 1955–1970." *Journal of Southern African Studies* 41, no. 2 (4 March 2015): 273–97.

Kemp, Amanda D., and Robert Trent Vinson. "'Poking Holes in the Sky': Professor James Thaele, American Negroes, and Modernity in 1920s Segregationist South Africa." *African Studies Review* 43, no. 1 (2000): 141.

Kerr, Alistair J. *The Customary Law of Immovable Property and Succession*. 2nd ed. Grahamstown: Rhodes University Press, 1976.

Khumalo, Vukile. "Ekukhanyeni Letter-Writers: A Historical Inquiry into Epistolary Network(s) and Political Imagination in KwaZulu-Natal, South Africa." In Barber, *Africa's Hidden Histories*, 113–42.

Kirkaldy, Alan. *Capturing the Soul: The Vhavenda and the Missionaries, 1870–1900*. Pretoria: Protea Book House, 2005.

Kriel, Lize. *The 'Malaboch' Books: Kgaluši in the "Civilization of the Written Word."* Stuttgart, Germany: Franz Steiner Verlag, 2009.

Krige, Eileen J. "Changing Conditions in Marital Relations and Parental Duties among Urbanized Natives." *Africa: Journal of the International African Institute* 9, no. 1 (1 January 1936): 1–23.

——. "Girls' Puberty Songs and Their Relation to Fertility, Health, Morality and Religion among the Zulu." *Africa: Journal of the International African Institute* 38, no. 2 (1968): 173–98. https://doi.org/10.2307/1157245.

——. *The Social System of the Zulus*. 2nd ed. Pietermaritzburg: Shuter and Shooter, 1950.

Krige, Eileen Jensen, and John L. Comaroff, eds. *Essays on African Marriage in Southern Africa*. Cape Town: Juta, 1981.

Krige, Sue. "Segregation, Science and Commissions of Enquiry: The Contestation over Native Education Policy in South Africa, 1930–36." *Journal of Southern African Studies* 23, no. 3 (1997): 491–506.

Kropf, Albert. *A Kafir-English Dictionary.* 2nd ed. Stutterheim, South Africa: Lovedale Mission Press, 1915.

Kros, Cynthia. *The Seeds of Separate Development: Origins of Bantu Education.* Pretoria: Unisa, 2010.

Kuper, Adam. "Traditions of Kinship, Marriage and Bridewealth in Southern Africa." *Anthropology Southern Africa* 39, no. 4 (2016): 267–80.

———. *Wives for Cattle: Bridewealth and Marriage in Southern Africa.* International Library of Anthropology. London: Routledge and Kegan Paul, 1982.

Kuzwayo, Ellen. *Sit Down and Listen.* London: Women's Press, 1990.

Laband, John. "The Rise and Fall of the Zulu Kingdom." In *Zulu Identities: Being Zulu, Past and Present,* edited by Benedict Carton, John Laband, and Jabulani Sithole, 87–96. Scottsville, South Africa: University of KwaZulu-Natal Press, 2009.

Lacey, Peter. *The Wedding.* New York: Grosset & Dunlap, 1969.

La Hausse de Lalouviere, Paul. *Restless Identities: Signatures of Nationalism, Zulu Ethnicity and History in the Lives of Petros Lamula (c.1881–1948) and Lymon Maling (1889–c.1936).* Pietermaritzburg: University of Natal Press, 2000.

Laidler, Percy W. "Bantu Ritual Circumcision." *Man* 22, nos. 6-7 (1922): 13–14.

Landau, Paul Stuart. *The Realm of the Word: Language, Gender and Christianity in a Southern African Kingdom.* Edited by Allan Isaacman and Jean Hay. Social History of Africa. Portsmouth, NH: Heinemann, 1995.

Laubscher, Barend J. F. *Sex, Custom and Psychopathology: A Study of South African Pagan Natives.* London: George Routledge & Sons, 1937.

Lawrance, Benjamin N., Emily Lynn Osborn, and Richard L. Roberts. "African Intermediaries and the 'Bargain' of Collaboration." SSRN Scholarly Paper. Rochester, NY: Social Science Research Network, 22 August 2006. https://papers.ssrn.com/abstract=1914787.

Leatt, Dhammamegha Annie. *The State of Secularism: Religion, Tradition and Democracy in South Africa.* Johannesburg: Wits University Press, 2017.

Leeb-du Toit, Juliette. *IsiShweshwe: A History of the Indigenisation of Blueprint in South Africa.* Scottsville, KwaZulu-Natal: University of KwaZulu-Natal Press, 2017.

Leone, Mark P. "Epilogue: The Productive Nature of Material Culture and Archaeology." *Historical Archaeology* 26, no. 3 (1992): 130–33.

Levin, Ruth. "Marriage in Langa Native Location." PhD diss., University of Cape Town, 1946. https://open.uct.ac.za/handle/11427/23447.

Lewis, Jack. "An Economic History of the Ciskei, 1848–1900." PhD diss., University of Cape Town, 1984.

———. "The Rise and Fall of the South African Peasantry: A Critique and Reassessment." *Journal of Southern African Studies* 11, no. 1 (1984): 1–24.

Lissoni, Arianna, Jon Soske, Natasha Erlank, Noor Nieftagodien, and Omar Badsha, eds. *One Hundred Years of the ANC: Debating Liberation Histories Today.* Johannesburg: Wits Press, 2012.

Lodge, Tom. *Black Politics in South Africa since 1945.* London: Longman, 1983.

Longmore, Laura. *The Dispossessed—a Study of the Sex-Life of Bantu Women in and around Johannesburg*. London: Corgi, 1966.

Lonsdale, John. "Mau Maus of the Mind: Making Mau Mau and Remaking Kenya." *Journal of African History* 31, no. 3 (1990): 393–421.

Lovett, Margot. "'She Thinks She's Like a Man': Marriage and (De)Constructing Identity in Colonial Buha, Western Tanzania, 1943–1960." *Canadian Journal of African Studies* 30, no. 1 (1996): 52–68.

Madikwa, Zenoyisa. "Mbalula Goes to the Mountain." Sowetan Live, 9 September 2008. http://www.sowetanlive.co.za/sowetan/archive/2008/09/09/mbalula-goes-to-the-mountain.

Magaziner, Daniel R. "'Black Man, You Are on Your Own!' Making Race Consciousness in South African Thought, 1968–1972." *International Journal of African Historical Studies* 42, no. 2 (2009): 221–40.

———. *The Law and the Prophets: Black Consciousness in South Africa, 1968–1977*. New African Histories Series. Athens: Ohio University Press, 2010.

Mager, Anne Kelk. *Beer, Sociability, and Masculinity in South Africa*. Bloomington: Indiana University Press, 2010.

———. *Gender and the Making of a South African Bantustan: A Social History of the Ciskei 1945–1959*. Social History of Africa, edited by Allan Isaacman and Jean Allman. Cape Town: David Philip, 1999.

———. "Youth Organisations and the Construction of Masculine Identities in the Ciskei and Transkei, 1945–1960." *Journal of Southern African Studies* 24, no. 4 (1998): 653–67.

Magona, Sindiwe. *To My Children's Children*. New York: Interlink Books, 1998.

Mair, Lucy. "African Marriage and Social Change." In *Survey of African Marriage and Family Life*. London: Cass, 1969.

Malan, Mia. "Medical Back-Up in Pondo Initiation." *M&G Online*, 28 September 2013. http://mg.co.za/article/2013-09-28-00-medical-back-up-in-pondo-initiation/.

Maluleke, Tinyiko Sam. "Black and African Theologies in the New World Order: A Time to Drink from Our Own Wells." *Journal of Theology for Southern Africa* 96 (1996): 3–19.

———. "Half a Century of African Christian Theologies: Elements of the Emerging Agenda for the Twenty-First Century." *Journal of Theology for Southern Africa* 99 (1997): 4–23.

Manicom, Linzi. "Ruling Relations: Rethinking State and Gender in South African History." *Journal of African History* 33, no. 3 (1 January 1992): 441–65.

Mann, Kristin. *Marrying Well: Marriage, Status and Social Change among the Educated Elite in Colonial Lagos*. Edited by J. Dunn, J. M. Lonsdale, and A. F. Robertson. African Studies Series. Cambridge: Cambridge University Press, 1985.

Manoim, Irwin Stanley. "The Black Press 1945–1963: The Growth of the Black Mass Media and Their Role as Ideological Disseminators." Master's thesis, University of the Witwatersrand, 1983. http://wiredspace.wits.ac.za/handle/10539/7460.

Marks, Shula. "From *Of Revelation and Revolution* to *From Revolution to Reconciliation?* A Comment." *Interventions* 3, no. 1 (2001): 55–64.

———. *Not Either an Experimental Doll: The Separate Worlds of Three South African Women.* Killie Campbell Africana Library Publications. Durban: Killie Campbell Africana Library and University of Natal Press, 1987.

Marshall, Ruth. *Political Spiritualities: The Pentecostal Revolution in Nigeria.* Chicago: University of Chicago Press, 2009.

Martens, Jeremy C. "Polygamy, Sexual Danger, and the Creation of Vagrancy Legislation in Colonial Natal." *Journal of Imperial & Commonwealth History* 31, no. 3 (2003): 24.

———. "Settler Homes, Manhood and 'Houseboys': An Analysis of Natal's Rape Scare of 1886." *Journal of Southern African Studies* 28, no. 2 (2002): 379–400.

Masola, Athambile. "'Bantu Women on the Move': Black Women and the Politics of Mobility in *The Bantu World*." *Historia* 63, no. 1 (May 2018): 93.

Matthews, Frieda Bokwe. *Remembrances.* Mayibuye History and Literature Series, no. 54. Bellville, South Africa: Mayibuye Books, 1995.

Matthews, Zachariah K. *Freedom for My People.* Cape Town: David Philip, 1981.

———. "Marriage Customs among the Barolong." *Africa: Journal of the International African Institute* 13, no. 1 (1940): 1–24.

Mayekiso, Andile. "'*Ukuba yindoda kwelixesha*' ('To Be a Man in These Times'): Fatherhood, Marginality and Forms of Life among Young Men in Gugulethu, Cape Town." PhD diss., University of Cape Town, 2017. https://open.uct.ac.za/handle/11427/24447.

Mayer, Philip. *Townsmen or Tribesmen: Conservatism and the Process of Urbanization in a South African City.* Vol. 2. London: Oxford University Press, 1971.

McAllister, Patrick A., and Dumisani Deliwe. "Youth in Rural Transkei: The Demise of 'Traditional' Youth Associations and the Development of New Forms of Association and Activity, 1975–1993." Working paper, Rhodes University, Institute of Social and Economic Research, 1994.

McClendon, Thomas V. *Genders and Generations Apart: Labor Tenants and Customary Law in Segregation-Era South Africa, 1920s–1940s.* Edited by Alan Isaacman and Jean Allman. Social History of Africa. Oxford: James Currey, 2002.

———. "Tradition and Domestic Struggle in the Courtroom: Customary Law and the Control of Women in Segregation-Era Natal." *International Journal of African Historical Studies* 28, no. 3 (1995): 527–61.

McCulloch, Jock. *Black Peril, White Virtue: Sexual Crime in Southern Rhodesia, 1902–1935.* Bloomington: Indiana University Press, 2000.

Mchunu, Mxolisi. "A Modern Coming of Age: Zulu Manhood, Domestic Work, and the 'Kitchen Suit.'" In *Zulu Identities: Being Zulu, Past and Present*, edited by Benedict Carton, John Laband, and Jabulani Sithole, 573–83. Scottsville, South Africa: University of KwaZulu-Natal Press, 2009.

Meaker, R. *Reports of the Native Appeal Courts, Volume III.* Cape Town: Cape Times, 1954. https://repository.up.ac.za/handle/2263/57595.

Meyer, Birgit. "Christianity in Africa: From African Independent to Pentecostal-Charismatic Churches." *Annual Review of Anthropology* 33 (2004): 447–74.

Mgqwetho, Nontsizi. *The Nation's Bounty: The Xhosa Poetry of Nontsizi Mgqwetho*. African Treasury Series 22. Johannesburg: Wits University Press, 2007.

Mills, Wallace G. "The Fork in the Road: Religious Separatism versus African Nationalism in the Cape Colony, 1890–1910." *Journal of Religion in Africa* 9, no. 1 (1978): 51–61.

———. "Missionaries, Xhosa Clergy and the Suppression of Traditional Customs." In Bredekamp and Ross, *Missions and Christianity*, 153–72.

"Mnakwethu Season 2 2021." Facebook, accessed 25 August 2021. https://www.facebook.com/groups/234054868351576.

Mokoena, Hlonipha. *Magema Fuze: The Making of a Kholwa Intellectual*. Scottsville, South Africa: University of KwaZulu-Natal Press, 2011.

Moodie, T. Dunbar, with Vivienne Ndatshe and British Sibuyi. "Migrancy and Male Sexuality on the South African Gold Mines." *Journal of Southern African Studies* 14 (1988): 228–56.

Morinis, Alan. "The Ritual Experience: Pain and the Transformation of Consciousness in Ordeals of Initiation." *Ethos* 13, no. 2 (1985): 150–74.

Morrell, Robert. "Masculinity in South African History: Towards a Gendered Approach to the Past." *South African Historical Journal* 37 (1997): 167–77.

Mqhayi, Samuel E. K. *Abantu Besizwe: Historical and Biographical Writings, 1902–1944*. African Treasury Series 24. Johannesburg, South Africa: Wits University Press, 2009.

Mtuze, Peter T. "Hidden Presences in the Spirituality of the AmaXhosa of the Eastern Cape and the Impact of Christianity on Them." Master's thesis, Rhodes University, 1999. https://core.ac.uk/reader/145053771.

———. "A Preliminary Annotated Bibliography of Xhosa Prose, Drama and Poetry, 1909–1990." *South African Journal of African Languages* 13, no. sup2 (1 January 1993): 14–26.

———. "The Promise of Happiness: Desire, Attachment and Freedom in Post/Apartheid South Africa." *Critical Arts: A South-North Journal of Cultural & Media Studies* 29, no. 2 (2015): 183–98.

Murray, Bruce K. "Wits as an 'Open' University 1939–1959: Black Admissions to the University of the Witwatersrand." *Journal of Southern African Studies* 16, no. 4 (1 December 1990): 649–76.

MzansiMagicOfficial. "You Are Not Welcome—Mnakwethu." Mzansi Magic, accessed 25 August 2021. https://www.youtube.com/watch?v=YxHm3qbAE84.

Ndabayakhe, Vuyiswa, and Catherine Addison. "Polygamy in African Fiction." *Current Writing: Text and Reception in Southern Africa* 20, no. 1 (1 January 2008): 89–104.

Nettleton, Anitra. "Ethnic and Gender Identities in Venda *Domba* Statues." *African Studies* 51, no. 2 (1 January 1992): 203–30.

Newell, Stephanie. *Literary Culture in Colonial Ghana: "How to Play the Game of Life."* Manchester: Manchester University Press, 2002.

———. *The Power to Name: A History of Anonymity in Colonial West Africa.* New African Histories. Athens: Ohio University Press, 2013.

Ntantala, Phyllis. *A Life's Mosaic: The Autobiography of Phyllis Ntantala.* Cape Town: David Philip, 1992.

Nyathi, Sue. *The Polygamist.* Cape Town: Logogog Press, 2012.

Odendaal, André. *Vukani Bantu! The Beginnings of Black Protest Politics in South Africa to 1912.* Cape Town: David Philip, 1984.

Oduyoye, Mercy Amba. "Christianity and African Culture." *International Review of Mission* 84, nos. 332/333 (1995): 77.

———. "Re-imagining the World: A Global Perspective." *Church & Society* 84, no. 5 (1994): 82–93.

O'Laughlin, Bridget. "Missing Men? The Debate Over Rural Poverty and Women-Headed Households in Southern Africa." *Journal of Peasant Studies* 25, no. 2 (1998): 1–48.

"One Man, Four Wives: The New Hit Reality TV Show." *BBC News,* 4 June 2017. https://www.bbc.com/news/blogs-trending-40136391.

Opland, Jeff. *Words That Circle Words: A Choice of South African Oral Poetry.* Parklands, South Africa: Ad. Donker, 1992.

———. *Xhosa Poets and Poetry.* Cape Town: David Philip, 1998.

Ortner, Sherry B. "Resistance and the Problem of Ethnographic Refusal." *Comparative Studies in Society and History* 37, no. 1 (1995): 173–93.

Pauli, Julia, and Rijk van Dijk. "Marriage as an End or the End of Marriage? Change and Continuity in Southern African Marriages." *Anthropology Southern Africa* 40, no. V1 (1 January 2017): 257–66.

Pauw, Berthold A. *Christianity and Xhosa Tradition: Belief and Ritual among Xhosa-Speaking Christians.* Cape Town: Oxford University Press, 1975.

———. *The Second Generation: Study of the Family among Urbanized Bantu in East London.* Cape Town: Oxford University Press, 1973.

Pearsall, Sarah M. *Polygamy: An Early American History.* New Haven, CT: Yale University Press, 2019.

Peel, John D. Y. "For Who Hath Despised the Day of Small Things? Missionary Narratives and Historical Anthropology." *Comparative Studies in Society and History* 37, no. 3 (1995): 581–607.

Peffer, John. "Together in the Picture," *Chimurenga Chronic,* 23 June 2015. https://chimurengachronic.co.za/together-in-the-picture/.

Peires, Jeff B. *The Dead Will Arise: Nongqawuse and the Great Xhosa Cattle-Killing Movement of 1856-7.* Johannesburg: Ravan, 1989.

———. *The House of Phalo: A History of the Xhosa People in the Days of Their Independence.* Johannesburg: Ravan, 1981.

———. "The Lovedale Press: Literature for the Bantu Revisited." *History in Africa* 6 (1979): 155–75.

———. "Traditional Leaders in Purgatory: Local Government in Tsolo, Qumbu and Port St Johns, 1990–2000." *African Studies* 59, no. 1 (2000): 97–114.

Penner, Barbara. "'A Vision of Love and Luxury': The Commercialization of Nineteenth-Century American Weddings." *Winterthur Portfolio* 39, no. 1 (2004): 1–20.

Peters, Christine. "Gender, Sacrament and Ritual: The Making and Meaning of Marriage in Late Medieval and Early Modern England." *Past & Present*, no. 169 (2000): 63–96.

Peters, Pauline. "Gender, Developmental Cycles and Historical Process: A Critique of Recent Research on Women in Botswana." *Journal of Southern African Studies* 10, no. 1 (1983): 100–122.

Peterson, Bhekizizwe. "The Bantu World and the World of the Book: Reading, Writing, and the 'Englightenment.'" In Barber, *Africa's Hidden Histories*, 236–57.

Peterson, Derek R. *Creative Writing: Translation, Bookkeeping, and the Work of Imagination in Colonial Kenya*. Edited by Alan Isaacman and Jean Allman. Social History of Africa. Portsmouth, NH: Heinemann, 2004.

———. "Culture and Chronology in African History." *Historical Journal* 50, no. 2 (2007): 483–97.

———. *Ethnic Patriotism and the East African Revival: A History of Dissent, c. 1935–1972*. African Studies. Cambridge: Cambridge University Press, 2012.

———. "Morality Plays: Marriage, Church Courts, and Colonial Agency in Central Tanganyika, ca. 1876–1928." *American Historical Review* 111, no. 4 (October 2006): 983–1010.

Peterson, Derek R., and Emma Hunter. "Introduction." In Peterson, Hunter, and Newell, *African Print Cultures*, 1–48.

Peterson, Derek R., Emma Hunter, and Stephanie Newell, eds. *African Print Cultures: Newspapers and Their Publics in the Twentieth Century*. Ann Arbor: University of Michigan Press, 2016.

Philip, John. *Researches in South Africa: Illustrating the Civil, Moral, and Religious Condition of the Native Tribes, Including Journals of the Author's Travels in the Interior, Together with Detailed Accounts of the Progress of the Christian Missions, Exhibiting the Influence of Christianity in Promoting Civilization*. New York: Negro Universities Press, 1969.

Phillips, Arthur, ed. *Survey of African Marriage and Family Life*. London: Oxford University Press, 1953.

"Placing the Film 'Inxeba—The Wound' in Historical Review." South African History Online, accessed 14 September 2021. https://www.sahistory.org.za/article/placing-film-inxeba-wound-historical-review.

Posel, Deborah. "Marriage at the Drop of a Hat: Housing and Partnership in South Africa's Urban African Townships, 1920s–1960s." *History Workshop Journal*, no. 61 (2006): 57–76.

Posel, Dorit. "Marriage and Bridewealth (Ilobolo) in Contemporary Zulu Society." *African Studies Review*, no. 2 (2014): 51.

Pretorius, Hennie, and Lizo Jafta. "'A Branch Springs Out': African Initiated Churches." In Elphick and Davenport, *Christianity in South Africa*, 211–26.

Price, Richard. *Making Empire: Colonial Encounters and the Creation of Imperial Rule in Nineteenth-Century Africa.* Cambridge: Cambridge University Press, 2008.

Prochaska, Frank K. *The Voluntary Impulse: Philanthropy in Modern Britain.* London: Faber and Faber, 1988.

Ramphele, Mamphela. *A Bed Called Home: Life in the Migrant Labour Hostels of Cape Town.* Cape Town: David Philip, 1993.

Ranger, Terence O. "The Invention of Tribalism Revisited: The Case of Colonial Africa." In *Inventions and Boundaries: Historical and Anthropological Approaches to the Study of Ethnicity and Nationalism,* edited by Preben Kaarsholm and Jan Hultin, 5–50. IDS Roskilde Occasional Papers. Denmark: University of Roskilde, 1994.

———. "Missionary Adaptation of African Religious Institutions: The Masasi Case." In *The Historical Study of African Religion: With Special Reference to East and Central Africa.* London: Heinemann Educational, 1972.

———. "Religious Movements and Politics in Sub-Saharan Africa." *African Studies Review* 29, no. 2 (1986): 1–69.

Redding, Sean. "Deaths in the Family: Domestic Violence, Witchcraft Accusations and Political Militancy in Transkei, South Africa 1904–1965." *Journal of Southern African Studies* 30, no. 3 (2004): 519–37.

———. "Peasants and the Creation of an African Middle Class in Umtata, 1880–1950." *International Journal of African Historical Studies* 26, no. 3 (1993): 513–39.

Resha, Maggie. *'Mangoana Tsoara Thipa Ka Bohaleng: My Life in the Struggle.* London: S.A. Writers, 1991.

Reyher, Rebecca Hourwich. *Zulu Woman: A Biography of Christina, Wife of Solomon, King of the Zulus. With a Portrait.* New York: Columbia University Press, 1948.

Reyher, Rebecca Hourwich, and Christina Sibiya. *Zulu Woman: The Life Story of Christina Sibiya.* Pietermaritzburg: University of Natal Press, 1999.

Rich, Jeremy. "My Matrimonial Bureau: Masculine Concerns and Presbyterian Mission Evangelization in the Gabon Estuary, c. 1900–1915." *Journal of Religion in Africa* 36, no. 2 (2006): 200–223.

Robbins, Joel. "What Is a Christian? Notes toward an Anthropology of Christianity." *Religion* 33, no. 3 (2003): 191–99.

Roberts, Richard L. *Litigants and Households: African Disputes and Colonial Courts in the French Soudan, 1895–1912.* Social History of Africa. Portsmouth, NH: Heinemann, 2005.

Robertson, Stephen. "Age of Consent Law and the Making of Modern Childhood in New York City, 1886–1921." *Journal of Social History* 35, no. 4 (2002): 781–89.

Ross, Robert. *Clothing: A Global History.* Cambridge: Polity, 2008.

Rudwick, Stephanie, and Dorrit Posel. "Contemporary Functions of Ilobolo (Bridewealth) in Urban South African Zulu Society." *Journal of Contemporary African Studies* 32, no. 1 (2014): 118–36.

Ruether, Kirsten. "Heated Debates over Crinolines: European Clothing on Nineteenth-Century Lutheran Mission Stations in the Transvaal." *Journal of Southern African Studies* 28, no. 2 (1 June 2002): 359–78.

Ryrie, Alec. *Protestants: The Faith That Made the Modern World.* New York: Viking, 2017.
Sales, Jane M. "The Mission Station as an Agency of 'Civilization': The Development of a Christian Coloured Community in the Eastern Cape, 1800–1859." PhD diss., University of Chicago, 1972.
———. *Mission Stations and the Coloured Communities of the Eastern Cape, 1800–1852.* Vol. 8. Cape Town: Balkema, 1975.
Sandwith, Corinne. "Reading and Roaming the Racial City: R. R. R. Dhlomo and *The Bantu World.*" *English in Africa* 33, no. 2 (1 November 2018): 17–39.
———. "Revolutionaries or Sell-Outs? African Intellectuals and *The Voice of Africa*, 1949–1952." *English in Africa* 33, no. 2 (2006): 67.
———. *World of Letters: Reading Communities and Cultural Debates in Early Apartheid South Africa.* Pietermartizburg: University of KwaZulu-Natal Press, 2014.
Saunders, Christopher. *The Annexation of the Transkeian Territories.* Archives Year Book. Pretoria: Government Printer, 1976.
———. *The Making of the South African Past: Major Historians on Race and Class.* Cape Town: David Philip, 1988.
Schapera, Isaac. *Married Life in an African Tribe.* London: Faber and Faber, 1940.
Schiltz, Marc. "A Yoruba Tale of Marriage, Magic, Misogyny and Love." *Journal of Religion in Africa* 32, no. 3 (2002): 335–65.
Schoeman, Willem J. "South African Religious Demography: The 2013 General Household Survey." *HTS Teologiese Studies / Theological Studies* 73, no. 2 (2017): https://hts.org.za/index.php/hts/article/view/3837/9239.
Selection of Cases Decided in the Native Appeal and Divorce Court: Cape and Orange Free State Division . . . with Table of Cases and Alphabetical Index. Cape Town: Juta, 1914.
Selection of Cases Decided in the Native Appeal and Divorce Court: Cape and Orange Free State Division . . . with Table of Cases and Alphabetical Index. Cape Town: Juta, 1929.
Selection of Cases Decided in the Native Appeal and Divorce Court: Cape and Orange Free State Division . . . with Table of Cases and Alphabetical Index. Vol. 5. Cape Town: Juta, 1933.
Selection of Cases Decided in the Native Appeal and Divorce Court: Cape and Orange Free State Division . . . with Table of Cases and Alphabetical Index. Cape Town: Juta, 1936.
Seton, Bridget E. "Wesleyan Missionaries and the Sixth Frontier War, 1834–1835." PhD diss., University of Cape Town, 1962.
Sewell, William H. *Logics of History: Social Theory and Social Transformation.* Chicago: University of Chicago Press, 2005.
Shadle, Brett L. *"Girl Cases": Marriage and Colonialism in Gusiiland, Kenya, 1890–1970.* Social History of Africa. Portsmouth, NH: Heinemann, 2006.
Shepherd, Robert H. W. *Lovedale, South Africa: The Story of a Century, 1841–1941.* Lovedale, South Africa: Lovedale, 1940.
Shropshire, Denys William Tinniswood. *Primitive Marriage and European Law: A South African Investigation.* London: Society for Promoting Christian Knowledge, 1946.

Simons, Harold Jack. *African Women: Their Legal Status in South Africa*. London: C. Hurst, 1968.

———. "Marriage and Succession among Africans." *Acta Juridica*, 1960, 312–33.

Skota, T. D. Mweli. *The African Yearly Register: Being an Illustrated National Biographical Dictionary (Who's Who) of Black Folks*. Johannesburg: R. L. Esson, 1931.

Smit, Alexia, and Tanja Bosch. "Television and Black Twitter in South Africa: Our Perfect Wedding." *Media, Culture & Society* 42, nos. 7–8 (2020): 1512–27.

Soga, John Henderson. *The Ama-Xosa: Life and Customs*. Lovedale, South Africa: Lovedale, 1932.

Solway, Jacqueline. "'Slow Marriage,' 'Fast *Bogadi*': Change and Continuity in Marriage in Botswana." *Anthropology Southern Africa* 39, no. 4 (2016): 309–22.

South African Law Reports, Decisions of the Local Division of the Supreme Court, Eastern Districts, 1913. Cape Town: Juta, 1913.

South African Native Affairs Commission, 1903–5: Report of the Commission. Cape Town: Cape Times, Govt. Printers, 1905.

Spear, Thomas. "Neo-traditionalism and the Limits of Invention in British Colonial Africa." *Journal of African History* 44, no. 1 (2003): 3–27.

Stanford, Walter Ernest Mortimer. *The Reminiscences of Sir Walter Stanford 1885–1929*. Edited by John Macquarrie. Vol. 2. Van Riebeeck Society Second Series 43. Cape Town: Van Riebeeck Society, 1962.

Stapleton, Timothy J. "The Expansion of a Pseudo-Ethnicity in the Eastern Cape: Reconsidering the Fingo 'Exodus' of 1865." *International Journal of African Historical Studies* 29, no. 2 (1996): 233–50.

STATSSA. "General Household Survey 2015." Pretoria, South Africa: Statistics South Africa, 2015. http://www.statssa.gov.za/?page_id=1859.

Stearns, Peter N., and Mark Knapp. "Men and Romantic Love: Pinpointing a 20th-Century Change." *Journal of Social History* 26, no. 4 (1993): 769–95.

Stewart, James. *Lovedale Missionary Institution, South Africa*. Edinburgh: Andrew Elliot, 1894.

Steyn, Anna F. *Die Banto in die Stad: Die Bantoegesin*. Pretoria: Suid-Afrikaanse Buro vir Rasse-Angeleenthede, 1966.

Steyn, Anna F., and Colin M. Rip. "The Changing Urban Bantu Family." *Journal of Marriage and Family* 30, no. 3 (1968): 499–517.

Stoner-Eby, Anne Marie. "African Clergy, Bishop Lucas and the Christianizing of Local Initiation Rites: Revisiting 'The Masasi Case.'" *Journal of Religion in Africa* 38, no. 2 (May 2008): 171–208.

Sundkler, Bengt. *Bantu Prophets in South Africa*. Cape Town: Oxford University Press, 1961.

Switzer, Lester, and Donna Switzer. *The Black Press in South Africa And Lesotho: A Descriptive Bibliographic Guide to African, Coloured and Indian Newspapers, Newsletters and Magazines 1836–1976*. Boston: G. K. Hall, 1979.

Switzer, Lester. *Power and Resistance in an African Society: The Ciskei Xhosa and the Making of South Africa*. Madison: University of Wisconsin Press, 1993.

Tallie, T. J. *Queering Colonial Natal: Indigeneity and the Violence of Belonging in Southern Africa*. Minneapolis: University of Minnesota Press, 2020.

———. "Queering Natal: Settler Logics and the Disruptive Challenge of Zulu Polygamy." *GLQ: A Journal of Lesbian and Gay Studies* 19, no. 2 (2013): 167–89.

Taylor, James Dexter, ed. *Christianity and the Natives of South Africa: A Year-Book of South African Missions*. Lovedale, South Africa: Lovedale Institution Press, 1928.

Ter Haar, Gerrie, and Stephen Ellis. "The Occult Does Not Exist: A Response to Terence Ranger." *Africa* 79, no. 3 (2009): 399–412.

Thomas, Lynn M. "Historicising Agency." *Gender & History* 28, no. 2 (2016): 324–39.

———. "Love, Sex, and the Modern Girl in 1930s Southern Africa." In Cole and Thomas, *Love in Africa,* 31–58.

———. "The Modern Girl and Racial Respectability in 1930s South Africa." *Journal of African History* 47, no. 3 (2006): 461–90.

———. "Modernity's Failings, Political Claims, and Intermediate Concepts." *American Historical Review* 116, no. 3 (2011): 727–40.

———. "'Ngaitana (I Will Circumcise Myself)': The Gender and Generational Politics of the 1956 Ban on Clitoridectomy in Meru, Kenya." *Gender and History* 8, no. 3 (1996): 338–63.

———. "Schoolgirl Pregnancies, Letter-Writing and 'Modern' Persons in Late Colonial East Africa." In Barber, *Africa's Hidden Histories,* 180–207.

Thornberry, Elizabeth. *Colonizing Consent: Rape and Governance in South Africa's Eastern Cape*. Cambridge: Cambridge University Press, 2018.

———. "Defining Crime through Punishment: Sexual Assault in the Eastern Cape, c.1835–1900." *Journal of Southern African Studies* 37, no. 3 (2011): 415–30.

Thorne, Susan. "The Conversion of Englishmen and the Conversion of the World Inseparable." In *Tensions of Empire: Colonial Cultures in a Bourgeois World*, edited by Fred Cooper and Ann Stoler, 238–62. Berkeley: University of California Press, 1997.

Tishken, Joel E., and Andreas Heuser. "'Africa Always Brings Us Something New': A Historiography of African Zionist and Pentecostal Christianities." *Religion* 45, no. 2 (2015): 153–73.

Tlali, Miriam. *Muriel at Metropolitan*. Johannesburg: Ravan, 1975.

Ukah, Asonzeh, and Tammy Wilks. "Peter Berger, *The Sacred Canopy*, and Theorizing the African Religious Context." *Journal of the American Academy of Religion* 85, no. 4 (30 December 2017): 1147–54.

Union Statistics for 50 years, 1910–1960. Pretoria: Bureau of Census and Statistics, 1960.

Urban-Mead, Wendy. *The Gender of Piety: Family, Faith, and Colonial Rule in Matabeleland, Zimbabwe*. Athens: Ohio University Press, 2015.

———. "'Girls of the Gate': Questions of Purity and Piety in the Mtshabezi Girls' Primary Boarding School in Colonial Zimbabwe, 1908–1940." *Le Fait Missionaire* 11 (2001): 75–99.

———. "Negotiating 'Plainness' and Gender: Dancing and Apparel at Christian

Weddings in Matabeleland, Zimbabwe, 1913–1944." *Journal of Religion in Africa* 38, no. 2 (2008): 209–46.

———. "Religion, Women and Gender in the Brethren in Christ Church, Matabeleland, Zimbabwe 1898–1978." PhD diss., Columbia, 2004.

Vance, Carol S. "Social Construction Theory and Sexuality." In *Constructing Masculinity,* edited by Maurice Berger, Brian Wallis, and Simon Watson, 37–48. New York: Routledge, 1995.

Van der Vliet, Virginia. "Traditional Husbands, Modern Wives? Constructing Marriages in a South African Township." In *Tradition and Transition in Southern Africa: Fechtschrift for Philip and Iona Mayer,* edited by Andrew D. Spiegel and Patrick McAllister, 219–41. Johannesburg: Wits University Press, 1991.

Van der Waal, C. S. (Kees). "Long Walk from Volkekunde to Anthropology: Reflections on Representing the Human in South Africa.." *Anthropology Southern Africa* 38, nos. 3–4 (7 October 2015): 216–34.

Van Kessel, Inneke, and Barbara Oomen. "One Chief, One Vote: The Revival of Traditional Authorities in Post-apartheid South Africa." *African Affairs* 96, no. 385 (1997): 561–85.

Vansina, Jan. *Paths in the Rainforests: Toward a History of Political Tradition in Equatorial Africa.* Madison: University of Wisconsin Press, 1990.

———. Review of *Review of Ethnography and the Historical Imagination,* by Jean Comaroff and John Comaroff. *The International Journal of African Historical Studies* 26, no. 2 (1993): 417–20.

Van Warmelo, Nicholas J., and Wilfred M. D. Phophi. *Venda Law.* Pretoria: Government Printer, 1948.

"Vat En Sit—Definition of Vat En Sit in A Dictionary of South African English—DSAE." Accessed 25 August 2021. https://dsae.co.za/entry/vat-en-sit/e07587.

Vincent, Louise. "'Boys Will Be Boys': Traditional Xhosa Male Circumcision, HIV and Sexual Socialisation in Contemporary South Africa." *Culture, Health & Sexuality* 10, no. 5 (2008): 431–46.

———. "Cutting Tradition: The Political Regulation of Traditional Circumcision Rites in South Africa's Liberal Democratic Order." *Journal of Southern African Studies* 34, no. 1 (2008): 77–91.

Vinson, Robert Trent. *The Americans Are Coming! Dreams of African American Liberation in Segregationist South Africa.* New African Histories. Athens: Ohio University Press, 2012.

Vinson, Robert Trent, and Robert Edgar. "Zulus Abroad: Cultural Representations and Educational Experiences of Zulus in America, 1880–1945." *Journal of Southern African Studies* 33, no. 1 (1 March 2007): 43–62.

Walker, Cherryl. "Women and Gender in Southern Africa to 1945: An Overview." In *Women and Gender in Southern Africa to 1945,* edited by Cheryl Walker, 1–32. Cape Town: David Philip, 1990.

Walley, Catherine J. "Searching for 'Voices': Feminism, Anthropology, and the Global Debate over Female Genital Operations." *Cultural Anthropology* 12, no. 3 (1997): 405–38.

Wauchope, Isaac. "'Primitive Native Customs.'" In *Isaac Williams Wauchope: Selected Writings 1874–1916*. Van Riebeeck Society for the Publication of South African Historical Documents, second series, no. 39. Cape Town: Van Riebeeck Society, 2008.

Weber, Max. *Protestant Ethic and the Spirit of Capitalism*. 2nd ed. London: Harper Collins Academic, 1930.

Welsh, David. *The Roots of Segregation: Native Policy in Colonial Natal, 1845–1910*. Cape Town: Oxford University Press, 1971.

White, Hylton. "The Materiality of Marriage Payments." *Anthropology Southern Africa* 39, no. 4 (2016): 297–308.

"Why Inxeba Was Assigned a Classification X18—FPB Appeal Tribunal—DOCUMENTS." Politicsweb, 23 February 2018. https://www.politicsweb.co.za/documents/why-inxeba-was-assigned-a-classification-x18--fpb-.

Wilhelm-Solomon, Matthew, Lorena Núñez, Peter Kankonde Bukasa, and Bettina Malcomess, eds. *Routes and Rites to the City: Mobility, Diversity and Religious Space in Johannesburg*. Global Diversities. London: Palgrave Macmillan UK, 2016.

Williams, Donovan. "Social and Economic Aspects of Christian Missions in Caffraria 1816–1854—Part 1." *Historia* 30 (1985): 33–48.

———. "Social and Economic Aspects of Christian Missions in Caffraria 1816–1854—Part 2." *Historia* 31 (1986): 25–58.

Willows, Joshua Peter. "Shaping the Boys' South African Identity: Suppressed Queer Space in *Spud* and *Inxeba*." Master's thesis, University of the Western Cape, 2020. http://etd.uwc.ac.za/xmlui/handle/11394/8143.

Wilson, Monica. "The Wedding Cakes: A Study of Ritual Change." In *The Interpretation of Ritual: Essays in Honour of AI Richards*, edited by J. S. La Fontaine, 187–201. London: Tavistock, 1972.

———. "Xhosa Marriage in Historical Perspective." In *African Marriage in Southern Africa*, edited by Eileen J. Krige and John L. Comaroff, 133–47. Cape Town: Juta, 1981.

Wilson, Monica, Selma Kaplan, Teresa Maki, and Edith M. Walton. *Social Structure*. Vol. 3 of *Keiskammahoek Rural Survey*. Pietermaritzburg: Shuter and Shooter, 1952.

"Wives Total 110, Not 600, Fon Says; Chief of Bikom Tribe Says Any May Go Home—Agrees to Ban Forced Marriage." *New York Times*, 28 January 1949, https://www.nytimes.com/1949/01/28/archives/wives-total-110-not-600-fon-says-chief-of-bikom-tribe-says-any-may.html.

Wolf, Jan Jacob de. "Circumcision and Initiation in Western Kenya and Eastern Uganda: Historical Reconstructions and Ethnographic Evidence." *Anthropos* 78, nos. 3/4 (1983): 369–410.

Wolpe, Harold. "Capitalism and Cheap Labour Power in South Africa." In *Segregation and Apartheid in Twentieth-Century South Africa*, edited by William Beinart and Saul Dubow, 60–90. London: Routledge, 1995.

Wright, Marcia. "Introduction." In *Zulu Woman: The Life Story of Christina Sibiya*, by Rebecca Hourwich Reyher and Christina Sibiya, ix–xvii. Pietermaritzburg: University of Natal Press, 1999.

Yarbrough Michael W. "A New Twist on the 'Un-African' Script: Representing Gay and Lesbian African Weddings in Democratic South Africa." *Africa Today* 67, no. 1 (2020): 48–71.

———. "Very Long Engagements: The Persistent Authority of Bridewealth in a Post-apartheid South African Community." *Law & Social Inquiry* 43, no. 4 (2017): 647–77.

Zimudzi, Tapiwa B. "African Women, Violent Crime and the Criminal Law in Colonial Zimbabwe, 1900–1952." *Journal of Southern African Studies* 30, no. 3 (2004): 499–517.

Index

Page numbers in italics refer to figures and tables.

Abantu-Batho, 171–72
African chiefdoms/kingdoms, 26, 58; Bhaca, 53; Eastern Cape, 26–27, 56; Mfengu, 52, 54, 56; Mpondo, ix, x, 26, 27, 53, 54, 144; Mpondomise, 26, 30, 52, 54, 128; Ndebele, 22, 113; Sotho-Tswana, 8, 52, 53, 68, 113; Thembu, 26, 38, 52, 54, *55*, 150, 153; Tswana, 14–15; Venda, 52; Xhosa, ix, 1, 3, 26–29, 52–60, 64–66, 191; Zulu, ix, 22, 27, 53, 59–61, 161–62
African Christianity: colonially complicit/resistant, 10; cosmopolitan, 15, 35–37; as field of inquiry, 8–11, 13–16, 33–34; forms/variation, 9; material benefits, 9; polygamy and, 177; roots, 28
African Christians: benefits, 187; chiefs/headmen, 7; Christian ideals/morality, 4, 5, 20–21, 62, 69–70, 152–53; clergy, 61, 62–63, 128–30, 162, 170, 185, 190; conversion patterns, 29; customs and (*see* circumcision; lobola; polygamy); denominational fluidity, 10, 11; early, 2, 28, 29, 32; identities, 5, 24, 32; marriage (*see* marriage; weddings); numbers, 5, 9, 10, 11, 32, 121; self-profession, 9; solidarity, 36; writing/writings, 15–16, 71, 188. *See also* newspapers
African converts (early), 18, 22, 28–29, 33, 82, 107; clothing, 150, 155; morality and, 102; tradition and, 4, 12, 165–68, 173, 184, 190
African independent churches, 4–5, 10–11, 15, 29, 64, 69, 122, 124–25, 173, 176
African Methodist Episcopal Church, 5

African National Congress, 7, 50, 93, 190
African Yearly Register, The (Skota), 47–48
Afrikaners, 13, 17, 25, 36
Afrikaner territories, ix, 29
agency: African, 14, 16; arenas, 19, 33; gender and, 97, 185; mission, 14; sexual, 76, 97; spiritual, 9; term, 33–34
amaKholwa. *See* African Christians
AmaNazaretha, 11, 15, 173
An African Tragedy (R. Dhlomo), 111–12
Anglican Church, 11, 28–31, 35, 50, 61–63, 68, 128, 131, 151, 166, 170–71, 173
Anglican Native Conference, 63
apartheid, ix, x, 6, 10, 17–18, 33, 178, 189

Bandela, Moses, 64–65
Bantu Education Act, 28, 108, 126
Bantu Social Institute, 44
Bantu World, 84, 100, 112, 138, 147–49, 158, 175, 190
Bhunga, 22, 27
Bible, x, 15, 16, 20, 67, 68, 71, 73, 139, 173
Biko, Steve, 12
Black Administration Act, 16, 17, *42*, 43, 93, 119–20, 126
Black Christians. *See* African Christians
Black consciousness, ix, 12, 16
Black elites: church government and, 7; church weddings (*see* weddings); class status, 32, 156–57; consumer culture, 147–48; courtship, 142; education and, 5, 28, 29, 68; identities, 5; lobola and, 122; women's curfews and, 136–37
Black middle class. *See* Black elites
Black press, 8, 16, 47, 51, 62, 132, 144, 174, 175, 194. *See also* newspapers

267

Black women: Christian modernity and, 76, 84, 92, 98, 109–10, 189–90; converts, 29–30, 33, 168, 175; courts and, 24, 38, 39, 40, 41, 49, 97–98; initiation, 52, 59, 70; lobola and, 112, 114–18, 137–40, 175–76, 190; migrant laborers, 6; polygamy, 161–63, 165, 170, 186, 193–94; precolonial, 2–3, 27, 54, 57, 77, 81–83, 109; roles, 4, 20; sex/sexuality, 16, 20, 69–70, 76–77, 81–83, 97–107, 110, 124, 160, 162, 170, 177, 189–90; status, 3, 16, 190; urban, 14, 17, 69–70, 135–37; writing, 16, 38–39, 138–39, 211. *See also* marriage; weddings
bogadi. See lobola
Bokwe (later Matthews), Frieda, 93, 94, 123, 146
Bokwe, Roseberry, 93, 94, 123, 151–52
Bokwe, Selbourne, 74–76, *78, 79, 80,* 81, 83, *88,* 88–98, 123, 142, 153
bridewealth. *See* lobola
British Kaffraria, 116, 120
Bulhoek Massacre, 69

Calata, Rev. James: on circumcision, 13, 50, 51, 58, 60, 67, 192; and ethnic nationalism, 64; on initiation, 58; on sexual behavior, 57–58, 62, 192
Cape Colony, 26, 58, 104; courts, 8, 27, 38, 40, *42,* 43–44, 75, 105; "liberalism," 27; marriage regime, 17, 120, 123, 127; missions, 28
capitalism, 4, 23, 33, 140, 148, 154, 157
Cattle Killing, 29
chiefs/headmen, 3, 22, 37–39, 56, 57, 164; Christianity and, 7, 61; precolonial councils/courts, 7–8, 22, 23, 27–28, 31, 40, 48, 75, 188; representative councils, 27. *See also* customary law
Christian cosmopolitanism, 24, 35–37, 47
Christian Council of South Africa (CCSA), 174, 176, 177
Christian Express, 47, 117, 129–30, 133, 171, 172, 176
Christianity (institutional), 7, 11, 19, 61, 98–101, 104, 128–32; access to public life and, 20, 22, 51, 188; church government, 7, 30, 34–35; Eastern Cape, 26, 28, 29–35; impact/reach, 5, 13, 19, 31–36, 46, 63, 122, 142, 159, 188; networks, 20, 31, 32, 36, 188
churches: Anglican, 11, 20–31, 35, 50, 61–63, 68, 128, 131, 151, 166, 170–71, 173;

Ethiopian, 10, 11, 64; evangelical (*see also* evangelical Christianity), 15, 28, 131; independent, 5, 10–11, 15, 29, 69, 122, 124, 125, 173, 176; Lutheran, 4; mainline (*see* mainline churches); Methodist, 4, 5, 15, 28, 29, 104, 171, 177; mission (*see* missions/missionaries); Presbyterian, 1, 4, 28–29, 34–35, 102, *143;* Wesleyan, 28, 74, 93, 102, 104, 175; Zionist, 10–12
circumcision, x, 20, 30, 191–92; Christianized, 72; female, 52; generational politics and, 58–60; newspaper discussions, 23, 50, 63–72, 73; practice/rite, 53–58, 60–61, 72; prevalence, 53; support for, 13, 50, 61–63, 72, 73; Xhosa, 52–58, 73. *See also* initiation; manhood
Ciskei / Ciskeian Territory, ix, 38, 85, 122, 146. *See also* Eastern Cape (province/region)
clergy: Black, 61, 62–63, 128–30, 162, 170, 185, 190; white, 129–30, 170, 173, 185
clothing, 118, 146, 149–51. *See also* weddings: dresses
Colenso, Bishop John, 166–67, 171, 172
colonialism, 13, 33, 72, 117, 140, 149, 165, 167, 172, 189–90; British, x, ix, 7, 26, 28, 58, 105, 113, 116, 120, 165; colonial law, 7, 28, 37–44, 75, 93, 120; Dutch, 26, 113; Eastern Cape region, 26–29; labor and, 118–19; missionaries and, 10, 14, 15, 104, 118; women and, 96–98
Commission on Native Law and Custom, 27, 53
Commission on Zulu Succession, 162
Conference of the Independent Ethiopian Congress Mission, 64
Conference on African Family Life, 17, 156, 177
Congregational Church, 29, 175
consumer culture, 143, 147–48, 154
courtship, 1, 83, 84, 95, 142, 162
customary law, 17, 39, 40–44, 49, 94, 120, 134, 169; courts/councils, 7–8, 22–24, 27–28, 31, 38, 40, 48, 75, 188

Dhlomo, H. I. E., 146, 180
Dhlomo, Reginald (R. R. R.), 111–12, 115, 117, 126, 138; *An African Tragedy,* 111–12
Drum, 147
Dube, John, 174, 175

Eastern Cape (province/region), ix–x, 99–100, 121, *145;* circumcision/initiation, 52–60; colonialism, 26–29; courts / court cases, 8, 20, 39, 41–43, 81, 84, 85–87, 114, 157, 191; missionaries, 14–15, 28–35, 61–62, 99, 102, 115–16, 129, 130, 154. *See also* Ciskei / Ciskeian Territory; Transkei / Transkeian Territories

Edinburgh World Missionary Conference, 36, 163, 167, 176

education: Christianity and, 22; identity and, 5, 12, 48; mission-driven, 8, 28–29, 46, 56, 104, 129, 194; state-controlled, 101. *See also* literacy (written)

Ethiopian churches / Ethiopianism, 10, 11, 64

ethnicity: ethnic nationalism, 27, 54, 64–65, 69; masculinity and, 20, 51–52, 56, 59–60, 69, 72–73, 191. *See also* identities: ethnic

evangelical Christianity, 14–15, 28, 131

faith: communities of, 31–33, 107–8; as historically causative, 9, 31, 66; personal, 4, 11, 14, 33; tradition and, 94, 113, 140, 165, 172, 177, 183, 192–93

female-headed households, 6, 14, 117

forced removals, 6, 178

Foreign Missions Conference of North America (FMCNA), 19

Free Church of Scotland, 29, 35

gender: gendered practices, 2, 4, 139, 149, 150, 189; history, 14–15; moral codes and, 4, 20–21, 76–81, 103, 106, 107, 152–53, 155, 189, 190; roles, 1, 4, 5, 20

General Missionary Council/Conference (GMC), 131–32, 173–76

generational politics, 3, 52, 58–61, 118, 126, 164

Golden City Post, 147

Government Commission on Native Law and Custom, 27, 53–54

Grant, E. W., 29–30

Great Depression, 16, 30

High Church Society of Saint John the Evangelist (SSJE), 30, 31

Hunter (also Wilson), Monica, 144, 146, 152, 174

identities: African, 73; Christian, 5, 19, 24, 32, 49, 73; ethnic (*see also* ethnicity), 20, 27, 32, 56, 73; literate, 83; masculine, 51, 52, 65; modern, 23, 46, 48; national, 73; political/social, x, 5; racial, 103; sexual, 76; weddings and, 150

Ilanga lase Natal, 47, 63, 67, 112, 132, 166, 174

Imvo Zabantsundu, 47, 63, 64, 148

Indaba / Kaffir Express, 46

industrialization, 5, 13, 113, 116, 130, 135, 144

influx control, 178

initiation (female), 52

initiation (male), 20, 21, 191–92; adulthood and, 56–61; clerical support, 61–63; control of, 59–61; debates, 15–16, 23, 30, 51, 52, 56, 60, 63–73; initiates, 54, *55;* migrant labor and, 56; pain and, 56, 60–61; practices, 52–56; public interest in, 70–71; secrecy, 56, 59, 61, 66, 70; traditional, 51, 52–58; Xhosa, 52–58, 60, 70. *See also* circumcision; manhood; masculinities

International Committee for Christian Literature (ICCLA), 71

International Missionary Council (IMC), 36, 37, 132, 140, 174–77

Intlalo xa Xosa, 1, 13, 54, 71, 119, 188

Isigidimi sama Xosa, 46–47, 133

izibongo (praise poems), 8, 36, 72

Izwi laBantu, 47, 63, 132

Jabavu, Wilson, 104–7

Jordan, A. C., 30, 141–42, 146, 148; *The Wrath of the Ancestors,* 30, 141–42

Kabane, Dorothy, 74–76, *79, 80,* 81, 83, 87–98, *88,* 106, 123, 142; wedding, 153, 190

kaDinuzulu, Solomon, 161–62

Khoikhoi people, 14–15, 28

kirk justice, 40–41

KwaZulu-Natal, ix, 15, 27, 115, 164. *See also* Natal

Le Zoute Conference, 37, 174, 175, 176

lineage politics, 2–4, 8, 58, 59, 82, 107

literacy (written), 6–8, 15, 16, 20, 25–26, 48, 109, 128, 171, 188, 190, 194–95. *See also* education

lobola, x, 2, 8, 21, 59, 159, 190, 195; Christianity and, 13, 21, 122–24, 172; commercialization, 116–17; court cases, 39, 41, *42,* 86, 94–95, 181–82; debates about, 21, 23, 71, 128–32, 140, 190, 195; gerontocratic power and, 115; missionary attitudes, 115–19, 131–32;

Index ∽ 269

lobola (*cont.*)
  precolonial, 112–15; support for, 5, 13, 123, 130–37, 179; urbanization and, 18, 110, 111–12, 176, 186; women and, 112, 114–18, 137–40, 175–76, 190. *See also* marriage; weddings
love affairs: Christian morality and, 76, 83, 94–96, 109–10, 142; church courts and, 103; civil courts and, 75–76, 84, 86, 93–98, 103–9; letters, 78, 79, 80, 81, 84–92, 88; modern, 83–84, 110; precolonial, 75–77, 81–83, 109; public vs. private, 20, 77, 81, 109; secrecy, 80–81, 109. *See also* sex and sexuality
Lovedale Institute, 28–29, 93, 103, 129, 146; Lovedale Bible School, 176; Lovedale Infant School, 74; Lovedale Literary Society, 68; Lovedale Press, 13, 46–47, 54, 71, 72; secondary school, 35, 98, 99
Lutheran Church, 4

Magistrates' Courts / magistrates, 16, 17, 28, 37–44, 75, 82, 98, 103; court marriages, 120, 126–28, 169–70, 191; lobola disputes, 39, 42, 123; polygamy and, 169–70; proceedings, 8, 38, 39, 43; as public spaces, 7, 21, 39, 40, 49; records, 8, 37, 39, 41, 42, 43, 85; seduction cases, 39–43, 85
mainline churches, 4–5, 10–12, 28, 104, 130; lobola and, 131, 132, 140; marriage and, 124–28, 140, 190; polygamy and, 21, 170, 171, 173, 176, 177, 180, 190
manhood, 50, 73; access to, 58–61; debates over, 51, 65–66; definitions, 51, 66; paths to, 58–63, 66. *See also* circumcision; initiation (male); masculinities
marriage, 1–4, 195; changing patterns, 6, 18, 21, 112–13, 140, 179, 190–91; church, 113, 119–30, 121–28, 142, 143; civil, 113, 123, 126–28; counseling, 127; customary, 12, 113–15, 120, 161–62, 164; forced, 116; missionary attitudes, 115–19; officers, 124–25; precolonial, 2–3, 112–15; regimes, 17, 43–44, 120–21, 126–28, 173, 189; by special license, 111, 113, 126; urbanization and, 134–37, 177–80, 186. *See also* lobola; polygamy; weddings
masculinities, 20, 191, 195; anxieties around, 63, 65–66, 69, 135–37; authority/power and, 60, 115; Christianity and, 51, 60; constructions of, 51, 52–53, 66, 72; contests over, 23, 47, 50–52, 60; national, 65; Xhosa, 20, 51–58, 60, 191; Zulu, 59–60. *See also* circumcision; initiation (male); manhood
masihlalisane, 163, 179, 180, 181
material culture, 25, 143, 146–48, 159
Matthews, Z. K., 94, 123, 146
Methodist Church, 4, 5, 15, 28, 29, 104, 171, 177
Mfengu people, 52, 54, 56
Mgqwetho, Nontsizi, 16, 70
migrant labor, 6, 13–14, 35, 56, 113, 117–19, 140, 144, 157, 179, 187
missions/missionaries, 2, 4–5, 10, 14–15, 83, 107–8, 130–32; Eastern Cape, 14–15, 28–35, 61–62, 99, 102, 115–16, 129, 130, 154; education, 8, 28–29, 46, 56, 104, 129, 194; evangelical, 14–15, 28; marriages and, 146–47, 150, 154–56, 162–77, 184, 190; presses, 24–25, 46–47, 64; schools, 99–101, 110, 126, 129–30; stations, 98–105; tradition and, 51, 61–64, 68, 73, 76, 114–19, 132, 136, 140
modernity: definitions, 12; performative spaces for, 7; sexual, 5, 6, 8, 16; vs. tradition, 5, 12, 67, 71, 141, 142, 148, 188–89; weddings and, 144; women and, 76, 84, 92, 98, 109–10, 139, 189–90
Mpondomise people, 26, 30, 52, 54, 128
Mpondo people, ix, x, 26, 27, 53, 54, 144
multipartner relationships, 21, 162, 163, 177–83, 184–86, 190–91

Natal, ix, 27, 29, 43, 58, 115, 116, 166; courts, 8, 44, 85; marriage regimes, 120, 122, 126, 127, 132. *See also* KwaZulu-Natal
nationalisms: Afrikaner, 13; Black/African, 17, 36, 46, 50, 172; cultural, 50; ethnic, 27, 64–65, 69; Khoikhoi, 15; Xhosa, 1, 50
National Party, 16, 17
Native Affairs Department, 128, 179
Native Appeal Court (NAC), 42, 75, 86, 181, 182
Ndebele people, 22, 113
newspapers, 44–49; advertisements, 45, 47, 63, 72, 147–49; discussions, 21, 23, 50–51, 63–73, 132–40, 154, 171–72, 175–76; languages, 18, 23; material/social impact, 23, 25; mission-driven, 24–25,

64; as public spaces, 23–26, 36–37, 72–73, 81, 112, 132–38, 147–49, 153, 188. *See also* Black press

orality, 8, 15, 24–25, 27, 39, 48, 75, 85, 116, 139, 188

patriarchy, 2, 11, 127, 128, 135, 136
Pentecostal churches, 10–11
polygamy, x, 2, 8, 21, 36, 190–91, 193–95; academic writing, 164; benefits, 162; Black Christian views, 11, 23, 36, 133, 175–77; challenges, 161–62; church policies/records, 170–71, 173–77, 184–85; contemporary, 194; court cases/records, 181–84, 185; discarded wives, 170, 172; forms, 164–65; masculinity and, 162; moral anxiety, 165–67, 171; multipartner relationships, 21, 162, 163, 177–83, 184–86, 190–91; newspaper writing, 171–72, 174; West African, 172–73; white Christian views, 12, 21, 116, 162–77, 184–85; women and, 161–63, 165, 170, 186, 193–94. *See also* marriage
polygyny. *See* polygamy
Pondoland, 29, 38, 128
precolonial society: chiefly forums, 7–8; councils, 7, 8, 27; cultural/political economy, 2; gift-giving, 21, 158; lineage politics, 2–4, 8, 58, 59, 82, 107; love affairs, 82, 109; manhood, 53; marriage, 2–3, 113–15; private/public concepts, 3, 78; punishment, 39, 83; sex/sexuality, 76–77, 81–83, 189; structure, 2–3; women and, 2–3, 27, 54, 57, 77, 81–83, 109
Presbyterian Church, 1, 4, 28–29, 34–35, 102, *143*
Protestant Christianity, 4, 8, 12, 51, 66, 163, 166, 168; ecumenism, 19, 28, 36–37, 188; evangelical, xii, 28; gendered teachings, 4, 51; industrial capitalism and, 4; missionaries, 115, 116–19; nonconformist, 8, 33, 36; written literacy and, 8, 24–26
public spaces, 3–4, 6–8, 16, 20, 162–63, 165, 191, 193; churches, 22–24, 29–37, 46, 49, 109, 128–29, 170–77, 188; courts, 21, 23–24, 37–44, 49, 76–81, 84, *86*, 93–98, 103–9, 121–24; newspapers, 23–26, 36–37, 44–51, 61, 72–73, 81, 112, 132–38, 148–49, 153, 188

Pule, N. M., 71–72

race and class (analytical mode), 3, 13–14, 25, 31
racial politics, x, 18, 24, 156, 160, 172
Rand Revolt, 64
Ross, Brownlee J., 129–30, 135

Selby-Msimang, Henry, 134–37, 174
settlers (white), 27, 113, 115, 167, 171
sex and sexuality, 1–3, 164, 166, 167, 171–72, 192; Christian morality and, 1–5, 20, 62, 105–10, 116, 117, 134–35, 144, 163, 180; modernity and, 5–6, 8, 16, 76, 83–85, 89, 91–92; nonconsensual, 39–41, 58, 100, 101, 142; public consequences, 98–102, 106, 109–10, 152–53; sexual cultures, 2–3, 11, 21, 56–58, 178; sexual misconduct, 40–41, 100–109; traditional, 2–3, 56–58, 62, 76–77, 81–83, 109; women and, 16, 69–70, 97, 110, 124, 160, 162, 170, 177, 189–90. *See also* love affairs
Shembe. *See* AmaNazaretha
Sibiya, Christina, 161–62, 164–65, 168
Skota, T. D. Mweli, 47–48
social capital, 144, 157, 160
Soga, J. H., 54, 58, 59, 62, 70
Soga, Tiyo Burnside (T. B.), 1, 12–13, 35, 54, 65, 71, 119, 130, 188; on circumcision, 54, 61, 67; on initiation, 57, 61, 71, 72; on lobola, 13, 174; on modernity, 12, 188–89; on polygamy, 172, 174, 177; on sexual morality, 58, 62, 172, 189; writing skill, 19, 71, 188
Sotho-Tswana people, 8, 52, 53, 68, 113
South African Native Affairs Commission (SANAC), 169, 171
Stanford, Walter, 37–39
succession, 3, 7–9, 38, 40, 119, 121, 123, 162, 170, 181. *See also* lineage politics
Survey of African Marriage and Family Life (Phillips), 144, 164, 177

Tambaram Conference of the International Missionary Council, 132, 163, 177
textuality, 24–26, 37–38, 44, 47, 93, 162, 179
Thembu people, 26, 38, 52, 54, *55*, 150, 153
traditional courts. *See* customary law: courts/councils
Transkeian Missionary Conference, 155

Index ~ 271

Transkei / Transkeian Territories, ix, 26, 27, *42*, 43, 85, 120, 122, 155, 165. *See also* Ciskei / Ciskeian Territory; Eastern Cape (province/region)
Tsala ea Becoana, 132
Tswana people, x, 14, 150

ubudoda. See manhood
ukushweshwa, 180
Umteteli wa Bantu, 44, *45*, 71–73, 137, 174; wedding notices, 148–49, 151–53, 190; women's writing, 138–39; writing about circumcision, 50–51, 63–67, 69, 70, 73; writing about lobola, 133, 138–39, 190; writing about polygamy, 175, 182
umtshato, 113, 127, 143–44
Union of South Africa, 7, 16, 26, 29, 36, 43, 119, 120, 121
United African Methodist Church, 172
urbanization, 5, 16, 18, 117–18; families and, 16–17, 125, 126, 140, 144, 177; lobola and, 117, 134–37; marriage/weddings and, 121–22, 128, 130, 140, 142, 144; polygamy and, 174, 177–83; relationships and, 163, 177–84, 191; urban life, 15, 112, 132, 140, 174; women and, 14, 16–17, 69, 135–37

Venda people, 52
volkekunde, 25

weddings: advertising, 147–48; aesthetics, 150–51; church/white, 13, 21, 123–25, 144, *145*, 146, 193; commodification, 141, 143, 144, 159, 160; consumer culture and, 146–48, 157; costs, 153–60; dresses, 149–53, 157, 160, 190; functions of, 144, 151, 153–54, 157; gifts, *45*, 148, 158–59; hybrid, 141–42, 144, 148, 151, 158; paraphernalia, 25, 143, 146, 155, 158, 159; racism and, 155–56; rituals, 21, 151, 160; shame and, 152–53, 160, 190; status and, 148–49, 151, 152, 160; symbolism, 141, 150; traditional, 143–44, 158, 193; writing about, 141, 142, 144, 146. *See also* lobola; marriage
Wezinto, Umboneli, 50–51, 65, 68
World Council of Churches, 36
World War I, 21, 47, 100, 130, 131, 142, 154, 171, 184, 188, 190
World War II, 17, 31, 135, 154, 156
Wrath of the Ancestors, The (Jordan), 30, 141–42

Xhosaland, 3, 22, 28, 39, 40, 82
Xhosa people, ix, 1, 3, 26–29, 52–60, 64–66, 191

Zionist Christian Church / Zionism, 10–12
Zulu, Robert, 111–12, 115, 117
Zululand, ix, 59, 61, 85, 128
Zulu people, ix, 22, 27, 53, 59–61, 161–62